EARLY CHRISTIAN TEXTS ON JEWS AND JUDAISM

Program in Judaic Studies
Brown University
BROWN JUDAIC STUDIES
Edited by
Jacob Neusner
Wendell S. Dietrich, Ernest S. Frerichs, William Scott Green,
Calvin Goldscheider, David Hirsch, Alan Zuckerman

Project Editors (Projects)

David Blumenthal, Emory University (Approaches to Medieval Judaism)
William Brinner (Studies in Judaism and Islam)
Ernest S. Frerichs, Brown University (Dissertations and Monographs)
Lenn Evan Goodman, University of Hawaii (Studies in Medieval Judaism)
William Scott Green, University of Rochester (Approaches to Ancient Judaism)
Norbert Samuelson, Temple University (Jewish Philosophy)
Jonathan Z. Smith, University of Chicago (Studia Philonica)

Number 194
EARLY CHRISTIAN TEXTS ON JEWS AND JUDAISM
by
Robert S. MacLennan

EARLY CHRISTIAN TEXTS ON JEWS AND JUDAISM

by

Robert S. MacLennan

Scholars Press
Atlanta, Georgia

EARLY CHRISTIAN TEXTS ON JEWS AND JUDAISM

BM
585
.M325
1989

© 1990
Brown University

Library of Congress Cataloging-in-Publication Data

MacLennan, Robert S.
    Early Christian texts on Jews and Judaism / by Robert S. MacLennan
    p. cm. -- (Brown Judaic studies ; no. 194)
    Includes bibliographical references (p.).
    ISBN 1-55540-414-6 (alk. paper)
    1. Judaism--Controversial literature--Early works to 1800.
2. Apologetics--Early church, ca. 30-600. #. Judaism--History-
-Talmudic period, 10-425--Sources. I. Title. II. Series.
BM585.M325 1989
239'.2--dc20   89-27029
                                      CIP

Printed in the United States of America
on acid-free paper

Table of Contents

FOREWORD	ix
PREFACE	xv
LIST OF ABBREVIATIONS	xxiii

INTRODUCTION

I. Introduction — 1
II. The New Methods Begun in the Study of the Bible — 3
   A. New Data — 3
      1. Archaeology and Biblical Studies — 3
      2. Ancient Texts and the Interpretation of the Bible — 3
      3. The Historical-Critical Method — 4
   B. The New Approaches — 4
      1. Reading the Bible More as Theology than History — 5
      2. Asking Sociological Questions — 5
      3. The University Context: Departments of Religious Studies and the Study of the Bible — 7
III. The Historical-Critical Method of Biblical Studies and the Study of Ancient Jewish and Christian Literature — 8
   A. New Data — 8
      1. Archaeology and the Jews in the Diaspora — 8
      2. Texts: Qumran and Nag Hammadi and the Study of Ancient Judaism — 9
   B. New Approach to the "Jewish Issue" — 11
      1. Theology is Not History — 11
      2. The Case of the Mishnah — 13
      3. The Sociological and Anthropological Questions and the Study of Ancient Jewish Literature — 14
IV. The New Approach Applied to a Study of Second-Century Christian *adversus Judaeos* Literature — 15
   A. Archaeological Data and the Study of *adversus Judaeos* Texts — 15
   B. The Sociological Question and the Texts — 16
   C. The Case of the City as Text — 17
   D. Nonconfessional Reading of Ancient Christian Texts — 18
   E. Reading the *adversus Judaeos* Texts in the Context of the University — 19
V. Conclusion — 19

CHAPTER ONE
BARNABAS: A MODERATE APPROACH
The *Epistle of Barnabas*, (115-117 C.E.)

I. Introduction and Summary of the *Epistle* — 21
II. The City of Alexandria as "Text" — 25
   A. The Evidence from Second-Century Alexandria — 25
   B. Literary Texts Used as Sources — 29

1. The Septuagint		29
2. Papyri		29
3. The Talmud		30
4. Philo and Josephus		31
5. Acta		32

III. The Jews of Alexandria ... 33
    A. The Romans and the Jews ... 36
    B. The "Greeks" and the Jews ... 37
    C. The Jews on the Jews ... 39
IV. The Christians of Alexandria ... 41
V. Conclusion: Barnabas Was a Moderating Voice in the Crisis ... 43

CHAPTER TWO
JUSTIN: AN APOLOGETIC ESSAY
The *Dialogue with Trypho a Jew*, (c. 160 C.E.)

I. Introduction ... 49
II. Trypho the Jew, and Justin, the Christian Philosopher: Some Issues ... 51
    A. Personal Characteristics ... 51
    B. A Time for Self-Definition ... 53
    C. Cities as Text ... 54
III. The Three Cities as Texts ... 55
    A. Justin's Birth: A Roman City: Neapolis ... 56
        1. Justin's Family and Samaritan Background ... 56
        2. The Bar-Kokhba War ... 59
        3. Jewish Christianity ... 61
        4. Eclectic Knowledge of Judaism ... 63
        5. The Jews in Neapolis ... 64
        6. The Jewish Texts ... 66
        7. The "Benedictions" ... 67
    B. Ephesus: The Hellenistic Context ... 69
        1. Hellenistic Christianity and Philo ... 70
        2. The Septuagint (LXX) ... 71
        3. No Mention of Paul in Justin's *Dialogue* ... 74
        4. Persecution of the Christians by the Jews ... 75
    C. Rome ... 78
        1. Christians Compromise with the Romans ... 80
        2. Justin Was Martyred in Rome c. 165 C.E. ... 81
        3. The Jews in Rome ... 82
IV. The *Dialogue* ... 84

CHAPTER THREE
MELITO: A POETIC DEFENSE
The *Paschal Homily* (c.180 C.E.)

I. Introduction ... 89
II. Jews and Pagans of Sardis in the Late Second Century ... 93
    A. The New Evidence ... 93

	B. The Venerable Jewish Community in Sardis	97
	C. A New Picture of the Jews in Sardis	98
III.	The Christians of Sardis in the Second Century: A Literary Approach	103
IV.	The *Homily* and the New Evidence	109
	A. Literary Form	109
	B. The Audience	112
	C. Themes and Purpose of the Homily	114
	1. The Proper Use of the Scriptures	114
	2. Christianity Replaced Judaism	115
	3. Evangelistic Intent	115
	4. Conclusions	115

CHAPTER FOUR
TERTULLIAN: A LEGAL DEFENSE
The *Answer to the Jews* (c. 197 C.E.)

I.	Introduction	117
II.	The City: Carthage, North Africa	120
	A. What Can Be Known from Extant Evidence	120
	B. The Necropolis and Other Evidence	123
	C. What the Evidence Does Say	124
III.	Jews and Judaism in Carthage	125
IV.	The Christians in Carthage	129
V.	The Relationship Between Christians and Jews in Carthage	133
	A. The "God-fearers" and Proselytes	133
	B. *Adversus Judaeos* and *Adversus Marcionem*	134
	C. "Jewish Legalism and Christian Legalism"	135
	D. The Persecutions of Christians by Jews	135
VI.	The *Answer to the Jews*	137
	A. A Biblical Commentary	137
	B. Jewish or Rabbinic Influences on the *Answer*	138
	C. The *Answer* as Greek Rhetoric	139
	D. The *Answer* Was Written for the Nations	140
VII.	Conclusion	141

CONCLUSION	145
APPENDIX	155
BIBLIOGRAPHY	159
Primary Sources	159
Barnabas	159
Justin	159
Melito	159
Tertullian	160
Primary Sources: General	160
Secondary Sources	162
INDEX	199

FOREWORD

There has been more progress in interfaith relations in the past 25 years than in the 2,000 years that preceded them. Clearly, with the courageous attitudes and actions of Pope John XXIII, the world of Christian-Jewish relations was radically altered. Until modern times Jews and Christians regarded each other with antipathy, anger, hostility, and hatred. With the papal encyclical in the early 60's, millions of Christians were given sanctioned permission to look at Jews in a different light. To be sure, there were Christians and Jews who had meaningful and positive relationships before then, but here was an official attitude, an authoritative intervention, an answer to the destruction and devastation, the deceit and damage that had resulted before.

It is not surprising, then, that in the past 25 years most dialogues between Jews and Christians have consisted of cautious attempts to find common ground, to determine and emphasize the things we share. Our values and dreams, our vision of a better world were the things that interfaith dialogue stressed. On the part of Christians, there was also an attempt to "atone" for the Holocaust, to beat their chests and say "we have sinned." This might have been necessary, but the time has come for Christian-Jewish dialogue to move beyond this stage.

It is appropriate for us to also understand our differences and distinctions, to create a respectful environment in which we can see why it is that we are different, that we see the world sometimes in very different ways. Interfaith relations in this area will not do damage to relationships, but will help us to grow to a mature level, where our own security with our religious faith will not be undone by an understanding of and respect for the other. We have come a long way in the last 25 years, but there is still a great distance to traverse.

People like Bob MacLennan are proof that there is hope for Christian-Jewish relations. Reverend MacLennan's book is a major contribution to the furtherance of interfaith relations. MacLennan's observations are based on an important presupposition, that the evidence for enhancing our relationships is there in the text, in its interpretation and its context. MacLennan makes it possible for us to relate in an honest way, without bias and hatred. As you read his work and are influenced in your thinking you, too, cannot help but become one of the people who will help to build a new era in Christian-Jewish relations.

Throughout the contents of this book, we find important breakthroughs in this kind of thinking. Already in his preface, he takes note of the Pharisees as a very misunderstood and misrepresented leadership of the Jewish people during the time of Jesus. One of the sources of anti-Semitism has been this misunderstanding of the Pharisees' role in Jewish life. The way they are described in the New Testament, in mostly negative terms, needs to be contrasted with their very positive role in Jewish thinking.

Many Jews today see themselves as heirs of the Pharisees, for it was the Pharisees who created rabbinic Judaism, the Judaism from which all modern Jewish religious movements have sprung. Contrary to their role in the New

Testament, the Pharisees had much better things to do with their time than to antagonize Jesus. They are the authors of the aphorisms of Pirke Avot; they are the creators of Jewish customs and ceremonies; they are the builders of the Judaism that was to continue to grow to this very day. Indeed, most of the teachings of Jesus were quite Pharisaic in nature and origin, and perhaps some of the resentment and hostility that the early Christian writers express about the Pharisees represent a regret that some of the teachings of Jesus were not so uniquely his.

Reverend MacLennan understands and explains quite well the importance of contextual study. He recognizes that past Christian and Jewish literature emphasize the texts too heavily, while ignoring the context. The texts are related inextricably to their context and cannot truly be understood without them. MacLennan asks us to think about the cities, themselves, as texts. The texts, in fact, take on a life of their own and represent not so much revelation, in and of themselves, but material for revelation, which is what occurs in the interplay of the reader and the text. While it may be prohibitive to some that so much effort must be exerted in order to study the text, it is obviously necessary to realize a better understanding of what it was the redactor wanted to relay.

The obvious conclusion is that not only was the social context important then, but today, too, for we cannot ignore the contemporary reality of the diversity of our social contexts. Jews and Christians living in contemporary America need to factor the place of interpretation into our understanding, as well. MacLennan is particularly courageous in recognizing the same biases and prejudices found in *adversus Judaeos* texts in modern discussions on the floor of the General Assembly of the Presbyterian Church today.

In MacLennan's description of the context of Barnabas's writings, it is easy to see an important truth---that, while many choose to see Jews in a negative light because of their activity in the cultural life of the community, it is just as possible to draw positive conclusions about Jews and the Jewish community. It all depends on one's pretext. This same principle was operative in Nazi Germany, when it would have been just as easy to point out the Jews' accomplishments as a positive incentive for others on which to model themselves rather than in negative volatile terms, as an incentive for envy and violence against them.

In MacLennan's analysis of Melito, he assumes that "Judaism was probably providing a rich spiritual resource for some Christians during the first and second centuries, and this disturbed Melito and other leaders of the church. When Melito spoke, "He was speaking to his Christian community in Sardis, attempting to present a rationale for his understanding of the Christian tradition, which best represented the original intention of the God of Israel against a venerable and compelling Judaism." Some scholars believe that Luther's turn against Judaism in his later writings was attributable to this kind of attitude. He was fearful that Lutherans would convert to Judaism because of its appeal and he needed to destroy that threat in whatever way possible.

Jews reading MacLennan's work will recognize that the phenomenon in Alexandria during Barnabas's days was not unlike the situation of Jews in American society today. "Some were trying to assimilate into the culture of Alexandria; others tried to maintain their uniqueness. Some were caught up in radical and fanatical movements in the city, while others hoped to go unnoticed."

The diversity of Judaism is something that is not only a factor today, but was evident even in the days of the early church. As MacLennan states so succinctly, "How could he [Justin] write a treatise or a dialogue about monolithic Christianity and Judaism when there were so many different kinds of Jews and Christians?" That same thinking will do wonders for Jewish-Christian dialogue and respect today.

The authenticity of Rev. MacLennan's book is found not only in the words that appear on the page, but in his life. MacLennan's scholarship and facility with verbal expression are derived from the goals of his ministry. This is a man who is dedicated to building positive relationships between Christians and Jews, and his words in the text find their authenticity and authority from his deeds. For example, he has spent years studying Rabbinic literature.

MacLennan observes in his assessment of Rabbinic literature, quite correctly, "The rabbis seemed to be indifferent to issues that were so important to the Christian writers, who were their contemporaries." This recognition is part of a scholarly understanding that the importance of Christianity was magnified by Christians, and that it not have the same kind of effect in the Jewish community that one would expect. This is especially hard to accept in modern times, when Christian-Jewish dialogue is so often directed toward Jews having to understand things in Christian terms. In retrospect, however, we can appreciate the fact that, for Jews, these issues were not of primary concern.

This book makes the significant distinction between the importance of theology in Christianity and in Judaism. In Christian terms, theology is of ultimate importance. For Jews, theology is something that is inherent in the Jewish way of life, not necessarily in treatises and tracts.

MacLennan explains that in ancient days during the times of the *adversus Judaeos* writings, Jews seemed to be a problem for Christians. For many Christians today, that is still the case. The existence and flourishing of the Jewish community is a problem, theologically, for some fundamentalist Christians. According to some, Jews are destined to suffer as a result of their rejection of Jesus. For Jews to continue to flourish today is therefore enigmatic.

MacLennan recognizes what many Jews have known all along, "Far too often, scholars have used these writings as hostile, anti-Jewish tractates." While MacLennan argues that they are not necessarily anti-semitic in their origin, these texts have been used through the ages for anti-Jewish purposes, and countless Jews have suffered and some even died because of them. In MacLennan's preface, his apologetic comment that the statements of the four texts he studied were not meant to be timeless statements about Jews and Judaism must also take into account that anti-Judaism is never all right, even if it is time specific.

The preface lists a number of anti-Jewish themes that have been derived from the texts he studied. These themes, unfortunately, still have some force in the modern world.

There is nothing that is more powerful and potentially damaging than the church's supersessionistic attitude about Judaism. Triumphalism and supersessionism are based on the essential tenet that Christianity has replaced Judaism. To believe that Christianity and the church have somehow taken the place of Judaism and obviated and precluded the significance of Jewish covenant with God makes it impossible to be respectful toward Jews and Christian-Jewish dialogue. To hold that view assumes that Jews do not understand their own covenant and have been totally abandoned by God. This is to believe that God somehow breaks promises. MacLennan is quite correct in recognizing the dangers of triumphalism and supersessionism and realizes that, in order for Christian-Jewish relations to improve, we must do the most difficult thing of all---change our attitudes about the other.

MacLennan also points out the anti-Jewish theme that states that Jews have erred by rejecting Jesus as the Christ. Too often, Christian perception of Jewish non-acceptance of Jesus as the Christ is seen as a negative act by the Jews, as a rejection. From a Jewish perspective, Jews' continuing to maintain hope that a Messiah is yet to come---that is that the world will be perfected and filled with peace and hope and harmony---is not to abandon the Jewish understanding of *brit*, of covenant. Jews have been faithful, not unfaithful, to their understanding of covenant with God by not seeing Jesus as their messiah.

The deicide charge is, of course, the most significant source of anti-Jewish prejudice. Believing that the Jews killed the Christ has given permission for the suffering of the Jews, many times at the hands of Christians. MacLennan recognizes what has seemed so clear to Jews throughout the ages---that the Jewish culpability in the death of Jesus represents more a theological tendency than an historical tradition.

Furthermore, the reinterpretation of certain prophetic passages has led to a total disregard for the Jewish understanding of the Bible. The stereotype that Jews are somehow lost in legalism has ignored the real heart of Jewish teaching and faith.

It is interesting to note that the *adversus Judaeos* literature makes the case that Jews no longer "have a share in the world to come." This very phrase is derived from Talmudic literature, where Jews are instructed to believe that all people have a share in the world to come and do not necessarily have to convert to Judaism to be considered in covenant with God.

Perhaps MacLennan's greatest contribution and observation in his work is that religious writings must be understood more as theology than history. When people in dialogue claim that their texts are entirely historically and scientifically accurate, it creates stumbling blocks to the humility that comes along with understanding that the texts are texts of faith, and not historical data. An important conclusion of MacLennan's work is to remind us that the examination of texts reveals much more about the intention of the last redactor of the work than it possibly could about the original writers of the texts themselves. The truth that is contained in religious texts is much deeper and more valuable than the mere superficial reliability of historical details. The greatest challenge that lies ahead is for us to engage in scholarly analysis in order to find that truth that lies beyond historical accuracy. This is not easy for it takes security of faith to accept this approach.

MacLennan also points out that the words Judaism and Christianity are not what they seem to be. Each of them is a pluralistic and diverse concept, which warns us of speaking too simplistically when we compare our faiths.

MacLennan's analysis of Watson's view of Paul helps us to understand why so-called "Messianic Jewish" congregations (Jews for Jesus, Hebrew Christians, etc.) are egregiously inappropriate in their attempts to evangelize and proselytize Jews. While Christianity may have begun as a "Jewish sect," the meaning of being a Christian soon evolved into something that was quite different from Judaism's expectation of Messianic fulfillment.

One of MacLennan's most admirable observations is when he sees each of the four writers "dealing with their particular views of Judaism in their particular place in time, portraying them as Bible people." Even today, many people think of Judaism as the religion of the "Old Testament." This leads to fossilization in respect for Judaism on the part of some Christians. The only way to truly understand Judaism is to look at Jews today, to talk directly to Jews today, and place them in relationship with the roots from which they have grown---that is, the Judaism that originated in the Jewish Bible, what Christians call the Old Testament. To do otherwise is to place Jews in a box, the same box that has permitted people to stereotype and to prejudice all of their interactions with members of the Jewish people.

MacLennan's final words of his book are, "One question remains. Can Christians define themselves in relation to the Jews without the supersessionistic or triumphalistic overtones? It is the intention of this book to make a start in the direction of answering that question in the affirmative." To that query I, as a Jew interested in interfaith relations, answer totally in the affirmative. MacLennan has done so quite admirably. You cannot but be moved and changed by the thinking that MacLennan forces you to do in the reading of this text. There is hope, and that hope starts in reassessment and re-evaluation of our conceptions and attitudes. MacLennan has done so, and so can we.

Rabbi Norman M. Cohen

Bet Shalom Congregation
Hopkins, Minnesota
February 5, 1990

PREFACE

In 1974 Professor Markus Barth, while teaching a seminar on "Jesus and the Pharisees," explained how only in the twentieth century have Christian scholars not conversant with Hebrew or Aramaic become familiar with the primary sources of ancient Jewish literature. This was due in part to the fact that the primary documents had previously not been accessible to them: the large corpus of rabbinic literature of late antiquity known as the Mishnah and its commentary, the Talmud (225-450 C.E.), had only recently been translated by European scholars into French (M. Schwab, 1871-1890), German (L. Goldschmidt, 1929-1936) and English (I. Epstein 1935-1952, and H. Danby, 1933).

Professor Barth went on to tell his students that the study of the rabbinic literature had made it possible for these scholars to look at Jesus and the Pharisees in a new way. No longer is it possible to describe the Pharisees in only negative terms, since most of the evidence discovered through a more thorough understanding of the rabbinic writings presented a positive view of the Pharisees.

Modern scholars are at the beginning of a process of reevaluation of first- and second-century Judaism and Christianity. The causes of the conflicts between Jews and Christians in late antiquity are just beginning to be reexamined. It was understandable that there would be tensions between two different peoples who were interested in establishing their place in the cities of the Greco-Roman world in which they lived. However, the precise nature of the conflicts, and of the persecutions which sometimes resulted, was still an unanswered question.

Questions about the circumstances leading to the conflicts have led scholars to find methodologies and new evidence that would help in a search for an answer. This search for this student began with a reexamination of the methodologies and interpretations proffered by other scholars: most prominently S. Baron, L.W. Barnard, H. Chadwick, W.H.C. Frend, H.J. Leon, G.F. Moore, J. Parkes, M. Simon, and H.A. Wolfson, among others, about the relationship between Jews and Christians in the first two centuries, and at the conclusions they drew from their readings of the early Christian and Jewish literature.

Many of these studies of early Christian and Jewish literature seemed to be examinations of the texts themselves, ignoring almost entirely the context of these texts. This was true even though biblical studies, especially Old Testament studies, for many decades, had insisted on studying texts in their context. More recently scholars are examining the New Testament more vigorously, using archaeological and historical evidence.

But for some reason, early Christian and Jewish writings were examined by scholars who used the historical critical methodologies less rigorously. They did not pay enough attention to the context. Further, most scholars seemed to read the ancient texts as if these ancient writers were describing in a literal way the events of their day. There seemed to be little concern for the nature of the literature being studied. I have wondered how one could read a satirical writing, for instance, as anything other than satire. It seemed to me that any conclusions which these scholars drew relative to the relationship between Christians and Jews would always be suspect.

In 1974, I began to read through the rabbinic literature myself and became directly familiar with those writings: the Mishnah and Tosefta, the Babylonian Talmud, Midrash Rabbah and Midrash like the Mekilta and the Talmud of the Land of Israel.

In the midst of this pursuit it became clear, from the rabbinic literature itself and the critical studies of this literature, that what I had been taught about the Jews and Judaism omitted many important aspects and distorted others. Briefly, teachers omitted mentioning the rich resources found in the rabbinic and other Jewish literature, and distorted my understanding of Judaism by explaining it from a Christian perspective only.

Rabbis---those teachers, scholars and others who produced the corpus of literature listed above---devoted little of their works to discussions of Christians and Christianity. For example, there were no extant anti-Christian documents composed by rabbis. There is no record in the texts themselves that rabbis argued with Christians over the meaning of the Bible, or over the assertion that Jesus was the Messiah, a central concern within Christianity. These rabbis seemed to be indifferent to issues that were so important to the Christian writers who were their contemporaries. Why was this?

Jacob Neusner has helped this writer become aware of a new methodology or approach to the rabbinic corpus and the reconstruction of early Christianity and Judaism of late antiquity. He suggests that the issues in the rabbinic discussions were more about the life circumstances of their communities than the theological meaning of Judaism. Rabbis were concerned about such things as seeds, food, cloth, property, bodily functions, women, issues of blood, what was clean and unclean. In the modern academy these were more the concerns of the cultural anthropologist than the theologian, the apologist, or the dogmatist. Neusner introduced the thought that the Mishnah and other rabbinic literature were records of the way one thought about the mundane, and not so much about theological dogmatics.

These discoveries have led me to attempt a reconstruction and create a more accurate picture of the relationship between Jews and Christians from a direct reading of early Christian or Jewish literary sources. The issue became one of the usefulness of these sources in understanding the conflicts. Could the Talmud (redacted finally in 450 C.E.), and the Christian writings which were theological and polemical, be useful in reconstructing the relationship of Christians and Jews in the second century? What data could be used to reconstruct the relationship between Jews and Christians? Something more was needed.

New Testament scholars had used archaeological and epigraphic data in their study of the Bible, and it made sense to study the early Christian and rabbinic writings using the same materials. A search was made for the available data and ways a study could be done in Christian and Jewish literature of late antiquity, taking advantage of what was already known in critical biblical scholarship.

However, even within these circles, there were some who had the new data, yet did not use it as thoroughly as they could. Many New Testament scholars, for example, simply use the critical editions of the Greek New Testament without concerning themselves with the context out of which these texts emerged. Nor did they use the new methodologies which are currently being developed by such scholars as Meeks, Theissen, Brown, Malina, and many others.

Later I began to read through the *adversus Judaeos* literature, which was viewed as a good test case for this new approach. *Adversus Judaeos* literature is an informal designation given by scholars such as J. Parkes, A.L. Williams, R. Wilde, H. Schreckenberg, J. Gager, and R. Ruether to those writings of early Christians against Jews and Judaism in the first five centuries of the common era. Some of these writings had actually been entitled *adversus Judaeos*. But most of them had other titles: a Dialogue, an Answer, an Epistle, and a Homily.

Nearly all of the major early Christian writers wrote something (a dialogue, an essay, a letter, a poem) "*adversus Judaeos*," "against the Jews." It seems that Jews are always a problem to Christians. I became interested in finding out exactly what the problem was by examining how Christians wrote about Jews and what they knew about Judaism.

As test cases for my study, I chose one specific anti-Jewish writing from each of four major early writers. The particular authors studied in this book are representative of the writers *adversus Judaeos* and are most often referred to by other early and later Christian authors. Justin, Melito, Barnabas, and Tertullian were major teachers in the early Church and that by itself demands that they be examined.

They are also from the same formative period, 113-197 C.E., a time when the early Church was emerging into the Greco-Roman world as a significant force. The precise degree of influence exerted by the Church on the pagan and Jewish cultures at the time is difficult to ascertain, but it is clear that the movement known as Christianity was beginning to establish itself throughout the Mediterranean world.

The four texts also represent a broad geographical setting. The major cities in the Mediterranean world, Carthage, Ephesus, Rome, Sardis, Alexandria, and one minor city, Neapolis in Samaria, are examined in this study. Each city has its special part to play in helping us understand the meaning of the particular *adversus Judaeos* text. The cities in which these writings were developed become a "text" in a sense, which can be "read" alongside each writing.

Two disclaimers are necessary at this point. First, in order to use a city as a "text" it is not necessary to reconstruct a "model Roman city." It is not the intention of this book to present a "model city," but to use the evidence from the cities in order to reconstruct the social and cultural elements that demonstrate the presence and the interaction of Jews, Christians, and others in a particular place. Second, it is also possible to use the questions which have been raised by the social and cultural anthropologists who study ancient texts without constructing an anthropological model. These questions from scholars working in the social sciences enable one to understand the texts in a much broader context.

As I thought about the structure for each chapter a similar outline for the discussion of each text was created. First, the contents of the individual writings would be summarized. Then the city in which it was written would be described, after which archaeological, epigraphical, and other historical data would be used to describe the kinds of Christian and Jewish communities in that particular town.

At first, it seemed possible to follow this outline for each chapter and come to some conclusions about the meaning of the *adversus Judaeos* writings, but as the research was done I discovered that each city and text required different questions that would not fit neatly into the original outline for each chapter. Each *adversus Judaeos* text demanded a slightly different approach, and so each chapter took on its own character.

In researching and drafting the discussion of the *Epistle to Barnabas*, it became clear that it was important to mention the tension which existed in Alexandria, Egypt, between the Jews and the "Greeks," as well as some concern about fanatical Jewish messianism which existed in Alexandria during the time Barnabas wrote his epistle.

It was also necessary to include some of the other historical sources of the first and second centuries which were related to Alexandria. This was material which at first might not have seemed directly related, or at best only peripheral, to an examination of the central issues in the *Epistle of Barnabas*, but as one studies the city and the other *adversus Judaeos* literature, the importance of these other sources becomes clearer.

In the study of Melito's *Homily* some unique problems have been revealed. The archaeological data brought to light by the late G.M.A. Hanfmann demonstrated that there is no archaeological evidence of a Christian presence in Sardis in the middle of the second century, the time during which Melito composed his *Homily*. Hanfmann also showed that there is a rich display of Jewish evidence in the same period.

The combination of the archaeological evidence and a reading of the *Homily* leads to a question: Why was Melito so hostile to the Jewish population there? Why would he have to denigrate them? If they were so venerable, as their impressive synagogue indicates, then why would Melito insist on declaring Jews in Sardis inferior? Was the Jewish community persecuting Christians in Sardis during the late second century? Was the "insignificant" Christian community overwhelmed by the Jewish presence there? These questions lead us to some new conclusions about the relationship between Jews and Christians in Sardis in the second century.

The third text studied for this essay was Justin Martyr's so-called dialogue with a Jew in Ephesus. The *Dialogue* and its author provide an interesting study. First, however, one has to deal with the question of the identity of the

Jew with whom Justin had the dialogue. What kind of a Jew was he? Why did he leave Israel during the Bar-Kokhba War? Was he more than one person? Did Justin create a Jewish teacher named Trypho? From this study it was discovered that it did not matter if Trypho was an individual or a representative Jew; what matters is what Justin thought was important about this "Jew" and his beliefs in relation to the audience Justin had in mind.

It is clear that any study of the writings of Justin demand an investigation of three cities (Rome, Ephesus and Neapolis), since Justin was influenced by each of them in some way. I do not know of any other scholar who has connected these three cities in a study of Justin's writings. Although no one can be absolutely sure if Justin ever visited these cities, let alone lived and worked in them, scholars are reasonably sure that he spent some time in each. A study of these cities gives us a "text" for the meaning of Justin's *adversus Judaeos* document called *Dialogue with Trypho the Jew*.

Some insights begin to emerge from this approach to Justin's *Dialogue*. For example, the traditions and various cultures which influenced Justin's thinking expressed in his writings may be discovered.

The last *adversus Judaeos* discussed is Tertullian's *Answer to the Jews*. Again, very special circumstances present themselves, not the least of which is the fact that the archaeological evidence in late second- to early third-century Carthage is very difficult to interpret. The city was destroyed many times, and the pieces from those devastated buildings (we might assume Christian dwellings and Jewish buildings; possibly some synagogues) were apparently used to rebuild other nonreligious structures, such as walls and roadways in Carthage.

To complicate matters further, most of the commonly held understandings about Christians and Jews in Carthage are usually taken from Tertullian's statements about them. His statements about the Jews are not very satisfactory for reconstructing what actually went on between Christians and Jews in that city.

Tertullian was an apologist for Christianity and as such seemed to want to defeat Marcion's form of Christianity more than Jews and Judaism; when he did refer to Jews he seemed to refer to those portrayed in the Bible.

As research was completed for each text, the methodological approach applied---using new data, analyzing texts in new ways and reading them in a postconfessional way, and using the city as a "text"---proved to be helpful in discovering the meaning and purpose of each particular *adversus Judaeos* writing.

This writer approaches the second century *adversus Judaeos* literature from three directions:

(1) The new archaeological and epigraphic evidence and other historical evidence,
(2) The new methods developed in the modern academy to study rabbinic literature, especially as it is now being applied by Jacob Neusner, and
(3) A postconfessional or nonreligious reading of the texts.

Far too often, scholars have used these writings as hostile anti-Jewish tractates. After a careful study of the texts using the new approach it is no longer necessary to see them as such. They are, rather, attempts on the part of the particular Christian writer, in a specific place, during a period of time, to say something about the uniqueness and importance of the Christian Way to the Christian community in whatever form that might have taken at the time. In them, Christians were talking with Christians about theological concerns which were later to grow into social and cultural anti-Jewish sentiments.

This last approach is especially important since one may now study these ancient *adversus Judaeos* texts as an attempt at Christian self-definition rather than as hostile anti-Jewish polemic or theological dogmatism.

This new approach can also help one understand the relationship or lack of relationship between Christians and Jews in the second century. It is necessary that Christians and Jews of each generation wrestle anew with the issue of the meaning of and relationship between Christianity and Judaism. The final resolution to the questions is not yet settled. But this new approach, if pursued further, can be a significant contribution to the ongoing work in the study of Christian and Jewish writings of late antiquity.

The problems encountered as one does his or her research centers mainly on the question of availability of archaeological and epigraphic data. It is difficult in some of the cities mentioned above to know exactly what the Jewish and Christian communities were like, since the archaeological evidence is not always abundant. Carthage and Alexandria are particularly difficult spots to "recreate" because of the lack of second century Christian or Jewish material. There is much more pagan evidence which makes it possible to reconstruct the social and cultural life of the cities of late antiquity.

There is ongoing archaeological exploration in each of the cities mentioned. Scholars continue to excavate in Alexandria and Carthage. Other cities in the Mediterranean world are also being explored and will reveal helpful information in the next few decades. It is reasonable to argue that the more archaeological and epigraphic information from these sites we have, the more clearly we will be able to reconstruct the past.

It is hoped that this contribution to the ongoing discussion of the meaning, purpose, and place of the *adversus Judaeos* writings helps one to see the different concerns of some early Christian writers. It was later Christian writers who were responsible for using the so-called *adversus Judaeos* texts as anti-Jewish tractates which were thought to literally refer to Jews and Judaism. It is not too uncommon a phenomenon to create myths which are used for political and other purposes.

I am grateful to friends and teachers who guided me through this process. A.T. Kraabel, my thesis adviser, helped me get beyond the conventional wisdom to insight. Theofanis Stavrou, my committee chair, guided me to *Ithaca* and taught me how to love Cavafy. Achilles Avramides taught me the beauty of the Greek writers. Tzvee Zahavy inspired me to appreciate the mystery in the Jewish texts. Robert Spencer always asked the hard questions and taught me the fun of anthropology. William A. Johnson supported me, cheered me on, and helped me over my fear of the defense. Lloyd Cooke encouraged me to see ideas from different angles and helped me write them clearly. James H. Charlesworth was generous with his time and resources. Jacob Neusner showed me another way to read the texts. Bill Peterson introduced me to Neusner. Norman Cohen of Minneapolis joined me in this adventure. The late Yigal Shiloh taught me how to listen to the ancient city. Donald Macleod of Princeton Seminary helped me get started. Wilbert R. Sykes taught me to believe in myself.

The people in the Center for Ancient Studies at the University of Minnesota supported me through the process. Librarians at the Wilson Library of the University of Minnesota, the Bodleian Library in Oxford, the Burke Library of Union Seminary, NYC, the Columbia University Libraries, the Firestone Library of Princeton University, the New York Public Library, and the Robert Speer Library of Princeton Seminary, led me through the caverns and the stacks of these great storehouses of information.

A number of people helped with the editing of this book. Joanna Tsuyuki, my administrative assistant, has been with this project from the beginning and has used computers, FAX, Express Mail, hours of her time beyond eight to five to complete this book. Jennifer Regan was the first to edit the manuscript. Judy Handelman prepared the text for the Ph.D. defense. Henry Engel edited the camera-ready copy for the publishers. Henry also did the index.

The people of Hitchcock Presbyterian Church in Scarsdale, NY, are the congregation who saw me through the Ph.D. oral examinations in November 1983, the writing of the Thesis from 1984 to 1988, and the final thesis defense on December 12, 1988. I thank them for being a supportive and celebrative community all along the way.

In 1983 I moved from Minneapolis and settled in Scarsdale. Jane, my wife, and Katie and Stewart, our children, took this journey with me. I thank them for making our house a home, and our family an experience in love. They love with all their hearts, minds and souls. It is good when a scholar can stay in touch with the ongoing realities of life. I dedicate this book to them.

LIST OF ABBREVIATIONS

A	*Archaeology*
AA	*The Acts of the Pagan Martyrs, Acta Alexandrinorum*, ed. H. Musurillo (1954)
AASOR	*Annual of the American Schools of Oriental Research*
AB	*The Anchor Bible*
ANRW	*Aufstieg und Niedergang der romischen Welt: Geschichte und Kultur Roms im Spiegel der neuren Forschung.* Edited by Hildegard Temporini and Wolfgang Haase. Berlin and New York: de Gruyter, 1984
ASR	*American Sociological Review*
AJ	Josephus, *Antiquitates Judaicae*
AJA	*American Journal of Archaeology*
Ap.	Josephus, *In Apionem*
ATR	*Anglican Theological Review*
Answer	Tertullian, *Answer to the Jews*
AusBR	*The Australian Biblical Review*
BA	*Biblical Archaeologist*
Barn.	*The Epistle of Barnabas.* In *The Apostolic Fathers.* LCL
BASOR	*Bulletin of the American Schools of Oriental Research*
BAR	*Biblical Archaeology Review*
BJ	Josephus, *Bellum Judaicum*
BJRL	*Bulletin of the John Rylands University Library of Manchester*
BJS	*The Brown Judaica Series*
BT	*The Babylonian Talmud*, followed by the name of the tractate; English translation ed. I. Epstein (1935-48)
CBQ	*Catholic Biblical Quarterly*
CC	*Christian Century*
CCARJ	*Central Conference of American Rabbis Journal*
CH	*Church History*
CIJ	*Corpus Inscriptionum Judaicarum*, ed. J.B. Frey (1936-1952)
ConJ	*Conservative Judaism*
CPJ	*Corpus Papyrorum Judaicarum*, editors, V.A. Tcherikover, A. Fuks and M. Stern, (1957-1964)
CQ	*The Classical Quarterly*
CQR	*Church Quarterly Review*
CW	*Classical World*
Dio	*Dio's Roman History*
EJ	*Encyclopaedia Judaica*, 16 vols. Jerusalem: Keter Publishing House Jerusalem Ltd., 1972
Eus., *DE.*	Eusebius, *Demonstratio Evangelica*
___, *HE.*	_____, *Historia Ecclesiastica*
___, *PE.*	_____, *Praeparatio Evangelica*
Fl.	Philo, *In Flaccum*, ed. H. Box (1939)
HTR	*Harvard Theological Review*

HUCA	Hebrew Union College Annual
ICC	The International Critical Commentary
IDBS	Interpreter's Dictionary of the Bible, Supplement
Int	Interpretation
JBL	Journal of Biblical Literature
JE	The Jewish Encyclopedia (1901-6)
JEA	Journal of Egyptian Archaeology
JEH	Journal of Ecclesiastical History
JES	Journal of Ecumenical Studies
JJS	Journal of Jewish Studies
JQR	Jewish Quarterly Review
JRH	Journal of Religious History
JRS	Journal of Roman Studies
JSJ	Journal for the Study of Judaism in the Persian, Hellenistic and Roman Periods
JSNT	Journal for the Study of the New Testament
JTS	Journal of Theological Studies
Dial.	Justin Martyr's *Dialogue with Trypho the Jew*
LCL	Loeb Classical Library
LTQ	Lexington Theological Quarterly
NT	Novum Testamentum
NTS	New Testament Studies
Numen	Numen: International Review for Religions
NYT	The New York Times
Orig., Cel.	Origen, *Contra Celsum*
PG	J. Migne, *Patrologia Graeca*
PL	J. Migne, *Patrologia Latina*
PRS	Perspective in Religious Studies
RE	Paulys Realencyclopadie der classischen Altertumswissenschaft
RSR	Religious Studies Review
RB	Revue biblique
RHE	Revue d'histoire ecclesiastique
RHPhR	Revue d'histoire et de Philosophe religieuses
SA	Scientific American
SBL	The Society of Biblical Literature
Scr.Hier.	Scripta hierosolymitana
SEv.	Studia Evangelica
Semeia	Semeia
SJT	Scottish Journal of Theology
SPB	Studia postbiblica
SP	Studia Patristica
T	Theologia
TDNT	Theological Dictionary of the New Testament, eds. G. Kittel and G. Friedrich
Tert. Ad.Jud.	Tertullian, *Adversus Judaeos*
___. Ad.Mar.	Tertullian, *Adversus Marcionem*

TS	*Theological Studies*
TT	*Teologisk Tidsskrift*
TU	*Texte und Untersuchungen*
TZ	*Theologische Zeitschrift.* Basel 1945ff
USQR	*Union Seminary Quarterly Review*
V	Josephus, *Vita*
VC	*Vigiliae christianae*
VT	*Vetus Testamentum*
ZNW	*Zeitschrift für die neutestamentliche Wissenschaft*

INTRODUCTION: Methodology

FOUR EARLY CHRISTIAN TEXTS ON JEWS AND JUDAISM IN THE SECOND CENTURY C.E.

I. Introduction

The purpose of this book is to examine four early Christian anti-Jewish writings, known as *adversus Judaeos* literature, applying new methods recently developed by scholars for the study of ancient religious literature.[1]

The period covered in this book is the second century of the common era. The texts to be discussed are writings which have been thought to be against Jews and Judaism. They have also been used by the Church in later centuries to support Christian anti-Judaism and to perpetuate misunderstanding between Jews and Christians.

The four *adversus Judaeos* writings selected for this study have been chosen because of their proximity in time, locale, and theme. Although their views were presented in various forms---a letter, a sermon, a dialogue, and an essay---they are all *adversus Judaeos*, joined by their distinctly anti-Jewish themes.[2]

---

1 In the course of this introduction the use of this method will be explained as it applies to the study of the Bible as well as the early rabbinic literature. For summaries of the most recent use of this method in the study of the Bible as well as early Jewish and Christian texts see D.A. Knight and G.M. Tucker, *The Hebrew Bible and Its Modern Interpreters*, (Chico, CA: Scholars Press, 1985); R.A. Kraft and G.W.E. Nickelsburg, *Early Judaism and its Modern Interpreters*, (Atlanta: Scholars Press, 1986) and E.J. Epp and G.W. MacRae, *The New Testament and Its Modern Interpreters*, (Atlanta: Scholars Press, 1989).

2 The major summaries of the *adversus Judaeos* literature are as follows: J. Parkes, *The Conflict of Church and Synagogue* (London: The Soncino Press, 1934); A.L. Williams, *The Adversus Judaeos, A Bird's-Eye View of Christian Apologiae Until the Renaissance* (Cambridge, England, 1935); R. Ruether, *Faith and Fraticide, The Theological Roots of Anti-Semitism* (New York: Seabury, 1974), 118; M. Simon, *Verus Israel: A Study of The Relations Between Christian and Jew in the Roman Empire (135-425)* [1964], trans. H. McKeating, (Oxford, 1986), 135-178; H. Schreckenberg, *Die christlichen Adversus-Judaeos-Texte und ihr literarisches und historisches Umfeld, (1.-11, Jh.)* (Frankfurt am Main: Peter Lang, 1982); J. Gager, *The Origins of Anti-Semitism* (Oxford: Oxford University Press, 1983), 155-156; and S.G. Wilson, *Anti-Judaism in Early Christianity 2, Separation and Polemic* (Ontario: Wilfrid Laurier University Press, 1986) and R. Wilde, *The Treatment of the Jews in the Greek Christian Writers of the First Three Centuries*, (Washington, D.C.: The Catholic University of America Press, 1949). Wilde summarizes the *adversus Judaeos* themes: "The Jews boasted at the death of Christ but without any right. Their Synagogue was in a figurative sense considered to be the mother of Christ. Christ was asked for deliverance from the bonds of death lest the Jews have reason to boast. The Jews are in their wretched condition because they put Christ to death. The wrath of God fell upon them because of their part in the death of Christ, and it brought with it the following punishments: eternal blindness, loss of the way which is Christ, eternal servitude to the Gentiles, and the destruction of the Temple. The Jews killed Christ with a violent and unjust death. Hence they should not be reckoned with their holy ancestors and the patriarchs. In the age to come the Jews will be horror-stricken at the punishment that they are to receive." (164). This is a summary of Hippo-

(continued...)

Anti-Jewish themes follow a particular line of reasoning. The four texts studied here hold the following point of view.

+ The Church has superseded the synagogue.
+ Jews have erred by rejecting Jesus as the Christ.
+ Jews are being judged by God for killing Jesus (Melito accuses Jews of "deicide") and have paid for their disobedience through the destruction of the Temple, dispersion from their land, and other experiences of condemnation.
+ The Old Testament is a Christian book because Jews have misunderstood it.
+ Jews are lost in legalism, their religion is sterile and useless.
+ Their synagogues are worn out.
+ God has turned from them.
+ Jews do not understand their own covenant and therefore God has given it to another people, the Christians, who now replace Jews and receive the blessing originally given to them.
+ Most *adversus Judaeos* writings view Jews' suffering as deserved, because of their rejection of Jesus.

The *adversus Judaeos* literature has often been viewed as making a case against Jews which tries to prove that they no longer have a share in the world to come. At the same time the Jews know that something is wrong. In their synagogues they perpetuate hate against God's people, the Christian Church. This makes the situation even worse. Some synagogues are the source of persecution (Tertullian).

The four writers' *adversus Judaeos* examined here are Barnabas, whose letter to a congregation in Alexandria, Egypt (c.115-117 C.E.), is the earliest example of an "anti-Jewish" writing outside the New Testament; Justin Martyr from Neapolis, Ephesus, and Rome, who recorded a dialogue with Trypho, a Jew (c.160 C.E.); Melito, Bishop of Sardis, who wrote a homily (c.180 C.E.); and Tertullian from Carthage, North Africa, who is represented by an essay, "Answer to the Jews," (c.197 C.E.).[3]

2(...continued)
lytus' *adversus Judaeos*, and yet it covers in broad outline the themes in the other *adversus Judaeos* writings.

3 Some of Tertullian's other writings contain anti-Jewish sections. See *Adversus Marcionem* and *Apology*. For a summary of his anti-Jewish views see D.P. Efroymson, "The Patristic Connection," in A. Davies, *Antisemitism and the Foundations of Christianity*, (New York: Paulist Press, 1979), 98-117.

Following is a brief description of the methods used by this book to study the *adversus Judaeos* texts.

II. The New Methods Begun in the Study of the Bible

A. New Data

1. *Archaeology and Biblical studies.* The impact of the archaeological and epigraphic discoveries since the Second World War, as well as the interaction between biblical criticism and more recent social scientific studies of the texts of early Judaism and Christianity, have contributed to the emergence of a new way of thinking about the meaning and interpretation of the Bible.

There is no significant biblical study which excludes this valuable work in archaeology of the Middle East.[4] It is clear that vast numbers of discoveries in the region since 1945 have decisively changed the way one views emerging Judaism and Christianity. Now scholars have found a balance between literary sources and archaeological evidence which is used to reconstruct the history of the past.[5]

Biblical scholars today readily accept that archaeology has helped them reconstruct the history of the ancient Near East. Discoveries like the ones at Qumran in recent years have clarified questions long thought unsolvable. Now documents, along with the ruins themselves, are combined to illuminate the complexities of the cultures of late antiquity.

Bricks and stone, graffiti and formal inscriptions expose the contents of a society only indirectly known from the writings themselves. The remains of Kirbet Qumran assist scholars to present a much more complete portrait of the way those pious Jews lived near the Dead Sea in the first century B.C.E. to the last quarter of the first century C.E. A far more complex picture of first-century Judaism has emerged as a result of these discoveries.

2. *Ancient Texts and the Interpretation of the Bible.* The Qumran scrolls themselves offer an even more complete description of those who lived at the "monastery" by the Dead Sea. These scrolls, as well as the Bar-Kokhba materials for a later period, have enabled scholars to reconstruct the organization and religious beliefs of the people who lived in the Qumran and the surrounding region.

---

4 See D.A. Knight and G.M. Tucker, eds., *Hebrew Bible* especially pages 31-74, and E.M. Meyers and A.T. Kraabel, "Archaeology, Iconography, and Nonliterary Written Remains," in R.A. Kraft and G.W.E. Nickelsburg, eds., *Early Judaism*, 175-210. These two volumes summarize the work which has been done in the fields of archaeology and the Bible and early Judaism and Christianity since the Second World War.

5 See E.R. Goodenough, *Jewish Symbols in the Greco-Roman Period*, (New York: Pantheon Books, 1965), vol. 12, 186, where a discussion of the balance between archaeological evidence and literary sources is spelled out. Note that recently J. Neusner and others are working on a reprint of Goodenough's works. For the use of new literary and archaeological data in Jesus Research, see J.H. Charlesworth, *Jesus Within Judaism: New Light from Exciting Archaeological Discoveries*, The Anchor Bible Reference Library, (New York: Doubleday, 1988).

Ancient Near Eastern texts included in a volume by J.B. Pritchard,[6] studies in Ugaritic poetry by Albright,[7] the newly discovered tablets at Ebla by Matthiae and Pettinato,[8] and the Nag Hammadi library edited by Robinson[9] are more literary sources used to reconstruct the philosophical, commercial, and religious views of the people in the ancient Near East.

The Bible is no longer read as literature conceived in a cultural vacuum. There are many texts that relate to it and help open its meaning and value. It is now seen as a collection of literary genre which is not unlike other literature written in the same period and locale. This understanding of how to read the Bible is now being used to read second-century Christian literature.

3. *The Historical-Critical Method.* With the growing number of archaeological and literary evidence, the historical-critical method continues to be refined and reshaped. From the mid-nineteenth century to the present, scholars have been working in different places in the world, revising their picture of the past. People like Y. Kaufmann[10] and U. Cassuto[11] are examples of Jewish scholars who lived in Israel and helped establish departments which examined critically the Bible and Israel's history.[12]

B. The New Approaches

The critical study of the Bible has led to radical rethinking concerning the meaning of the text---such questions as: How were the Gospels developed and written down?[13] Where did the Israelites get their epics?[14] Can one reconstruct

---

6 J.B. Pritchard, *Ancient Near Eastern Texts*, 3d.ed. (Princeton: Princeton University Press, 1969).

7 W.F. Albright, *Yahweh and the Gods of Canaan*. (Garden City, NY: Doubleday, 1968).

8 See P. Matthiae, "Ebla in the Late Early Syrian Period: The Royal Palace and the State Archives." *BA* 39 (1976): 94-113 and G. Pettinato, "The Royal Archives of Tell Mardikh-Ebla." *BA* 39 (1976): 44-52.

9 J.M. Robinson, Director, *The Nag Hammadi Library in English*, (New York: Harper & Row, 1977).

10 Y. Kaufmann, *The Religion of Israel*, trans. M. Greenberg, (Chicago: University of Chicago Press, 1960).

11 U. Cassuto, *Biblical and Oriental Studies*, vol. 2: *Bible and Ancient Oriental Texts*, (Jerusalem: Magnes, 1975).

12 The recent anniversary volumes by Scholars Press have extensive bibliographical material outlining these works. See D.A. Knight and G.M. Tucker, *Hebrew Bible* and R.A. Kraft and G.W.E. Nickelsburg, *Early Judaism*.

13 M. Dibelius, *From Tradition to Gospel*, [1919] trans., B.L. Woolf, (Cambridge and London: James Clark and Co., 1971) and R. Bultmann, *The History of the Synoptic Tradition* [1921] trans., J. Marsh, (New York and Evanston: Harper & Row, Publishers, 1963).

a history of Israel?[15] These and other questions reopened the study of the Bible and provided some insights into the meaning and intention of the text.

1. *Reading the Bible More as Theology than History*. Reading the Bible with the historical question in mind permits scholars access to its primary intention. It was not written to describe events as they happened, but to interpret events that had happened. The Gospels, for example, are no longer viewed simply as biographies of Jesus. Rather, it is now the consensus that their contents are influenced by faith. The authors were driven first of all by the conviction that Jesus was the Messiah, the Lord, the Son of God, the Word of God in the flesh, and as such had made an impact on the world.

H. Conzelmann is a typical example, a New Testament scholar who saw the Gospel of Luke as "theology"[16] which reflected Luke's view of Jesus in the context of the early Church. Luke wrote his gospel to speak to the needs of his congregation, and to present his particular view of the events of his day. He wrote theology and some scholars have used it as if it were a record of what actually happened.

Other biblical scholars mentioned in the recent summaries of the Hebrew Bible and the New Testament[17] are consistent in this approach. There is a consensus on the fact that the biblical material is to be read as more theology than history.

2. *Asking Sociological Questions*. Recent studies have also demonstrated the value of the sociological study of the Scriptures. N.K. Gottwald in the Hebrew Bible and W. Meeks in the Pauline corpus have presented popular and readable monographs employing a sociological approach to the study of Scripture.[18]

14(...continued)
14 A. Alt, *Die Ursprünge des israelitischen Rechts*. Berichte über die Verhandlungen der Sächsischen Akademie der Wissenschaften zu Leipzig. Phil.-hist. Klasse 86/1. Leipzig S. Hirzel. Reprinted pp. 278-332 in *Kleine Schriften zur Geschichte des Volkes Israel*, 1. (Munich: C.H. Beck, 1968) and F.M. Cross, *Canaanite Myth and Hebrew Epic: Essays in the History of Religion*, (Cambridge, MA: Harvard University Press, 1973).

15 M. Noth, *Geschichte Israels*, (Göttingen: Vandenhoeck & Ruprechte, [Eng., trans., 1958] 1950) and G. von Rad, *Old Testament Theology, I: The Theology of Israel's Historical Traditions*, [1962], trans., D.M.G. Stalker (Edinburgh and London: Oliver & Boyd, 1962).

16 See H. Conzelmann, *The Theology of Luke*, (New York: Harper and Brothers, 1960); F.F. Bruce, "The Acts of the Apostle: Historical Record or Theological Reconstruction?" In *ANRW* 2.25.3 (1984): 2570-2603 and J.T. Sanders, *The Jews in Luke-Acts*, (Philadelphia: Fortress Press, 1987).

17 D.A. Knight and G.M. Tucker, *Hebrew Bible* and E.J. Epp and G.W. MacRae, *New Testament*.

18 See N.K. Gottwald, *The Tribes of Yahweh: A Sociology of the Religion of Liberated Israel 1250-1050 B.C.E.* (Maryknoll, NY: Orbis Books, 1979) and W. Meeks, *The First Urban Christians*, (New Haven: Yale University Press, 1983).
See the more recent summary of the sociological method used to study the meaning of Paul's letters in F. Watson, *Paul, Judaism and the Gentiles: A Sociological Approach*, SNTS
(continued...)

Although this book is not meant to be another study of the social scientific investigation of ancient texts,[19] it is important to mention briefly the impact of cultural anthropology on the study of "religious" texts.

Basically, the varied way of studying the ancient texts has opened up the possibility of approaching them more deeply. Cultural anthropology insists that we view the text in a "contextual"[20] way by placing the writing in a larger social and cultural setting.[21]

Now biblical scholars are aware that where there is a lack of clear documentation or evidence about the context of a given biblical author or work, careful attention paid to the manner in which ordinary interpersonal and community interaction take place can uncover the tacit meanings held by the communities in and for which various biblical writings were produced.[22]

This concentration on the "ordinary" which has been given religious symbolic value can be seen in the influential work of anthropologist Mary Douglas.[23] She has encouraged combining the work of cultural anthropology and textual criticism.[24] New Testament scholars such as W. Meeks and B. Malina

---

18(...continued)
Monograph Series, 56 (Cambridge: Cambridge University Press, 1986) and the works of H.C. Kee, especially his *Miracle in the Early Christian World: A Study in Sociohistorical Method*, (New Haven and London, Yale University Press, 1983).

See also the works by John Gager, Peter Berger, and Daniel Harrington which deal mainly with the sociological-anthropological approach. Kümmel's *The New Testament: The History of the Investigation of its Problem* (Philadelphia: Westminster Press, 1973), is a standard summary of the history of the use of historical-critical method in the study of the New Testament.

19 For an outline of the methodologies used for such a study see the summaries in Kraft and Nickelsburg, *Early Judaism*.

20 The term "thick description" is used by C. Geertz in his book *The Interpretation of Culture*, (New York: Basic Books, 1973), 3-30, as a way of describing the social and cultural concerns, groups within society, and struggles between the groups as particularly important parts of the study of a text. After one views these concerns external to the text itself, one has a thicker view of the text itself. There is more to the literature than simply the words on the page, or the structure of the text. For clarity, "contextual" has been used instead of "thick description."

21 See W. Meeks's comment on thick description in his essay "A Hermeneutics of Social Embodiment," in *Christians Among Jews and Gentiles*, ed., G.W.E. Nickelsburg and G.W. MacRae, (Philadelphia: Fortress Press, 1986), 178. See also J. Neusner's comments about "Anthropology and the Study of Talmudic Literature" in *Method and Meaning in Ancient Judaism, BJS 10* (Missoula: Scholars Press, 1979): 21-40.

22 For a recent study summarizing this method see L.J. White, "Grid and Group in Matthew's Community: The Righteousness/Honor Code in the Sermon on the Mount," *Semeia* 35 (1986): 88.

23 See M. Douglas, *Purity and Danger* (London: Routledge and Kegan Paul, 1966) and *Natural Symbols* (New York: Vintage Books, 1973).

24 See the recent discussion of the "Social-Scientific Criticism of the New Testament and its Social World" in *Semeia* 35 (1986). This whole issue is dependent on the work of M. Douglas.

have demonstrated the values of these connections in their recent monographs.[25]

By studying the "interpersonal... community interactions" and the "texture of life in particular times and places"[26] which are the concerns of the anthropologists, scholars can examine ancient texts in a broader and deeper way. This provides a much richer context to work with, namely the social and cultural concerns and questions, groups within society, and the struggles between groups and the particular political and intellectual climate in a particular city.

The urban centers, with all of their complexities, provide in themselves contexts in which biblical scholars discover keys that unlock the meaning of a particular text. The city can be used as a text that is read for an understanding of literary texts.[27]

Questions which would not ordinarily be asked are now part of the examination of an ancient text. One becomes concerned with social codes, myths, and symbols, even eating habits, and the structure of a city as a whole, issues not ordinarily raised in the examination of ancient texts. The city, with all of its variety and social levels and interchange, is becoming more and more important as a context in which scholars study a particular biblical text.

G. Theissen, a pioneer in using sociological methods in the study of the New Testament, summarizes one of the implications of his methodology as follows: "the more clearly the general background can be established, the more clearly individual elements stand out from what is universal and typical."[28] What this book does is to place early Christian *adversus Judaeos* writings in their "general background."

3. *The University Context: Departments of Religious Studies and the Study of the Bible.* This book is being written in the context of the University of Minnesota Center for Ancient Studies. It is required to be an interdisciplinary

---

25 See W.A. Meeks, *Urban*; J. Neusner, *Ancient Judaism: Debates and Disputes*, BJS 64 (Chico, CA: Scholars Press, 1984), and B.J. Malina, *Christian Origins and Cultural Anthropology: Practical Models for Biblical Interpretation* (Atlanta: John Knox Press, 1986). See also the works of W.S. Green, *Approaches To Ancient Judaism: Studies in Judaism and Its Greco-Roman Context*, BJS 32, (Atlanta: Scholars Press, 1985) and F. Watson, *Paul*. Geertz in his studies found in *Interpretation*, Peter L. Berger and T. Luckmann, *The Social Construction of Reality*, (New York: Anchor Books, 1967), have also influenced this new direction in the study of New Testament and patristic texts.

26 See W. Meeks, *Urban*, 2.

27 A more complete description of the "city as text" as well as its application as a context will be discussed below.

28 See Theissen, *Sociology of Early Palestinian Christianity*, trans., J. Bowden, (Philadelphia: Fortress Press, 1978), 4-5; F. Watson, *Paul*, and J.T. Sanders, *Jews* are more recent monographs which ask the sociological questions in their studies. These studies have indicated how these "questions" illuminate not only the "life situation" of the text but the probable intention of the writers.

study. The readings and the discussions on the topic take place within the context of five different but related academic disciplines.

There is great advantage in working in such a setting. Not all departments of Religion in universities offer an interdisciplinary context. One benefits from the various academic disciplines and access to different points of view.

Pastors and rabbis are coming to see that teaching the Bible in the context of a yeshiva, a seminary, a church, or a synagogue, can be a very different and important endeavor. In those settings, one teaches from his or her confessional point of view for the spiritual nourishment of the participants. That is one of the ways of using this literature.

But a nonconfessional or postconfessional study of these same texts can also be helpful in understanding how those writings can be and have been used in anti-Jewish ways or in deprecating the "other." When they are used to denigrate the other, then a resounding "no" must be said in order to put an end to the long-standing hostilities which have existed between Church and Synagogue.

III. The Historical-Critical Method of Biblical Studies and the Study of Ancient Jewish and Christian Literature

A. New Data

1. *Archaeology and the Jews in the Diaspora*. In the early 1950s, E.R. Goodenough suggested in his study of Jewish symbols[29] that Jews of late antiquity in the Diaspora could be found living in every level of Roman society: they were among the wealthy class as well as the poor; some were at home in the Greek culture, while others were isolated in their own communities separated from non-Jewish groups.

More recent discoveries confirm Goodenough on this point and suggest that Jews and Judaism in the Greco-Roman world were much more diverse and integrated than had previously been realized. In some places, Sardis in particular, Diaspora Jews were well integrated into the society in which they lived. They may have been important contributors to the social and intellectual activities of those towns throughout the Roman and Parthian empires from the first through the seventh century C.E.[30]

---

29 E.R. Goodenough, *Jewish Symbols*.

30 See the study of Sardis by G.M.A. Hanfmann, *Sardis from Prehistoric to Roman Times: Results of the Archaeological Exploration of Sardis, 1958-1975*, (Cambridge, MA and London: Harvard University Press, 1983) where there is a study of the evidence of Diaspora Judaism and a Diaspora Jewish community. For comments about the diversity of the Jews in the Roman world see E.R. Goodenough, *Jewish Symbols*, I:16-17. See the recent study on the stele in Aphrodisias by J. Reynolds and R.F. Tannenbaum, *Jews and God-fearers at Aphrodisias: Greek Inscriptions with Commentary* (Cambridge, England: Proceedings of the Cambridge Philological Society Supplement, 1987).

Introduction   9

Philo of Alexandria is one outstanding example of a Jew who was conversant in Greek letters and made contributions to his non-Jewish culture.[31] The evidence suggests that some Jews were "at home" in various parts of the Roman world even though they were in different positions in those cities. They fit into some cities as they were, and made contributions to those urban settings where they lived.[32]

Goodenough's observations, based on the new data collected from the Jewish and Christian sites of late antiquity, demonstrated the importance of applying the historical-critical methods developed by biblical scholars to the late Christian and Jewish texts. Later scholars would continue the work of applying new data and the historical-critical method to Jewish and Christian texts of late antiquity. J. Neusner and his pioneering work have already been mentioned.

2. *Texts: Qumran and Nag Hammadi and the Study of Ancient Judaism.* The discovery of the sectarian Jewish *Dead Sea Scrolls* in Israel and the gnostic Christian *Nag Hammadi* texts in Egypt is a major contribution to the study of early Judaism and Christianity. As the *Nag Hammadi* texts[33] have changed our view of early Christianity, so the documents from Qumran[34] have changed

---

31 See the outline of his views and the bibliography of current works on Philo in M.E. Stone, ed., *Jewish Writings of the Second Temple Period: Apocrypha, Pseudepigrapha, Qumran Sectarian Writings, Philo, Josephus.* (Philadelphia: Fortress Press, 1984), 233-282. S.J.D. Cohen, *From the Maccabees to the Mishnah*, The Library of Early Christianity (Philadelphia: Westminster Press, 1987), also mentions these contributions of Philo in his study.

32 A.T. Kraabel in his "The Diaspora Synagogue: Archaeological and Epigraphic Evidence since Sukenik", in *ANRW* II.19.1: 483, suggests that "Dura [Europos] remains a 'source' for ancient Judaism more puzzling than the Dead Sea Scrolls, and no less important."

For summaries and the most complete descriptions of the Dura Synagogue, as well as its contribution to a better understanding of a particular kind of Jewish community and Judaism in the second and third centuries, see J. Guttman, ed., *The Dura-Europos Synagogue: A Reevaluation (1932-1972)*, (Religion and the Arts 1: Missoula: Scholars Press, 1973); E.R. Goodenough, *Jewish Symbols*, vols., 9-11; C.H. Kraeling, *The Synagogue (The Excavations at Dura-Europos. Final Report VIII.1)*, (New Haven, 1956). Also see the article on "Dura-Europos" in *EJ*, 6 (1972) 275-298 and, in general, Clark Hopkins, *The Discovery of Dura Europos*, (New Haven: Yale University Press, 1979). These accounts of a city on the Persian border demonstrate how involved the Jews were in the culture by arguing against the notion that religious Jews were somehow unable to use art to portray biblical stories. They apparently did not see the use of art as a violation of the prohibition against portraying images. A new picture of Jews and Judaism in the Greco-Roman world is beginning to emerge, thanks to the use of the methods long used by biblical scholars on the evidence and texts of postbiblical literature.

33 See, for example, J.M. Robinson, *Nag Hammadi*, which presents an introduction and texts of this material.

34 W.F. Albright, *From Stone Age to Christianity, Monotheism and the Historical Process*, 2nd. ed. (New York: Doubleday, 1957), suggests that his view has only been confirmed by the discoveries at Qumran. See J.A. Fitzmyer, *The Dead Sea Scrolls Major Publications and Tools for Study* (Missoula: Scholars Press, 1977), for an excellent bibliography for the study of the scrolls. An early pioneer in making the connection between Qumran and New Testament studies is F.M. Cross, Jr., whose book *The Ancient Library of Qumran and Modern Biblical Studies* (New
(continued...)

our view of early Judaism. The words "Judaism" and "Christianity" do not have the same meaning scholars once thought they did. It is no longer possible to speak simplistically about Judaism as if there was a "normative"[35] or "orthodox"[36] Judaism. These texts support the argument made by Goodenough more than forty years ago,[37] and strengthen his assertion that there was a pluralism of thought and life-style in Palestine and Egypt among Jews in the second and third centuries.

After these discoveries it is difficult to use terms like "normative" or "orthodox" when describing Jews and Judaism of late antiquity. These texts have given scholars of late antiquity direct access to the history and philosophy of one segment of the Jewish and Christian communities, heretofore limited to indirect knowledge. Now it is possible to read about the Qumran community written by those who lived there.[38]

34(...continued)
York: Doubleday, 1958), is very helpful. Also see the work by J.H. Charlesworth, *The Pseudepigrapha and Modern Research with a Supplement 7S* (Chico, CA: Scholars Press, 1981) and M. Hengel, *Judaism and Hellenism*, II, *Notes and Bibliography*, (Philadelphia: Fortress, 1974).

35 See G.F. Moore *Judaism in the First Centuries of the Christian Era, The Age of the Tannaim*, 2 vols. ([1927] New York: Schocken, 1971) and Neusner's critique of his position in his works. See bibliographical references to Neusner's works. For an excellent discussion of the use of terms to describe early Judaism and a critique of the use of terms such as "orthodox" and "normative," see S.J.D. Cohen's *Maccabees*, 35-41.

36 See R.F. Tannenbaum's use of this term in his recent article "Jews and God-Fearers in the Holy City of Aphrodite," *BAR* 12.5 (1986): 54-57. It is unfortunate that Tannenbaum still seems to insist on maintaining the view that God-fearers were numerous and uses the "new evidence" from Aphrodisias to perpetuate that view. Even though Tannenbaum is aware of the new data and discoveries that prove a diverse first-century Judaism, old ways of describing Judaism of the first century still persist in his writings.

37 See the comments that support Goodenough's thesis made by Robinson, *Nag Hammadi*, 7, relative to the influence of both the Dead Sea Scrolls and the Nag Hammadi texts on our understanding of Gnosticism and early Christianity and Judaism. Also see A.F. Segal, "Judaism, Christianity, and Gnosticism," in S.G. Wilson *Anti-Judaism*, 133-162, on Gnosticism in relation to both Christianity and Judaism. See E.R. Goodenough, *Jewish Symbols*, 13 vols.

38 For studies which evidence a revision of the old way of looking at Jews and Christians in the first three centuries see W.D. Davies, *The Gospel and the Land*, (Los Angeles: University of California Press, 1974); S. Freyne, *Galilee from Alexander the Great to Hadrian 323 B.C.E. to 135 C.E.*, (South Bend: Notre Dame University Press, 1980); Hengel, *Judaism*; and H. Koester, *Introduction to the New Testament*, 2 vols., (Philadelphia: Fortress Press, 1982).

The article which has outlined what those changes must be is found in A.T. Kraabel, "The Disappearance of the 'God-fearers'," *Numen* 28 (1981): 113-126; "The Roman Diaspora: Six Questionable Assumptions," *JJS* 33 (1982): 445-464 and his "Impact of the Discovery of the Sardis Synagogue," in Hanfmann's *Sardis*, 178-190.

Several joint projects must also be consulted, such as W.A. Meeks and R.L. Wilken, *Jews and Christians in Antioch In The First Four Centuries of The Common Era*, (Montana: Scholars Press, 1978); J. Neusner and E. Frerichs *"To See Ourselves as Others See Us" Christians, Jews, "Others" in Late Antiquity*, (Chico, CA: Scholars Press, 1985); G.W.E. Nickelsburg and G.W. MacRae, *Christians*; E.P. Sanders, ed., *Jewish and Christian Self-Definition*, 3 vols. (Philadelphia:
(continued...)

B. New Approach to the "Jewish Issue"

1. *Theology is Not History*. The New Testament, as well as the *adversus Judaeos* texts used in this book, are theological interpretations. As such, the persistent error in New Testament and early Christian literary studies of accepting theological interpretations as historical records must be corrected.

J.T. Sanders and F. Watson have recently written books which make a contribution to a correct understanding and use of the New Testament writings. Their works concentrate on Luke-Acts and the writings of Paul. Their arguments are based on two standard methodological presuppositions about the New Testament texts: First, they restate an accepted premise that the New Testament is not concerned about being a history book, reporting accurately on Jews and Judaism, so much as it tries to present a point of view.[39] Second, they suggest that the New Testament is best understood when the reader pays close attention to the social context of the text. Sanders and Watson use "social history" as a guide to the study of the text.[40]

On the first point, Sanders argues this way: "Luke's altering the received tradition of the passion narrative in the direction of greater Jewish culpability in the death of Jesus represents more a theological tendency than a historical tradition. Furthermore, the fact that the same Jewish religious leaders appear so routinely in Acts rather woodenly working the same mischief on the church that they worked on Jesus casts a thick shadow of doubt on the historicity of those accounts."[41]

The "God-fearer" debate over the last decade is another example of how Luke-Acts has been read as history rather than theology. The outlines of the "debate" have been most clearly drawn by A.T. Kraabel, who in his article "The Disappearance of the 'God-fearers'"[42] suggests: "at least for the Roman Diaspora, the evidence presently available is far from convincing proof for the existence of such a class of Gentiles as traditionally defined by the assumptions of the secondary literature."[43]

38(...continued)
Fortress Press, 1980-1982); B.A. Pearson and J.E. Goehring, Jr., *The Roots of Egyptian Christianity*, (Philadelphia: Fortress Press, 1986); Wilson, *Anti-Judaism*; and Kraft and Nickelsburg, ed., *Early Judaism*. These studies summarize the work which has gone on in the study of early Christianity and Judaism, as well as suggesting new directions for the study of this period.

39 See J.T. Sanders, *Jews*, 19.

40 See F. Watson, *Paul*. For a review of F. Watson, *Paul*; P.F. Esler, *Community*, and J.T. Sanders, *Jews*, see A.T. Kraabel in the forthcoming (1989) *Religious Studies Review*.

41 J.T. Sanders, *Jews*, 18-19.

42 *Numen*, 28 (1981):113-126.

43 Ibid., 121.

Kraabel has pointed out that Acts has been used as history and as "evidence" for the growth of Christianity from the synagogues of the Diaspora.[44] The use of theologically driven texts for a historical reconstruction has been the basis for most scholars' perception of the emergence of early Christianity.

In support of the second methodological approach, Watson suggests that it is important for the student of Paul to recognize the "social reality underlying Paul's statements about Judaism";[45] these social realities have determined Paul's way of arguing and reflect the reader's concerns. In Paul's case they are more "sociological than theological."[46] This means that when contemporary scholars try to interpret Paul they must look for the underlying social realities and questions which were experienced by Paul's audience.

For Watson, "Paul's aim was to persuade the Jewish Christians to recognize the legitimacy of the Gentile congregation and to join with them in worship, even though this would inevitably mean a final separation from the synagogues."[47] Thus Paul's aim was to speak to a specific first-century audience and not to a universal and timeless church.

Scholars who read the New Testament texts with these two methodological concerns in mind begin to view the content of these writings differently. It is becoming clear that their reasons for being anti-Jewish are different from modern ones. Watson and Sanders have helped make this distinction for New Testament studies.

To read the New Testament solely as a history book, and not reflect on the theological concerns and motivations, is not only a problem for students of first-century sacred literature but one for scholars of later Christian and Jewish literature as well.

Even a careful scholar like W.H.C. Frend uses the ancient writings as "historical" evidence.[48] He uses these texts to reconstruct the past without cri-

---

44 The "debate" can be followed in the following works: A.T. Kraabel, "Disappearance": 113-126; R.S. MacLennan and A.T. Kraabel, "The God-Fearers -- A Literary and Theological Invention?" *BAR* 12.5 (1986): 46-53. The responses to this article were made by R. Tannenbaum, "God-Fearers," 54-57 and L. Feldman, "The Omnipresence of the God-Fearers," *BAR* 12.5 (1986): 58-63. See also J.A. Overman, "The God-Fearers: Some Neglected Features, *JSNT* 32 (1988): 17-26; T.M. Finn, "The God-fearers Reconsidered." *CBQ* 47 (1985): 75-84; J. Gager, "Jews, Gentiles and Synagogues in the Book of Acts," in *Christians*, edited by G.W.E. Nickelsburg and G.W. MacRae: 91-99; A.T. Kraabel, "Greeks, Jews, and Lutherans in the Middle Half of Acts," in *Christians*: 147-157 and J. Reynolds and R.F. Tannenbaum, *Aphrodisias*.

45 Watson, *Paul*, 177.

46 Ibid. 177-178.

47 Ibid.

48 In commenting on Juvenal's *Satires*, Frend writes: "On this score as well, the Dispersion Jews showed themselves to better advantage. They were intensely keen to propagate their religion, hawking proselytism and groceries from door to door (Juvenal, *Satires* (ed. Owen) vi. 543-545) and influencing those around them long after they ceased to be politically dangerous." See W.H.C. Frend, *Martyrdom and Persecution in the Early Church*, (Oxford, 1965), 189. See M.

(continued...)

Introduction

tically evaluating their adequacy as historical reports in the twentieth-century sense.[49] His conclusions, then, rest on the tenuous assumption of the historical reliability of theological or philosophical texts.

2. *The Case of the Mishnah*. Jacob Neusner has been a pioneer in using the critical method from biblical studies and from other disciplines of the humanities applied to the study of rabbinic literature. He has consistently worked to clarify the philosophical, sociological, and theological purposes of rabbinic texts using methods employed by most biblical scholars.[50]

Neusner suggests that confusion results when one attempts to use these specialized writings to reconstruct the past. The most one can do from the text itself is try to find the intention of the last redactor of the work. One must remember that the writings of the rabbis, in their present forms as Talmud, Mishnah, Midrash, or any other rabbinic literature, are products of the last person who put them together. The finished text tells the reader more about the last editor of the material than about the original writers who are quoted in the document.

Most critical biblical scholars agree that the writings of the Bible are the result of the last redactor and may reflect that redactor's point of view more than that of the person they are supposed to be quoting. Neusner agrees with this statement. A fourth-century rabbi quoting a first-century teacher may be giving the reader his view, and not that of the person he quotes.

Thus, it appears that the written texts from late antiquity are not reliable sources of the period they are supposed reflect. They primarily reflect the concerns of the last redactor.[51]

48(...continued)
Stern, ed. and trans., *Greek and Latin Authors on Jews and Judaism*, 3 vols., (Jerusalem: The Israel Academy of Sciences and Humanities, 1976-1984), 2:94-95, who warns the reader about Juvenal's intent: "Juvenal could not tolerate either the pliability of the Greeks, or the part played by the Egyptians or Syrians parvenu in the life of Rome. Particularly abhorrent were Egyptians, whose barbarian behavior appeared in such glaring contrast to the cultural society of the West (XV, 110f). It was only to be expected that such a writer would include Jews among the targets of the satire."

49 Frend, in *The Rise of Christianity*, (Philadelphia: Fortress Press, 1984), is consistent in interpreting texts without questioning the adequacy of their use for reporting what actually happened. An earlier work by M. Baney (*Tertullianius, Africa Romana: Some Reflections of Life in North Africa in the Writings of Tertullian*, (Washington, D.C., 1948)) tried to reconstruct Carthage using Tertullian's writings. She introduces her doctoral thesis by admitting that "the present study of Tertullian as a witness to his times is an endeavor to exact from his writings those details which give evidence of the life of the people of his day and to present their material in a systematic fashion." (Baney, *Tertullianius*, v). See note on J. Neusner below.

50 J. Neusner has many monographs and books describing his method and arguing his case for the use of the critical method in the study of rabbinic texts. See *The Talmud of the Land of Israel*, vol. 35, *Introduction Taxonomy*, English translation J. Neusner, (Chicago: The University of Chicago Press, 1983), 49, for a summary of his method.

51 See Kelber, "Narrative as Interpretation and Interpretation of Narrative: Hermeneutical Reflections on the Gospels," in *Semeia* 39 (1987):107-133. In this article Kelber supports the
(continued...)

As the study of rabbinic texts and other Christian and Jewish texts from late antiquity continues to rely on the historical-critical method used by biblical scholars,[52] the discussions around the purpose and meaning of those texts will heat up. Already there is much discussion around Neusner's writings and critical assessment of what has gone on in the field of rabbinic studies in the seminaries and yeshivas.[53]

3. *The Sociological and Anthropological Questions and the Study of Ancient Jewish Literature.* Another interest of J. Neusner is his critical study of rabbinic texts, applying the social scientific methods to them.[54] In his book *Judaism: The Evidence of Mishnah*,[55] Neusner concludes with a critique of Moore's study of Judaism in the first century by suggesting that Moore fails to "take account of the evidence of the Halakah, that is, of Mishnah, of the second-century authorities" and omits "the social and political context of a religious structure and system. For the law of the Mishnah deals precisely with that---the construction of society, the formation of a rational, public, normative way of life."

The so-called "construction of society, the formation of a rational, public, normative way of life," is an important insight for the reading of rabbinic texts as Neusner makes amply clear throughout his many works.

51(...continued)
idea that a text is a dynamic in itself. One cannot simply read a text and receive evidence from it for the setting to which it was written. The writer is usually working on an interpretation of something else as well. See especially pages 127ff.

52 For a summary of the critical work done on the Bible, see the Scholars Press anniversary volumes by D.A. Knight and G.M. Tucker, *Hebrew Bible*, and E.J. Epp and G.W. MacRae, *New Testament*. See also W.G. Kümmel, *New Testament*, which presents a history of the use of historical criticism in the study of the New Testament.

53 See the Bibliography for J. Neusner references to the critical study of the rabbinic texts. Also see R.A. Kraft and G.W.E. Nickelsburg, *Early Judaism*, especially A. Saldarini's article, "Reconstruction of Rabbinic Judaism," 437-477. See S.J.D. Cohen, "The Political and Social History of the Jews in Greco-Roman Antiquity: The State of the Question," in the same volume.
   J. Neusner admits in his *Pharisees* that "the study of the Talmudic and related literature for historical purposes stands conceptually and methodologically a century and a half behind biblical studies. When Talmudic literature was studied in universities, it was mainly for philological, not historical, purposes." (322). See Cohen, "Political," 31-56 for a critical view of Neusner's position.

54 See J. Neusner, *Method* 10, 21-40. See also Cohen, *Maccabees*, for an overview of this period. See also R.A. Kraft and G.W.E. Nickelsburg, *Early Judaism*, for a summary of the methods used to study rabbinic literature. Refer to the listing of Neusner's writings used for this thesis in the bibliography. See also Cohen's critique of Neusner's conclusions in "Jacob Neusner, Mishnah, and Counter-Rabbinics, A Review Essay," *Con.J.* 37.1 (1983): 50-51. See also Lightstone's positive comment about Moore's careful scholarship in "Judaic Context," 105.

55 J. Neusner, *Judaism, The Evidence of the Mishnah*, (Chicago and London: The University of Chicago Press, 1981) 12.

The sociological questions applied to the study of ancient texts have been skillfully used by Neusner and have opened the way for other scholars to look more carefully at other literature outside of the biblical writings in the same way.

IV. The New Approach Applied to a Study of Second-Century Christian *adversus Judaeos* Literature

A. Archaeological Data and the Study of *adversus Judaeos* Texts

The studies of early rabbinic Judaism have provided another model for the study of texts of late antiquity. These studies have used and developed the historical-critical methods most biblical scholars have used. It is now possible to take advantage of the insights of earlier studies and determine the value of those studies in using the same methodologies when working with the second-century Christian *adversus Judaeos* texts.

Major works have been published in the last two decades which have added more information about the settings in which these writings were produced (the list of works is in the first footnote above, and additional works are listed in the Bibliography below). This new information, along with the reinterpretation of the old data in light of the new methods and information, demands that these second-century texts be examined anew.

The following chapters suggest what the new archaeological data and methods have contributed to the study of the *adversus Judaeos* texts. It will also be suggested that it is necessary to view differently the way Jews and Christians related to each other in the second century.

From a review of many studies of second-century rabbinic and Christian literature, this writer concludes that not all scholars have taken advantage of the new data or the historical-critical methods in approaching these "postbiblical" texts. Instead, archaeological, epigraphic,[56] and nonliterary written materials have been referred to by some serious scholars, but have not used them sufficiently in their studies of the emergence of Christianity and Judaism in the first three centuries C.E.[57]

---

56 See description and dates of some relevant epigraphic materials given by J. Reynolds, "Roman Inscriptions, 1981-1985," in *JRS*, 76 (1986): 124-146. There is plenty of new data and stimulating methods developing out of this new data, but few scholars seem to incorporate this information into the interpretation of ancient Christian and Jewish texts. See footnote 57 below about W.H.C. Frend's work.

57 See W.H.C. Frend, "Archaeology and Patristic Studies," *SP* 18.1, *Papers of the 9th International Conference on Patristic Studies*, Oxford, 1973, ed. Elizabeth A Livingstone, (Kalamazoo, Mich. 1985), 9-21, in which Frend describes the importance of archaeology in the study of ancient patristic texts, but never really says what it has done to influence his understanding of the "received views" from other scholars. Even though his lecture was given prior to more recent publications on the subject, Frend does not make note of these works in an updated comment, which would have been possible in 1985 when it was finally published. See for instance, the ground-breaking works of G.M.A. Hanfmann, *Sardis* and E.M. Meyers and J.F.
(continued...)

When the new data and methodologies are used to review the relationship between Jews and Christians in late antiquity, a different picture of the relationship of early Judaism and Christianity begins to emerge. The picture is more balanced and not all one way. Different cities and regions present their unique history of the relationship between the two groups.[58]

B. The Sociological Question and the Texts

Each *adversus Judaeos* text will be examined as a product of a particular and influential social setting, much as F. Watson and J.T. Sanders did with the New Testament.[59] It will be appropriate to ask the sociological questions in each case: Where was it written? When was it written and what seems to be the social reality that stimulated such a writing?

The underlying sociological realities will be sought. An attempt will be made to determine what the author wanted his audience to do as a result of reading his text. Did he want the Christians to stay away from the Synagogue because they were being lured away from the Church? Did the writer want his readers to make more converts from the Jewish community? Did he want to set up a school that would compete with the more venerable school run by Jewish teachers across the street? What information do we have about the town or city in which the author lived or worked that would help explain the nature of his arguments?

When one studies the texts from the perspective of these sociological questions, it becomes clear how much the point of the particular writing is determined by that social context. If the context is changed, the meaning of the text is changed. It is no small matter, then, to study the context as well as the text itself to come to an understanding of the meaning of early Christian and Jewish literature.[60]

57(...continued)
Strange, *Archaeology, the Rabbis, and Early Christianity: The Social and Historical Setting of Palestinian Judaism and Christianity*, (Nashville: Abingdon, 1981). Each one of these scholars has gone further than Frend in explicating the value of archaeology in changing the methods with which one views the ancient texts. Also, Frend does not mention the social-scientific works that influence the way one interprets data.

58 For studies which have provided models in the use of the new data and historical-critical method see Kraft and Nickelsburg, *Early Judaism*, and M.I. Finley, *Ancient History: evidence and models*, (New York: Viking Press, 1986). Finley is careful in the way he uses the social sciences to study ancient history.

59 F. Watson, *Paul*, 19-23 and J.T. Sanders, *Jews*, both provide the kind of model being used in biblical studies today when approaching a text employing sociological questions in addition to theological and historical concerns.

60 See the summaries of this approach in *Interpretation* 36.3 (July 1982), especially the articles by John Gager, "Shall we marry our enemies? Sociology and the New Testament", 256-265, and W A. Meeks, "The Social Context of Pauline Theology", 266-277. Also refer to J.S. Kselman, The Social World of the Israelite Prophets: A Review Article", *RSR* 11.2 (April, 1985):
(continued...)

C. The Case of the City as Text

This writer has several times stated that it is imperative, when interpreting or analyzing documents written in any period, to relate the writings to the historical, political, economic, intellectual, and religious characteristics of the particular community at a specific time. This admonition, best expressed by Jacob Neusner in the study of rabbinic literature, has helped lead the writer to this book, a new approach to the study of the four *adversus Judaeos* writings.

Neusner insists that the 'place' or the 'community' in which the writers were doing their work, the 'time' and 'circumstances' as well as the cultural setting in which they were written, are important for an understanding of the content of the rabbinic texts.[61] (Some New Testament scholars have also used this approach---with early Christian texts.[62] However, even though this method is known, it has not been used consistently for the study of patristic literature from the second to the third centuries).

For example, no one has yet done a "contextual"[63] study of a particular place and then examined the *adversus Judaeos* literature in the light of the particular cities and time when they were written. This book intends to fill that gap and offer a new interpretation of the purpose and significance of those writings.

A "contextual" study of a town or country includes everything that happens in a particular place. It examines the conflicts, the economics; the military, political, and religious conditions; special relationships, and a variety of other factors which are important to help the interpreter to come to conclusions about a particular literary text. The city itself, then, becomes a setting which can be "read" as a kind of text.

Reading an *adversus Judaeos* text within the light of this "contextual" work means that a literary text which can be placed in a particular geographical and sociopolitical context and time period is adequately interpreted. Without such information, one is left to the whims and predispositions of the reader. As a

---

60(...continued)
120-128, which deals with the Old Testament but has applications for the New Testament as well. See also the articles in the recent *RSR* 2.4 (October 1985) and *Semeia* 35 and the work of Malherbe, *The Social Aspects of Early Christianity*, 2d. ed. (Philadelphia: Fortress Press, 1983). There is the summary by R.A. Kraft and G.W.E. Nickelsburg, *Early Judaism* that gives an overview of the various methods used to study ancient Jewish and Christian texts.

61 See J. Neusner "The Experience of the City in Late Antique Judaism," *Approaches to Ancient Judaism* V, BJS 32, edited by W.S. Green, (Atlanta: Scholars Press, 1985), 37-52.

62 For the Old Testament see N.K. Gottwald, *Tribes*, and for the New Testament see W.A. Meeks, *Urban*.

63 See C. Geertz, *Interpretation*, 3-32 and his lectures, *Works and Lives: The Anthropologist as Author*, (Stanford: Stanford University Press, 1988). The term "contextual" has been used throughout this thesis to clarify Geertz's phrase, "thick description." See footnote 20 above on "thick description."

result, the reader becomes the context of the text, and his or her predispositions determine how the text will be interpreted.

Therefore, to use the city as a text and read the *adversus Judaeos* literature in that context, the following factors can be used effectively:

- The *history of the city*, especially events which were contemporaneous with the place of the literature being studied.
- *Archaeological evidence* may be used to help the scholar understand more completely the circumstances of the city.
- The *literature from the city*.
- *Ancient writings about the city* might help.
- *Special places* within the city---synagogues, churches, libraries, graves, are particularly useful sources for an understanding of what the city had in the way of Christian and Jewish places of worship.

Readers of this book, pursuing the four analyses following, should be able to recognize the writer's application of "Cities as a Text" and gain from those cities insights into the intention of the writing.

D. Nonconfessional Reading of Ancient Christian Texts

The texts will also be read in the context of the academic setting. This means that a critical view of the writer's intention will be held throughout. There are confessional and religious views which are being expressed in these texts which must be seen in their own context.

J.T. Sanders suggests that there is "doubt on the historicity" of many of the accounts in the Gospel of Luke and opposes accepting theological interpretations of the New Testament as historical records.[64] The *adversus Judaeos* writings analyzed in this book are also documents which have been produced as confessional statements against the Jews and Judaism of the second century. Far too often this specific theological intention has not been recognized by later Christian writers and has lead to a perpetuation of an anti-Jewish and anti-Judaism attitude within the Christian community. It is the task of this writer to demonstrate this theological or confessional intention in the second-century *adversus Judaeos* texts and work to show its intention in the particular time and location in which the writer of those documents worked.

They were not meant to be timeless statements about Jews and Judaism; rather they were time-specific, space-specific. This will be discussed in the following four chapters.

---

64 J.T. Sanders, *Jews*, 19.

E. Reading the *adversus Judaeos* Texts in the Context of the University

An attempt has been made to read the *adversus Judaeos* texts as literature, learning to appreciate their value as religious documents in a sociopolitical context. The sociological questions which are raised in the texts themselves have been given special attention.

These texts are also "religious" writings. They were written for faith or for the faithful. They were meant to say something to the spiritual needs of individuals who were struggling with their own identity as Christians or Jews. This "religious" purpose was also this writer's concern.

Also, it is possible to learn something about the way early Christians viewed the Jews and Judaism from these *adversus Judaeos* texts, and to realize that social condition creates negative feelings between people from different groups. These negative feelings and attitudes do not need to be perpetuated, though, and should be challenged. Insecurity on the part of some groups, which some of the studied texts demonstrate, causes individuals and communities of people to distrust and finally hate the other.

It is possible, in the context of the academic and religious settings, to gain insights from the texts of late antiquity that can help people today live more peacefully with each other.

V. Conclusion

It is expected that this study will demonstrate a valid and useful way to examine Christian *adversus Judaeos* texts and gain new insights into the relations between Jews and Christians in the second century. This new view can influence the way scholars examine all Christian literature when it speaks about Jews and Judaism.

This book will also provide examples of the way to look at the *adversus Judaeos* literature and thus allow the reader a new approach to the study of these texts.

It will also enable the scholar to reexamine other similar texts and raise questions about the meaning of Jew and Judaism or Christian and Christianity when it appears in those texts.

As a contribution to the ongoing debate about the methods and use of ancient texts, this book provides one example of a trajectory from the already well established historical-critical method, when applied to text other than the biblical literature. J. Neusner has contributed much to the study of religious texts of late antiquity and has been an example who inspires many of us to take the next step: examining all Christian and Jewish literature of late antiquity in light of the *developing* historical-critical method.

CHAPTER ONE

BARNABAS: A MODERATE APPROACH
The *Epistle of Barnabas* (c. 115-117 C.E.)

I. Introduction and Summary of the *Epistle*

The so-called *Epistle of Barnabas* has been characterized as one early Christian writing which reflects a "distinctly anti-Judaic bias."[1] It was probably written within the context of a school or "club" in Alexandria, Egypt, sometime before the Bar-Kokhba War (115-117 C.E.) in the land of Israel.[2] The *Epistle*

---

1 See the summary of the purpose, provenance, and date of the *Epistle* in B.A. Pearson "Earliest Christianity in Egypt: Some Observations," in The *Roots of Egyptian Christianity*, edited by B.A. Pearson and J.E. Goehring, (Philadelphia: Fortress Press, 1986): 150-151, where he contends that the *Epistle of Barnabas* was written around 115-117 C.E. in Alexandria. Pearson also suggests that it reflected the final split between church and synagogue. Because of Pearson's recent (1987) and ongoing involvement in the archaeological exploration in Alexandria, and his balanced presentation of the data, as well as his knowledge of the literary evidence, greater weight has been given to Pearson's arguments here than to those who suggest another provenance and date for the *Epistle*. But see M.B. Shukster and P. Richardson, who disagree and suggest that it was written around 98 C.E. in the provenance of Syro-Palestine: M.B. Shukster and P. Richardson "Temple and Bet Ha-midrash in the *Epistle of Barnabas*," in *Anti-Judaism*, 17-31. See also P. Richardson and M.B. Shukster, "Barnabas, Nerva, and the Yavnean Rabbis", in *JTS* 34 (1983):31-55, which examines the same theme. See A.F.J. Klijn, "Jewish Christianity in Egypt," in B.A. Pearson and J.E. Goehring, *Roots*, 173, nn. 71, 72, where it is suggested that the Hellenistic Judaism in Syria and Alexandria were probably very similar. (see n.72). H. Koester, *Introduction* 2:277-279 is inconclusive about author, date, and provenance of the *Epistle*. But see R.M. Grant "Theological Education at Alexandria," in B.A. Pearson and J.E. Goehring, *Roots*, 181, who agrees with Pearson's view that the *Epistle of Barnabas* was written in Alexandria around 115-117 C.E.

2 H. Räisänen in *Paul and The Law*, [1983] (Philadelphia: Fortress Press., 1986): 220, points to several sections of the *Epistle of Barnabas* (14.5, 16.7, and 4.9) that indicate that the author was a Gentile Christian. It is not possible to determine conclusively from the text itself who the author is (cf. M.A. Shukster and P. Richardson, "Temple," 16ff, who try to discover the author by locating the *Epistle* in the "provenance of Syro-Palestine." They suggest that the *Epistle* reflects the intellectual concerns which originated in that region). See also, Klijn, "Jewish Christianity," 166, n. 28, where he indicates that there is a debate over the provenance of the *Epistle*. See K. Wengst, *Tradition und Theologie des Barnabasbrief*, (Berlin, 1971), 55ff., who locates the *Epistle* in Alexandria, Egypt. See also the notes in the critical text of K. Bihlmeyer, *Die apostolischen Väter*, Neubearbeitung der Funkschen Ausgabe, *SQS*, 2, Reihe 1, (Tübigen, 1956) and R. Wilde, *Treatment*, who consider the author of the *Epistle of Barnabas* to have been a Jewish Christian. See also J. Jervell, *The Unknown Paul, Essays on Luke-Acts and Early Christian History*, (Minneapolis: Augsburg Publishing House, 1984), 26-51, where he suggests that Jewish Christianity was a very strong force in the development of the early Church in the first two centuries. This is part of the problem in coming to an understanding of who the Jews are in early Christian writings. Were they Jews who did not accept Jesus as the Messiah? Or were they Jewish Christians?

For the idea that the early Christians gathered in "schools" or "clubs" for their work and mutual support, see W. Meeks, *Urban*, 31. This idea is referred to below in the chapter on

(continued...)

includes historical allusions which seem to reflect the time and events of the early part of the second century C.E.[3]

The contents of the *Epistle* may be divided into two unequal sections: The first part (1-17) is a theoretical and dogmatic section which deals with the concerns of a Christian community intent on proving that its form of Christianity (as outlined by Barnabas) is superior to Judaism. This theme is present in all *adversus Judaeos* literature.

2(...continued)
Justin. See the discussion of Valentinus (c. 100-175) in B. Layton, *The Gnostic Scriptures* (New York: Doubleday & Company, 1987): 217 where it is suggested that he may have written and published in Alexandria during the years Barnabas was working there.

3 For a reference both to the destruction of the Temple in 70 C.E. and the promise of rebuilding the Temple c. 117 C.E. See *Barn.* 16.3-4:
> That is happening now. For owing to the war it was destroyed by the enemy; at present even the servants of the enemy will build it up again.

Also see the summary of the promise of the rebuilding of the Temple in H.H. Ben-Sasson, *A History of the Jewish People*, (Cambridge: Harvard University Press, 1976), 331, and more recently E.M. Smallwood, *The Jews Under Roman Rule, From Pompey to Diocletian*, Studies in Judaism in Late Antiquity 20, (Leiden: Brill, 1981), 435, who suggests the idea of rebuilding the Temple during this period came from Jewish legends or hope that it would be rebuilt. Compare P. Richardson's comments ("Barnabas," *JTS* 34 (1983):47-49, where he discusses who the Emperor was during Barnabas's work. He suggests it was Nerva, c. 96 C.E. and that Barnabas was living at the time of the short-lived fear (by Christians) that the Temple would be rebuilt. This would trouble Christians because they were taught to think of the destruction of the Temple as God's punishment of those Jews who did not accept Jesus as the Messiah. This position is challenged by the thesis of this chapter that Barnabas is more concerned about a growing fanatical messianism than the actual rebuilding of the Temple.

See also B.A. Pearson, "Earliest Christianity," 132-156, where the argument for an Alexandrian provenance and date around 117 C.E. is convincingly made. M.B. Shukster and P. Richardson, "Temple," 22, argue the other view, that Barnabas at 16.4 is "alluding to the Yavnean authorities who were no doubt perceived as instrumental in securing and supporting the Romans' endorsement of the rebuilding venture" (23).

Still others have suggested the rebuilding of the Temple to be around 117 C.E. Both dates could be in the memory of the author of Barnabas no matter which date he wrote his work. Compare J.J. Gunther, "The *Epistle of Barnabas* and the Final Rebuilding of the Temple," *JSJ* 7.2 (1976): 150-151: "Therefore, on neither exegetical nor historical grounds should *Barn.* 16.3-4 be understood to refer to rebuilding of a temple of stone during Hadrian's reign. The passage should not be used either for dating the *Epistle* or for understanding the history of the Temple." See the following studies of the *Epistle of Barnabas*: L. W. Barnard, "The Date of the *Epistle*---A Document of Early Egyptian Christianity," *JEA* 44 (1958): 101-107; "Is The *Epistle of Barnabas* a Paschal Homily?" *VC* 15 (1961): 8-22; *Studies in Church History and Patristica*, Patriarchal Institute for Patristic Studies. (Thessaloniki, 1978): 63-72; R.A. Kraft, "Barnabas' Isaiah Text and Melito's Paschal Homily," *JBL* 80, (1961): 371-373; Pearson, "Earliest Christianity," 132-161; A.P. O'Hagan, "Barnabas: A Christian Theology of History," *Material Re-Creation in the Apostolic Fathers, SP* (=*TU* 100), (Berlin, 1968): 44-67, who argues for the Alexandrian authorship of a "pagan convert to Christianity" (44-45), and yet makes clear that its roots are deep in the same Jewish tradition out of which Philo emerged; Quasten, *Patrology* 1:90-91; and H. Räisänen, *Paul*, 121 and 220.

The second part (18-22) deals with moral teachings of the Christian community.⁴ This part of the *Epistle* could easily be from Jewish or Christian sources. It is similar to the *Didache* or *Teaching of the Twelve Apostles* which was composed sometime during the early part of the second century C.E.⁵

The *Epistle* is a "short letter" that attempts to help the readers find a way for their knowledge to be "perfected along with their faith" (1.5). This would be done in a time when the "worker of evil himself" (2.1) was in power. The reader, Barnabas suggests, should take heed of his teachings and "bear patiently in them for this is what the Lord wants" (2.3).

Some have suggested that the *Epistle* is a "theological tract,"⁶ or "academic treatise" in the form of a letter, on the relation between Christianity and Judaism, and does not imply a threat to Christianity from Judaism.⁷ It has also been viewed as presenting an anti-Judaic bias which reflects a final split between Church and Synagogue.⁸ Many references in the *Epistle* support this view. One is told from the beginning that he should not "err like them"(2.9) and that "we should not be shipwrecked by conversion to their law"(3.6).⁹ The Covenant was not theirs but ours (4.7; 6.16, 19.) because they have turned to idols (4.8) and abandoned the Covenant (4.14). The position of this book is that the *Epistle* is a tract written to moderate a Christian and Jewish fanatical

---

4 For a general description of the outline and contents of the *Epistle* see J. Quasten, *Patrology*, 1:85-92 and H. Schreckenberg, *Adversus-Judaeos-Texte*, 174-178.

5 See R.H. Connolly, "The Didache in Relation to the Epistle of Barnabas," *JTS* 33 (1932): 237-253.

6 Quasten, *Patrology*, 1:86.

7 Räisänen, *Paul*, 220. Even though there may not have been a threat from Judaism itself, tensions still could exist between the two communities. The nature of that tension is the concern of this chapter.

8 See B.A. Pearson "Earliest Christianity," 151. But see the provocative discussion by Shukster and Richardson, "Temple," 17ff., who suggest that Barnabas was written to Syro-Palestine Christians who defined themselves over against the Jews who were thinking about rebuilding the Temple. The hostility in the writing "is related to identifiable historical circumstances" (17); the rebuilding of the Temple which would make "Judaism a dangerously attractive alternative to Christianity" (30). This is a compelling argument based solely on literary analysis of the Jewish and Christian texts. The danger in this kind of analysis is finding the correct date for the origin of these writings. The basic thesis of this chapter is that the *Epistle* was written in Alexandria, for one of the Christian communities in that city around the second decade of the second century. See Pearson, "Earliest Christianity," 150-151; Grant, "Theological Education," 181; and Klijn, "Jewish Christianity," 166, in B.A. Pearson, and J.E. Goehring, *Roots*.

9 There is a problem with this text (3.6). The sense is that we are either in danger of becoming "resident aliens" (*epelutoi*) of their law or as *codex Sinaiticus*, s. IV has it, that we become proselytes (*proselutoi*) of their law. On the discussion of these two words see *TDNT* 6: 729-730 and the critical notes in *Epistola di Barnaba Introduzione, testo critico, traduzione, commento, glossario e indici a cura di Francesco Scorza Barcellona*. (Torino: Societa editrice Internazionale 1975), on 3.6.

messianism both within and outside of Barnabas's community or "club" in Alexandria.

Barnabas continues by telling his readers that the synagogue is a place of the wicked (5.13) and those who are in the synagogue are unable to understand clearly the covenant (10.12), or correctly interpret its meaning.

Christians are the ones who are brought into the good land (6.16) and therefore are the heirs of the covenant (6.19). The problem is that "they" (the Jews to whom the *Epistle* is referring) have looked at the scriptures in the wrong way, that is, literally and not symbolically, and therefore have always been unable to understand them properly.

Barnabas then uses examples of how the text should be understood: through allegory and typology. "They" erred in their understanding of circumcision (9.4), the food laws (10.1, 3, 9), the meaning of Sabbath (15.5-9) the purpose of the Temple (16.1, 10.10) and the meaning of most Scriptures.[10] Barnabas offers an exegesis of the scripture and traditions which is similar to the arguments of Tertullian, Justin, and Melito.

It would be easy to assume from a reading of the *Epistle* that the author argues for the superiority of Christianity over Judaism. After all, he did tell his readers that the Covenant belongs to the Christians and not the Jews (4.7; 6.16,19; 4.14; 13.1). But the superiority of one tradition over the other does not seem to be the consuming passion of Barnabas's argument as much as he wants to make sure that one has the correct understanding of the tradition. Barnabas has the correct view of the tradition. His opponents do not hold the proper view of it.

In the discussion below, several concerns are raised which suggest that perhaps Barnabas is not speaking about all Jews and every form of Judaism, but to a *particular* form of Judaism: one which he encountered in a specific place (Alexandria) at a particular time (115-117 C.E.) and which, for whatever reasons, was seen as some kind of threat[11] to the emerging Christian community. The close quarters in Alexandria and the nature of the Jewish community, as well as the climate of unrest in the city in this period, certainly contributed to the tension between the two groups.[12]

---

10 Barnabas tells his readers that the whole scripture refers to Christ. The two goats (7.8-11) are a type of Jesus, Numbers 19 is talking about Jesus, (8.1-2), Numbers 21 is about the Cross of Jesus (12.2,5). Contrary to Shukster and Richardson, "Temple," 28-30, these typological arguments are not limited to a Syro-Palestine or Egyptian provenance. See Klijn, "Jewish Christianity," 173, nn. 71, 72, who suggests, correctly, a more universal provenance of ideas. In one way this makes the work of discovering the specific context of a particular text much more difficult.

11 This view is contrary to Räisänen, *Paul*, 121, 220.

12 See Map 1 in the Appendix, Ancient Alexandria, with relevant early Jewish and Christian sites in Pearson, "Earliest Christianity," 158-159. See the discussion of the revolt of 115-117 in Smallwood, *Jews*, 389-427.

II. The City of Alexandria as "Text"

A. The Evidence from Second-Century Alexandria

A reading of the *Epistle* reveals certain characteristics which call for a particular kind of literary and theological milieu, one resembling Alexandria more closely than the other most commonly suggested provenance, Yavneh, Palestine.

The *Epistle* grew out of a city where there was a long Hellenistic tradition with an eschatological orientation; it uses the Greek language and shows an understanding of Semitic thought; it is anticultic and interested in salvation history; and it is diligent in the study of scripture and at the same time preserves literature and hymns which originated in its own particular tradition.[13]

These observations and literary analysis of the *Epistle of Barnabas* from R.A. Kraft led him and this writer to suggest that Alexandria, and not Syria or some community in the region of Yavneh, for that matter, provides the most satisfactory milieu for the *Epistle*.[14]

This list of "satisfactory milieux" has been expanded and improved upon by R.M. Grant and B.A. Pearson in their recent studies of Egyptian Christianity,[15] and provides further support of this thesis. T.A. Robinson's criticism of Bauer and Koester's ideas about the origin of Christianity in Alexandria has

---

13 These observations are from R.A. Kraft, Review of P. Prigent, *Les Testimonia dans le Christiennes primitif: l'Epitre de Barnabe i-xvi et ses sources*, *JTS* 13 (1962): 406-407. See also the discussion in Pearson, "Earliest Christianity," 150, n. 103: "For a social description of the house churches in the Pauline mission see Meeks, *Urban*, 75-81. Much of what Meeks discusses would apply also to Alexandrian Christianity." This comment by Pearson opens the way for a broader view of provenance. It could be that most any Hellenistic city around the Mediterranean could be the provenance for the *Epistle*. Certainly, even Jerusalem in the second century could be considered a Hellenistic city in some ways.

See the standard discussion of the Jews in the Diaspora, especially in Alexandria, Tcherikover, *Hellenistic Civilization and the Jews*, translated by S. Appelbaum, (New York: Atheneum, 1977), 296-332; Smallwood, *Jews*, 224-250; Tarn, *Hellenistic Civilization*, third revised edition by the Author and G.T. Griffith. (New York: New American Library, 1975), 210-238. It is difficult to read this history and the description of the city and not be impressed with how perfectly, or nearly perfectly, the *Epistle of Barnabas* fits into this provenance.

14 See L.W. Barnard's comments on Wengst's view in "Review of *Barnabasbrief* by Klaus Wengst, *JEH* 23 (1972): 345. Compare L.W. Barnard, *Studies in the Apostolic Fathers and their Background*, (Oxford, 1966), 53ff; O'Hagan, "Barnabas," 44-67; and R.A. Kraft, *The Apostolic Fathers. A New Translation and Commentary*, vol. 3, *Barnabas and the Didache*, (New York: 1965), 54-56. See also the discussions in Pearson and Goehring, *Roots*, 150-151, and in the same volume, Klijn, "Jewish Christianity," 166 and Grant, "Theological Education," 181. Compare Shukster and Richardson, "Temple," 17-32, and the relevant footnotes above.

15 Pearson, "Earliest Christianity," 132-159; and in the same volume, Grant, "Theological Education," 178-189. "Probably one should locate the *Epistle of Barnabas* at Alexandria too. Certainly the writer of this epistle is devoted to a rather intensive use of the allegorical method, with his famous exegesis of Abraham's 318 servants and his insistence that 'no one has received a more excellent lesson from me.' It cannot be said that his work is notable for cogency of thought, however." (181).

also provided a basis for establishing Alexandria almost with certainty as the city in which Barnabas lived and wrote his *Epistle*.[16]

H.I. Bell's early study of Alexandrian context[17] outlines the problems with this view:[18] "Unfortunately Alexandria, on the sea coast, cannot be expected to yield any papyri. We have, indeed, a good many documents written there, but they were all of them discovered elsewhere, and they form an insignificant proportion of surviving papyri. For early Christianity in Alexandria we are dependent on literary sources, scanty and for the most part ambiguous in character."[19] And as B.A. Pearson points out "[t]he evidence for the existence of church buildings in Alexandria before the fourth century is very slim."[20]

For more than forty years now, the emergence of Alexandrian Christianity, and its relationship to Jews and Judaism in that same city, has been an enigma to scholars.[21] It is as if the sea air has dissolved the evidence. One is

---

16 For a discussion of the problem with the Bauer thesis that earliest Christianity in Egypt was gnostic (and Koester's acceptance of that thesis) see T.A. Robinson, *The Bauer Thesis Examined, The Geography of Heresy in the Early Christian Church*, (Lewiston/Queenston: The Edwin Mellen Press, 1988): 59-69. Robinson agrees with C.H. Roberts in *Manuscript Society and Belief in Early Christian Egypt*, (London: Oxford University Press, 1979) that there is not enough evidence to establish Gnostic Christianity as the earliest form of Christianity in Egypt and suggests further that early Christianity was probably closely tied to Judaism in Alexandria. See also Barnard, "*Barnabasbrief,*" 347, which accepts the view that the *Epistle of Barnabas* was written in Alexandria. See also H.I. Bell, ed., *Jews and Christians in Egypt, The Jewish Troubles in Alexandria and the Athanasian Controversy*, (London, 1924), 187. But see A. Harnack who is quoted in W. Bauer, *Orthodoxy*, 44, and has this to say: "The most serious gap in our knowledge of primitive church history is our almost total ignorance of the history of Christianity in Alexandria and Egypt . . . until about the year 180 (the episcopate of Demetrius). It is only at that time that the Alexandrian church really emerges for us into the light of history. . . Eusebius found nothing in his sources about the primitive history of Christianity in Alexandria. We can with more-or-less probability, suppose that certain very ancient Christian writings (e.g., The *Epistle of Barnabas* . . . [*et alia*]) are of Egyptian or Alexandrian origin, but strictly speaking, this can hardly be demonstrated for any one of them." See also Bauer, *Orthodoxy*, 47ff, who is referring to A. Harnack's, *The Missionary Expansion of Christianity in the First Three Centuries*, ET J. Moffatt, 2nd ed. vol. II (New York 1908), 159-160.

17 Bell, *Jews*, 187.

18 Compare the recent comments in Pearson, "Earliest Christianity," 145-156.

19 See H.I. Bell, "Evidence of Christianity in Egypt During the Roman Period," *HTR* (July 1944) 208. See also Bauer, *Orthodoxy*, 44-60 who suggests through a literary analysis that there were gnostics in Alexandria until 180 when the "orthodox" Christians became dominant. See also T.A. Robinson, *Bauer Thesis*, 61 and 64 and C.H. Roberts, *Manuscript* for another view of the early Christian community in Alexandria.

20 Pearson, "Earliest Christianity," 151. On the reason for lack of evidence of Church structures in the Roman Empire before 325 see G. Snyder, *Ante Pacem, Archaeological Evidence of Church Life Before Constantine*, (Macon, GA: Mercer University Press, 1985): 1-10.

21 T.A. Robinson, *Bauer Thesis*, 64-69, follows C.H. Roberts's view that early Christianity in Alexandria was closely tied to Jews and Judaism in that city. Even though the evidence is sparse, it is well known that there was a large Jewish community in Alexandria (66).

faced, then, with the problem of how to use this well-known and third-largest city in the Roman empire as a "text" for the study of the *Epistle of Barnabas* if the evidence for early Christianity and its relationship to Jews and Judaism is so scanty.

The answer proposed here is that ancient written non-Alexandrian, and a number of Alexandrian, sources which have been preserved do indicate a climate conducive to such contact and interaction.[22]

It is well known through various sources that Alexandria in the early second century (113-138 C.E.) was a lively commercial, literary, and political center in the Roman Empire.[23] It is also known that there was great personal and social unrest in the city during the early decades of the second century.[24] The literary evidence for the first third of the second century supports this view.[25] These internal tensions between the "Greeks," "Egyptians," and the

---

[22] For meager evidence available for churches in second-century Alexandria see A. Calderini, *Dizionario dei nomi geografici e topografici dell'Egitto greco-romano*, Milan: Cisalpino-Goliardica, 1935, 1/1:165-78, and A. Adriani, *Reportorio d'arte dell'Egitto greco-romano*. Series C, 2 vols, Palermo:Fondazione "Ignazio Mormino" del Banco di Sicilia, 1966, 1:216-217. These are referred to in Pearson, "Earliest Christianity," 151, n.106. See also Robinson, *Bauer Thesis*, 59-69.

But for a complete collection of Greek and Latin authors on the Jews in Alexandria see Stern, *Authors*, vols. 1-3. The literary evidence, along with papyri and some inscriptions gathered by Stern, suggest a rather lively Jewish community in Alexandria until the tragedy of the revolt around 113-117 C.E. After this period, the Jews seem to have been reduced in number, but certainly not in influence. There is evidence that during Hadrian's time some Jews had moved to Palestine to establish themselves there for business reasons. See Smallwood, *Jews*, 517. See also Stern, *Authors* 2:153-155, for a summary of the history of the Alexandrian Jews during 113-117 C.E. Stern points out that Arrian (early second century C.E.) and Appian (second century C.E.) both write about the Jewish revolt in Alexandria (see Stern, *Authors*, 2:150f and 178ff.) but do not seem to vent much hatred against the Jews. Appian is an Alexandrian who was loyal to Rome and opposed the Greeks or any other ethnic groups which opposed Rome. He was aware of the Jewish revolt, but does not display any particular hatred toward the Jews in his extant writings.

[23] See Stern, *Authors* 3:103, where the importance of Alexandria is catalogued and references are made to the variety of events, visitors, and ethnic groups. It was the host of many Roman emperors, a mix of cultures, a place for scholars and diplomats from all over the world.

[24] See V.Tcherikover, A. Fuks, M. Stern, eds., *Corpus Papyrorum Judaicarum*, 3 vols. (Cambridge: Harvard, 1957-1964) 2:57, where mention is made of the hatred of the Jews in Alexandria during the first part of the second century. "This hatred of the Jews was a permanent feature in the political *credo* of the Alexandrians in the Roman period; it would be a waste of time for an Alexandrian writer to explain to his fellow citizens why Jews ought to be hated. The anti-Semitic feelings of the Alexandrian population could, therefore, easily be used as a means of political propaganda for other purposes." This hatred led to the counter-attack by the Jews. See also Smallwood's description of this period in *Jews*, 389ff.

[25] See Smallwood, *Jews*, 516-519 and notes. See also, Stern, *Authors* 2, Arrian (150ff), Appian (178ff), *Scriptores Historiae Augustae* (a 4th-century writing about an earlier period). Cassius Dio (387ff). See Meeks, *Urban*, 38 for a brief history of first-century Alexandria and the letter of Claudius. Also for a description of this period (34-117 C.E.) and the *Letter of Aristeas* see *The Old Testament Pseudapigrapha*, vol. 2, edited by J.H. Charlesworth, (New York:
(continued...)

"Jews" seemed to stem from a variety of causes. One might be that the "Greek"[26] population in Alexandria was struggling for its own existence against Rome and vented its frustrations on the Roman overlords indirectly by attacking the Jews, since they seemed to be favored or protected by the Emperor. There is no reason to think that Christians would remain detached from the turmoil and social hostility.

Beginning with Claudius's letter to the Alexandrians in 41 C.E.,[27] the *Acts of the Alexandrian Martyrs* (c. 115-120), and continuing through the Roman codes, one is able to read about the transition taking place in the city.[28] In the midst of this change, literary and cultural activities in the early second century were responsive to the transitions.[29] J. Gager suggests that one can observe the process of assimilation among Jews during the later part of the second to the early third century. This would be a way some Jews would attempt to protect themselves against any violence which may have been stirred by latent or active anti-Semitism in the city.[30]

25(...continued)
Doubleday, 1985): 7-34. This work is both an update and a revised bibliography of R.H. Charles's *The Apocrypha and Pseudepigrapha of the Old Testament in English*, 2, (Oxford: Oxford University Press, 1913): 83-122. Refer also to Tarn, *Hellenistic Civilization*, 210-238, for an overview of hellenism and the Jews, especially in Alexandria. For other documents which are relevant to a study of the *Epistle of Barnabas* in relation to other literary sources of the first- and second-century Alexandria, see J.H. Charlesworth, *Old Testament Pseudapigrapha*, vols. 1 and 2. For Josephus's comments on the status of the Jews in Alexandria see *Ant.* 19.279

26 See Stern, *Authors* 1:403ff., where there is a discussion about the different groups in Alexandria in the first part of the second century C.E. There are distinctions made between Greeks, those non-Egyptians who live in the city, the Egyptians, and the Jews. This leads to a discussion about citizenship in the city. Jews were not considered citizens (408). See also Smallwood's discussion on this same topic in *Jews*, 228-229.

27 See Bell, *Jews*, 2-37; H. Last, "The Study of the 'Persecutions'," *JRS* 27 (1937): 80-92 and Tcherikover and Fuks, *CPJ* 2:55-107. Also V.A. Tcherikover, *Hellenistic Civilization*, 325-332.

28 See Smallwood, *Jews*, 390-392, 406-412; and the discussion of the appreciation of Hadrian for the reestablishment of the Jewish community in Alexandria after the revolt (115-117 C.E.) 409 n.76. The reference is to the *Sibylline Oracle* 5.46-50 which is an early second-century Oracle.

29 The basic works on the Alexandrian topography and archaeology used in this book are: A. Adriani, "Saggio di una pianta archeologica di Alessandria," in Ann. Mus. Gr.-Rom. 1, (Alexandria, 1934); *Repertorio d'arte dell'Egitto Greco-Romano*, Ser.C, 2 vols. (Palermo: 1966); A. Bernand, *Alexandrie la Grande* (Paris: 1966); P.M. Fraser, *Ptolemaic Alexandria*, 3 vols. (Oxford: 1972). Also see the summary of the work done by the Polish and French archaeologists in K. Michalowski, *Art of Ancient Egypt*, translated and adapted from the Polish and French by N. Guterman, (New York: H.N. Abrams, 1969): 501-505. Also see the historical overview of the city, *Alexandrien: Kulturbergenungen dreier Jahrtausende im Schmelztiegel einer Mediterranien Gross-Stadt*, edited by N. Hinske. (Aegyptiaca Treverensia: Trierer Studien zum Griechisch-Römischen Ägypten, 1.) (Mainz am Rhein: Verlag Philipp von Zabern, 1981):3-12.

30 See J. Gager, *Origins*, 54.

So the literary sources can be consulted to help reconstruct Alexandria as a "text" for the *Epistle of Barnabas*.

B. Literary Texts Used as Sources

What are the literary sources that can be used to help reconstruct Alexandria as a "text"? There are some pagan and Christian (although this may be disputed) literary sources. If Tcherikover is still accurate (and there is no evidence to dispute his statements), there are Jewish sources which survived from Alexandria in this period.[31]

1. The Septuagint. The Greek translations of the Old Testament were used as inspired scripture for both Christians and Jews in the western Diaspora.[32] They were also a source for Greek culture and philosophy, as H. Koester points out:

> But the translation of the Hebrew Old Testament into Greek created more than a book that was useful for Jewish services of worship; it also provided a basis for a new departure of Jewish theology in a new cultural environment, and made it possible that the ferment for renewal, already present in the tradition of Israel and in postexilic theology, could further develop within the horizons of Hellenistic culture and religion.[33]

One cannot read the literature of the second-century Christian writers without recognizing the debt these writers owe to the Septuagint and the other Greek translations of the Old Testament.

2. Papyri. A collection of papyri from the period 100-140 C.E. is contained in the second volume of Tcherikover's *Corpus Papyrorum Judaicorum*.[34] This collection contains "dialogues" between Jews and the Emperor as well as a "trial before Commodus" (No.159) which give an interesting perspective of the

---

[31] See *CPJ*, 1, v. where it is stated this way: "We have adopted the title, *Corpus Papyrorum Judaicarum* (*C.P.Jud.*), although we are aware of its inaccuracy, since it may give the impression that the documents included were written by Jews, whereas most of them are not of Jewish authorship, but relate to Jews and Jewish affairs."

[32] For the documentation of the use of the Septuagint in the *Epistle* see Swete, *An Introduction to the Old Testament in Greek*, [1902] Revised by R.R. Ottley. (New York: KTAV Publishing House, Inc., 1968): 411ff. For the importance of the Septuagint in Alexandria see H. Koester, *Introduction 1*: 252-255; Schürer, *The History of the Jewish People in the Age of Jesus Christ (175 B.C.- A.D. 135)*, 3.1. A New English Version Revised and Edited by G. Vermes, F. Millar, and M. Goodman. (Edinburgh: T & T Clark Ltd., 1986):474-480; and S. Jellicoe, *The Septuagint and Modern Study*, (Oxford: The Clarendon Press, 1968). Further discussion of the place of the Septuagint may be found in Chapter 2 n. 101 below.

[33] Koester, *Introduction* 1:253.

[34] *CPJ*, 2, nn. 155-159b.

continuing effort of the Jews to defend their cause before the Roman Emperor.[35] From this material one observes that there was tension between pagans and Jews and (possibly) Christians and Jews in Alexandria in the first part of the second century C.E.

3. *The Talmud*. The Talmud, even though it was redacted late in the fifth century C.E. in the Land of Israel and Babylonia, is another source which has been used to express a Jewish point of view on the condition of Jews in second-century Alexandria.[36] Barnard, for one, uses the rabbinic sources as if they were straight historical reporting, as his use of the Tosefta to describe the Great Synagogue in Alexandria[37] makes vividly clear. He comments on the Tosefta and at the same time illustrates the problem of using it or any of the Talmudic materials as a source for historical reconstruction.[38] For the

---

[35] Philo also championed the cause of the Jews in Alexandria before the Emperor. See *De Legatione ad Gaium* and the comments about Philo in P. Borgen, "Philo of Alexandria," in *Jewish Writings of the Second Temple Period*, edited by M.E. Stone. (Philadelphia: Fortress Press, 1984): 252ff.

[36] See Tcherikover, *The Jews in Egypt in the Hellenistic-Roman Age in the Light of the Papyri*, (Hebrew), (Jerusalem, 1945), for a summary of this period. See also, Barnard, *Studies*, 47-48, n.64 who makes the following comment: "That their architectural style was Greek is confirmed not only by the evidence of archaeology but also by the description in the Talmud of the Great Synagogue at Alexandria which is said to have been destroyed by Trajan in *A.D.* 116. 'Rabbi Judah (b.Illai) taught: He who has not seen the double colonnade at Alexandria has never see the glory of Israel. It was made like the great basilica, one colonnade within another. Often there were as many as twice the number which went out of Egypt in the exodus. Seventy-one golden chairs were in it, [the great synagogue] corresponding to the seventy-one elders. Each chair cost 250,000. In the middle stood a wooden platform upon the top of which stood the Chazen of the Synagogue. He had a scarf in his hand which waved when a person took up (the scroll of the Torah) to read, whereupon all the people responded Amen. At each distinct benediction he waved the scarf and all the people responded Amen. They did not however sit together promiscuously but goldsmiths by themselves carpet-makers by themselves, so that if a stranger came he associated himself with his profession in order to get his livelihood.' (*Tosefta*, Sukkah IV.6:198)." See Neusner's translation of this section in Neusner, *Tosefta*, "Sukkah", 4.6, (New York: KTAV, 1981): 224.

For an example of how to use the Talmud as a source for second- or third-century Alexandria, see E.R. Goodenough, *Jewish Symbols*, 2:85-87. Goodenough makes sure that these statements are not taken literally but are "suggestive" of the way the great synagogue might have been.

[37] For a discussion of the evidence for this and other synagogues in Alexandria see Pearson, "Earliest Christianity," 147, n. 82; Smallwood, *Jews*, 395, n.33, 499; *CPJ* 2:93, n.37; and *Encyclopaedia Judaica*, 3d Printing, s.v. "Synagogue". For an overview of the research of Diaspora synagogues see A.T. Kraabel "Diaspora Synagogue" *ANRW* 2.19.1: 477-510. See also the comments about the Great Synagogue in Alexandria in Stern, *Authors* 2:387ff, with notes, and Goodenough *Jewish Symbols* 2:85-87.

[38] Similar to the earlier footnote about the variety in the New Testament writers is Jacob Neusner's demonstration throughout his works that the rabbis in their writings may have been uninterested in the events around them. They were not writing essays about the times; rather they were focusing on God's order in a chaotic world. The rabbis were not trying to solve all the problems of the outside world; they were trying to solve their own problems with the world.

(continued...)

purposes of this chapter it is assumed that the Talmudic materials are referred to and are helpful in presenting what the last redactor thought of the Jewish community in Alexandria. When references are made to Alexandria in the Talmuds they will be considered "suggestive" and not taken as literally descriptive of what actually happened.

4. *Philo and Josephus*. Philo and Josephus[39] are sources which should be used with care. Obviously, Philo was deeply involved in the intellectual, spiritual, and political life of Jews in Alexandria from c.20 B.C.E. to 45 C.E. His works, from his biblical commentaries to his diplomatic correspondence in the Roman empire, are the most important Jewish writings of this period (50 B.C.E. to 100 C.E.). Philo may or may not have made important contributions to Judaism in Alexandria,[40] but his extant writings present important information regarding at least one of the Jewish theological or philosophical expressions in Alexandria of the time. It is clear from most of the recent and earlier research on Philo and his environment that Philo made a significant impact on Jewish and, later, Christian thought in the city.

Overlapping Philo by a few years, but living until the early part of the second century C.E., was a Jewish historian, biblical commentator, and chronicler, Josephus. He wrote his history of the Jews from the beginning of the world to his death around 98-100 C.E. as an apologetic; he was concerned that his readers see the Jewish people as civilized and cultured.[41] His more immediate intent was to defend himself as well as his people in the context of

---

38(...continued)
Neusner summarizes the difference between the Mishnaic and the Talmudic way of thinking in one of his latest books: "My interpretation of the matter---beyond the evidence---is this: The Mishnah speaks of stasis and eternity to whom it may concern. The Talmud addresses Israel in the here and now of ever-changing times, the gross matter of disorder and history." See Neusner ed., *Talmud* 35:49.

39 See the discussion of Josephus and Philo in M. Stone, *Jewish Writings*, 185-282, and bibliographies. See also the more recent study, B.L. Mack and R.E. Murphy, "Wisdom Literature," in R.A. Kraft and G.W.E. Nickelsberg, *Early Judaism*, 387-395. See the comments on Josephus in Cohen, *Maccabees*,144-147. Also see the comments about Philo's wide appeal in the Diaspora in Goodenough, *Jewish Symbols*, 12:189, and the way Goodenough uses Philo as a source in *Jewish Symbols*, 2:87ff.

40 See H.A. Wolfson, *Philo, Foundations of Religious Philosophy in Judaism, Christianity, and Islam*. 2 vols. (Cambridge, MA: Harvard University Press, 1947); E.R. Goodenough, *An Introduction to Philo Judaeus*, 2d ed rev. (Oxford: Basil Blackwell, 1962); and S. Sandmel, *Philo of Alexandria, An Introduction* (New York, 1979), for the various views of Philo's contribution to the life of the Jewish community in Alexandria. Goodenough, for example, sees Philo as marginal to the Judaism in Alexandria. See the summary of views in Stone, *Jewish Writing*, 281. For a recent assessment of Philo and his impact on Alexandrian exegesis see B.L. Mack "Philo Judaeus and Exegetical Traditions in Alexandria" in *ANRW* 2.21.1 (1984): 228-271. This work includes an extensive bibliography for the study of Philo.

41 See the discussion of Josephus's views in H.W. Attridge, "Josephus and His Works," in M.E. Stone, *Jewish Writings*, 185-232.

the Roman rule in Palestine in the late first and early second centuries. He was probably close enough in time to Barnabas to be aware of the origins of the political and social movements which were still influencing Barnabas's work (115 C.E.).

Josephus was also concerned with defending the Jews as a people who were chosen for a very special mission in the world. In his *Against Apion*, he defended not only Jewish antiquity and scholarship but the Jews themselves as people of integrity and seekers of truth. In fact it is from the Jews, Josephus argues, that one can find an accurate history of the world. The Greeks, he observes, have been lost in myths and fables and cannot really report what happened.[42]

Josephus is often used as the major (and sometimes only) source for events during his lifetime. Many modern scholars have discovered that Josephus was accurate in presenting the events of his day. Archaeological studies have confirmed his historical descriptions.[43]

The importance of Josephus as a source must not be underestimated. He noted how the world misunderstood the Jews and set out to correct those false impressions. Even though he has his biases, he makes an attempt at objectivity and historical accuracy.

5. *Acta*. Another literary source which provides insight into the second-century social climate of Alexandria are the *Acta*. H.A. Musurillo has gathered *The Acts of the Pagan Martyrs*[44] and made some important observations for our purposes. If the general population was hostile to the Jews during certain periods, causing riots and unrest in Alexandria, then Christians were more than likely involved.[45]

---

42 See *Ap.* 1.3-8.

43 Y. Yadin's *Masada, Herod's Fortress and the Zealot's Last Stand*, (New York: Random House, 1966) demonstrates the accuracy of Josephus's comments about the places and events in first-century Palestine.

44 See H.A. Musurillo, *The Acts of the Pagan Martyrs*, (Oxford: Clarendon Press, 1954) and *CPJ* 2, Nos. 154-159 which present the "Acts of the Alexandrian Martyrs", with notes and a bibliography.

45 See Musurillo, *Pagan Martyrs*, 257-258, where Musurillo writes: "But it is especially the propaganda motifs, anti-Semitic and anti-Roman, which set the *Acta* in a class apart, not only from the novel but also from the mime and the simple protocol. With regard to the question of anti-Jewish feeling, it should be remarked that this motif is found only in those fragments in which Jews are actually concerned [which is] a characteristic mark of the *Acta Alexandrinorum* in general. Secondly, I do not believe that anti-Semitism was merely "*eine sekundare Nebenerscheinung*," as Wilken once wrote. (*Antis.*, p. 825. cf also pp. 263f. below). It was this and more; for the *Acta* reflect tensions which actually existed at Alexandria and which became more acute at certain times. The anti-Semitic overtones in the *Acta*, where they exist, represent perhaps a more primitive stage in the textual evolution of the *Acta*. But it is particularly the anti-Roman bitterness---to be found in no other extant literature to such a degree---which has led recent scholars to classify *Acta* as the most violent anti-Roman propaganda." Tessa Rajak makes this comment in "Was There a Roman Charter for the Jews?" *JRS* 74 (1984), 123: "The *Acta*
(continued...)

The *Acta* allow the reader to appreciate the complexity of the tensions which existed in this multiethnic city. Dio Cassius has a vivid account of tensions that led to the Roman intervention in Alexandria.[46] Obviously, Dio has painted a rather crude picture of the enemy (the Jews) in preparation for the supposed slaughter, by Emperor Trajan's general Lusius, which took place in 117 C.E. Other pagan sources[47] corroborate a picture of unrest between the Jews and their fellow citizens in Alexandria of this period.

III. The Jews of Alexandria

From these sources one is able to reconstruct some of the attitudes which influenced Jews and Christians in Alexandria. The story of the Jews of Alexandria in the early second century C.E. can be restructured by using a variety of literary sources including (with reservation and caution) the Talmud, which seems to contain references to Alexandria in this period.[48] The so-called *Letter of Aristeas*[49] is the primary source for understanding the origin of the Septu-

---

45(...continued)
then, are the product of struggle, and animosities within Greek cities of a kind which we know (as at Alexandria and in the conflicts of 66-73 in many cities) could issue in serious and bloody riots. That is why Josephus, in his last work, *Contra Apionem* is able to distinguish the Law of the Jews from that of the Greeks by the fact that Jews are prepared to die rather than abandon any part of their's. One can readily see that for those who lived in such circumstances and with such convictions, every battle for rights and privileges was a battle for their law and therefore, potentially, for their physical survival."
See also T. A. Robinson's observation that Jews and Christians were probably closely tied to each other in Alexandria. Robinson, *Bauer Thesis*, 66-67.

46 See Stern, *Authors*,2: No. 437.

47 Ibid. 178ff, where Appian of Alexandria a loyal Roman citizen (Nos. 343-352) expressed his contempt for those who opposed the Romans. There is little in the way of hatred toward the Jews in Appian's extant writings. See Smallwood, *Jews*, 389-427, for a discussion of the revolt under Trajan.

48 See the *Babylonian Talmud*, gen. ed. I. Epstein (London: Soncino Press, 1948-1952), Sukkah 51b where reference is made to the great synagogue before its destruction in the early second century. See also Stern, *Authors* 2, 387. Also there are many references to Greek and Latin authors who mention the Jews in Alexandria in the early second century in Stern, *Authors* 1-3. See footnotes above for specific references. See *CPJ* I 48-93, II no. 435-450, 452, 186-187 (which provides evidence of Jews in Alexandria). Smallwood, *Jews*, 224-230, (ns. 20 and 41 for references to other sources for the Jews in Alexandria); A. Kasher "The Jews in Hellenistic and Roman Egypt," Institut de recherche de la Diaspora 23 (Tel Aviv: 1978) and the collection of relevant first- and second-century Alexandrian writings in J.H. Charlesworth, *Old Testament Pseudepigrapha*, 2 vols. Also the papyri and inscriptions are gathered in *CPJ*, 3 vols.

49 See the bibliography and introductory notes to the *Letter* in J.H. Charlesworth, *Old Testament Pseudepigrapha*, 2:7-34. For a briefer outline of the *Letter* and date, as well as intended audience, see G.W.E. Nickelsberg, *Jewish Literature Between the Bible and the Mishnah*, (Philadelphia: Fortress Press, 1981), 165-169.

agint, but also provides insights into the make-up of the Jewish community in the city.[50]

According to R.J.H. Shutt, the *Letter* is far more than simply the statement about a translation of a Hebrew text into Greek: "its importance goes further . . . because it raises a question implicit in Judaism that emerges in times of special crisis: If Jews are God's special people, a chosen race, how are they to regard non-Jews? Can they live with them, or must they simply remove themselves and live exclusive lives? Is there any temporary arrangement of mutual recognition and respect that can be evolved? The case for the Jewish Law and attitude is set out in this work, and in confirmation of this, an appeal is made to the history of the Jews in Egypt and Alexandria, with special reference to the Law and its translation into Greek."[51]

Thus the *Letter* suggests that many Jews in the Diaspora were comfortable within a Hellenistic setting and would naturally want their most sacred texts in the language they understood.[52] The Diaspora should not be seen as an exile, as much as it was a time to establish a much broader and more inclusive world view within Judaism itself.

Some have suggested that the Jews in Diaspora were more liberal than those in Palestine.[53] This does not necessarily need to be so. But it is true that Jews living in Diaspora were exposed to Hellenistic culture and the ways of various peoples in the Roman empire more directly and had to accommodate, or, as John Gager suggests,[54] assimilate to life more peacefully in their host city.

Greek was the language of most Jews in the Diaspora, and this led to the development of apologetic literature within the various Diaspora Jewish communities. Philo was so enthusiastic about the Greek translation of the Bible that he announced that it was inspired[55] in the same way as the Hebrew

---

50 See Koester, *Introduction* 1:252f. and the revised edition of Schürer, *History* 3.1:474-504.

51 R.J.H. Shutt's introduction to the *Letter of Aristeas* in *Old Testament Pseudepigrapha*, vol. 2, edited by J.H. Charlesworth, 9. See also Nickelsberg, *Jewish Literature*, 168, who states that Aristeas wanted to present a story that would affirm the notion that "it is possible for Jews to coexist and interact with them to the mutual benefit of both [Jew and Greek]."

52 See Tarn, *Hellenistic Civilization*, 210-234 and Tcherikover, *Hellenistic Civilization*, 296-332. Both of these authors describe the situation of Jews within Hellenistic culture. On the purpose of Aristeas's *Letter* see Nickelsberg, *Jewish Literature*, 189, n. 24.

53 *Old Testament Pseudepigrapha* 2, edited by Charlesworth, 7.

54 Gager, *Origins*, 54.

55 *Mos.* 2.26-44

text,[56] which indicates a positive acceptance of Greek as a language which can be used for biblical and theological discussions.

Philo, a lifelong resident of Alexandria and an example of a Hellenistic Jew, is the most important source for knowledge of Jews and Judaism in Alexandria in the first century.[57] Philo's survival, attributable to the good graces of the Christians, probably indicates that not all his fellow Jews in Alexandria appreciated his point of view.

It is clear from Philo's writings that he thought that Greek Philosophy should be subordinate to the exegesis of the Pentateuch.[58] Moses was the great Lawgiver not only for the Israelites but for all nations.[59] Philo's works reflect a skilled interpreter of one philosophical tradition to a group who do not necessarily hold the same views.[60] It is possible that in the statement that

---

56 See *Encyclopaedia Judaica*, 3d Printing, s.v. "Bible". For a bibliography on modern studies of the origin of the Septuagint see J.H. Charlesworth, *Modern Research*, 78-80 and the bibliography in *Old Testament Pseudepigrapha*, 2, ed. J.H. Charlesworth, 11. Cohen in *Maccabees*, 210 makes the following comment: "The purpose of the translation, then, was not to make Judaism accessible to non-Jews but to make it accessible to Jews, and in all likelihood this same purpose governed the production of the Greco-Jewish literature that followed the Septuagint."

57 E.R. Goodenough, *Jewish Symbols* 2: 86 demonstrates the use of Philo as one who provided historical data useful for reconstructing the nature of one Jewish community within Alexandria of the first century.

58 See the discussion of Philo and his exegetical work in Stone, *Jewish Writings*, 264-274.

59 See Philo *De Vita Moses* 1.158; *De Opicio Mundi* 3; *De Vita Moses* 1.157. The idea that Moses is the Lawgiver for all nations grew into the concept of Israel as the priest for all nations; *De Specialibus Legibus* 2.166-167; *De Vita Moses* 2.196; *De Specialibus Legibus* 1.97. See the universal application of this fact in *De Posteritate* 11; *De Abrahamo* 79f.; *De Somniis* 1.68 and *De Legatione ad Gaium* 6.

60 In his study of *Jewish Symbols*, E.R. Goodenough has given much evidence to the integration of these two cultures. See especially *Jewish Symbols* 12:186-197. On page 197 Goodenough states:
"Outside the circles of rabbinic teaching, as we have hitherto envisioned it, there seem to have been a great number of Jews everywhere who had been influenced by paganism, to the point not only that, like Philo, they expressed their religious aspirations in the language of Greek mystery and metaphysics, but also that they found the symbolic vocabulary of later Greco-Roman art equally suitable to their thinking."
Wolfson summarizes his view of Philo with these words:
"With a single exception, none of the people who after the conquest of Alexander began to participate in Greek Philosophy contributed anything radically new to it. All they did was to master its teachings and furnish teachers . . . The single exception was the Jewish population in Alexandria. This Alexandrian Jewish population produced out of its midst a school of philosophers who consciously and deliberately and systematically set about remaking Greek philosophy according to the pattern of a belief and tradition of an entirely different origin." "The rise of this school and the continuity of its existence for about three centuries, from the translation of the Pentateuch into Greek (c. 260 B.C.) to the end of the activity of Philo (c. A.D. 50), was made possible by the nature of the dominate element, if not the basic stock, of the Jewish population in Alexandria and by the nature of the social economy of the Alexandrian Jewish Community." H.A. Wolfson, *Philo*, 1:3-4. But see Stone, *Jewish Writing*, 233, where another view is expressed. Borgen, the author of the article on Philo in Stone's collection,

(continued...)

"Philo was not only the culmination point of a literary tradition within Alexandrian Judaism, he was also the end of it,"[61] a great loss to philosophical thinking, Jewish as well as Greek, was recorded.

After Philo's death (c. 45 C.E.) it seems from the available evidence that something negative began to happen to the Jewish community in Alexandria. This lively[62] and populous community of Jews grew restive and, for reasons unknown to historians, rebelled against the Roman protectors.[63] Thirty years before the destruction of the temple in Jerusalem, the Greek and Egyptian population, as well as the Romans, expressed great dissatisfaction with the Jewish presence in their city.[64]

A. The Romans and the Jews

In 41 C.E. Emperor Claudius wrote a letter to the Alexandrians:[65] "I bid the Jews" he wrote, "not to busy themselves about anything beyond what they have held to hitherto, and not henceforth as if you and they lived in two cities to send two embassies---a thing such as never occurred before now---nor to strive in . . . games, but to profit by what they possess, and enjoy in a city not their own an abundance of good things, and not to introduce or invite Jews who sail down from Syria or Egypt, thus compelling me to conceive the greater suspicions; otherwise I shall by all means take vengeance on them as fomenting a general plague for the whole world."[66]

60(...continued)
insists that Philo's main contribution was to Jewish exegesis and not Greek philosophy at all.

61 P. Borgen, "Philo" in Stone, *Jewish Writings*, 279-280.

62 This is according to Wolfson, who relies solely on Philo. He gives no archaeological or epigraphic information about the Jewish community which was thought to be so influential. For the Greek and Latin authors' view see the collection of writings in M. Stern *op.cit*. See also the well-documented study of the Jews in Alexandria by M. Smallwood, *Jews*, 224-250, 359-364 who agrees with Wolfson's assessment.

63 See the extensive discussion of the Jewish revolt in Smallwood, *Jews*, 389-466. See also the related revolts in the east which are summarized by Stern, *Authors*, 2:152-154.

64 See Stern, *Authors* 2:154ff for a summary of the wars in the east in which the Jews were the most trouble for the Romans. Trajan wanted them completely destroyed.

65 See W. Meeks, *Urban*, 37-38 on this topic.

66 This translation by Bell is found in "Evidence," 189 (=*CPJ* No. 153). See also the description of this event in Josephus *AJ* 19.280ff. A complete discussion of Claudius's letter and other decrees also found in Suetonius (Stern, *Authors* 2 No. 307) is discussed in Stern, *Authors* 2:113-117. Also see Stern, *Authors* 1:400-403. Stern thinks that "Claudius first intended to expel all Jews from Rome, and even published an edict to that effect. But under pressure from the Jews, and perhaps especially from Agrippa I, to whom Claudius owed so much that year (41 C.E.), he reversed the order of expulsion and changed it into a restriction of the Jewish right to assembly" (116). Some probably left before Claudius changed the order (as it is recorded in Acts 18.2) but most stayed.

Salo Baron suggests that "Claudius' unfriendly remark need not indicate his real antagonism to the Jews, but rather his growing impatience with this ever troublesome group of subjects."[67] The literary evidence suggests that the Jews may have been perceived as a privileged class in the city[68] and boasted a large impressive synagogue in Alexandria.[69]

Some scholars suggest that Jews occupied two of the five sections of Alexandria[70] and were probably financially well off compared to some of the other citizens of the city.[71] After the destruction of Jerusalem in 70 C.E. Vespasian sent Jewish slaves to work in the mines in Egypt; that increased the size of the Jewish population in the city. But their presence did not add to the social stability of the Jewish community there; rather the strain it caused was part of the reason for its disruption and disintegration.[72]

B. The "Greeks" and the Jews

The so-called "Greek citizens,"[73] or other part of the population in Alexandria during 41-130 C.E., had a slightly different reaction to the Jews. The city seemed to be at peace (except during the period 113-117). Social harmony was more or less a given. And yet, because the Jews in "Alexandria were regarded as aliens who sought to dominate the rest of the population by virtue of their numbers, affluence, and solidarity,"[74] tensions began to grow.

---

67 See S.W. Baron, A Social and Religious History of the Jews, vol. 1, (New York: Jewish Publication Society, 1952): 246.

68 See *CPJ* 2:1-24 where the social, economic, and political position of Jews in Alexandria is discussed. Jews were on all levels of society, but seemed to have privileges even beyond those given to most other citizens. Fuks states: "The problem is rather why the Jews who had their own autonomous courts had nevertheless recourse to non-tribunals." (2:5).

69 See *CPJ* 1:93 n. 37. *TP* Sukka, v, 55b and Stern, *Authors* 2:387 for the major sources and references to the Great Synagogue in Alexandria.

70 See Philo *In Flaccum* 8 and A.C. Johnson, *Roman Egypt to the Reign of Diocletian*, 2 vols. (Baltimore, 1935), 247.

71 See the discussion of the social and economic condition of Jews in Alexandria in the second century in Smallwood, *Jews*, 224-250, 359-364; *CPJ* 2:1-24; B.A. Pearson and J.E. Goehring, *Roots*, 110-111 and notes.

72 See Smallwood, *Jews*, 364-368, 389-396, 407-408.

73 See the full discussion of the three levels of inhabitants in Alexandria from 41-130 C.E. in Stern, *Authors*, 1:401-403. The three major groups were the Jewish (*politeuma*), the Greek citizens, and the lower-level Egyptian population. Also, John Gager in his *Origins*, 43-54, discusses "Anti-Semitism and Anti-Romanism in Egypt" and proposes a similar argument to the one in this chapter.

74 Baron, *Social* 1:188.

Viewing the Jews as alien, the Greek citizens and, perhaps, the Egyptian population, were in a position to see the Jews as partly at fault for their troubles with Rome. The Jews became a safe scapegoat. "Over against the Alexandrians stood the Jews. The 'good boys' of the Empire, with all their Alexandrian privileges, their Council of Elders, archives and law courts, and in addition enjoying the general concessions which the Roman Government made to their religious scruples . . . not merely because the Greeks hated the Jews but because to attack the Jews seemed a safer and less direct way of attacking the authority of Rome."[75]

Tcherikover, commenting on the *Acta*, suggests "the main purpose of these fragments is to incite hatred against the Roman Emperors or to ridicule them; the hatred against Jews is merely a matter of subordinate significance."[76] As in most movements which choose a scapegoat and launch a destructive campaign against a particular people, the perpetuators are either very insecure about their own place in society and have to find someone to blame for their problems, or they are looking for a way to get out from under the oppressors' power. It is possible that in Alexandria the Greek citizens used the Jews as a scapegoat to cover up their own insecurity and possibly their jealousy of the privileges which Jews had gained within the Empire.[77]

---

75 H.I. Bell, "Anti-Semitism at Alexandria," *JRS* 31 (1941): 4-5. J. Gager, *Origins*, 43 suggests a similar view: "Ironically, it was precisely this Roman power, [in the later part of the first century] together with the policy of protecting the special status of Judaism, that created the conditions in which Alexandrian anti-Semitism came to life." Also see H.Z. (J.W.) Hirschberg, *A History of the Jews in North Africa*, vol. 1, *From Antiquity to the Sixteenth Century* 2d revised edition, translated from the Hebrew (Leiden: E.J. Brill, 1974): 29 for a comment about the revolt during the reign of Trajan.

76 See *CPJ* 2 nn. 154-159. See also V. Tcherikover, *Jews*, 18. See H.A. Musurillo, *Pagan Martyrs*, 257-258, where a similar view is mentioned.

77 In the Melito chapter below it has been suggested that the old and venerable Jewish community in Sardis caused the weak and rather insignificant Christian Community great trouble. The Messiah had come, according to the Christians, Easter was behind them, and yet the Jewish community was being influenced by a powerful, lively form of Judaism as well as a very creative and intelligent Jewish community which might not have anything to do with life in the Synagogue. The presence of the Synagogue does not tell one everything about Jews in Sardis, but it does suggest that there was enough financial and social support to maintain a rather significant house of worship and community center. The Jewish community had stature and influence in Sardis.

At the end of his chapter on "Roman Policy toward Judaism and Christianity," John Gager makes this statement:

"In general, and despite the inevitable tensions associated with missionary activity, the dominate mood of Caesarea was open and cosmopolitan; Jews were respected in the community. Indeed, Levine's concluding note sounds strikingly like Kraabel's assessment of the Jews in Sardis:

". . . the Caesarean Jewish community formed one of a long line of acculturated Jewish centers which were integral parts of the Jewish world. . . . While remaining 'Palestinian,' Caesarean Jewry anticipated a uniquely Diaspora phenomenon, a striking example of the city's dual heritage." J. Gager, *Origins*, 101. The quotation from Levine is L. Levine, *Caesarea Under Roman Rule*, (Leiden: Brill, 1975): 106.

C. The Jews on the Jews

How did the Jews view themselves in Alexandria?[78] From the evidence which has been gathered it is clear there was some unity and loyalty among them.[79] From 40 B.C.E. to the revolt of the Jews in North Africa (115-117 C.E.) and Palestine (135 C.E.), Jews seem to know about the trauma of Jews in other places but do not mount a unified campaign to save them in war-torn areas. This is partly because of the uniqueness of Jewish settlements throughout the Roman empire. A large city like Alexandria hosted a large and diverse Jewish population. Jews in Alexandria, as well as Jerusalem were not bound to one view of Judaism, nor were they bound to one strata of society.[80]

The Jews' own view of the Jews in Alexandria emerges as a rather diverse portrait. The evidence from the papyri, inscriptions, and literary sources indicates forms of Judaism often independent and sometimes in conflict with each other. It has already been suggested that after Philo the Jewish community in Alexandria went into decline. Certainly the revolts in Egypt and North Africa did not help relations between Jews and other Jews.

Diversity within the Jewish communities is assumed in this book, and yet it is this diversity that was a source for tension and civil war, as well as part of what makes the community interesting and vital.

Tcherikover suggests that the Jewish community in Alexandria was not completely destroyed, as some writers have held.[81] Rather, he thinks that the tensions and despair experienced by many Jews led to the hope and created an enthusiasm (sometimes a fanaticism) for the rebuilding of the Temple and the reestablishment of the Jewish community in Jerusalem.[82] Also, if the

---

78 See *CPJ* 2:1-24, nn. 142-149. There is not complete agreement on the origin of these documents that deal with land sale, birth, divorce, and other social concerns. In *CPJ* they are treated as Jewish documents because they were found in a Jewish section of the city and use Jewish names. Nn. 435-450, are documents which talk about the Jewish revolt in 115-117 C.E. *CPJ* 3, contains some documents and an appendix of inscriptions which Tcherikover considered Jewish, even though some have suggested they are of dubious origin. They might be Christian in origin.

79 See Wolfson, *Philo*, 1:85 and compare Barnard, *Studies*, 42.

80 The fact that Josephus and Philo were both preserved by the Christian Church indicates that variety within Judaism of the first century. The discovery of the Dead Sea Scrolls further demonstrates the variety within Judaism of Palestine. Philo represents a Hellenistic form of Judaism in Alexandria which later would form the basis for Christian thought in Alexandria. See P. Borgen, "Philo," in M.E. Stone, *Jewish Writings*, 233-282.

81 See Tcherikover, *Jews*, 26 and *Hellenistic Civilization*, 356-377 and *CPJ* where much evidence is gathered for the existence of a strong and vital Jewish community in Alexandria and other parts of Egypt through 337 C.E. See also Eus., *HE*, 4.2, *Dio Cassius*, 68.32, Papyri, and *Acts of Paulus and Antonius* which are the sources that Tcherikover refers to in his comments.

82 See J.J. Collins, *Between Athens and Jerusalem, Jewish Identity in the Hellenistic Diaspora*, (New York: Crossroads, 1983), especially his discussions on the content of Alexandrian Jewish

(continued...)

Midrash R. Genesis 64.10 reflects a real promise orally given to the Jews in Palestine during the early part of the second century, then it is conceivable that that hope could have flamed Jewish enthusiasm during this time.[83]

The Jews of Alexandria, like the Jews in Sardis, were a formidable community and probably made impressive intellectual, cultural, religious, and commercial contributions to their host city.[84] Yet from the literary sources it is clear that Jews in Alexandria did not have an easy time of it. They seemed to be constantly on the defensive for one reason or another.[85] This may be due to Alexandria's proximity to Palestine and the possibility of a more intimate contact with the Jews there. Quite possibly the Jews in Alexandria made pilgrimages "home"[86] from time to time, while the Sardian Jews were more permanently "at home" in Sardis. The Jewish presence in Sardis seemed peaceful in comparison to the chaotic circumstances for Jews in Alexandria.

82(...continued)
literature pp.103-134. See also, G.W.E. Nickelsburg, *Jewish Literature,* 161-202.

83 See L.W. Barnard, *Studies in Church History,* 45, n.59 and Baron, *Social* 2:97 where he states: "He [Hadrian] also sought to pacify the Jewish masses by holding out some vague promises of rebuilding their Holy City and, perhaps, even reconstructing their Temple." Baron, like most every other secondary source, is probably referring to *R. Genesis* 64.10 where there is a reference to the rebuilding of the Temple during Hadrian's time: "In the days of R. Joshua b. Hananiah the [Roman] State ordered the Temple to be rebuilt . . . " *Midrash Rabbah Genesis* 64.10, general eds. H. Freedman and Maurice Simon, vol. 2.2 (London: Soncino, 1939):579. It is difficult to establish the historical value of this Midrash. If it is indeed from the time of Hadrian, then one can understand the enthusiasm this might have generated among large numbers of Jews and part of the cause for Barnabas's concern for a rising fanatical messianism that generated support, later, for Bar Kokhba as a messiah.

Shukster and Richardson in "Temple," 17ff, base their argument for the provenance and date of the *Epistle of Barnabas* on the premise that Nerva (c. 90s) was the emperor and the promise of rebuilding the Temple was the reason Barnabas wrote his letter. The rebuilding of the Temple would "threaten to undermine his [Barnabas's] community's understanding of the covenant by obscuring the political signs of Christian supersession. . . .any suggestion of the continuity of Jewish covenantal claims is dangerously retrograde, [for Barnabas] and must be dealt with aggressively" (24). See R.A. Kraft, *The Apostolic Fathers,* 3:42-43, for the suggestion that 16.4 can be used to prove the promise of the rebuilding of the Temple. Kraft argues that this places the *Epistle* in Palestine during Nerva's time. For a discussion of the Jewish legend that the Temple would be rebuilt see Schürer *History* 1:535-536.

84 See Barnard, *Studies in Church History,* 40, and his readings of Josephus, *BJ* 2.18.7, where he describes the Jews in Alexandria living in a "special quarter separated from the rest of the city 'in order that they might be able to live a purer life by mixing less with foreigners' (Josephus)." Barnard goes on to report that some Jews did live among the Greco-Egyptian population and "occupied positions of considerable eminence in the metropolis."

85 See the discussion of the "Jewish Revolt of A.D. 115-117" in Smallwood, *Jews,* 389-427. Smallwood carefully explains the development of this so-called revolt. There was a long history of discontent both from the side of the Jews and the Greco-Egyptian (Barnard's phrase in *Studies in Church History,* 41) population.

86 See S. Cohen's comments about Philo's pilgrimage to the "mother-city" (Jerusalem) in *Maccabees,* 6, n.2.

IV. The Christians of Alexandria

The concluding words of Pearson's discussion on "Earliest Christianity in Egypt" point to the limitations of one's knowledge of first-century Alexandria. "But the limitations upon future expansion of our knowledge of Judaism and Christianity [including this period] must finally be acknowledged. Perhaps we shall never be able finally to lift that obscurity that veils the early history of the Church of Egypt."[87]

According to Eusebius, the foundations of Christianity in Egypt go back to the writer of the second Gospel.[88] H.I. Bell, commenting on the text from Eusebius 2.2.16, writes: "This would be conclusive if we could rely on it, but it is not mentioned by either Clement of Alexandria or Origen, [and occurs first] in Eusebius, in the fourth century. Negative evidence is rarely conclusive, but it is certainly surprising that Clement and Origen should ignore the foundation by St. Mark if it were a fact, and we must regard the tradition as at least extremely doubtful."[89]

Yet, more recently, W.H. Kelber in discussing the "pre-canonical synoptic transmission" observes that "[t]he fragmentary *Letter to Theodore*, attributed to Clement, and discovered and published by Morton Smith, depicts Mark as a circumspect literary agent of his written notes (*hypomnemata*)."[90] This new evidence would shake the position that there is only negative evidence for the origin of the Church in Alexandria. It is possible that Mark may have had something to do with it. But still, there is only indirect knowledge of its origins. That is at least a step up from "negative" evidence.

The *Acts of the Apostles* (2.10), a late first-century New Testament writing, has been used to suggest another way that the Church might have begun: by pilgrims returning from their unique Pentecost experiences with the Christians in Jerusalem. Then, during the Jewish revolt under Trajan, the Christian com-

---

87 B.A. Pearson, "Earliest Christianity," 156, quoting C.H. Roberts, *Manuscript*. T.A. Robinson thinks that Roberts's thesis is correct and challenges Bauer's thesis that Gnostic Christianity was the earliest Christianity in Egypt. Robinson also assumes that Christianity was in close contact with Jews and Judaism before the chaos of 113-117 C.E. See Robinson, *Bauer Thesis*, 64-65.

88 Eus., *HE* 2.2.16. See also Bauer, *Orthodoxy*, 44-60.

89 H.I. Bell, *Cult and Creed in Greco-Roman Egypt*, (Liverpool, 1953), 79. For a more recent discussion of the evidence see T.A. Robinson, *Bauer Thesis*.

90 See W.H. Kelber, *The Oral and Written Gospel: The Hermeneutics of Speaking and Writing in the Synoptic Tradition, Mark, Paul and Q*, (Philadelphia: Fortress Press, 1983): 22. Kelber is referring to M. Smith, *Clement of Alexandria and the Secret Gospel of Mark*, (Cambridge, MA: Harvard University Press, 1973): 446. Smith's translation of the text is as follows: "But when Peter died a martyr, Mark came over to Alexandria, bringing both his own notes and those of Peter, from which he transferred to his former book things suitable to whatever makes for progress toward knowledge" (446).

munity which existed in the city may have come to a temporary end.[91] T.A. Robinson writes: "In the Jewish War of A.D. 70, perhaps as many as 50,000 Jews in Alexandria were killed, and in the revolt under Trajan, heavy fighting occurred throughout Egypt, with tremendous losses. Roberts thinks that, given this situation, the early Christians (who appeared to outsiders as a Jewish sect) would not have been able to attract gentiles into the church."[92]

A discussion of emerging Christianity in Alexandria is lost in "obscurity." In fact there is no textual or epigraphic evidence about a church in Alexandria until after 180 C.E.[93]

H.I. Bell may be correct in his observation [which agrees with T.A. Robinson] that Christianity temporarily ended around 115, leaving not a trace. The *Epistle of Barnabas* could be both an apologetic writing and an *adversus Judaeos* text written for the newly emerging Christian community in need of guidelines[94] and distinctiveness; that is, a movement of "sons and daughters."[95] Followers of the Lord are not Jews who live a certain way following a pattern that both alienates them from Rome and their fellow Alexandrian citizens, but the "sons and daughters of (our) Lord Jesus Christ."[96]

Further, during the later part of the second century, and probably after the *Epistle of Barnabas,* there was much ferment in the emerging church in Alexandria. Bauer and Koester suggest that Gnosticism was on the rise, the great Catechetical School was developing, and a Christianity dependent on the classical tradition began to be a force to be reckoned with in the city.[97] The materials from the *Cairo Geniza*[98] suggest contact between Palestine and Egypt dating back to the time of the Dead Sea Scrolls, which seems to add credence to this suggestion. It is likely that this contact was never broken within the Jewish community. Certainly communication between Alexandrian Christians and Christians in Palestine and Egypt was inevitable.

---

91 Bell, *Cults,* 79. See also T.A. Robinson, *Bauer Thesis,* 68 n. 90.

92 Robinson, *Bauer Thesis,* 68.

93 The first known head of the Catechetical School at Alexandria was Pantaenus (d. 190 C.E.). See Eus., *HE* 5.10.1-4. See also Bauer's quotation from Harnack in *Orthodoxy,* 44.

94 The "Two Ways" chapters in the second half of the Epistle (18.1-21.9), for example, indicate that the author was concerned about the discipline of the Christian community. See the study by Connolly, "Didache," 237-253, of a possible connection between the two documents.

95 *Barn.* 1.1.

96 See R.A. Kraft, *Apostolic Fathers,* 3:80, n. a.

97 See Bell, *Cults,* 81. See also Bauer, *Orthodoxy,* 49-60 and Koester, *Introduction,* 2:220.

98 See P.E. Kahle, *The Cairo Geniza,* [1947], (Oxford: Clarendon Press, 1959). It deals with texts of a later period, and yet Kahle supports the notion that there was a continual exchange of ideas and texts between Palestine and Alexandria.

The suggestion that Christianity grew out of the God-fearers is not supportable with any evidence from Alexandria and therefore not a consideration for the beginnings of Christianity in the city.[99] The evidence does not support the idea that there were God-fearers in Alexandria in great numbers.

Although it has been suggested that the early development of Christianity in Alexandria must remain in obscurity,[100] still it is possible, based on what is known in later evidence, to make several assumptions about its character in the second century. First, the sophisticated Christianity of the third and fourth centuries suggests that in the earlier years of formation the Church had a fairly sophisticated constituency. The famous "schools" in Alexandria[101] emerged out of a culturally rich and pluralistic society. Certainly if the Christians were identified with the Jews in that city during the revolt from 115-117, then it might be possible to assume that they received the same treatment after the revolt, and possibly even made their way back into the city after the tensions cooled down.[102]

Second, the Alexandrian church produced teachers for the later church who held differing views. It is clear that Christianity in the Roman empire, as well as in Alexandria, was not monolithic; one must assume that Barnabas represents one Christian position among many, and that Christianity was multifaceted from the beginning.[103] Gnosticism, Orthodoxy, Arianism, and Barnabas's form of Orthodoxy and later monastic movements in Egypt (fourth century) were the result of what seems to be rather fluid and varied beginnings for Christianity in Egypt.[104]

V. Conclusion: Barnabas Was a Moderating Voice in the Crisis

---

99 See Barnard, *Studies in Church History*, 46 where he makes the following comment: "However, behind the agitators and the leaders of the Jewish community stood not only the thinkers who sought to introduce Hellenistic ideas into the interpretation of their ancestral faith but also the great mass of Jewish population who followed in the ways of their fathers. Among these folks and among the God-fearers who attached themselves to the synagogues Christianity began to take root."

100 See Bell, "Evidence," 187-204, and the more recent studies by Pearson, "Earliest Christianity," 156.

101 See R.M. Grant, "Theological Education", 178-189.

102 See Robinson, *Bauer Thesis*, 68.

103 There is evidence for this in the New Testament as well. It is not insignificant that there are four Gospels, and writings from a variety of authors in the New Testament. James Robinson and Helmut Koester's *Trajectories through Early Christianity*, (Philadelphia: Fortress Press, 1971), 114-157, is an excellent discussion of the ways early Christianity emerged from a variety of viewpoints and sources. There was not a monolithic Christianity any more than there was a monolithic Judaism in first- and second-century Alexandria.

104 Robinson and Koester, *Trajectories*, 114-157.

The *Epistle of Barnabas* read in the city of Alexandria in the early part of the second century is best viewed as a "letter" written by a moderate Christian teacher resisting the growing messianic fanaticism both in Jewish and Christian circles.[105] This tension is reflected by Barnabas in his description of the times as "evil days" (2.1; 4.9; 8.1), his encouragement to his readers to "flee from the works of wickedness," his view of the synagogue as a place of the "wicked" (5.13; 6.6; 11.2), the experience of the Christians as one of "pain and suffering" (7.1), and his emphasis throughout his *Epistle* on holding on and keeping away from "the errors like them" (2.9; 4.6, 8). The last section of the Two Ways (28-30) seems to encourage his readers to develop a disciplined life style in a time of chaos.

The urgency in the *Epistle* is expressed in the apocalyptic language of Daniel 7 (*Barn.* 4.3, 5), and *Enoch* 89 and 90 and cryptically in the reference to "evil and wicked" days (2.1; 8.6). Both uses of language were meant to warn Christians (and perhaps Jews) about their place in the struggle.

The struggle would have been complicated in Alexandria, since it meant that Christians were caught in the middle, between Jews with hostile feelings toward them on the one hand, and Greeks or "Greco-Egyptians" on the other, who might mistake Christians for a Jewish sect. Thus they would be vulnerable to the same abuse Jews were experiencing.[106]

The conflict was over Barnabas's view of messianism and the covenant and not stimulated primarily by a revolt during Trajan's reign (98-117). These two issues were not simply abstract theology, but political and social commentary. Barnabas insisted that his way was the appropriate inheritor of the covenant; it is "ours and not theirs" (4.6). Barnabas was quite emphatic when he reminded his followers that they had now taken over the place of "them" (4.7; 6.19).

After this statement, the rest of the Epistle systematically demonstrates how "Jews" had lost the real purpose of all of their traditions and laws and how they had turned to follow the way of their ancestors when they left Egypt and "turned to idols" (4.8). Christianity, the way Barnabas interpreted it, clearly had the appropriate and adequate understanding of Scripture (5.2; 10.12). This proper understanding of the Bible was accomplished through a typological interpretation.[107]

The messianic hope among some Jews in Alexandria (and in other parts of the Roman Empire) during the early part of the second century C.E., stirred by the possibility of the rebuilding of the Temple by the Romans, was

---

105 See Goodenough's discussion of the reference to *JT* Sukkah 55a and 55b, that in 116 Trajan destroyed the Great Synagogue in Alexandria. Could this insult to the Jews cause a fanatical or apocalyptic Judaism to emerge, creating greater tension for some of the Christians in that city? See Goodenough, *Jewish Symbols* 2:86.

106 See *Barn.* 7.11; 8.6; 2.1. Also see T.A. Robinson, *Bauer Thesis*, 68 n. 90.

107 See Barnabas's use of typology in 7.3-11, and 8.7. *et al.*

probably seen by Barnabas as engendered by "wicked men" who "erred by putting their hope on the building, and not on God who made them, and is the true house of God. For they consecrated him in the Temple almost like the heathen," he contended (16.1-2).

This is contrary to Shukster's insistence that Barnabas was speaking as a teacher/exegete and had become like the rabbis of Yavneh.[108] Shukster and Richardson also point to a "tone of urgency" which pervades the *Epistle*.[109] But their reasons for this view differ from this writer's in that they think that the tension was caused by the struggle between Barnabas's view of the Christian community as a kind of *Beth ha-midrash* in competition with the rabbinic *Beth ha-midrash* somewhere in the provenance of Syro-Palestine during the reign of Nerva (96-98 C.E.).[110]

The reference that Shukster and Richardson make to Barnabas as a polemic against the Temple and the Beth ha-midrash could also be used in a similar way to support Paul's argument in his letter to the Corinthians (see I Corinthians 12-15) about the spiritual and carnal body. Barnabas did not necessarily refer to a particular "*Judaism redivius*" in Yavneh[111] around 90 C.E., but to a form of Judaism (and Christianity) in Alexandria between 115 and 117 C.E. that had become more hostile and fanatical.[112]

Also Barnabas was not trying to argue "as a rabbi" as Frend suggested.[113] It is unclear from a reading of the *Epistle* if Barnabas knew any rabbis or if he had contact with rabbis (like the ones in Palestine) during the time he wrote the *Epistle*. To propose that he was a sectarian in the mode of the

---

108 See Shukster and Richardson, "Temple," 31, and the discussion about how one should view Barnabas. It is the view of this writer that Barnabas was more like a sectarian (Kraft) than a Yavenian rabbi (Shukster, Richardson, Frend, and Lowry). The importance of this point of view is (1) Barnabas is not arguing with the *Beth ha-midrash* in the style of a rabbi, and (2) he does not see himself as the head of a rabbinic school in Alexandria, but as one who is trying to moderate the growing messianic fanaticism. See notes on Smallwood, *Jews*, below.

109 Shukster and Richardson, "Temple," 23. See also L.W. Barnard, *Studies in Church History*, 46. For another view of the provenance of Barnabas, see Shukster and Richardson, "Temple," 17ff, where the authors locate Barnabas in the provenance of Syro-Palestine and the tension is between Barnabas as a teacher/exegete and those Jews of the Beth Ha-midrash who anticipated the rebuilding of the Temple under Roman sponsorship, (30-31). The view of this chapter as discussed above, is that the epistle was written in and for Alexandrian Christians. For support of this view see Pearson, "Earliest Christianity," 134f. Barnabas's report that he lived in "evil days" (2.9; 3.1-6) reflected the revolt under Trajan, (115-117). It is possible that Christians during that revolt may have been mistaken for Jews and therefore forced into exile or death along with their Jewish fellow "citizens."

110 Shukster and Richardson, "Temple" 20-31.

111 As Shukster and Richardson do in their argument in "Temple" 23-31.

112 See Smallwood, *Jews*, 397. For literary evidence of these disturbances see *CPJ* 444 and 449.

113 Frend, *Rise*, 122.

people of Qumran, as Kraft suggests,[114] may be closer to the truth. He wrote as one who stood by himself against "they" and "them" the same way the Qumran people stood against "those" priests in Jerusalem who had misused the tradition.

An argument similar to Frend's is given by G. Alon, as described by S. Lowy this way:

> Furthermore it has been proved by Alon that Barnabas used a Jewish written tradition current among the Jews in Alexandria which was attached to the whole scripture. It was a kind of midrash written in Greek, interlocated into the scripture (6.3-7; 8.1-4; 10.7; 15.1) and considered as an entity with it. Similar phenomena of midrash interwoven into scripture and fused into one unit we find also in the books of the period (e.g., Jubilees, liber Antiquitatum biblicarum etc.). Alon suggested that the source which Barnabas used was probably similar to the Targum of Pseudo-Jonathan, but composed in Greek; for in that paraphrase we also have Halaka and 'Aggada grafted into the verses of scripture.

In conclusion, S. Lowy states what is probably closest to the intent of the *Epistle* and with a few exceptions provides a fairly accurate view of Barnabas's works.

> The *Epistle* was written as an answer to the Jewish messianic movement which prophesied the early reconstruction of the Temple, the ingathering of the exiles, the coming of the messiah, political freedom, etc. These aspirations were given a fillip by certain political and social events, which could be explained as forming Jewish hopes, and they were consequently used as a proof that such hopes were going to be fulfilled. The Roman Empire was considered as being in favor (consciously or otherwise) of these hopes. By its preaching, prophecies and supposed success, the movement drew converts and sympathizers to Judaism and the Law, including some from the rank and file of Christianity. The similarities between the two religions at this period increased the danger, to check which the author wrote his extremist *Epistle* to prove: (i) that there was never a Jewish covenant and that, (ii) all Jewish hopes were based on a misunderstanding.[115]

The *Epistle* was written as an answer to one particular type of Jewish messianic movement which prophesied the early reconstruction of the Temple. But Lowy's argument does not make this perspective clear and leads one to

---

114 Kraft, *Apostolic Fathers*, 3:55.

115 See S. Lowy, "The Confrontation of Judaism in the Epistle of Barnabas", *JJS* 11 (1960): 32. Also see G. Alon, "Halacha in Barnabas Epistulae," (Hebrew), *Tarbiz* 11 (1939): 23-28.

conclude that Barnabas is "extremist" and "anti-Jewish"; which is the opposite of this writer's view.

Barnabas was vehemently against one form of Jewish (and possibly Christian) religious enthusiasm precisely because it was extremist and would probably lead to and end up in a bloody revolt (115-117 C.E.). But he was not against all forms of Judaism and Christianity.

As the Qumran sectarians, a Jewish movement, were not against all Jews and Judaism, but only those who abused the Temple, so Barnabas is against fanatical messianic Jews or Christians.[116]

At stake here is a broader understanding of Judaism and the Law. It is not Judaism that sympathizers would be attracted to but that kind of Judaism which stirred up hope for the rebuilding of the Temple. Barnabas was not against Judaism, and certainly not the Law (he uses it much the same way as Philo did); rather, he was distressed over certain directions some Jews and Christians were taking.

Lowy's conclusions about the *Epistle* are accurate: "(1) The *Epistle* is not extremist, but corrective; the covenant belongs to those who understand it the way he (Barnabas) does and not some other exclusive way. Barnabas may sound extreme because he is reacting to extremists on the other side. (2) The *Epistle* does not say that 'all Jewish hopes were based on a misunderstanding,' but that a particular form of fanatical Judaism among the Jews was based on a misunderstanding."

Barnabas's desire was to demonstrate the superiority of his brand of Christianity over the others. He called Christians to hold on in these "evil days" (2.1) and "err like them" (2.9). Barnabas told his readers that they should "enquire concerning our salvation, in order that the evil one may not achieve a deceitful entry into us and hurl us away from our life" (2.10).[117]

Barnabas was a moderating voice, in a dangerous and fanatical era prior to 115 C.E., for Alexandrian Jews and Christians. His exegetical concern was aimed at other schools which were stirring their students into a kind of messianic frenzy.[118] According to some scholars the rabbinical school at Yavneh would not stir up a messianic fanaticism anyway.[119]

---

116 For another view see Gunther, "*Epistle of Barnabas*", 150-151.

117 It seems likely that this is a reference to the "messianic crusades" (Smallwood, *Jews*, 397) which were taking over the Cyreniacan Jews during this period (c.116).

118 Shukster and Richardson argue that Barnabas wanted to set up such a school to compete with Yavneh. See "Temple," 30.

119 See the comments by S.J.D. Cohen in "Yavneh Revisited: Pharisees, Rabbis and The End of Jewish Sectarianism" in *SBL 1982 Seminar Papers*, (Chico, CA: Scholars Press, 1982): 45-62. Cohen suggests that there was an attempt to encourage a broadening of one's understanding of Judaism and a break from the sectarianism of the past. They too, then, wanted a moderate Judaism in the face of a growing fanaticism.

Barnabas offered a balanced critique of what appeared to him to be a distortion of Judaism and Christianity. It is possible that part of the reason for his views may be found in his childhood experiences with an inclusive and moderate form of Judaism; the Judaism he knew may have known the tradition as a matter of the heart and not simply the flesh (10.12).

Therefore, the *Epistle* is not an "early Christian writing which reflects a distinctly anti-Judaic bias";[120] rather, it is a letter seeking a way to moderate Jewish and Christian fanatical and extremist ideas.

---

[120] See Pearson, "Earliest Christianity," 150-151 and the extensive bibliographical materials in the first few footnotes of this chapter.

CHAPTER TWO

JUSTIN: AN APOLOGETIC ESSAY
The *Dialogue with Trypho a Jew* (c.160 C.E.)

I. Introduction

Justin Martyr's *Dialogue with Trypho a Jew*[1] is one of the so-called early Christian *adversus Judaeos* writings. It was probably composed sometime around 160 C.E., twenty-five years after the dialogue took place. The *Dialogue* is one of the first fully developed theological statements by a Christian philosopher to debate the relative merits of Christianity over Judaism. Many scholarly works describe and interpret Justin's *Dialogue* as an example of the ongoing relationship between Christians and Jews in the second century.[2] Most of these studies are textual.[3] They either compare the *Dialogue* with contempo-

---

1 The critical texts which have been used for this book are *Justin Dialogue avec Tryphon. Texte Grec.*, translated by G. Archambault, editors H. Hemmer and P. Lejay, "Texte et Documente pour l'Etude Hist. Chr.," 2 vols. Paris, 1909, and *Justin Martyr, Die ältesten Apologeten, Texte mit kurzen Einleitungen*, edited by E.J. Goodspeed (Göttingen: Vandenhoecht Ruppert, 1914).

2 See the following studies: A. Hulen, "The Dialogue with the Jews as sources for the early Jewish argument against Christianity," *JBL* 51 (1932): 58-71; A. von Harnack, *Judentum und Judenchristentum in Justins Dialog mit Trypho, (TU* 39, 1939): 47-98; E.R. Goodenough, *The Theology of Justin Martyr* (Jena: Frommansche Buchhandlung, 1923); M.S. Enslin, "Justin Martyr: An Appreciation," *JQR* 34 (1944): 179-205; J. Neusner, "A Life of Rabbi Tarphon, c. 50-130 C.E.," *Judaica* 17 (1961): 141-167; H. Chadwick, "Justin Martyr's Defence of Christianity," *BJRL* 47 (1964-65): 275-297; L.W. Barnard, "The Old Testament and Judaism in the Writings of Justin Martyr," *VT* 14 (1964): 395-406; W.A. Shotwell, *The Biblical Exegesis of Justin Martyr* (London: SPCK, 1965); A.J.B. Higgins, "Jewish Messianic Belief in Justin Martyr's *Dialogue with Trypho*," *NT,* 9 (1967): 298-305; P.J. Donahue, *Jewish Christian Controversy in the Second Century. A Study in the Dialogue of Justin Martyr* (Diss. Yale Univ.), New Haven, 1973 (Donahue uses the primary sources uncritically. See his use of the Talmud and other rabbinic materials, 62f. He has not benefited from the more recent works of scholars like J. Neusner); E.F. Osborn, *Justin Martyr* (Tübingen: Mohr-Siebeck, 1973); Ben Zion Bokser, "Justin Martyr and the Jews," *JQR* 64 (1973-1974): 97-122, 204-211; T. Stylianopoulos, *Justin Martyr and the Mosaic Law* (SBLDS 20; Missoula: Scholar Press, 1975); J. Nilson, "To Whom is Justin's *Dialogue with Trypho* Addressed?" *TS* 38 (1977): 538-546; C. Cosgrove, "Justin Martyr and the Emerging Canon," *VC* 36 (1982): 209-232; H. Koester, *Introduction,* 2: 242-245; W. Horbury, "The Benediction of the Minim and Early Jewish-Christian Controversy," *JTS* 33 (1982): 19-61; D. Trakatellis, "Justin Martyr's Trypho," in *Christians Among Jews and Gentiles,* edited by G.W.E. Nickelsburg, (Fortress Press, Philadelphia, 1986), 287-297. See also Räisänen's comments on Justin in his book on *Paul,* 223 and Segal's summary of Justin that agrees with the thesis of this chapter. See Segal "Judaism, Christianity, and Gnosticism," in S.G. Wilson, *Anti-Judaism,* 143.

3 See the brief literary analysis of H. Schreckenberg, *Adversus-Judaeos-Texte,* 182-200; G.N. Stanton, "Aspects of Early Christian-Jewish Polemic and Apologetic," *NTS* 31 (1985): 377-392; D. Trakatellis, "Justin," and Remus, "Justin Martyr's Argument with Judaism," in S.G. Wilson, *Anti-Judaism,* 59-80. Each of these scholars give an excellent analysis of Justin's *Dialogue* and
(continued...)

rary literature or examine the text in light of the conventional wisdom about Jews and Christians in the second century. Most deal only with the theological content of the *Dialogue*, with little or no attention given to the social, economic, and cultural context of the document or the individuals involved in the "dialogue."[4]

The aim of this chapter is to reconsider the purpose of the *Dialogue* by paying closer attention to the people and places that produced it. But first it will be necessary to present some basic information about the content of and theological questions raised in the document itself. After a few preliminary comments about the *Dialogue*, it will be discussed, using three cities as a text and context. As this is done the cultural, social, and religious context for each of those cities will enhance one's understanding of the *Dialogue*.[5] This discussion of people and places enables the reader to read the text taking advantage of many levels of a particular social context, which can enhance the context of the text. Reading the text this way raises the question of the nature of the dis-

---

3(...continued)
interpretation of it from a study of the *Dialogue* itself and other so-called contemporary works.

4 See H. Remus's "Justin," in S.G. Wilson, ed. *Anti-Judaism*, 59-80. Remus suggests that it is helpful to look at the Dialogue through the "conceptuality of the sociology of knowledge" (60) and "Rather than rehearsing these issues once again, the remainder of this essay will seek to illuminate Justin's argument with Judaism by focusing especially on the social and cultural rooting and dimensions of that argument and viewing it as an expression of a conflict between competing communities and their respective social and cultural worlds." (66). See also A.L. Williams, *Justin Martyr*, 31, and L.W. Barnard, *Justin Martyr, His Life and Thought*, (Cambridge, England, 1967), among other scholars, seem to approach the *Dialogue* with a sense of religious awe, which throughout their writings creates distortions as to the meaning of the text in its social, political, and cultural context. In his introduction to *Justin Martyr*, vii, Barnard wrote: "I have found much food for thought and also encouragement from the example of this Apologist who rose so triumphantly above his material and who, in one bold stroke, summed up the whole history of the human race in Christ." It seems that the "whole history of the human race" would include Jews (not to mention the other ethnic and religious groups of the Mediterranean world). One can appreciate Barnard's concern with theological issues since he is a leader of a Church and is trying to interpret the writings of Justin for a faith community; but when a book such as his is an attempt to present an academic study of Justin Martyr, then it is important for him to try to present a somewhat detached analysis which would help our understanding of the text. The following scholars may not use the *Dialogue* in the same biased way but they do quote from it uncritically as if Justin said it and therefore it must have happened that way. See W.H.C. Frend, *The Early Church*, (London, 1965), 75-76, and "The Old Testament in the Age of the Greek Apologists A.D. 130-180" *SJT*, 26 (1973): 141, where Frend simply makes historical comments from a theological text.

5 See the sociological approach of F. Watson, *Paul*, and the concern for the urban setting of Meeks, *Urban*, and Sanders theological/sociological approach to Luke-Acts in *Jews*. These authors insist on examining the documents in the context of the social setting as well as in the light of the sociological questions. An ancient text is more than a text, it is a product of a specific environment.

cussion Christians and Jews would have in a particular place at a specific time. What were they doing in that city at the time the *Dialogue* was written?[6]

The last section of this chapter summarizes the overall purpose and intent of the *Dialogue*.

II. Trypho the Jew, and Justin, the Christian Philosopher; Some Issues

A. Personal Characteristics

In comparison to other *adversus Judaeos* literature, the *Dialogue with Trypho a Jew*, is the most agreeable in tone.[7] Only two serious altercations take place in the whole work (64.1, 79.1). Generally Justin is supportive and pastoral, concluding with a cordial farewell (142). Even though Justin tends to use harsh language from time to time and is very critical of Trypho and "your people," for the most part this blatant criticism is not a source of irritation to Trypho (85.6, 87.1, 118.5), who occasionally even silences his fellow (Jewish?) listeners who were mocking Justin (8.3, 9.2).[8]

Beyond the tone of the *Dialogue*, the reader is given some insights into Trypho himself. For instance, at the beginning Trypho tells Justin that he was a "Hebrew from the circumcision, and having escaped from the war that is presently going on, I am living in Greece, mainly in Corinth" (1.3).

Later in the first part of the discussion Trypho summarizes his fundamental beliefs:

> If, then, you are willing to listen to me (for I already consider you a friend) first be circumcised, keep as has been enacted, the Sabbath, and the feasts and the new moons of God; and in a word, do everything that is written in the Law, and then you shall obtain mercy from God. But Christ, if he has indeed been born and exists anywhere, is not known, and does not even know himself, and has no power until Elias comes to anoint him and make him manifest to all. And you, having accepted a groundless report, make up a Christ for yourselves and for his sake, are heedlessly perishing (8.4).

---

6 See the discussion of "thick description" and the "city as text" above.

7 See Trakatellis, "Justin," 289-290, which presents Justin's view of Trypho as a worthy opponent. Trakatellis suggests that this contact was not necessarily the prevailing one between Christians and Jews but does not present a discussion for the "philosophically inclined, and in cultural milieux." (297).

8 Trakatellis's "Justin," 294, is the source of this observation about the tone of the *Dialogue*. "Whether he accuses Justin or whether he listens or whether he raises sharp questions, Trypho is portrayed by Justin as a gentleman and as a willing and eager explorer of the truth, enjoying deeply the ongoing theological interaction with his Christian interlocutor, agreeable and yet uncompromising."

In 9.3 Trypho is presented as a person who is open and fair-minded even though he opposes his mocking companions. Trypho continues to speak cordially and intensely with Justin, and does not avoid difficult theological or personal conversations.

The underlying mood of the *Dialogue* is one of open discussion with Justin, the Christian philosopher, who throughout is portrayed as the one who understands the true meaning of the Scriptures and Israel's tradition.[9] Even Trypho seems to agree more than disagree with Justin's interpretations of the text.

Another aspect of Trypho's personality is revealed in the statement about his "escape from the war lately carried on there" (Palestine). It seems clear that the "war" mentioned in the *Dialogue* (1.3 and 9.3) is Bar-Kokhba's revolt against the Romans.[10] This is a revealing insight into the kind of person Trypho may represent, suggesting that he did not agree with the rebellion there.

What kind of a Jew,[11] then, was Trypho? Was he a traitor to his nation during the traumatic experience of the war with Rome in 135 C.E.? Would Rabbi Akiba, a contemporary of Trypho and Bar-Kokhba, have looked with disdain on him for betraying the cause of freedom?[12] A case could be made

---

9 See 29.2 where Justin tells Trypho that the Scriptures belong to the Christians. There are references throughout which suggest that the Christians are the ones who have received the "prophetic gifts which have been lost by Israel (82.1), and have become the holy people of God (11.2,3,4,5, 12.3,6,7, 123.6,7,9, 119-120). The Christians have actually replaced Israel 135.3,6, and are the only true worldwide religion now (117).

10 See *Apol*. 1.31 where Justin refers to the "Jewish war" which was led by Bar Kokhba and *Dial* 1.3, 9.3, 16.2-4 which refer to the same war in Judea. Also see Eus., *HE* 4.8. For a discussion of the use of *Dial*. 1.3 and 9.3 as a reference to the war see E.M. Smallwood, *Jews*, 453 n. 99 and D. Trakatellis, "Justin," 289 and notes.

11 The word "Jew" (*Ioudaios*) appears in the *Dialogue* only a few times (72.3, 77.3, 80.4, 103.3, 5). Each of these references is to Jews in a very technical or historical sense and does not refer to Jews in a general way. Justin never refers to Trypho as a Jew. Instead the references to Jews are to Israel (past and present, as if they were one and the same (132.1) or "your people" (46.5, 48.2) or people of your race. It seems that the designation "Jew" was probably a later addition to the discussions with and against the Jews.

E.R. Goodenough, *Jewish Symbols*, I.53 n.117, suggests that Trypho is an interesting example of the diversity of Judaism in the Roman Diaspora. He suggests that Trypho, at least the way Justin describes him, would be more comfortable with Philo's thinking than with the rabbis in Palestine. He seems to exhibit a mixture of rabbinic and nonrabbinic Jewish thoughts. It is clear, too, that Trypho did not know (or use) Hebrew. Goodenough summarizes Trypho's form of Judaism with these words: "Justin's Trypho seems to me typical of diaspora Judaism, not primarily because of the specific points of Hellenism or legalism that he expresses, but because his Judaism is such a mixture of elements from hellenistic and halachic traditions, a mixture which in any individual might have had more or less of one or the other element." Also, see his earlier work on Justin Martyr, *The Theology of Justin Martyr*, Jena, 1923.

12 Louis Finkelstein, in his romantic novel about *Akiba, Scholar, Saint and Martyr* (New York: Atheneum, 1936), 269, suggests that "Akiba himself did not long resist the contagion of Messianism. When he saw Roman legions yield to untrained Judean youths, new hope blossomed in his heart. 'Yet once, it will be a little while,' he quoted from Haggai (2:6), 'and I will

(continued...)

that Trypho did not represent the thoughts and feelings of those within Judaism who supported the war. But one can not be certain about the "kind" of Judaism Trypho represented.

What is clear, though, is that Trypho was not one of those "Rabbis" contemporary with Akiba who supported the war.

B. A Time for Self-Definition

Probably the best way to describe what was happening in the *Dialogue* is that the writer was reporting the struggle of one Christian with the meaning of his tradition. It has been argued[13] that the issues in the *Dialogue* do not represent a real exchange between Christians and Jews as much as an "exposition of Christian philosophy for pagans" or, on the other hand, simply an indication of the relevant issues between Jews and Christians from a Christian's perspective.[14]

As one reads through the *Dialogue* it seems that the latter is more likely to be the case, namely that Justin used dialogue as a means of making clear theological and philosophical issues essential for Christian self-definition.[15]

12(...continued)
shake the heavens and the earth, and the sea, and the dry land.' (B. Sanhedrin 97b) He went so far as to encourage the popular delusion concerning the miraculous role to be played by the new leader and applied to him the verse (Num. 24:17), 'The star hath trodden forth out of Jacob.' (Yer Ta'anit 4.7, 68b; Lament R. 2.2) Once he even said outright, 'This is the Messianic King.'" It would appear from the more recent studies of Neusner and others that Finkelstein's comments on Akiba are more fanciful history. But it is apparent that there was a feeling by those who wrote the Talmuds that Bar Kokhba stimulated much discussion and was obviously seen by some people, perhaps even Akiba, as a messianic figure. Trypho represented one perspective of the war among the Jews during the period of the war. Akiba represented another view. Even Neusner in "Rabbi Tarphon," 141-167, tends to write a fanciful history of Tarphon. In Neusner's later writings he improves his method of dealing with these tests. See Neusner, *Method 10*, 51 and his *In Search of Talmudic Biography: The Problem of the Attached Saying, BJS* 70. (Chico, CA: Scholars Press, 1984) and *The Peripatetic Saying: The Problem of the Thrice-Told Tale in Talmudic Literature, BJS* 89. (Chico, CA: Scholars Press, 1985) for further comments on the development of Neusner's method.

13 Stanton makes this observation in his essay, "Aspects," 377-392: "Two very different conclusions have been reached. On the one hand Harnack believed that by Justin's day genuine discussion and debate between Christians and Jews was virtually over and that the dialogue with Trypho was in truth the monologue of a victor. 'Nicht der Gegner selbst spricht mehr; Justin lässt sich spechen.' (A. Harnack, *Judentum*). On the other hand some scholars have insisted that the polemical character of the Dialogue is so very strong that it cannot have been addressed to Jews; rather, it was intended to be an exposition of Christian philosophy for pagans. (E.R. Goodenough, *Justin Martyr*)." Stanton insists that "the Dialogue contains a considerable amount of invaluable information about the issues at stake between Christians and Jews in the middle of the second century."

14 See Trakatellis, "Justin," 296-297.

15 For a discussion of Jews and Christians in the second century working on self-definition see M.R. Greenwald, "The New Testament Canon and the Mishnah as Consolidation of Knowledge in the Second Century C.E." *Seminar Papers SBL 1987*, Number 26, Atlanta: Scholars
(continued...)

The *Dialogue* is not a common form either in Christianity or in Judaism. The reader is left with the impression that the issues discussed in the *Dialogue* need further comment. Justin and Trypho would meet again for their discussions.[16] Therefore the discussions, and even the long debate by Justin in the *Dialogue*, may be seen not as the end of an encounter between two friends, but as a beginning of polemic and dialogue between some Christians and Jews in western Asia Minor in the mid-second century.[17]

C. Cities as Text

According to the opening words by Justin, the *Dialogue* took place in Ephesus[18] during the "war lately carried on there [Palestine]" (1.1,3). Yet there are other cities which inform the reader and stand behind the text. Neapolis, located near ancient Schechem in northern Palestine,[19] is one of those cities.

15(...continued)
Press, 1987: 244-254. Greenwald suggests that both Christians in the process of canonizing the New Testament and Jews in creating a written Mishnah were establishing their own authority and legitimization (253-254).

16 This comment is based on an assumption about the *Dialogue* which will be discussed in more detail below. The assumption is that in the *Dialogue* Justin seemed to struggle with certain issues he held to be important to Christians and Jews, and the dialogue with a Jew named Trypho was simply a way he had of framing those issues. The questions which Trypho placed before Justin seem to be questions which Justin himself wanted to answer. In other words, Trypho's comments permitted Justin to carry on his exposition and thus work out his own point of view of Christianity and Judaism as the dialogue unfolded. Another possibility is that Justin posed those questions in the responses by Trypho and the others which were predictable questions raised by Jews who objected to Christianity. The *Dialogue* survived because Justin's answers provided the responses that a number of Christians wanted and used to predictable questions posed by some opponents.

17 See Stanton, "Aspects," where this thesis is developed. See Remus's comments in "Justin," 72, where he states: "the extended, developed arguments in the *Dialogue* point to significant contact between Justin and Jews, with his arguments hammered out in conversations and disputes with them."

18 L.L. Welborn suggests Corinth as the place of the *Dialogue*. See "On The Discord in Corinth: I Corinthians 1-4 And Ancient Politics" *JBL* 106.1 (March 1987): 85. Welborn's comments are admittedly tentative.

19 J. Neusner makes the following comment in his *Judaism in the Matrix of Christianity* (Philadelphia: Fortress Press, 1986), 17: "In both the second and the fourth centuries the matter reached full symbolic realization in the name by which the Land of Israel would be known. In the second century the Land of Israel became 'Palestine.' Israel was defeated, so Rome renamed the Land. In the fourth century the Land of Israel became, for Christian Rome that ruled, 'the Holy Land.' Therefore the use of the word 'Palestine' here, is not to be considered a modern political comment. It is important to be aware of people's sensitivities today when referring to the nations of the Middle East. There is a problem for people today, as there was for people in Justin's day, in referring to Israel or the Holy Land or Palestine with the technical name 'Palestine,' but for the sake of accuracy and so that it can refer to the text of the city properly, it is necessary to use this name which is distasteful for some."

It was the place where Justin reports he was born (120.6).[20] It is possible that this city of his childhood influenced the way he viewed the Jews and what he knew of Judaism. The perspective from this Roman diplomatic outpost could be very important for Justin's early understanding of Israel's religious traditions.

Trypho was also born in Palestine, but chose for some reason to live and carry on his work outside his homeland. It is possible that he left Palestine as a political exile. He had fled from the war. It could be that he was not in agreement with the politics of his colleagues and wanted to go to a more neutral place to live and work. This decision to leave the war zone was certainly not something unique to Trypho. Other early rabbinic sources suggest[21] that during the last days of Jerusalem in 70 C.E. Johanan ben Zakkai left that city and established the rabbinical school at Yavneh.

These cities were more than contexts in which two persons argued; they were vital places where certain social, political, economic, philosophical, and religious conditions existed, questions were raised, and attitudes held that influenced the kind of person one became. The cities Justin lived and worked in offer important information about the *Dialogue*.[22]

III. The Three Cities as Texts

Three cities were important in Justin's life and work: Neapolis in Samaria, Ephesus in western Asia Minor, and Rome.[23] Each of these cities played a significant role in Justin's discussions with Trypho. A brief examination of these cities, tied together by Justin's experiences in them at different times in his life, suggests the origins of some of his attitudes about Jews and Judaism.

---

20 See the more complete discussion of Neapolis below in the section on that city.

21 See the account of Yohanan ben Zakkai's request for Yavneh as it was told in *The Father According to Rabbi Nathan*, translated by Judah Goldin, (New York:Schocken Books, 1974) 4: 32-39. See also *Lamentations Rabbah* 1.5.31, translated by J. Rabinowitz, *Midrash Rabbah* (London, 1956), ed. H. Freedman and M. Simon, VIII, 100-105.

22 See W.A. Meeks, *Urban*; W.A. Meeks and R.L. Wilken, *Jews and Christians*; and F. Watson, *Paul*, which asks sociological questions which must be posed when looking at a text and the context of a city.

23 R. Murray in his essay "Jews, Hebrews and Christians; some needed distinctions," *NT* 24 (1982): 207 and 208, makes the following statement: "The whole 'map' of early Christianity, in all its forms and connections, calls for more sociological analysis, and that of the greatest possible perceptiveness and command of relevant detail. [At this point in Murray's statement he makes reference to D.J. Harrington, "Sociological concepts and the Early Church," *TS* 41 (1980): 181-190]. Precious data such as Justin's analysis of the conditions for compatibility of Christianity with Jewish practice (*Dial*.47) . . . must be brought into relationship with relevant details from many sources---historical, religious, epigraphic and so on . . . In the second century the Christian Churches had to define themselves not only over against their Jewish and 'Hebrew' cradles, but also against movements of over-reaction in the form of Marcion's violently anti-Jewish dualism and gnostic denial of the goodness of this world."

This section will review specific social, economic, political, religious, or cultural characteristics of these cities which would be relevant influences on Justin's life and work.

A. Justin's Birth: A Roman City: Neapolis

1. *Justin's Family and Samaritan Background.* Most scholars agree that Neapolis,[24] located near ancient Schechem and founded by Vespasian in 72 C.E., was the place of Justin's birth around 100 C.E. The city was given the status of a Roman *colonia* in the middle of the third century, but seemed to be a cultural center before that date.

The recent discovery of a theater[25] built in the second century that could seat 6,000 to 7,000 people provides a clue for the level of social life in Neapolis. The evidence seems to indicate a cosmopolitan setting for Justin's early childhood.

Justin himself refers to "my people" when referring to the Samaritans.[26] This "intimate" reference seems to reveal a feeling of involvement with the Samaritans with whom he lived. It also suggests that the Roman diplomats may have had a special relationship to them.[27] This social information about

---

24 For a recent and general article on Neapolis, but lacking in a bibliography, see *The Archaeological Encyclopedia of the Holy Land*, revised edition, edited by A. Negev, (Nashville: Thomas Nelson Pub., 1986) 138-139. See also a brief comment on Neapolis in M.J.S. Chiat, *Handbook of Synagogue Architecture*, BJS 29, edited by J. Neusner, (Chico, CA: Scholars Press, 1982): 197-198. Another reference to Neapolis is found in M. Stern, *Authors* 2, where Neapolis is mentioned by Ptolemy, 2nd century C.E. (No. 337a) and the *Expositio Totius Mundi et Gentium* 30 (No. 477), c. 350 C.E., as one of the cities of the Roman Empire in Judea and "as a famous and very noble city." See the extensive footnote on Neapolis (*Authors* 2:497 n.30) which describes the history and other references to the city. Apparently it was a very beautiful and important city in the second through sixth centuries. Josephus mentions Neapolis in his *Wars* 4.449. Besides these references there are no other studies or descriptions of the city in the second and third centuries C.E. Therefore, lacking information, the discussion of Justin's birthplace is extremely limited to what scraps of information can be carefully pieced together.

25 According to A. Negev, *Archaeological*, 139, the theater was excavated by Y. Magen in 1979. It could accommodate 6,000 to 7,000 people and was 330 feet in diameter. Some of the seats were labeled in Greek and the orchestra was paved in colored marble. It was constructed in the second century.

26 For a summary of the modern study of the Samaritans, see J.D. Purvis, "The Samaritans and Judaism," in Kraft and Nickelsburg, *Early Judaism*, 81-98. Also see the article and bibliography in the *IDBS* by R.J. Bull about Mount Gerizim in the second century. By then the "Temple" on the Mountain had become a pagan temple to Zeus Hypsistos. See I *Apol.* 1.1 and *Dial.* 120.6 where there is a reference to "my people, that is, the Samaritans" (*oude gar apo tou genous tou emou, lego de ton Samareon*).

27 This "special relationship" may be due to their anti-Jewish attitude. But it is also possible that there was some anti-Roman feeling among the Samaritans living in Neapolis since Hadrian built a large temple to Zeus Hypsistos on Mount Gerizim. See R.J. Bull's article "Gerizim, Mount" in *IDBS*. Also see his studies: R.J. Bull "A Preliminary Excavation of an Hadrianic Temple at Tell er-Ras on Mount Gerizim," *AJA* 71 (1967): 387-393; "The Excavation of Tell er-Ras on Mt. Gerizim", *BA* 31 (1968): 58-72 and R.J. Bull and E.F. Campbell, Jr., "The Sixth

(continued...)

the Samaritans in Justin's writings, coupled with the fact that Justin was born in Neapolis, a stronghold for Samaritan influence, gives a clue to the background of Justin's view of the Jews and Judaism.

It is also possible that Justin's father and grandfather were Romans, who were sent to Neapolis to live in the rebuilt Roman town.[28] There is evidence that the Samaritans were very active in the business and diplomatic communities in Roman cities outside of Palestine. Neapolis may have been an important "home base" for many Samaritans who were serving both diplomatic and commercial interests.[29]

It is possible that Justin's family was part of a "diplomatic" community sent from Rome to Neapolis, where the family became friends with local Samaritans who were working in the "diplomatic corps." A new picture of Samaritans emerges from the evidence found in their community on Delos.[30] If they were a cosmopolitan community in a number of Roman cities, then it is possible that Neapolis had a sophisticated community of Samaritans too.

The large theater, Temple to *Zeus Hypsistos*[31] and the evidence of Samaritans outside of Palestine indicates that the Samaritans were probably more sophisticated than previously indicated in studies of these people.[32]

Within this sophisticated and genteel diplomatic atmosphere in Neapolis Justin learned about the Jews and Judaism. Justin's study of the Bible, understanding of Jewish practices, and knowledge of Samaritan traditions may come from his early childhood contacts with Samaritans in Neapolis.[33]

27(...continued)
Campaign at Balatah (Shechem)," *BASOR* 190 (1968): 2-41.

28 See Baron, *Social* 2: 341, n.39.

29 See the article by A.T. Kraabel on Samaritan Diaspora, "New Evidence of the Samaritan Diaspora has been found on Delos," *BA*, 47, (1984): 44-46, which tends to support the idea that Samaritans for some reason (business, diplomacy, political exile, etc.) lived outside Palestine during this period. See also Meyers and Kraabel, "Archaeology," 185-186.

30 An island in the southern part of the Aegean Sea.

31 Bull, "Excavation," 58 and "Preliminary Excavation," 392.

32 See Bull, "Excavation," 58-59. Also Kraabel's comment in his article on the Samaritans in Delos is very provocative in this regard. He writes: "What were Samaritans and Jews doing on Delos? The evidence indicates that they were inhabitants, not just a transient population. The island is small, less than two square miles, but significant in cult (it is the legendary birthplace of Artemis and Apollo), in political and military history, in international relations and international trade. Its foreign colony in this period included Romans, and others from various locations in the Aegean and the Mediterranean. I suspect that it was trade and, to a lesser extent, international politics that brought Samaritans and Jews here to settle." (See Kraabel, "New Evidence," 46).

33 P.R. Weis, "Some Samaritanisms of Justin Martyr," *JTS* 45 (1944): 199, is bold when he suggests that there may be some connections between Justin's life in Neapolis and the way he interpreted the Scriptures. To support this idea Weis cites *Dial.* 120.6, 40.3, 103.5, I *Apol.* 34,
(continued...)

The importance of the Samaritan environment[34] as a context for Justin and his later works is indicated by the many intentional "Samaritanisms" in the *Dialogue*.[35] This suggests a close tie between Justin and the Samaritans both in his birthplace and later in other cities.

This childhood contact most likely influenced his later anti-Jewish bias as he argued for the Christian position. These early experiences, first impressions, and connections between the Samaritan background and Justin's feelings about the Jews later expressed in his *Dialogue*[36] form the basis for a more accurate understanding of his conclusions about Jews and Judaism. Subtle anti-Jewish and anti-Judaism attitudes could have been learned from childhood playmates and experiences in Neapolis.[37]

33(...continued)
73. These texts are used to demonstrate a knowledge of local ideas, which indicate that Justin had some childhood experience with Aramaic and the Samaritans. Weis continues: "It is hardly conceivable, however, that anyone living in Palestine in Justin's time and possessing Justin's presumed knowledge of post-biblical Judaism (The Judaism which emerged after the Maccabean revolt, c. 165 B.C.E. and was expressed in various writings, including Philo, Josephus, the Pseudepigrapha, the Dead Sea Scrolls and other writings of the period between 165 B.C.E. to 135 C.E.), should be capable of errors of the kind attributed to him. May not the simple explanation be that Justin, having been born and brought up among the Samaritans in Shechem has quoted Samaritan practices as Jewish; more especially, the line of demarcation between the two was in many cases rather indistinct? It is here submitted that this is actually the case." A recent study by Stylianopoulos, *Justin Martyr*, confirms this. Later in his note Weis concludes: "The assumption that Justin occasionally had recourse to Samaritan tradition may help us also to explain some of his chronological inaccuracies (see I *Apol.* 21, 31). Justin's assertion that in connection with the translation of the 70 elders, King Ptolemy sent ambassadors to Herod, may find some explanation in the fact that according to Samaritan tradition the name of Ptolemy's lieutenant in Palestine was Herod." Compare E.N. Adler and M. Seligsohn, "*Une Nouvelle Chronique Samaritaine*," *REJ* 45 (1902): 73. For more recent discussions of the Samaritans and the Jews see R.J. Coggins, *Samaritans and the Jews*, (Oxford, 1975); R. Pummer, "New Evidence for Samaritan Christianity," *CBQ* 41 (1979): 98-117; R.J. Coggins, "The Samaritans and Acts," *NTS* 28 (1982):423-434. Coggins, *Jews*, 133, suggests that Samaritanism may express an even more conservative form of Judaism which suggests that all of the heretical doctrines of the Samaritans may be an attempt on the part of the Jews who make the criticism to react against an excessive formalism on their part.

34 See Stylianopoulos, *Justin Martyr*, 97, n.46; Baron, *Social* 2: 341, n.39; Bokser, "Justin Martyr," 97, where it is suggested that Justin lived in a place which was hostile to the Jews and therefore this background stimulated his later anti-Jewish sentiments. Bauer, *Orthodoxy*, 232; Murray, "Needed Distinctions," 208; and Coggins, "Acts," 423-432.

35 Stylianopoulos, *Justin Martyr*, 97.

36 Coggins, *Jews*, 153, suggests that Joshua was a favorite hero of the Samaritans, which is unusual in itself, since the consensus is that the Samaritan Bible does not include books beyond the five books of Moses. Justin constantly refers to Joshua as a type of Christ, which adds more evidence for a connection between Justin and the Samaritans. (see *Dial.* 49.6,7; 61.1; 62.4,5; 89.1; 90.4; 113.1,2,7; 116.3; 120.3; 131.4).

37 Bokser, "Justin Martyr," 97, wrote about Justin's birth and childhood in Neapolis and its effect on him: Neapolis was "long a center of Samaritan population which practiced a dissident Judaism and felt hostility to the Jewish community, and its pharisaic and rabbinic lea-
(continued...)

These negative feelings toward the Jews were part of his early childhood experience and may be part of the reason for his anti-Jewish sentiments. This fact, along with his growing appreciation for Christianity and its need to define its uniqueness against whatever form of Judaism he was experiencing,[38] suggests that it may have been easy for Justin to be friendly with Jews and supersessionistic at the same time.

2. *The Bar-Kokhba War*. Besides the Samaritan context of Justin's early years was the later traumatic experience of the Second Revolt of the Jews against the Romans led by Bar-Kokhba ('son of a star' or 'son of a liar').[39] Apparently (*Dial*. 1.3) not long after the Revolt, Justin was in Ephesus talking with Trypho, a Jew, about matters other than the war. And yet, when Justin does comment on the war, he is clear that the defeat of the Jews by the Romans is a result of their refusal to accept Jesus as the Christ.[40] If his family had served the Romans in diplomatic service in Neapolis, it is understandable why he would not be supportive of those "fanatical" Jews who "caused" the Revolt.

Two factors must be kept in mind as one considers the possible impact of the Bar-Kokhba War on Justin. First, the bitter hostilities which constantly plagued the social and political life in Palestine during the time between 70 and 134 C.E. might have caused the proliferation of many factions among Jews and Samaritans.[41] Second, the presence of a number of messianic pretenders among the Jews might have caused Justin to think that the Jews (in Palestine, at least) were in disarray theologically.

37(...continued)
dership." Coggins, *Jews*, 133, suggests that this "dissident Judaism" was in fact a more conservative form of Judaism. If Justin was following a Samaritanism which was a more conservative form of Judaism, then it seems reasonable to suggest that his line of reasoning in the *Dialogue* was following what he considered to be a truer form of Judaism in Christianity.

For another view of the relation between Jews and Samaritans in Palestine see R. Doran, "2 Maccabees 6:2 and the Samaritan Question," *HTR* 76.4 (1983): 481-485. Doran suggests that Hellenistic Samaritanism had a good and nonhostile relation with Jewish neighbors. The evidence seems slim and not reliable.

38 The texts in the *Dialogue* which are explicitly negative and hostile towards Jews and Judaism are: *Dial*. 39.1; 67.8; 68; 95; 97.4; 110; 114.4; 123.4; 130; and 136.

39 A full description of the Revolt with ample archaeological and literary evidence is found in Y. Yadin, *Bar-Kokhba, The rediscovery of the legendary hero of the last Jewish Revolt against Imperial Rome*, [1971], (Jerusalem: Steimatzky's Agency Ltd.), 1978. See also the reviews of a book on the coinage of the Bar-Kokhba War; W.E. Metcalf and G.W. Bowersock review of *The Coinage of the Bar-Kokhba War* by Leo Mildenberg, edited by P.E. Mottahedeh, (Arrau/Frankfurt-am-Main/Salzburg: Verlag Sauerlander, 1984) in *AJA* 90 (1986): 254-256.

40 Among other references see *Dial*. 16.4; 17.1; 92; 108.

41 See R.J. Coggins's suggestion that Samaritans were a faction of emerging Judaism in *Jews*.

As to the first of these two factors, Justin was born thirty years after the destruction of the Temple in Jerusalem (70 C.E.). It is possible that he was aware of the hostile feelings among Jews, Samaritans, and Romans in Palestine during the early part of the second century. Apologists like the Jewish writer Josephus, who also tried to tell his readers that the Romans were a noble people even during the war, may have come out of this same milieu; Josephus was searching for a way to live at peace with the political realities of his day.

Josephus gave support to the notion that the Romans were victims of Jewish fanaticism. This, of course, was not a popular position and led him to believe that extreme anti-Roman sentiments on the part of his fellow Jews may have created an irrational anti-Roman war.

In describing the War with the Romans, Josephus's[42] pro-Roman bias led him to report that the Jews were as vicious with each other as they were with the Romans. In his view, Jews probably caused as much or more harm to themselves than the Romans did.

Social and political chaos was a reality in Palestine during Josephus's and Justin's lifetime (66-135 C.E.). There were conflicts between Jews and Samaritans, Jews fighting against Romans, and Jews in a civil war with fellow Jews.[43] Josephus presents a picture of confusion in Palestine at the end of the first century. Therefore it is possible to view the Bar-Kokhba War, in part, as a civil war as well as a revolt against the Romans.[44]

Justin may have viewed these events as caused by Jews' rejection of Jesus as their messiah. If they had not gone after other messiahs then there would have been no war.[45] Justin seems to suggest this in his answers to Trypho.[46]

---

42 See BJ, 5.71, 5.98ff, 5.248ff, 5.277-278, 5.429-445.

43 Ibid.

44 *Dial* 1.3. tells us that one Jew, Trypho, left the land of Israel for the safety of Corinth. In an article on "The Causes of the Bar-Kokhba Revolt," *JQR* 58 (1967-1968):225, H. Matel suggests: "Our aim in this paper is to show that Eusebius is right. It was not the decrees of Hadrian that caused the Bar-Kokhba revolt, but the reverse is true: Hadrian's decrees constituted a reaction of the Romans to the Jewish revolt." Matel suggests that a war was in process even before the decree by Hadrian, and that many years of preparation for that war under the leadership of Bar-Kokhba had been taking place in Palestine.

45 Eusebius suggests that, according to Justin, Christians were directly involved in the war. "The same writer mentions the war of that time against the Jews and makes this observation, 'For in the present Jewish war it was only Christians whom Bar Chocheba [sic], the leader of the rebellion of the Jews, commanded to be punished severely, if they did not deny Jesus as the Messiah and blaspheme him.'" Eus., *HE.*, 4.8.4. It is possible to see this statement by Eusebius as an expression of his own anti-Jewish bias.

46 See the discussion in Simon *Verus Israel*, 158-163 and Schürer *History* 1:534-535. Justin gave an explanation for these events in his *Dialogue*. The Jews were suffering justly because they did not follow Christ. *Dial.* 92.2; 110.6; 108.3; 18.2; 46.7.

The second factor in the Bar-Kokhba War which influenced the way Justin interpreted its meaning was the exclusivistic and fanatical messianic claims for Bar-Kokhba among some Jews. B.Z. Bokser suggests that Jewish attitudes, such as the one reflected in R. Akiba's inferences about Bar-Kokhba as the Messiah, a commentary on Numbers 24.17, made Justin extremely hostile to these Jews who ran after other messiahs but could not accept Jesus.[47] This, along with "the unwillingness of the Jews to desert their own faith and enter the church," and the irritation produced by this dissent, caused hostility and rationalizations for speaking out against the Jews.[48]

Justin was urgent about defending his view of the Christian faith and the superiority of Christianity over Judaism; to do this, he used the traumatic events and the emerging Jewish messianic notions (*Dialogue* 48-108) to support his case. It is likely that his reaction to these two factors was a significant part of his anti-Jewish argument in the *Dialogue with Trypho*.

3. *Jewish Christianity*. There is a third factor which may have influenced the way Justin viewed the Jews in his early years and that is the challenge from Jewish Christians.

Even though Eusebius reports that the Christians who were in Jerusalem went to Pella around 70 C.E., soon after the destruction of the Temple by the Romans,[49] it is clear from recent studies that not all Jewish Christians left during that time. According to some scholars, Jewish Christians were still a threat to some Jews who moved with R. Johanan ben Zakkai to Yavneh.[50]

The *Dialogue* in some places is ambiguous enough to make it difficult to know Justin's view of Jewish Christians. Did he consider them as full members of the Christian family, or were they outsiders, like the Jews who did not accept Jesus as the Messiah?[51] Or were they suffering from some kind of a

---

47 See Bokser, "Justin Martyr," 100.

48 See Bokser, "Justin Martyr," 205. See *Dial.* 137; 96; 108.1,3; 39.1; 37.8.

49 Eus., *HE.*, 3.5.3-5. See also S.G.F. Brandon, *The Fall of Jerusalem and the Christian Church* (1951): 168-173; S. Sowers, "The Circumstances and Recollection of the Pella Flight", *ThZ* 26 (1970): 305-320 and R.H. Snaith, "A Sarcophagus from Pella: New Light on the Earliest Christianity", *Archaeology* 26 (1973): 250-256.

50 See G. Alon, *The Jews in their Land in the Talmudic Age* (70-640 C.E.) 1, trans. G.Levi, (Jerusalem: Magnes Press, 1980), 288-307 where he discusses the Jewish Christians including a description of and discussion of the *Birkat ha minim*. Based on his own assertions and generalizations, Alon provides detailed descriptions of the various forms of Jewish Christians and asserts that the "sages of Yavneh placed them outside the Jewish fold because they (minim) were apostate and could no longer be called Jews" (307).

51 The ambiguity is caused by the translation of the phrase in *Dial.* 48.4. In 48.2 Justin has mentioned *apo tou genous humon* which is obviously referring to Jewish Christians ("from your race"), but in 48.4 Justin is again referring to "race" but does not give a pronoun with the word "*genous*" (race). *ANF* translates the phrase "our race," but the note (5) suggests "your race," which would mean that the criticism which follows this phrase is meant for Jewish Chris-
(continued...)

"weakness of mind," did not know any better, and could therefore be excused for their shortcomings?[52]

The issue between Justin and the Jewish Christians seems to revolve around the way some Jews view Christ and still need to follow the Mosaic Law. This, according to Justin, seemed to be a weakness. Justin wondered why Jewish Christians had to be faithful to that Law when they had Christ.[53] It may be, too, that Justin needed to make clear distinctions between the form of Judaism he had encountered, the Christianity he represented, and the Jewish Christians who in his view were confusing these distinctions. Thus when Justin summarized his arguments about Christians and Jews, it would appear that he viewed the Jewish Christians as "outsiders."

If Justin thought of Jewish Christians from the perspective of Samaritan Christians,[54] then it is possible to understand why he resisted the notion of a

---

51(...continued)
tians and not some gentile from "our race" who, like Marcion (*Dial.* 35) has strayed from the form of Christianity held by Justin. If 48.4 is referring to "your race," then Justin could be made to seem negative about Jewish Christians, or at least considering them not completely inside the Christian family. See 47.1-2.

52 See *Dial.* 47.1-2, where Justin seems to argue that the Jewish Christians were still holding on to Jewish rituals. But the main concern of this section is not with the Jewish Christians as much as it is with those Jews who "have anathematized and do anathematize this very Christ in the synagogues, and everything by which they might obtain salvation and escape vengeance of fire." *ANF* 47.4b. (Cf. Goodspeed, *Justin Martyr*, 47.4-5).

53 In an appendix to Bauer's *Orthodoxy*, Appendix 1, "On the Problem of Jewish Christianity," 241-285, Strecker states: "On the Problem of Jewish Christianity" presents a summary of Justin's view criticizing those Christians who combine the observance of the Jewish law with faith in Christ. The summary is worth mentioning here since many points made in this chapter about the Samaritan context and the feelings that environment conveyed are apparent in this description. The following five points are presented by G. Strecker, summarizing Justin's view: "(1) Jewish Christians can be saved if they hold fast to the Jewish law without demanding such observances from others nor regarding it to be necessary for salvation (47.1). (2) Jewish Christians who force their gentile brothers to keep Jewish observances or who withhold fellowship from them are not acknowledged as true Christians by Justin (47.3). (3) For those who have been misled by Jewish Christians to accept Jewish observances, salvation is possible if they hold fast to the confession of Christ (47.4a). (4) Christians who have turned to Judaism and forsaken faith in Christ and who are not converted prior to their death will not be saved (47.4,6). (5) The descendants of Abraham who live in accordance with the Jewish Law and who are not converted to Christ, but in their synagogues curse the believers in Christ will not be saved, (47.5)" (273-274).

This last reference, (5), is probably to the *Shemoneh Esreh*, or one of the benedictions said against Christians in the synagogue. For a more complete discussion of the Benediction see, Horbury, "Benedictions," 61 and G. Alon, *Talmudic Age*, 280-290.

Also see the contrary opinion by Cohen, *Maccabees*, 227-228, where Cohen suggests: "Furthermore, although by the fourth century the "benediction against heretics" was directed against Christians or some Jewish Christians' sects, its original version was a generic denunciation of all heretics. The intent was not to single out Christians or any other specific group, but to proclaim the end of sectarianism."

54 See Pummer, "New Evidence," 98-117, where he suggests that the "evidence for
(continued...)

Jewish exclusivistic view of salvation which included the Jews' claim to sole proprietorship of the Temple in Jerusalem. In reaction to this Jewish exclusivistic attitude, Justin set commitment to Christ beyond Jewish rituals as all-important.

Merely obeying the Law of Moses, according to Justin's view in the *Dialogue*, did not lead one to salvation. Thus conditioning his readers about some forms of Christianity---namely Jewish Christianity---Justin was narrowing the definition of an "insider."[55]

4. *Eclectic Knowledge of Judaism*. A difficult question to answer is: "What form of Judaism did Justin know?" One can ascertain Justin's familiarity with Samaritans and Jewish Christianity, but what kind of Judaism did Trypho represent?

It is possible that in the *Dialogue* Trypho represents an eclectic Judaism; that is, a Judaism which Justin put together from his encounters with various forms of Judaism and his "Samaritan" view of it. The rabbinical schools, in a modest way, were active in Israel at the time Justin was a child in Neapolis.[56] It is understandable that the Samaritans living around those "schools," in reaction to the emergence of rabbinic Judaism, would be very protective of their own traditions.

Justin's use of the Septuagint[57] suggests that he, along with most Jews in the Diaspora in the second century, thought that a Greek translation of the Scripture was adequate. It is possible that Justin had access to the Targumim, or Aramaic translations, and the Hebrew texts in Neapolis; nevertheless he quotes almost exclusively from Greek texts.[58]

Several reasons might be given for his lack of enthusiasm for the use of Aramaic or Hebrew besides the fact that he seems to find the Greek Bible adequate. One reason could be that his family was in Neapolis for only a short period and left when Justin was very young, thus precluding his learning Hebrew and Aramaic. Or it is possible that the Samaritan and Jewish popu-

---

54(...continued)
Samaritan Christianity is for the time being minimal," (117). This means that it is very difficult for one to be certain about the existence and beliefs of Samaritan Christianity.

55 See *Dial.* 44-47.

56 See the early work of Neusner, *Yohanan ben Zakkai*, for a discussion of the development of the schools.

57 There are several references in the Dialogue to the Septuagint. See especially, 71.3; 68.7; 84.3; and Justin's argument for the use of the Septuagint in 131.1. See the summary of Septuagint studies in Kraft and Nickelsburg, *Early Judaism* by E. Tov, "Jewish Greek Scriptures," 223-237, with bibliography.

58 See Barnard, *Justin*, 43. Most scholars agree that the languages in Palestine would include: Hebrew, Aramaic, Latin, and Greek. See Greenwald, "New Testament," 249 for a discussion of the use of Greek after 130.

lations living in Neapolis were similar to other communities in the Roman Empire, and used Greek almost exclusively, even in their synagogues.[59]

Whatever the reality was, it seems that Justin did not know or use Hebrew and Aramaic. This would mean that he was not interested in and had no knowledge of, the rabbinic discussions in those early years when the Mishnah was being formulated. Rabbinic Judaism, then, may have been known to him, if at all, through discussions and hearsay.[60]

The Judaism which Justin knew would be the Judaism of Trypho which Goodenough suggests is "a mixture of rabbinic and Philonic Judaism."[61] This, of course, assumes that Trypho was not a "straw man." The *Dialogue* does permit the reader to see Trypho as a composite similar to the Jews depicted in the New Testament. It is clear that Justin poses questions and gives answers in his *Dialogue*, which represent a mixture of many Jewish traditions.[62]

5. *The Jews in Neapolis*. Another view of Neapolis comes from the Jews who were living near the city in the first decade of the second century. Most scholars agree that significant conflict existed between Samaritans and Jews, both in Galilee and Judea. The New Testament is full of allusions to this tension.[63] Josephus refers to the conflict many times in his writings.[64] Their individual traditions played a significant role in creating tension between Samaritans and Jews and in the politics of the country.[65]

Neapolis was a Samaritan center[66] and therefore might influence the way

---

59 Goodenough, *Jewish Symbols* 1:53-54 suggests, again as he does throughout his writings, that the "overwhelming majority of Jews [living outside Palestine] of the period" spoke and worked in Greek. In fact it is not clear if they knew Hebrew or Aramaic.

60 Those discussions were probably in Hebrew or Aramaic and would not be public. What the rabbis would discuss in public would range through different topics and would not necessarily be in the more formal issues presented later (c. 225 C.E.) in the written form of the Mishnah. See the discussions of the formation of the rabbinic traditions in J. Neusner, *Method, BJS* 41 and *Method, BJS* 10. See the reference to Neusner's works in Greenwald, "New Testament," 253 n. 29.

61 Goodenough, *Jewish Symbols* 1:52.

62 For a discussion of rabbinic Judaism see J. Neusner's *Judaism, the Evidence of the Mishnah*, (Chicago and London: The University of Chicago Press, 1981). The discussions in Kraft and Nickelsburg, *Early Judaism*, by Cohen (33-51); Purvis (81-98) and Saladarini (437-477) outline the most recent study of multifaceted Judaism. In a way, Justin may have been in a position to observe many different forms of Judaism as he traveled.

63 The Gospel of Luke is particularly clear about this tension between Jews and Samaritans. See Luke 10 and 15, and especially 9:51-56.

64 *AJ* 2.111; 18.85-87; 20.118-119, 121-122, 125-130, 131-132, 134-135.

65 But see the discussion by Doran, "Samaritan Question," 485, who suggests that in the 2nd century B.C.E. there were peaceful relations between Jews and Samaritans.

66 M.J.S. Chiat, *Handbook*, 197 makes this comment about the formation of Neapolis: "The
(continued...)

a Jew would view Justin and his family, who lived as Roman diplomats in that community. Neapolis was a Roman city in Justin's day, located near the ancient center of Schechem. It was also the site of a Samaritan Temple, which competed with the Temple in Jerusalem.

It is understandable, then, that Jews would not be comfortable in Neapolis. They probably would feel the same way today in modern Nablus on the West Bank. It was a place which challenged their religious, political, and cultural traditions.[67]

Samaritans were also influential and competitive with their Jewish neighbors around the Roman world. Recent discoveries,[68] as mentioned above, have made it clear that Samaritans were present not only in southern Samaria, but lived in various places in the Diaspora. It is not clear what the relations were in the Diaspora, but there is enough evidence to suggest that the Samaritans seemed to maintain their own identity. It is reasonable to assume that this need for differentiation from their Jewish cousins meant some discomfort for the Jews.

The issues facing Jews in Palestine may have been raised again in other places. S. Baron suggests the following:

Samaritans remained only a minor sect within (*sic*) the Jewish people. Their very attachment to the locality became increasingly a handicap. They seem never to have succeeded in maintaining their Diaspora communities for any length of time,[69] except in Damascus with its strange immemorial ties to northern Palestine. Just as their deported forefathers were unable long to preserve their identity outside of Palestine, so all Samaritan settlements in the later Diaspora seem to have been short-lived . . . the same reasons which, throughout the ages, brought about Jewish emigrations from Palestine, also affected Samaritans. Forced repeatedly to leave the Holy Land and to estab-

---

66(...continued)
formation of the city-territory of Sebaste by the Romans left the southern area of ancient Samaria in the control of the Samaritans. Because Samaritans chose not to support the Jews in the first revolt, Vespasian rewarded them by founding a new city in their territory, Flavia Neapolis, on the site of ancient Maabartha (Josephus, *BJ* 4.449). The new city territory became known as Neapolis." It appears that this preference from the Roman ruler left a residual hostility behind. Jews living in that region would be aware of the preferential treatment shown to the Samaritans for their loyalty to Rome, a loyalty which was the cause for continued tension between the two groups. A description of the excavations on the Temple in Mount Gerizim is found in R.J. Bull, "Preliminary Excavation," 387-393 and "Excavation," 58-72.

67 S. Baron, *Social* 2:26ff., presented a rather extensive discussion on this matter.

68 See Kraabel, "New Evidence," 44-46. See the bibliography for further information about the Samaritans. See also Kraft and Nickelsburg, *Early Judaism*, 185-186.

69 But see Kraabel, "New Evidence," where he suggests another view. The few known Samaritan communities, the new evidence suggests, might have had (on Delos), a lively diplomatic or commercial settlement outside of Palestine.

lish settlements abroad, they always saw these settlements vanish[70] after a few generations. Until recently they survived exclusively around Nablus (*sic*), and here in steadily diminishing numbers. The most tenacious vitality could not save on foreign soil a people that had experienced neither the Exile nor the prophetic emancipation of religion from its territorial roots.[71]

This rather lengthy "quotation" presents a respected modern Jewish scholar's "tension" with the Samaritans even to this day.

If there are "Samaritanisms" in Justin's *Dialogue*, as some have suggested,[72] then it is understandable why some Jews would be offended. The offense has two parts: Justin argues like a Samaritan, echoing anti-Jewish feelings, and then as a Christian who speaks about his supersessionistic theology.

Along with being put off by the negation of the Mosaic Law as an adequate way to salvation, the Jews in Neapolis also experienced political hostility. Bar-Kokhba, as has already been suggested, was fighting for freedom from Roman rule. Trypho, as presented by Justin, refused to be involved in the Bar-Kokhba revolt against the Romans. This suggests that Justin knew some Jews who were opposed to the "popular" policies of other Jews.

The ambiguity of Trypho's particular form of Judaism allows for the view that not all Jews supported the war effort. Some Jews, and possibly all Samaritans, simply tired of the war effort (*Dial.* 1.3) and fled. It seems that there was much confusion in Neapolis among Jews and Samaritans about political and religious topics.

6. *The Jewish Texts*. There is also some confusion about the extent to which Justin and other Christian writers knew about rabbinic texts. In Palestine and Babylonia, the period 70-200 C.E. is considered by most scholars of ancient Judaism to be a fertile time for emerging rabbinic Judaism.[73] Judah the Prince (c.225 C.E.) codified their legal traditions into the Mishnah.[74]

Yet one wonders if Justin had any knowledge of the emergence of rabbinic Judaism in the early stages of that development. Many scholars simply assume that he did. They express this idea in the following ways:

Justin was acquainted with certain Jewish practices which are not found in the Old Testament. In *Dial.* 16.4; cf. 108.4; 107.3, he refers to the cursing of the Christians in the synagogues. This accords with the Palestinian form

---

70 But see Kraabel, "New Evidence" for a contrary view based on new evidence.

71 S. Baron, *Social* 2:34-35.

72 See Stylianopoulos, *Justin Martyr*, 97 and Weis, "Samaritanisms," 199, 204.

73 For a discussion of emerging rabbinic Judaism and the patristic writers and the reason these rabbinic texts cannot be used as parallels to the New Testament, see J. Lightstone "The Judaic Context," 103-132.

74 See Neusner, *Evidence*, and his many other books written on emerging rabbinic Judaism.

of the Twelfth Benediction in the *Shemoneh 'Esreh* which prayed that Christians (notzrim) may perish and be wiped out of the book of life. [see T.B. *Berakoth* 29a]. It is arguable that notzrim strictly refers to Nazarenes, i.e. Jewish Christians, but Justin assumes that it refers to all Christians, Gentile as well as Jewish. There is no reason to doubt the correctness of his information, although equally many Jews seemed to have remained in friendly contact with Christians in spite of the command of the rabbis not to hold discussions with Christians. To which Justin refers in *Dial*. 38.1 and which is confirmed by T.B. *Aboda Zara* 27B: "Let a man have no dealings with the heretics (*minim*) nor get healing of bodily diseases from them---for heresy (*minuth*) attracts".[75]

This statement makes use of rabbinic texts as if they were parallel to Justin's concerns. L.W. Barnard continues his remarks in this way:

They also appear to reflect fresh details concerning the ceremonies observed on that Day found in the Mishnah Tractate *Yoma*, which in its present form dates from c. A.D. 200. This Tractate may well reflect genuine earlier traditions, as the Temple ritual, at the time *Yoma* was written, was no longer applicable to Jewish life and therefore had been less overlaid with comments by later tannaim and less exposed to the possibility of revision (cf. *Yoma* xvi,a).[76]

S. Sandmel in his essay "Parallelomania"[77] suggests that too often New Testament scholars have jumped to conclusions that the rabbinic sources are closely allied with the New Testament sources in ideas and theological background. This "parallelomania" seems to be a unique problem with New Testament scholars who use the rabbinic texts as background of, or parallel to New Testament thought.[78] The same can be said of those who use the rabbinic sources as parallels to the thoughts found in the early Christian writers.

7. *The "Benedictions"*. Another case of "parallelomania" might be found in the suggestion that Justin knew about the so-called "Eighteen Benedictions."[79]

---

75 Barnard, *Justin*, 44-45.

76 Ibid. 45-46.

77 S. Sandmel, "Parallelomania," *JBL* 81, (1962): 1-13.

78 W.D. Davies does this in *Paul and Rabbinic Judaism*, London, 1962. His view has been somewhat corrected by E.P. Sanders, *Paul and Palestinian Judaism*, Philadelphia, 1977, who acknowledges that there is a different kind of Judaism, and suggests looking at what Paul says on his own terms, and what Palestinian Judaism is on its own terms, and not trying to enter the old debate of which one is better. (see 13). The most obvious work on the parallels between Judaism (rabbinic) and Christianity (the New Testament) is Strack and Billerbeck's *Kommentar zum Neuen Testament aus Talmud und Midrash*, 4 vols., München, 1924 and subsequent years. See Jack Lightstone's critical comments on parallelomania in his recent essay: "Christian Anti-Judaism in its Judaic Mirror: The Judaic Context of Early Christianity Revised" in *Anti-Judaism* 2, edited by S.G. Wilson, 106.

79 A discussion and list of the "Benedictions" as well as a revised bibliography may be found in Schürer, *History* II:454- 463. The note in *History* (462-463 n. 164) suggests that Justin

(continued...)

These *Shemoneh 'Esreh* [Eighteen] Benedictions were considered, in part, to be curses on Christians which emanated from synagogues.[80] Horbury states: "The anti-heretical benediction is interpreted by its context in the Tefillah [Prayer], which is marked by the zeal for the mission and unity of the brotherhood also found in the early Christian congregations. The effects of this zeal on both sides are illustrated by Justin's allusions to the propaganda, counter-propaganda and disciplinary measures which characterize the beginning of Jewish-Christian controversy."[81]

This view has been questioned by a number of scholars who suggest that the Benediction was actually not meant for non-Jews but instead was intended for Jewish sectarians.[82] Certainly there was tension between Jews and Christians, as the *Dialogue* amply demonstrates, but a statement that Justin had specific knowledge of the Benedictions cannot be based on any substantial evidence. It is unclear which Jews Justin had in mind.

Second, were the *Shemoneh 'Esreh* widely known among the Diaspora communities, or was Justin referring to some other early Christian writers (*Dial.* 16.4) when he wrote: "you do not now have the power to lay hands on us, on account of those who now have the mastery"? Is this a reference to the New Testament[83] notion that Jesus allowed the Jews of his day to arrest and

---

79(...continued)
making reference to the Benedictions in his *Dialogue* is out of the question. This writer agrees. See the evidence Schürer gathers to prove his point. See also Remus, "Justin," 73, n.58 for a bibliography for the study of the "Benedictions." Also there are extensive discussions of the Eighteen Benedictions in the *Encyclopaedia Judaica* (see 2.841ff on *Amidah* and 4.1035 on the *Birkat ha-minim*).

80 The comments in the *Dialogue* which are considered to be references to the Benedictions are 16.4; 96.2; 47.5; 95.4; 96.2; 133.6 among others. See Schürer, *History*, II:462 n. 164, for the supposed references to the Benediction in Justin's *Dialogue*. See also R.E. Brown, *The Community of the Beloved Disciple* (New York: Paulist Press, 1979), 173, for a brief reference to the *Birkat ha-Minim* (Curse on the deviators) c.85 C.E., as a way of identifying one group in the Gospel of John. Also the more detailed recent description of the "Benediction" by Horbury, "Benediction," 19-61.

But see another view in Cohen, *Maccabees*, 114-115, and especially 127-128 where Cohen suggests that the Benediction really declares the end of sectarianism and was not intended as a malediction against Jewish-Christians, or Christians. See C. Thoma, *A Christian Theology of Judaism*, trans. Helga Croner (New York: Paulist Press, 1980), 146, who suggests that the vehemence in the "Benediction" has to do with Jews and never non-Jews.

81 Horbury, "Benediction," 19ff.

82 See Cohen, *Maccabees*, 114-115 and C. Thoma, *Christian Theology*, 146. Simon *Verus Israel*, 198-199, suggests that the insertion into the *Shemoneh 'Esreh* was meant to root out those Jews of the Nazarenes (Christians) in the synagogues who could not repeat the "formula condemning the minim."

83 See James 5.6 and John 19.10-11 which are New Testament references to the power that Jesus had given to the "Jews" which enabled them to arrest him and kill him.

kill him? It seems that Justin, like Tertullian, has used Biblical notions to make his point (See *Dial.* 132.1; 46.5; 48.2).

If Justin is referring to the Jews in the Bible, then the "curse" mentioned in the *Dialogue* is not the "Benedictions" of the rabbis, but a more general statement about first-century Jews living in Palestine who arrested and killed Jesus.

B. Ephesus: The Hellenistic Context

The next city to be considered is Ephesus. Justin tells his readers that Ephesus was the place of his conversion[84] and his dialogue with Trypho.[85] Was there some special significance that it was set in this particular city where both John and Paul worked?[86] The evidence suggests[87] that Ephesus was a very important center for the Jews. In some ways the Jewish communities of Ephesus and Sardis were similar.[88]

Ephesus was a very active governmental, commercial, and academic center for Rome in Asia Minor. It boasted libraries, theaters, lecture halls, and various centers for domestic and foreign cults. One of the seven wonders of the world, the Temple to Artemis, was there. Clive Foss observes that Ephesus was the "greatest city of Roman Asia Minor . . . and was the terminus of two great highways connecting the Aegean coast with the interior of Asia Minor and the lands of the east: the ancient Persian Royal Road and the *Koina hodos*, the main trade route of the Romans which led up the Maeander valley

---

84 *Dial.* 3-6. For a complete bibliography on Ephesus see R.E. Oster, ed., *A Bibliography of Ancient Ephesus* (Metuchen, NJ and London: Scarecrow Press, 1987). Also see C. Foss, *Ephesus after Antiquity: A late antique, Byzantine and Turkish City* (Cambridge: Cambridge University Press, 1979). See the brief description of the city by D. Knibbe, "Ephesos", *RE* (1970): 293-297.

85 *Dial.* 1.1, 9.3, 142.2.

86 On Paul's work in the city, see Meeks, *Urban*, 44, n.224. On John's work in Ephesus, see R.E. Brown, *The Gospel According to John*, 2 vols. (New York: Doubleday, Anchor Bible 29 and 29A, 1966 and 1970). References in Josephus which refer to the Jews in Ephesus may be found in *Antiquities* 14-16 and *Apion* 1-2. *RE Suppl.* 12 (1970) 248ff., 297ff. and 1588ff., provide background materials for the city during the second century. Goodenough, *Symbols* I, 52ff., has a brief comment which gives the reason for Trypho escaping to Ephesus during the Bar-Kokhba war. He suggests that Trypho, like many Jews in this period, was looking for contact with Hellenistic philosophy. Ephesus was a center for learning and teaching. Acts 19 provides the New Testament story of Ephesus. Eus., *HE* 4.18.6-7 reports the dialogue between Justin and Trypho, the "most distinguished Jew (*Hebraion*) of the day."

87 A.T. Kraabel, "*Hypsistos* and the Synagogue at Sardis," *Greek, Roman and Byzantine Studies*, 10 (1968): 81-93 gives references to evidence for Jews in Ephesus. See also T.A. Robinson, *Bauer Thesis*, 93-121 for a discussion of early Christianity and Judaism in Ephesus.

88 See Meeks, *Urban*, 44.

to the plateau.... Under the *Pax Romana*, therefore, Ephesus had grown to become a great center of trade, finance, and industry."[89]

Paul worked very hard in and around the city but did not seem to be very successful there.[90] The Jews had a large community which apparently was not very cordial either to Paul or to Justin. Throughout the *Dialogue*, Trypho's Jewish companions laugh at Justin or walk away in amazement and disgust (see *Dial.* 16.4; 9.2; 8.2; 56; 122). Jews are mentioned in the literature about Christians and Jewish relations in Ephesus but there is no evidence to date to establish a Jewish presence there.[91]

In order to appreciate Ephesus as a "text" which can be read as a context for the *Dialogue*, it is necessary to understand four social and cultural characteristics, which will be mentioned: Hellenistic Christianity and Philo; the use of the Septuagint; the absence of explicit mention of Paul in the *Dialogue*, and the persecution of Christians by Jews in Ephesus (or anywhere in the Diaspora).

1. *Hellenistic Christianity and Philo*. E.R. Goodenough suggests in his work on *Jewish Symbols* that Jews throughout the Diaspora drew upon their cultural context when interpreting their tradition to themselves and their neighbors. Philo is certainly one of the premier examples of this process.[92] Justin was himself influenced by those same ideas, as is obvious in the opening chapters of the *Dialogue*. But he was also deeply impressed by Alexandrian Jewish ideas as known mainly from Philo.[93] L.W. Barnard summarizes the most recent dissent on this matter.[94] He reports that most recent studies have concluded that Justin's openness to contemporary philosophy was important,

---

89 See the description of the city of Ephesus in C. Foss, *Ephesus*, 3-102.

90 On Paul and his work in Ephesus, see M. Barth, *Ephesians 1-3*, Anchor Bible 34, (New York: Doubleday, 1974). See J.M. Ford, *Revelation*, Anchor Bible 38. (New York: Doubleday, 1975), 388-389, where there is a discussion about the influence of John the Baptist in Ephesus.

91 See C. Foss, *Ephesus*, 45.

92 See E.R. Goodenough, *Jewish Symbols* 1:52-53, 12:80, 4:72,74 and many other reference in this work where Goodenough details the interaction between Jews and their host cultures.

93 For an early recognition of this notion see P. Heinisch, *Der Einfluss Philos auf die Älteste Christliche Exegese*, (Muenster, 1908), 36. More recently a study has been done by Lightstone, "Christians' Anti-Judaism," in S.G. Wilson, *Anti-Judaism*, 112-113, where he summarizes his understanding of the world-view of Hellenistic Judaism and Goodenough's contribution to the study of Philo's form of Hellenistic Judaism. A detailed study of Philo's exegetical tradition is by B.L. Mack, "Philo Judaeus" in *ANRW* II.21.1: 228-271. S. Sandmel in the same volume has demonstrated how Philo has influenced the early Christian writers, especially the New Testament writer, in his "Philo Judaeus: An Introduction to the Man, his Writings, and his Significance," 3-47.

94 Barnard, "Recent Study," 153-157.

for it meant that Platonism as well as Judaism was seen as preparation for the gospel.[95]

Mixing of Greek philosophical thinking with one's own tradition, or using Hellenistic ideas as a context for the construction of one's theological framework in Justin and Philo, suggests that there were some authors in both early Christianity and emerging Judaism willing to attempt an apologetic of their traditions for a larger audience.[96]

In dealing with the influence of Philo on Justin, Barnard suggested that "direct influence of Philo's *logos* doctrine on Justin is unlikely . . . Justin's uses for *logos* are more likely taken directly from biblical tradition. Philo's *logos* is ultimately Stoicism or middle Platonism blended with the Old Testament 'Word of God.' Justin's *logos* is Jesus Christ understood in the light of the same Old Testament 'Word of God' and Greek Philosophy."[97]

It is difficult to establish this point of view. In fact, Simon suggests that there are similarities in method and interpretation of specific biblical texts which may suggest a closer bond than most would accept.[98] Other scholars have suggested that Christians and Jews in the Mediterranean world were "playing the same game" in the "same ballpark", meaning they were both influenced by the same philosophical ideas, namely, Stoicism and neo-Platonism.[99]

Ephesus was a center of Hellenistic thought and discussion. There one could not help being influenced by the "marketplace" of ideas. Justin admits that he spent many years studying at the feet of several philosophers. Even though he later moved on to a different view of life, he still writes his apologetics and his *Dialogue* using their ideas.[100]

2. *The Septuagint (LXX)*. The consensus among most scholars is that Christians and Jews in Diaspora used the Septuagint not only as Scripture but as a basis for theological and philosophical discussions. Greek was the language for the worship life as well as for commerce and discourse in the marketplace.[101] Therefore Jews and Christians in Ephesus, as well as the other

---

95 Ibid., 156. The problem with Barnard's comment is that he does not define what kind of Judaism he is referring to when he explains Justin's view of Judaism. It may be reasonable to assume that Barnard is thinking about rabbinic Judaism.

96 See *Dial*.2.1. Also see A.T. Kraabel, "New Evidence," 46, where he suggests that the Samaritan community in Delos was probably cosmopolitan in its outlook.

97 Barnard, "Recent Study," 157.

98 See Simon, *Verus Israel*, 161 ns. 41-47.

99 For a full discussion of the influence of Hellenistic philosophy on Judaism and Christianity, see Lightstone, "Christian Anti-Judaism," 103-132.

100 See Justin's comments about his studies in philosophy in his early years in *Dial*. 2.1ff. See Koester, *Introduction* 2:342-345.

101 For recent discussions of the place of the Septuagint and other Greek versions of the
(continued...)

cities of the western Diaspora, could converse about many different topics including their understanding and interpretation of the Scriptures. It is well known that Justin used the Septuagint for his *Dialogue*.[102]

Until the Septuagint became a text used by the Christians against Jews, and the rabbis in Palestine sought another Greek text,[103] Christians and Jews in Ephesus were influenced by the same philosophical perspective found in the Greek translation of Hebrew words. As far as Christians were concerned, the struggle over the Old Testament was not necessarily over the possession of it but over the interpretation of the texts.[104] The *Dialogue* consistently makes this point clear.[105]

One example of this struggle is found in the detailed discussion between Justin and Trypho over the question of "young woman" and "virgin" in Isaiah 7.14. The Septuagint refers to "*parthenos*" (virgin) and not "*neonos*" (young woman). This debate is over the translation of the Hebrew word *almah* (young woman) into the Greek *parthenos* (virgin).[106] Justin obviously wants to

---

101(...continued)
Hebrew Scriptures among Greek-speaking Jews, as well as a Bibliography, see E. Tov, "Jewish Greek" in Kraft and Nickelsburg, *Early Judaism*, 223-237. For its use among Greek-speaking Jews and Christians in the second century C.E., see the bibliographical references in J.H. Charlesworth, *Modern Research*, 78-81; Koester, *Introduction*, 1:252-255; the extensive updated bibliography in Schürer, *History*, III.1, 491-493 and O. Eissfeldt, *The Old Testament, An Introduction*, translated by P.R. Ackroyd (New York: Harper & Row, 1965): 701-715. Also see comments on the Septuagint in Simon, *Verus Israel*, 59-60. The standard works on the Septuagint are H.B. Swete, *Introduction*, and S. Jellicoe, *Septuagint*.

102 See Koester, *Introduction*, 2:342-345 and for the extensive documentation see Swete, *Introduction*, 417ff.

103 See the discussion of this process in Simon, *Verus Israel*, 59-61, 153-154, 267-268, and 373. See also Simon's comments about Justin's interpretation of the Septuagint, 158-160. See Schürer's references to the Aquila translation in *History*, III.1, 493, where he refers to Justin's *Dialogue* 68; 71 and elsewhere as an example of "Christian theologians who exploited the uncertain text of the LXX [sic] in their own interests." This, according to Schürer, was one of the reasons "the Jews" wanted another Greek translation of the Hebrew Bible.

104 One scholar says this about the struggle: "Despite a purely Hellenistic upbringing, Justin shares an astonishingly wide knowledge of contemporary Judaism, and his writings, especially the *Dialogue* written perhaps as much as twenty-five years after the event in 160, throws light on the intricacies of the struggle which was still being carried on with the Jews for possession for the LXX." W.H.C. Frend, "Old Testament," 139. See *EJ*, s.v. "Bible" and *IDB*, s.v. "Septuagint".

For a discussion of the meaning and purpose of the "Aquila" translation (c. 143 C.E.) of the Hebrew Bible see Schürer, *History*, III.1: 493-497; Eissfeldt, *Old Testament*, 715f.; Simon, *Verus Israel*, 59-61, 153-154, 267-268 and 373 and Koester, *Introduction*, 254-255.

105 See *Dial.* 68.2.; 71.3; 68.7; 84.3; 131.1; 137; 67.1.

106 The discussion between Justin and Trypho on these two words (virgin and young woman) takes place for the most part in 43, 56, 66, 67, 71, 75, and 86. Justin is obviously trying to prove that Isaiah is referring to Christ and not to Hezekiah. The argument is over the interpretation and translation of a certain text. It was the allegorical interpretations of the Septu-
(continued...)

hold to the view that the text refers to Jesus and his virgin birth. Trypho was supposedly (68.7) defending the idea that it referred to a young woman who was the mother of King Hezekiah.

The debate over the translation of the word *almah* was supposed to have taken place in Ephesus.[107] Even though such a debate could have stimulated hostility and violence between the contestants, it is not recorded as such in the *Dialogue*. Rather, issues are discussed and points of view expressed, in a friendly manner.[108]

It is conceivable that the dialogue or debate between Christian and Jew in Ephesus was creative until one group was threatened by the existence of the other. It is the view of this writer that one reason for the emergence of Christian anti-Jewish writings in the early second century was the Christians' growing awareness that Judaism in Sardis, Ephesus, and Alexandria during the second century was not only permanent---it was vital. This vitality was a threat to the Christians' own self-understanding as the true Israel who had become the chosen of God. The Christian writers have to explain why Jews continued to flourish if they were no longer God's chosen vessels. (See *Dial.*, 82.1; 29.2; 119; 123; 135; 124.1; 134).[109]

The Septuagint, then, was used by Justin to prove the correctness of his interpretation to demonstrate the legitimacy of the Christian position against the Jewish view. Trypho, in the *Dialogue*, represents a typical Jewish position, according to Justin.

106(...continued)
agint that led the rabbis in Palestine to be receptive to a new Greek translation of the Bible. See the discussion of this transition in Simon, *Verus Israel*, 59, and in Swete, *Introduction*, 30.

107 See W.A. Meeks, *Urban*, in which he talks about Ephesus and other cities of Paul as centers for lively human cross-fertilization on all levels. Meeks provides an extensive bibliography.

108 J.S. Sibinga, *The Old Testament Text of Justin Martyr, 1. The Pentateuch* (Leiden: Brill, 1963):149, makes clear the possibility of cross-fertilization in the discussion between Greek and Jew in the following remark: "But in Justin's citations from the Pentateuch there is much material which is both ancient and valuable. A good part of it, including those variants which may be called archaic, belongs to a stage of the LXX's history which mainly antedates the date in our codices. This material enables the student to view, for example, the possibility that not only Hebrew texts influenced the Greek traditions already before Origen, but that influences may also have worked the other way about."

109 See Simon, *Verus Israel*, 69, where he makes a similar comment. Also see Hanfmann, *Sardis*, on the Jews in Sardis. Also J. Neusner has written a multivolumed work entitled *A History of the Jews in Babylonia*, 5 vols. (Leiden: Brill, 1966-1970) which presents a view of the Jews in the East. Even though Neusner himself looks with a critical eye on his own work, feeling that it was an effort of his younger, less experienced years, this study still provides valuable information about Jews in Babylonia. Neusner's other works on rabbinic Judaism provide much more information about the vitality of at least one form of Judaism in the first three centuries C.E.

3. *No Mention of Paul in Justin's* Dialogue. One would think that a Christian teacher working in Ephesus only a few decades after Paul's visit would refer to the Apostle and his writings to Christians in that city.[110] But in the *Dialogue*, Justin does not refer to Paul or quote directly from any of his writings. Goodspeed's Greek text of the *Dialogue* refers to the letters of Paul in his footnotes,[111] but nowhere in the text of Justin's writing is a direct reference made to Paul, his epistles, his work in Ephesus, or his activities in any other "Pauline" city.

This seems strange in light of the extensive work Paul did in that city, according to Acts 18-19. The reason that there is no mention of Paul in Justin's *Dialogue*, where similar issues to Romans 9-11 are dealt with, is probably due to several factors.[112] A review of other second-century Christian literature, such as Polycarp (*Philadelphia* 3), Irenaeus (*Against Heresies* 3.15), Marcion[113] (according to Tertullian's *Against Marcion*), Ignatius (*Ephesians*[114]), and a late New Testament letter that some consider a second-century writing (2 Peter 3.15),[115] all mention Paul and his importance to their work.

Even though this is the case, there is some indication that Paul might not have played a major role in the Church after his initial missionary work until sometime later.[116] Origen (c. 240 C.E.) wrote the first major commentary on

---

110 The textual variants in the critical apparatus of the Nestle-Aland, *Novum Testamentum Graece*, 26, 1979 edition *pros ephesious* 1:1 does not include *en epheso* in the better texts (see page 503).

111 There are forty two references to the epistles of Paul in the footnotes of Goodspeed's Greek Text (1914) and only three of them are references to the epistle to the Ephesians.

112 See E. Dassmann, *Der Stachel im Fleisch: Paul in der frühchristlichen Literature bis Irenäus* (Münster: Aschendorff, 1979), in which Dassmann presents an overview of scholarship on the use of Paul's epistles and on the character of Paul himself in Christian literature of the first two centuries. Peter Gorday has reviewed this book in *The Second Century* 5.4 (1985/1986) 243-244.

113 Marcion was, of course, Paul's most avid second-century "disciple."

114 See the comments about the use of Paul in Ignatius by W.R. Schoedel in *Ignatius of Antioch: A Commentary on the Letters of Ignatius of Antioch* (Philadelphia: Fortress Press, 1985): 9-10. Schoedel suggests that "certain usage by Ignatius of Paul can be established only for I Corinthians (see on *Eph.* 16.1; 18.1; *Rom.* 5.1; 9.2; *Phd.* 3.3). But Ignatius knew that Paul was the author of more than one letter (cf. *Eph.* 12.2), and it is possible that we should be more generous" (9).

115 This view is supported by M. Green in his *The Second Epistle General of Peter and the General Epistle of Jude.* (London: Tyndale, 1968): 145-146.

116 See T.A. Robinson, *Bauer Thesis*, 97-98, and notes 17 and 18 where it is suggested that Paul's influence diminished in the second century. Also see Brown and Meier, *Antioch and Rome: New Testament Cradles of Catholic Christianity*, (New York: Paulist Press, 1983): vii-viii. See M.M. de Boer, "Images of Paul in the Post-Apostolic Period," *CBQ* 42 (1980): 359-380 for a study of Paul's influence on the late New Testament Pauline writings.

Paul's letter to the Romans. Marcion's negative influence on the early Church, and his adoption of Paul's letter as central to his Christian scriptures, may have unsettled a large number of Church writers.

It is possible that Paul was not important to Justin's arguments and therefore Justin had no reason to quote him or refer to his work among the Ephesians. If there is any historical value to the record of Paul's visit to Ephesus in Acts (19), then it is possible that Justin did not want to bring up distasteful memories as well.

The footnotes in Goodspeed's text of Justin's *Dialogue*[117] refer constantly to the Pentateuch and Prophets and very infrequently to the New Testament. It appears that Justin was not trying to prove his point from the earliest Christian writings but from those texts which were accepted by both Jew and Christian in the Diaspora.

It is generally accepted that various traditions were emerging during the second century and Justin represented one of those "trajectories."[118] Thus Paul might be part of another tradition within the Church, and not useful to Justin's understanding of the tradition in the middle of the second century. Even though there are certain similarities between Justin and Paul's view of the Law, still Justin represented an independent and later direction within the Church.

4. *Persecution of the Christians by the Jews*. Did Jews persecute Christians in Ephesus during Justin's time there?[119] A few sections in the *Dialogue* of

---

117 Goodspeed, *Justin Martyr*.

118 See W. Bauer's comment on this issue in *Orthodoxy*, 212. For a discussion of "trajectories" in early Christianity. see the provocative book by J.M. Robinson and H. Koester, *Trajectories*, 100-101.

119 W.H.C. Frend, in his book *Martyrdom*, 189-191, describes the persecution of Christians by Jews. Some sections of this book are quoted here to summarize Frend's point of view. "On this scene as well (Frend refers to the Roman Jews in this quote. He then goes on to generalize from the experience of Christians in one city to the whole Roman Empire), the Dispersion Jews showed themselves to better advantage. They were intensely keen to propagate their religion, hawking proselytism and groceries from door to door (Juvenal, *Satires* (ed. Owen) vi. 543-545),) and influencing those around them long after they ceased to be politically dangerous . . . In these proselytes, the Jews had their firmest allies in the struggle against the Church. . . they after all, had everything to lose by the latter's victory, and Justin records that those whom he came across preserved a double portion of hatred for Christians. (*Dial.* 122.2)." (See Frend, "Old Testament," 141 and "Martyrdom," 192. Compare another view in Baron, *Social* 2, 394, n.49.

Frend continues with this conclusion: "These deadly rivalries resulted in constant strife between Jew and Christian. In the province of Asia, persecution of the Christians by the Jews seems at times to have been severe, and it was supported by fierce polemic against the person and work of Jesus Christ . . . while the debate with 'false Jews' (Ignatius, *Phil*. 6), was continuous, the threat of imprisonment and death at their hands was never far absent." (Frend, *Martyrdom*, 189, 192).

The evidence Frend uses for this "deadly rivalries resulted in constant strife between Jew and Christian" and "the persecution of the Christians by the Jews" is found in Justin's *Dial.* 16.4; 47.4; 95.4; 135.6, and Revelation 2:9-10.

(continued...)

Justin, as well as some passages of the New Testament, indicate that persecution of Christians by Jews in Asia Minor was severe.[120]

But is there enough evidence to support the notion that, as some would suggest, the Jews were generally violent against the Christians?[121] Salo Baron in a footnote suggests a contrary view.[122]

119(...continued)
Another comment from Frend which points to inter-Jewish conflict: "Such people (Hellenistic Jews) were anathema to the extremists who had risen in Palestine and the school behind them, and Trypho was a refugee in Ephesus," (*Dial.* 1.3), Frend "Old Testament," 141.

It is likely that some rabbis, Akiba included, believed that Bar-Kokhba was the Messiah, but Akiba could not be described as an "extremist". This insight is important because it suggests that the struggles going on within the Jewish and Christian communities were not only against each other (if indeed they were) but were also internecine conflicts as well.

120 See persecution of Christians by Jews in Acts 4.23-31; 5.17-42; 8.1b-3 and John 8.41-47, 51. J. Gager, *Origins*, 152 suggests that John 8 indicates tensions between the synagogue and the neighboring church. Possible references to the persecution of Christians by Jews may be seen in *Dialogue* 96.2; 108.3; 16.4; 17. For a discussion of the legal roots of the persecution of Christians by Romans see T.D. Barnes, "Legislation Against the Christians" and "Pre-Decian *Acta Martyrum*," both in *Early Christianity and the Roman Empire* (London: Variorum, 1984): II and I. In the first article Barnes concludes: "It is in the minds of men (*sic*), not the demands of Roman law, that the roots of the persecution of the Christians in the Roman Empire are to be sought" (50). This statement agrees with the premise of this book.

121 See the well-known passage describing Polycarp's persecution in Eus., *HE* 4.15.29 and 4.15.41 where Jews are portrayed as almost universally enthusiastic about persecuting Christians. Obviously this Christian source would not give a pro-Jewish report of the event if even one Jewish person happened to be involved.

122 See S. Baron, *Social* 2, 394, n.49. There is a more recent statement by D.R.A. Hare, "The Relationship Between Jewish and Gentile Persecutions of Christians," *JES* 4 (1967): 446-456, that states the problem and suggests a solution. "The following authors have argued that Jews instigated Nero's persecution of Christians [in Rome]: A. Harnack (1904); F. Huidekoper (1906) in *Judaism at Rome: BC 76 to A.D. 140* (1877); H.B. Workman (1906); C.H. Canfield (1913); E.T. Merrill (1924); M. Simon, *Versus Israel*, (1948, 1963.2, trans. 1986); W.H.C. Frend (1965); P. Allard (1903) (although Allard seems to be on both sides of this issue)."

After reviewing this literature, Hare states his position: "One manifestation of Christian anti-semitism to which scholars are becoming more sensitive is seen in uncritical statements concerning the persecution of the early church by the synagogue. After reviewing the evidence the present writer is convinced that this persecution was by no means as severe as frequently alleged by a number of Christian authors. It need not be doubted that intense hostility was aroused in Jewish communities by Jewish Christian evangelists, but the paucity of martyrdoms attributable to Jewish agency witnesses to the restraint with which 'the Christian problem' was dealt with by the synagogue." On this same point see D. Rokeah, *Jews, Pagans and Christians in Conflict*, (Jerusalem-Leiden: The Magnes Press, The Hebrew University and E.J. Brill, 1982): 63, 66, 69.

To make this point even clearer, Hare quotes A. Harnack's strong words: "Unless the evidence is misleading, they (the Jews) instigated the Neronic outburst against the Christians; and as a rule whenever bloody persecutions are afoot in later days, the Jews are either in the background or the foreground."

Hare points out that Harnack uses (uncritically) Justin's *Dialogue* (16) for his support and makes the following conclusion: "It seems probable that from the time of Justin, if not from the time of Acts, the proposition that Jewish hostility was primarily responsible for the church's
(continued...)

The large Jewish share in anti-Christian persecutions before Constantine, under Julian, and later on, a recurrent literary theme in patristic letters, is often accepted by modern scholars. Apart from many contradictions and intrinsic improbabilities appearing in this record of accusations, it is utterly unsupported by any reliable neutral source. The often-invoked testimony of Tacitus, for example, concerning the alleged Jewish role in the earliest Christian sufferings under Nero, is extremely dubious. . . . The part played by Jews in anti-Christian persecutions is plausibly reduced to minor proportions.

In spite of these warnings, many Christian scholars continue to be guided by their theological conventions and political agenda which are used to dictate how they reconstruct the past. Jewish persecution of Christians was an early theological convention which has been accepted and never challenged. The idea that Jews directly persecuted Christians throughout the second century and beyond has become part of conventional wisdom.[123]

But the evidence does not support such notions.[124] The archaeological data and inscriptions from Ephesus do not suggest that Jews were actively persecuting the Christians. Only writings which have a particular anti-Jewish bias are available as evidence for Jewish persecution of Christians.[125] A different view of the Jews in Ephesus and their relation to Christians emerges when one examines the archaeological evidence.[126]

Furthermore, the notion that Jews in Ephesus persecuted Christians assumes that Jews were anxious to see that Christians were silenced. The famous story about the persecution of Polycarp[127] suggests that Jews were enthusiastic in their participation with pagans to do away with Christians. But

---

122(...continued)
sufferings was a *theological convention* requiring little or no evidence in its support. The continuing influence of the theological attitude is reflected in Harnack's uncritical acceptance of the traditional charge against the Jews."
    These rather long citations from Hare's article (446-456) are included here because the case is clearly stated in these arguments.

123 See Frend, *Rise*, 98, 109, 147, 183, and 254. For another more balanced view see Smallwood, *Jews* 507-507 and 543 and notes; Simon, *Verus Israel*, 120-125 and Gager *Origins*, 253. See also D. Rokeah's thesis that Jews were neutral toward Christians and were not actively persecuting them, especially after the Bar-Kokhba persecution in Palestine of Christians who would not join the war against the Romans (Rokeah, *Jews*, 63 and 67).

124 See Foss, *Ephesus*, 36. Roman persecution of Christians did not begin in Ephesus until the third century.

125 Ibid., 33, n. 10 and 11. Also see Eus., *HE* 3.33.5-6.

126 Ibid., 45, ns. 43-49.

127 See Eusebius *HE* 4.15.29 where the Jews are described as anxious to be done with Christians and ready to assist the pagans who were burning Polycarp "as was their custom." This is a fanciful description of the Jews, created to parallel the Passion narrative of the death of Jesus. See *HE* 4.15.49 for a similar description.

the story is told for reasons other than to hold Jews responsible for the persecution of Christians. Fox suggests that "the ideal of martyrdom"[128] stimulated Christians for centuries in the development of a "theology of those who die for the faith."

From the Sardis evidence, it is clear that Jews were a secure and dominant group in that part of Asia Minor,[129] and probably in most of the cities in that area, and had no reason to be threatened by or to threaten Christians.

These are some of the major issues which help to illuminate the meaning of Justin's *Dialogue* with Trypho in Ephesus.

C. Rome

Rome, like Ephesus, was a cosmopolitan center with a pluralistic culture and Hellenistic society, influenced by the Greek Philosophical schools.[130] But Rome, unlike Ephesus, was the center of the Empire in the mid-second century and therefore all roads led to Rome. There are some unique contributions Rome makes to the study of Justin's *Dialogue*.

B. Layton, in his recent study of Gnostic scripture,[131] reminds his readers that "the Roman Christian community at mid-second century was noteworthy for the great variety of its theologians and for their acrimonious debates with one another." It is likely that Justin was part of this crosscurrent of debate and discussion. Justin's "school" in Rome was active during the first half of the second century (110-160 C.E.).[132]

---

128 Fox, *Pagans*, 420.

129 The evidence for Jews in Ephesus is of two kinds, inscriptions and Josephus. See Smallwood, *Jews*, 191 and 226 for one example of a reference to Josephus, and page 508 n.7 for the evidence from inscriptions. Both of these sources indicate that the Jews in Ephesus enjoyed protection under Roman law and the respect of fellow citizens in the community. See also the very interesting autobiographical comment in Kraabel, "Greeks," 150. Kraabel outlines his own change in his view about the "God-fearers" when confronted with the evidence, or lack of it. See also V. Tcherikover, *Hellenistic Civilization*, 287-288; Robinson, *Bauer Thesis*, 112-113 and Juster, *Les Juifs* 1:188-190.

130 For a study of Rome and Ephesus see Robinson, *Bauer Thesis*, 77-83 (Rome) and 93-121 (Ephesus). Against Bauer and Brown in *Antioch and Rome*, 105-127, Robinson argues that "I have offered this sketch of the Christianity in Rome primarily to show that our information is simply too incomplete or mute to allow us to reconstruct the character of the earliest form of Christianity in Rome" (81).

131 B. Layton, *Gnostic Scriptures*, 221.

132 For a general description of the Roman cities, including Rome itself, see the recently translated (1983) *Roman Cities* by Pierre Grimal. See especially pages 31-40 for a description of the emergence of Rome into a magnificent city known by 113 C.E. as the "Queen of the Cities." The bibliography in *Roman Cities*, which was originally titled *Les villes romaine* (1954), has been revised by G. Michael Woloch and has entries up to 1980. See Remus, "Justin," 73, n. 57, where a bibliography is provided for the importance of the city of Rome as the center of the Empire. For information about the Jews and Christians in Rome during the first part
(continued...)

Prior to 135 C.E., Roman citizens were experiencing unrest within and outside the Roman Empire. After the Second Revolt, or the Bar-Kokhba War, the evidence suggests that a calm came over the Empire which lasted for a century.[133]

During the early part of the second century there were two major disruptions between Jews and Romans, one in North Africa (115 C.E.) and the other in Palestine (132 C.E.).[134]

The revolt in 132 in Palestine may have been indirectly caused by Rome's extension of her boundaries to the east with a war against the Parthians (114-117 C.E.).[135] These campaigns did not disturb Christians and Jews living in other parts of the Diaspora, but did make them uncertain about their status.[136] In the midst of storm and stress, the Christians maintained a certain respect among the Romans. An observation of the third-century writer Cassius

---

132(...continued)
of the second century see: E.R. Goodenough, *Jewish Symbols* 2; H.J. Leon, *The Jews of Ancient Rome*, (Philadelphia: Jewish Publication Society, 1960); V. Tcherikover, *Hellenistic Civilization*; W.H.C. Frend, *Rise*, 164-184; and M. Simon *Verus Israel*, especially his analysis in chapter 4, 98-132. Each of these works deals primarily with the legal or social view of Jews and Christians within the Empire.

For a brief overview of the history and the culture of Rome see M.M. Eisman, "A Tale of Three Cities," *BA* 41.2 (June, 1978): 56-60. Eisman suggests that the situation in the city of Rome was closely tied to the condition of the Roman Empire.

For a review of works done on epigraphic records and other studies of the Roman Empire and the city of Rome in late antiquity, see J. Reynolds, Mary Beard, and Charlotte Rouché, "Roman Inscriptions," 124-146. Still a valuable resource is M. Rostovtzeff, *The Social and Economic History of the Roman Empire*, 2 vols., 2d ed., revised by P.M. Fraser. (Oxford: Clarendon Press, 1957). W.A. Meeks's *Urban* has a useful bibliography and specific references to the city of Rome (see 29 n. 276 and 207 n. 162). For archaeological evidence of Church life before Constantine, see G.F. Snyder, *Ante Pacem*.

For an overview of the Jews in the Roman Empire from Pompey to Diocletian, see Smallwood, *Jews*.

133 See Simon, *Verus Israel*, 102 and notes.

134 See Dio Cassius, *Dio's Roman History*, trans. E. Cary, LCL, (Cambridge, MA: Harvard, 1925), LXVIII and LXIX. Also there are extensive footnotes and explanations in Stern, *Authors* 2, 439, 440. See also M. Smallwood's treatment of these conflicts in *Jews*, 389-427 and 428-466.

135 For a discussion of Arrian's lost but fragmentary *Parthia*, a description of the Roman war with Parthia and their relationship with the Jewish population in the East at the time of Trajan, see M. Stern, *Authors* 2:150-156.

136 W. Bauer, *Orthodoxy*, 129, makes this comment about the unity of the Church in Rome around the last half of the second century: "Essentially unanimous in the faith and in the standards of Christian living, tightly organized and methodically governed by the monarchical bishop, the Roman church toward the close of the second century feels inclined and able to extend further the boundaries of her influence." See W.H.C. Frend, *Rise,* 40ff, for a similar view. It is possible that Christians during the middle of the second century discovered enough support from the Romans to work more boldly to expand their influence. M. Smallwood's *Jews* is a well-documented study of the political relations between Jews and Romans from Pompey to Diocletian.

Dio (c.160-230 C.E.), that Christians were shown great respect and honor "in which Hadrian had been wont to hold them,"[137] supports this notion.

The fact that Rome was the "Queen of the cities" and the most important city for the Empire means that Rome itself is a very important "text" to be read for an understanding of Justin's *Dialogue*.

1. *Christians Compromise with the Romans*. It is generally agreed that Justin was an apologist on behalf of Christianity to the Roman authorities and Roman public opinion.[138] It was for the survival and mission of the Church that it had a good relationship with the ruling powers. Therefore the *Dialogue* reflects support for the Roman authorities.

Persecution of Christians on a broad scale did not take place during the middle of the second century.[139] Polycarp and other heroic stories about the martyrs are isolated and were not the rule.[140] It is possible that the New Testament letters by Paul and Peter (Romans 13.1-7 and I Peter 2.13-17, respectively) reflect an early[141] Christian attempt at living with a potentially hostile Roman government. Paul's epistle to the Romans (13), the letter of First Peter (2) and Luke-Acts are all favorable comments about Rome and Roman authorities. Christians were told in these New Testament writings to support the good intentions of the Emperor.

Another New Testament writing, Revelation 13, written during a later period (c. 96 C.E.), reflects a different relationship to the Roman authorities and was not as supportive of the Emperor. Yet, even though there is strong opposition to the Roman government, open rebellion on the part of Christians is discouraged because it was not necessary: God would judge those who disobey God's Law. The Church's reticence to accept Revelation into the Canon

---

137 *Dio's Roman*, 70:3.1-3.

138 For a summary of Justin's views as an apologist on behalf of Christianity to the Roman public see Simon, *Verus Israel*, 118.

139 See Fox, *Pagans*, 419-422.

140 This view is supported by Simon in *Verus Israel*, 118, and is generally supported by the primary sources. The Martyrdom of Polycarp is more a heroic story of one person than a pogrom against Christians. The persecution of Christians after the murder of Alexander Severus is a more organized campaign. For a study of the persecution and martyrdom of Christians in the second century, see R.L. Fox, *Pagans*, 419-492. Also see Koester, *Introduction* 2:334-337. For another view of the persecution of Jews and Christians, see Stern, *Authors*, 2:113-114.

141 For a discussion of the date of I Peter, see F.W. Beare, *The First Epistle of Peter*, (Oxford, 1970), 28-37, 212-229. Also, see J.M. Ford, *Revelation*, for a well-documented discussion of Revelation and its place and date. See C.E.B. Cranfield, *The Epistle to the Romans, ICC*, 2 vols. (Edinburgh: T & T Clark, 1979). For a discussion of the early Christian attitude toward Rome, see *IDB*, s.v. "Rome" and *IDBS* s.v. "Rome," see Fox *Pagans*, 434-450. For a discussion of Luke-Acts and its view of Rome, see P.F. Esler, *Community and Gospel in Luke-Acts: The Social and Political Motivations of Lucan Theology*. SNTS Monograph Series 57. (Cambridge: Cambridge University Press, 1987), 201-219.

may reflect the need for the Church in the later second and early third centuries to remain on friendly terms with Rome. It is possible that Revelation's harsh anti-Roman bias was an embarrassment to the early Church.

One of the major concerns of some later writers in the New Testament was to establish good will between the emerging Christian community and the Roman Empire. It is important to Luke-Acts, for example, that the Romans not be held totally responsible for the death of Jesus. As mentioned above, Paul and Peter had their own reasons for maintaining peace with the Roman authorities. Persecution of the Christians during this period was sometimes overstated, for perhaps theological or even propagandistic reasons. Even though Revelation was written as a polemical tract against the Romans, the overriding emphasis in the Church and the New Testament in general was accommodation, rather than confrontation.[142] The *Dialogue* supports the notion of peace with the Roman authorities.

2. *Justin was Martyred in Rome c. 165 C.E.* The exact date of Justin's death is unknown, but most scholars accept the year 165 C.E. In any case, according to some sources, shortly before his death he became involved in a bitter debate with a Cynic philosopher named Crescens (2 *Apol.* 3.1), and this ultimately may have contributed to his arrest and arraignment at Rome.[143]

It is not clear why Justin was put to death. It is well known that Christians were viewed as atheists and strangely private or secretive about their religious exercises; they did not share in the public services to the Roman gods, which was viewed as antisocial behavior. The refusal to honor the Roman gods made Christians and Jews appear to be disloyal and even subversive.[144]

The *Acta* give a reason for Justin's trial and judgment. Rusticus's judgment reads like a formal declaration that has been staged: "Those who have refused to sacrifice to the gods are to be scourged and executed in accordance with the laws."[145] If Justin was a martyr, and died a horrible death, then it is

---

142 L.W. Barnard, in comparing the relation of Jews and Christians to the Roman Empire under Hadrian, reminds us that "the evidence has shown that Hadrian was not as hostile to the Christians as he became toward the Jews in his later years because Christianity was not as fanatical and was not intent on opposing the Emperor's ideas of unity within the Roman World." See L.W. Barnard's section on "Hadrian and Christianity" in *Studies in the Apostolic Fathers*, 149-150.

143 The founder of the Bollandists, Jean Bolland, (1596-1665) suggested that our *Acta* depict the death of another Justin, and that Justin Martyr had perhaps been murdered by Crescens himself (cf. Eus., *HE*. 4.16.7-8). It is a theory, however, that has not found acceptance among many scholars. See H.A. Musurillo, *The Acts of the Christian Martyrs*, (Oxford: Clarendon Press, 1972), xviii. Justin's death, along with the martyrdom of other early Christians, is fanciful and given to heroic story-telling. On this see Fox, *Pagans*, 419- 440.

144 See the many references to this in Stern, *Authors*, 3 vols., especially *Authors* 1:97; 2:88f., 108 and 113-115.

145 Musurillo, *Christian Martyrs*, 47, v.

possible to argue that he had offended civil religion and religious practices and was considered antisocial.

Justin's death, though, like Polycarp's martyrdom a year (?) later, can also be viewed as a particular event and does not need to be an indication of a much broader persecution of Christians in Rome.

For some reason Justin offended those in power, and was considered by some Romans as one who deserved death for his behavior. The critical tone of the *Dialogue* in Justin's argument with Trypho suggests the possibility that he could have offended Crescens, who in rage simply killed him. This view would agree with the seventeenth-century Bollandists who thought that Justin had been murdered by Crescens.

However one may settle this dispute, the *Acta* survived as evidence that some Christian leaders were persecuted and perhaps martyred by the Roman authorities. It is not possible, though, from these writings, to reconstruct what actually happened.

3. *The Jews in Rome*. The Jewish community[146] was well established in the

---

146 See H.J. Leon, *Jews*, 1-55, 75-91, 135-191, 229-259. The center of the Roman Empire, and the city in which representatives from all over the world lived, was Rome. Most of the sources report a long history for the Jews in Rome. See, for example, *EJ*, s.v. "Rome." Also see Leon, *Jews*, 229-260. In spite of the tension caused by the Jews in Judea, there was relative peace for the Jews in Rome.

Scholars have suggested that passages from Cassius Dio's History "constitute the main and most consistent survey of the Jewish revolt under Hadrian existing in ancient literature" and therefore are important to mention at this point in the argument. (see Stern, *Authors* 2:393.) "At Jerusalem he [Hadrian] founded a city in place of the one which had been razed to the ground, naming it *Aelia Capitolina*, and on the site of the temple of the god he raised a new temple to Jupiter. This brought on a war of no slight importance nor brief duration, for the Jews deemed it intolerable that foreign races should be settled in their city and foreign religious rites planted there. So long, indeed, as Hadrian was close by in Egypt, and in Syria, they remained quiet, some in so far as they purposely made of poor quality such weapons as they were called upon to furnish, in order that the Romans might reject them and they themselves might thus have the use of them; but when he went further away, they openly revolted. To be sure they did not dare try conclusions with the Romans in the open field, but they occupied the advantageous positions in the country. At first the Romans took no account of them." Dio continues with the story, reporting that a general from Britain was brought to Palestine (Severus) and how he completely devastated the Jews. "Very few of them in fact survived." The whole of Judea was desolate. This was the end of the war with the Jews. (Stern, *Authors* 2 para. 440).

Two issues emerge in this "Roman" view of the Jews and Judaism which are important for an understanding of the Jews in Rome during the Bar-Kokhba war: 1) Dio had knowledge of the importance of the Temple mount to the Jews. It was, as is generally known by most people today, a symbol of religious national identity. (See the Dead Sea Scrolls and the Mishnah for other examples for the Temple as a national and religious symbol.) 2) The Jews in Judea and Alexandria were restless with foreign rule, and did not maintain a comfortable relationship with their Roman overlords. But it is interesting to note that this did not always affect the relation of the Jews with people in other parts of the Empire.

Most of the evidence about Jews in the cities of the Empire suggests that they held a prominent place in pagan society. See Hanfmann, *Sardis*, and Fox, *Pagans*, 482.

Imperial city.¹⁴⁷ The main source for our knowledge of Judaism in Rome is the catacombs. Until late in the third century, most of the inscriptions on the tombs were in Greek or Greek letters used for Hebrew words, which indicates that Jews in Rome, like the rest of the Western Diaspora, used Greek as the language for everyday conversation as well as for religious ceremonies and rituals.¹⁴⁸

It is possible that Justin's fellow Christians in Rome may not have associated Jews in that city with any particular religious labels. Some Jews may have been more or less "assimilated" into the life of the city.¹⁴⁹ Jews certainly had a religious identity (viewed as a superstition) which was given them by their host city, but it was very difficult then, as it is today, to put all Jews into one category.¹⁵⁰

Therefore it is difficult to suggest that Justin in the *Dialogue* directed his arguments against Jews in Rome (or Ephesus). It is more likely that there were specific issues between Justin and a particular form of "Judaism" which he encountered or invented for the sake of his arguments.¹⁵¹

Some of Justin's arguments may have been heard, if they were heard at all, with indifference or disdain by Jews in general or by those Jews who bothered to listen to Christian rhetoric. A newly discovered synagogue in

---

147 See Leon, *Jews*, vii. See also A.T. Kraabel, "Jews in Imperial Rome: More Archaeological Evidence from an Oxford Collection," *JJS* 30 (1979): 41-58, where it is argued that two pieces from the Wilshere Collection at Oxford, along with all of the other data collected to date, adds to the already considerable evidence of Jews in the catacombs in Imperial Rome. For a lengthy discussion of this topic, see E.R. Goodenough, *Jewish Symbols*, 13 vols. See his concluding statements in *Jewish Symbols* 12:185ff., and 2:30ff., where he reminds his readers that the evidence for Judaism in the catacombs of Rome is "more reliable evidence for Jewish thought in Rome and Dura than are the Mishnah and early Midrashim of the rabbis in Palestine." This insight suggests a direction for the study of early Judaism in Rome and other cities of late antiquity, for that matter. The evidence for Jewish thought and even Jews' way of life can be read on the ancient stones under the city. The evidence reports that they lived there in great numbers, spoke Greek, and accepted many local images through which they expressed their religious beliefs.

For the literary evidence of Jews in Rome, see the 3 volumes of Stern, *Authors* especially 2: 109, 113-117 (Suetonius) and 365, 367, 378f. (Cassius Dio).

148 On the language of the Jews in Rome during this period, see Leon, *Jews*, 75-92. E.R. Goodenough, *Jewish Symbols*, 12:4ff., has a brief discussion about the use of Greek by Jews in Rome.

149 See Leon, *Jews*, 92. "The Jews formed no linguistic Island in Rome." See Kraabel "Jews," 41-58.

150 See the discussion in Stern, *Authors* 2:113-117, of Jews and Christians in Rome. Both were considered superstitious.

151 For a study of Paul's concern with a particular kind of Judaism, see F. Watson, *Paul*; Meeks, *Urban*, and the many other recent writings on Paul. See the Bibliographies in each of these works.

southern Italy[152] confirms once again that Jews were apparently present at important crossroads in the Empire and do not appear to have been intimidated by the early Church.

Most Jews in Rome and the surrounding regions in the mid-second century may have been almost totally unaffected by the Christian mission. It is possible that by that time the Christian community had more completely broken its Jewish connections and was no longer busy with a mission within the synagogues of Rome.[153] This would mean that the Church was becoming more and more Gentile and probably less tolerant or knowledgeable of its Jewish roots. Marcion, in the same century, was hard at work removing any Jewish connections.[154]

IV. The *Dialogue*

When one views the cities as a "text" to be "read" as the context for Justin's *Dialogue*, certain observations can be made about its purpose and meaning.

Clearly the *Dialogue* is an apologetic essay written to Christians to help them appreciate their own tradition in the context of multireligious, multiethnic and cosmopolitan cities.[155] The three cities, Neapolis, Ephesus, and

---

152 Recently a synagogue has been found in Bova Marina, Italy, by Dr. Elena Lattanzi, superintendent for archeology for the Calabria region. Dr. Lattanzi made a formal presentation of the excavation at the end of March, 1986, in Rome. (See Roberto Suro, "Italian Synagogue May Be Oldest in Europe," *The New York Times*, Tuesday, March 4, 1986, C3.) Clearly, Jews were living in a variety of settings throughout the Roman Empire, with places of worship, apparently undisturbed. What were they doing there? Were they a part of the commercial life of the Empire? The *NYT* article says that "Communities of Jewish merchants developed in Italy as early as the second century B.C." "Rabbi Toaff (chief rabbi of the Roman Synagogue) speculated that the newly discovered Jewish settlement was founded as an agricultural or commercial community and then perhaps prospered by providing a resting point for Jews on their way north." This writer has written to the *NYT*, as well as the scholars involved in this project, for more scholarly information on this dig, but to date no response has been forthcoming.

153 See Acts 28.

154 See S.G. Wilson, "Marcion and the Jews", in *Anti-Judaism* 2:45-58.

155 G.N. Stanton has given an excellent commentary on the *Dialogue* and agrees that it is an early Christian apologetic. See Stanton, "Aspects," 385, where a summary of his position is outlined. "Attention has already been drawn to important parallels between the Testament of Levi and Dialogue 108. I now want to suggest that this chapter of the Dialogue contains a further example of the S-E-R pattern. Justin roundly condemns the leaders of the Jews for their anti-Christian actions (Sin) and asserts that the capture of Jerusalem and the ravaging of the land are a punishment from God (Exile). But finally, quite unexpectedly, Justin expresses the hope that his Jewish opponents will repent and find mercy from a compassionate God (Return)." At the end of this essay Stanton concludes: "If the suggestions are plausible, there are implications for the origin and purpose of these early Christian writings. We need not conclude that Justin is so polemical that he cannot be engaged in genuine dialogue, nor need we conclude that his expressions of hope for the conversion of Trypho are simply an artificial devise dictated

(continued...)

Rome influenced the way Justin spoke to the issues and carried on his conversations with a "Jew" in the *Dialogue*.

Yet the precise audience is still difficult to establish. What kind of Jew was he referring to? Was he concerned about Jews and Judaism in general or a particular kind of Judaism? A careful reading of the *Dialogue* reveals that Justin spoke to an eclectic form of Judaism and was simply opening the doors for further discourse with "Jews" and "Judaism."

So the *Dialogue* is to be seen as a "friendly exchange" between two persons discussing the meaning of the tradition of Israel in the light of the Christian claims as Justin understood them.[156] The audience was any interested seeker[157].

It is as if each disputant in the *Dialogue* wanted the other to fare well so that arguments could be clarified through a process of dialogue similar to the "Socratic" methods of an earlier day.[158]

Was the *Dialogue* meant to be an *adversus Judaeos* writing and not a "friendly" conversation between friends? Several approaches to this problem have been suggested.

One group of scholars considers the *Dialogue* directed to a Jewish audience, with various reasons given for its purpose. H.P. Schneider says that one

---

155(...continued)
by the dialogue form. The S-E-R pattern of ch. 108 is an important form of early Christian apologetic vis à vis Judaism. Justin is engaged in a genuine dispute and NT scholars will do well to read him carefully." (389).

There are several scholars who insist that the *Dialogue* is apologetic: Enslin, "Appreciation;" H. van Campenhausen, *The Fathers of the Greek Church*, (London, 1963); Chadwick, "Justin Martyr's"; Higgins, "Messianic Beliefs," 298-305; Osborn, "Response," 37-54; Horbury, "Benediction," 19-61, and Cosgrove, "Justin Martyr." Of these writers C.H. Cosgrove provides the most lucid summary of this position:

"Stylianopoulos, however, on the basis of his research into Justin's view of the Mosaic Law, understands the *Dialogue* to contain a set of arguments previously used against Christian heretics such as Marcion, now employed against Jews. Nevertheless, in the light of the previous audience analysis, these arguments are best construed as leveled against Jews and Marcionites within the context of the intra-church monologue not a Jewish Christian dialogue. Justin addresses "orthodox" Christians with polemics against two groups of "outsiders", Jews and Marcionites. For the claims of both are of critical moment within the Roman Church itself" (220).

This argument is similar to Horbury's views in "Benediction," 61, where he suggested that the "Benediction" was not so much asking Jews to curse the "outsiders" as much as it was an attempt to offer encouragement and support for their own community. Horbury writes: "As has appeared from *Dial*. xlvii, Gentiles, including some who had joined the church, more inclined to regard Judaism and Christianity as alternative versions of the same biblical faith over against paganism," (52). The *Dialogue* is Justin's attempt to correct misunderstandings about Christianity to Roman officials and the general public, and in this sense is an apologetic.

156 *Dial*. 142.

157 A "seeker" like Justin. See his opening chapters in the *Dialogue* 1-9.

158 As Stanton points out at the conclusion of his essay on Justin ("Aspects," 389), the two disputants left each other with a hope that the other would fare well. In fact Justin promised to pray for Trypho and his friends. The parting was cordial (142).

must take a middle position between E.R. Goodenough's view that it is apologetic and others' view that it is anti-Judaic. He suggests that Justin took his arguments to the extreme and did not mean to be as anti-Judaic as he was.[159]

Bokser, on the other hand, thinks of the *Dialogue* as a "defensive writing" and, even though Justin was not an extremist as an anti-Jewish writer, "he stood midway between the New Testament and the rapid anti-Jewishness which eventually became part of Christian Culture."[160] The obvious question here is did Justin help the "rapid anti-Jewishness" to emerge? Or was he used by someone else to fan the hostile feelings already present in some Christian communities?

W.H.C. Frend includes the anti-Judaism polemic among Justin's anti-gnostic and anti-Marcion stance.[161] In other words, Frend thinks that Justin had a concern for the truth of the gospel and this truth had to be defended against all other false faiths. Judaism was not necessarily false, but because it rejected Jesus as the Messiah, Christianity superseded it.[162]

Hulen views the *Dialogue* as anti-Jewish, but he carefully explains what he means by that. There are three stages in the arguments against the Jews in the early church: (1) *expository*, addressed in large measure to the seed of Abraham, aiming at their conversion, and designed to prove to them the truth of Christianity out of the Old Testament---finished examples of this type being Cyprian's "Three Books of Testimonies" and Eusebius's "Demonstrations of the Gospel"; (2) *argumentative*, dealt largely with Jewish objections to the new religion represented by Justin Martyr's "Dialogue with Trypho the Jew"; and (3) *denunciatory*, based on the assumption that the Jews were a people abandoned by God whose conversion was hopeless, works like Chrysostom's "Eight Orations Against the Jews."[163]

From these three stages, with Justin somewhere in the middle, Hulen has helped one to appreciate a direction which the church appeared to take as it became a significant force in the Western world. Anti-Jewish views emerged as the church grew and no longer had to defend or define itself in the Roman Empire.

The so-called *adversus Judaeos* writings, as they emerged in the form that Justin wrote, or in the more virulent forms of Tertullian, Melito, and Barnabas, contributed to this rising anti-Judaism in the Church.

T. Stylianopoulos expresses the view that is directly counter to Cosgrove:

---

159 See H.P. Schneider, "Some Reflections on the Dialogue of Justin Martyr with Trypho," *SJT* 15 (1962): 164-175.

160 Bokser, "Justin Martyr," 204.

161 Frend, "Old Testament," 134.

162 Frend, *Rise*, 164.

163 Hulen, "Dialogue," 58.

However, the *Dialogue* as a document is primarily addressed to Jews in general, rather than to Jewish Christians in particular, not only because its setting is a dialogue between a Christian and a Jew, but also because of Justin's view of the Jewish eschatological remnant which as we shall now see, pertains to the Jews as a people rather than to sectarian Jewish Christians specifically. This is not to deny that Justin has something to say to all the groups or fronts mentioned above.[164]

Of the three objections to this thesis, Cosgrove's third seems most appropriate: "Justin's portrayal of Trypho and Jews in general makes it difficult to imagine that he writes the *Dialogue* as an evangelistic appeal to Jews. At points Trypho and his fellow Jews are cast in an extremely unfavorable light."[165]

It would be easy at this point to suggest a middle way to all of the arguments over the purpose of the *Dialogue* relative to the Jews but there is something more that has been said above and must be observed now.

The three cities provide a "text" for an answer to the question: To whom did Justin intend his *Dialogue*? Was it for the Christian community: an essay for both Gentile and Jewish Christians? Was it written for those who needed to learn the difference between Judaism (as Justin understood it) and Christianity? Was it intended to be anti-Jewish?

The answer is that it is not an *adversus Judaeos* or anti-Jewish essay as much as it is written to anyone, pagans or Jews who were favorably disposed to both Christianity and Judaism. The *Dialogue* argues in favor of Christianity over one particular form of Judaism, which is partly constructed by Justin from his experience and from the Bible because that Judaism has been surpassed by Christianity in all ways.[166]

The *Dialogue* was written not only to help "potential Gentiles . . . see the difference between Judaism and Christianity" but to help them see the differ-

---

164 Stylianopoulos, *Justin Martyr*, 39 n.73.

165 Cosgrove, "Justin," 218.

166 Nilson, "Justin's *Dialogue*," 538 and 546, suggests the following: "The hypothesis which this essay seeks to support is this: Justin's *Dialogue with Trypho* is addressed primarily to a non-Christian Gentile audience at Rome which is very favorably disposed towards Judaism and Christianity, yet is unable to adequately distinguish the one from the other. The *Dialogue* seeks to assist these readers not only to grasp this distinction but, further, to understand that to become a Jew is to convert to a religion which was intended solely as a preparation for Christianity. Christianity is thus superior to Judaism and, in fact, has supplanted it.

"Consequently, the *Dialogue* reflects a situation in mid-second-century Rome in which Christians found their efforts at evangelization hampered by Jewish competition for the same group of potential Gentile converts and the understandable inability of this group to see the difference between Judaism and Christianity. Thus the *Dialogue* is written against the Jews, not to them or for them" (539).

ence between Christianity and the particular form of "Judaism" which Justin has encountered and read about in the Bible. The impact of this suggestion is that there might be forms of Judaism, not encountered by Justin, that would answer the questions he raised in the *Dialogue* in a different way, and not much different than the "religion of Jesus." What then?

In a footnote[167] Hulen quotes A.C. McGiffert, "Dialogue between a Christian and a Jew" (Marburg, 1889):

> In fact, if we wish to learn the actual attitude of the Jews toward Christianity, we must seek elsewhere than in the Christian works which have been directed against them ... of the real attitude of the Jews toward the Christians, of the nature of their polemics against Christianity, their works tell us nothing.

Trakatellis[168] suggests:

> What if the whole *Dialogue* is pure literary fiction? In that case, certainly an unlikely and extreme one, we would have Justin's *Dialogue* and his Trypho as the noble vision of a refined Christian thinker. It is important that a central person in this vision is a Jew, that the creator of the vision is a Christian, and that the setting of the vision is a dialogue.

It is precisely the importance of these characters in Justin's *Dialogue*, a Jew and a Christian, and not that the *Dialogue* is *adversus Judaeos*, that is the key to a proper understanding of his writing.[169]

---

167 Hulen, "Dialogue," 64 n.8. See also G.F. Moore, "Christian Writers on Judaism," *HTR* 14.3 (1921): 197-254, on this same topic.

168 Trakatellis, "Justin," 297.

169 See J.L. Marshall,"Some Observations on Justin Martyr's use of testimonies" in *Studia Patristica, Texte und Untersuchungen* 15-16.2. Papers presented to the Seventh International Conference on Patristic Studies held in Oxford, 1985 (Berlin: Akademie Verlag, 1985):197-200. In this short lecture Marshall argues that Justin wrote the *Dialogue* before the Apologies and learned that "any attempt to present Christianity in a philosophical dress must inevitably mean the abandonment of the greater part of the traditional package of Jewish-Christian ideas" (200).

CHAPTER THREE

MELITO: A POETIC DEFENCE
The *Paschal Homily* (c. 180 C.E.)

I. Introduction

Eusebius of Caesarea, (c. 263-340 C.E.), is the only extant early source, outside of Melito's own writings, available for Melito's life and work.[1] Melito, according to Eusebius, was the "Bishop of the parish of Sardis," and wrote some very important essays for the Church in that area during the late second century C.E.[2] One of his writings, a homily entitled *Peri Pascha*, "Concerning the Passover,"[3] influenced the work of another early Christian writer, Clement of Alexandria.[4] Beyond these few scraps of literary evidence very little is known about Melito.

A Greek text of the *Homily*, discovered fifty years ago, has made it possible to have more direct access to the thoughts of some Christians in Sardis.[5] Most of these studies are literary and theological.[6]

---

1 Eus., *HE*. 4.26.1-14. See Bauer, *Orthodoxy*, 152-155.

2 Eus., *HE*. 4.26.1-3.

3 "Pascha has no English equivalent. It is the Greek form of the Aramaic *pasha*. It can denote the Passover festival, the Passover meal, the Passover lamb, or the Christian feast (Holy Week and Easter) which continues and replaces Passover" (3). See S.G. Hall, ed. and trans., *Melito of Sardis ON PASCHA and Fragments* (Oxford: Clarendon Press, 1979). With so much ambiguity about the meaning of the one word, *pascha*, one can already understand the difficulty ahead for anyone who is trying to understand the meaning and purpose of the whole *Homily*. The translation in this book, "Concerning the Passover," is intended to give this author's understanding of the meaning of the *Homily* in light of the new evidence from Sardis. Melito was trying to speak concerning the Passover as he understood it from the Christian point of view, over against the Jewish point of view, so he spoke "concerning" the Passover.

4 See Eus., *HE*. 4.26.4 and 6.13.9.

5 C. Bonner, *The Homily on the Passion by Melito Bishop of Sardis and some Fragments of the apocrypha Ezekiel* (Studies and documents 12, London and Philadelphia, 1940); M. Testuz, *Papyrus Bodmer XIII, Meliton de Sardes, Homilie sur la Paque*, Geneve, 1960. An up-to-date and critical edition of the Homily is from Hall, *ON PASCHA*; see page xvii in that volume for a description of the discovery of the text.

6 See the literary interpretations of the *Homily* in such works as Bonner, *Homily*; O. Perler, *Meliton de Sardes, sur la Paque et Fragments* (Paris, 1966); and G.F. Hawthorne, "A New English Translation of Melito's Paschal Homily," in *Current Issues in Biblical and Patristic Interpretation* (Studies in Honor of Merrill C. Tenney) (Michigan, 1975): 147-175. Other scholars rely on these basic studies. See Ford, *Revelation*, 408-413; Hall, *ON PASCHA*, xxiii-xxvii; Schreckenberg, *Adversus-Judaeos-Texte*, 201-204; Frend, *Rise*, 240-241. See also, S.G. Wilson, "Melito and Israel," in *Anti-Judaism* 2:81-102.

The *Homily* was a sermon in poetic form, used as a commentary on the meaning of the Exodus 12, the Passover, for Christians.[7] The *Homily* argued that everyone who read the Exodus story knew both the "old" way of looking at the event of the Exodus, and a "new" way of looking at it.[8]

The second half of the *Homily*, beginning with section 72[9], is anti-Israel.[10] There are many phrases in this section which would lead one to assume that Melito was trying to stir up hostile feelings among Christians toward Jews in Sardis. The text seems to support this notion. For example, Melito wrote:

---

7 See F.L. Cross, who considered the *Homily* a Christian Passover Haggadah. F.L. Cross, Review of "Die Passa-Homilies des Biscofs Meliton von Sardis," by B. Lohse, *JTS* 11 (1960): 162-163. S.G. Wilson makes the following comments about the homily: "A Consideration of Melito's view of Judaism falls naturally into two parts corresponding to two of the main sections of his work: the typological exposition of the Exodus story (1-45) and the charge of deicide (72-99)," Wilson, *Melito*, 84-85.

8 See 1.1-20. Part of this section (1.5-18) states:
Understand, therefore, beloved,
  how it is new and old,
    eternal and temporary,
    perishable and imperishable,
    mortal and immortal, this mystery of Pascha:
  old as regards the law,
    but new as regards the word;
  temporary as regards the model, (*tupos*)
    eternal because of grace;
  perishable because of the slaughter of the sheep,
    imperishable because of the life of the Lord;
  mortal because of the burial in earth;
    immortal because of the rising of the dead.
        (trans. S.G. Hall)
This is one example of the way Melito presented his argument. This comparison between the new and the old, or use of typology, may be found throughout the *Homily*: cf. 9.54-62; 36.226-235, 39.260; 40.265; 43.275-279; 44.280-289; 58.413-60.424; 69.479-488.

9 The argument at this point in the *Homily* changes from a description of the meaning of Christ and his work to a condemnation of Israel. Hall, *ON PASCHA*, suggests in a note (39, n.40): "[t]hroughout [paragraphs] 72-99 Melito shares with *Evangelium Petri* the tendency to attribute the crucifixion directly and exclusively to Israel."

10 "Israel" is used here in order to stay consistent with Melito's language in describing Jews. Schreckenberg, *Adversus-Judaeos-Texte*, makes a very interesting distinction in describing the *Homily*: "*Als solche war das Werk zwar kein ausgesprochen antijüdischer Traktar, es gehörte aber zweifellos in den Umkreis der antijüdischen Apologetik . . .* "(201). Schreckenberg goes on to explain that Melito was a part of the anti-Marcionite orthodoxy of the second and third-century church and was arguing out of his understanding of the OT. He was not condemning Jews, as such, but asking them to reconsider their understanding of the biblical texts. This seems like a worthwhile distinction when one is considering the meaning of the anti-Israel discussion in the *Homily*. Frend suggests that the *Homily* was early evidence of Christian anti-Semitism, Frend, *Rise*, 241. He does not make the same distinction one finds in Schreckenberg. S.G. Wilson characterizes sections 72-99 as containing a "charge of deicide against the Jews." (See Wilson, "Melito," 85).

It is he that has been murdered.
And where has he been murdered? In the middle of
   Jerusalem.
By whom? By Israel.
Why? Because he healed their lame
and cleansed their lepers
   and brought light to their blind
   and raised their dead,
      that is why he died.[11]

But as is discussed below, one cannot draw the conclusion from the extant literary evidence that "Melito intended" to stir up hostile feelings toward Jews in Sardis.

Two other issues, which may also be found in other *adversus Judaeos* writings, are prominent in the *Homily*.[12] These are important for an understanding of Melito's arguments against Jews in Sardis: 1) the parochialism of Judaism and 2) the allegation that Christianity has superseded Judaism.[13]

In the section on Jerusalem and the Temple Melito wrote:

The Jerusalem below was precious,
   but it is worthless now because of the
   Jerusalem above;
the narrow inheritance was precious,
   but it is worthless now because of the
   widespread bounty.
For it is not in one place nor in a little plot
   that the Glory of God is established,
but on all the ends of the inhabited earth
   his bounty overflows,
and there the almighty God has made his dwelling
   through Christ Jesus;
   to whom be glory for ever. Amen.[14]

---

11 Translation by Hall, *ON PASCHA*, see 72.505-512. There are many other equally harsh words used by Melito against Israel. See 79.505; 81.631; 92.677; 94.693-96.716; 97.717; 96.715 (This text was used by Werner, "Deicide," to prove that Melito was the first poet of deicide; the one who articulated the idea that Jews killed Jesus who is God); 93.692.

12 Judaism as parochial: *Barn.* 16.1,4; *Dial.* 52.4; 74; 117.5; *Answer*, 7.9; 14.12. Christianity has superseded Judaism: *Barn.* 4.6-7; 6.16-19; 5.7; 7.5; 15.5,8; 16.8-10; *Dial.* 82.1; 29.2; 116; 119; 123.6; 135; *Answer*, 6.1-4; 13.13; 13.19. These are a few examples from the other texts in this study of *adversus Judaeos*. They are cited here to suggest the similarity of argumentation among the second-century Christian writers.

13 See especially the summary in Wilson, "Melito," 84-95.

14 Hall, *ON PASCHA*, 45.290-300.

Notice that the "inheritance was precious" but is now worthless because the bounty is now widespread and not limited to the "little plot." This sounds similar to the ideas in Justin and Tertullian, which accuse Jews of being too narrowly focused on their own land and race.[15]

The other claim was that Judaism had been superseded by Christianity.[16] This is a view of Judaism still held by much of the Church to this day.[17] Part of Melito's argument on this issue was the fact that everything in Israel's history was a "prefiguration"[18] of the reality to come. The reality, of course, was the Church. "[T]he Temple below precious, but it is worthless now because of the Christ above" (44.288-289).[19]

From a reading of the *Homily*, and without any reference to the new evidence found in Sardis in the last several decades, one could conclude that the Christian presence was a forceful part of the community and a major threat to Jews living there.

But there are many other factors one must consider before reaching this conclusion. Questions have been raised as to the meaning and purpose of the *Homily*, as well as its supposed anti-Jewish contents.

Several preliminary conclusions are presented here to deal with the origin and audience of the *Homily*. Each of these views is not exclusive of the other, but they add to an understanding of the text.

(1) Some suggest that the *Homily* was Greek rhetoric[20] of the tradition of the "Second Sophistic," a movement very influential in the Church writings at the time. Melito was considered to be responsible for introducing Christians to this rhetoric as a form of discourse in Christian worship.

---

15 See *Dial.* 52.4; 74; 117; 117.5 and *Answer*, 7.108; 14.12, where Justin and Tertullian suggest that Judaism was too parochial and lacked a worldwide mission.

16 See Wilson, "Melito," 89-90.

17 Recently the 199th General Assembly of the Presbyterian Church (USA), meeting in Biloxi, Mississippi, from June 8-16, 1987, began to modify the position of supersessionism in its paper "A Theological View of the Relationship Between Christians and Jews."

18 *Homily*, 34-45, 36.226-234; 39.360; 40-43; 43.275-279; 44.28-45.300.

19 Wilson, "Melito," 91, suggests that Melito demonstrated a positive view of Judaism in the past, but because of Jews' rejection of Jesus as divine in the present, Melito must reject them now.

20 Hall, *ON PASCHA*, xxiii; Hawthorne, "Paschal Homily," 149. See also Wilson, "Melito," 96, where Wilson suggested that "Melito's rhetorical skills, probably the result of formal training in the traditions of the Second Sophistic, contribute significantly to the tone, if not the content, of his work. Scarcely a paragraph of *Peri Pascha* is formulated without resort to a formal rhetorical device designed to dramatize and enhance its effects."

(2) Others think that the *Homily* was a "Christian liturgy,"[21] a form of writing used in the communal gathering of Christians.

(3) Still others consider it a Christian haggadah[22] which was used to combat the Gnostic and Marcionite influence among Christians.[23]

(4) Finally, the *Homily* was seen as part of the ongoing discussion or polemic between Christians and Jews in Sardis in the middle of the second century.[24]

Each of these approaches has merit. Yet the problem and issues mentioned above still remain. One is still not sure what kind of Christian community spawned the *Homily*. It was thought by some scholars to indicate a strong Christian presence, with open conversations and access to the Jewish community, in Sardis. As the Jewish and Christian communities grew stronger and stronger, tension increased. In the middle of the second century there was supposedly an "articulated and well organized Christian community capable of upsetting Jews in Sardis."[25] The assumption was that "the seeds of anti-semitism were sown" by Melito's *Homily*.[26] It seemed that "the closer the two communities resembled each other the more deadly the enmity became."[27]

The new evidence found in Sardis[28] presents a somewhat different picture of Jews, pagans, and Christians there and indicates some different conclusions about the meaning and intention of the *Homily*.

II. Jews and Pagans of Sardis in the Late Second Century

A. The New Evidence

---

21 O. Perler, "Typologie der Leiden des Herrn in Melitons *PERI PASCHA*," in P.Grandfield and J.A. Jungmann (eds.), *Kyriakon*, vol. 1 (Münster: Aschendorff, 1970), 257-265.

22 Cross, "Review," 162-163.

23 See Hall, *ON PASCHA*, xxvi. Wilson suggested that the "Anti-Marcion concerns" were actually a background for the homily. (Wilson, "Melito," 98-99).

24 Hall, *ON PASCHA*, xxvii.

25 This is conventional wisdom supported by the more popular scholars like Frend, *Rise*, 162-163 and summarized in well-known volumes like *IDBS*, s.v. "Sardis" and *IDB*, s.v. "Sardis." But see the conclusions in Wilson, "Melito," 100-102, who suggests the relationship is not clear and therefore it is difficult to establish that there was an "articulated and well organized Christian community capable of upsetting the Jews in Sardis."

26 See E.Werner, "Melito of Sardes, The First Poet of Deicide," *HUCA* 37 (1966):191-210.

27 Frend, *Rise*, 163.

28 See Hanfmann, *Sardis*, which is the definitive work on Sardis to 1975.

Wayne Meeks and Robert Wilken begin their study of Jews and Christians in Antioch in the first four centuries[29] with this comment: "In reality, however, both early [Diaspora] Judaism and early Christianity were mostly urban movements, streetwise and cosmopolitan."[30] This comment is made for the Jews and Christians in Antioch in the fourth century of the common era, but probably can be used in a cautious way to describe the Christians and Jews of other cities in earlier centuries. It is mentioned here to suggest the starting place for the discussion of Jews and Christians in Sardis in the middle of the second century.

When one examines the evidence for the Christian and Jewish communities in Sardis, the question is raised as to which group would be considered the most streetwise and cosmopolitan. Recent studies of Christians in Asia Minor have suggested that in the middle of the second century the Christians were a formidable movement within the cities of this region, and that they were winning converts in the context where Judaism had failed, or had, for some reason, lost its appeal. On the other hand, this position holds, Christians had broad appeal and were a source of hope for confused Gentiles.[31]

The evidence recently found in this region,[32] though, suggests a different view of Jews and Judaism in Sardis of mid-second century. Early attempts to describe what the new evidence means demonstrate some of the problems with interpreting the archaeological data. D.G. Mitten, commenting on the Jewish community and its synagogue in Sardis, suggests that "we obtain a picture of a proud, prosperous and highly respected Jewish community, active in civic and commercial affairs, who were influential enough to build and maintain this huge house of worship in a location unparalleled elsewhere."[33] "The synagogue formed the focus of a thriving bazaar area, [s]tretching along the north side of the colonnaded street for 200 meters ... The existence of a large Jewish community at Sardis is known as early as the 1st century B.C. ...

---

29 Meeks and Wilken, *Jews and Christians,* 37, n.1.

30 See Neusner's comments about this book in his recent article, "The Experience of the City in Late Antique Judaism," 37-52. Neusner cautions the reader about viewing Judaism as having its origins in the cities of the Empire. He writes that the basic Jewish writings come from a more rural and town setting. It is the opinion of this writer that it is not an either/or problem. One must be sensitive to the fact that both town and country influenced the emergence of early Judaism and Christianity.

31 This is the view held by Frend in his recent study, the *Rise*. See also C. Foss, *Byzantine and Turkish Sardis*, (Cambridge, MA: Harvard University Press, 1976): 31, where Frend's view is supported.

32 The late G.M.A. Hanfmann's *Sardis* is the best summary of the new evidence.

33 D.G. Mitten, "A New Look at Ancient Sardis," *BA* 29.2 (1966): 65. A complete study of Sardis is found in Hanfmann, *Sardis*.

It was from this community that the first Christians, to whom the letter of St. John was addressed, must have come."³⁴

These statements captured the relatively new view (since 1966) of the second-century C.E. Sardian Jews,³⁵ as well as indicating a problem which still exists within the scholarly study of the evidence, namely, the unexamined assumption that Christianity somehow grew out of the synagogue in Sardis. But the evidence does not allow for this conclusion.³⁶ It is true that the old view could be taken to suggest that there was not a very significant or distinctive Jewish presence in Sardis³⁷, and that the Jews living there were either assimilated or, worse, following some of the pagan cults. In any case, the Jews were considered not to be a significant part of the Sardian culture. This limited and even negative view of Jews has changed with the archaeological discoveries made in Sardis by the late G.M.A. Hanfmann and his team.³⁸

The archaeological evidence reveals an ancient and venerable Jewish community, but is at best meager for the early centuries of the assumed "vibrant Christianity" in Sardis. And yet, the writings of Melito have been used by some observers, along with the New Testament book of Revelation, to give

---

34 See Mitten, "Ancient Sardis," 65. Mitten's confidence about the origin of the Christian community demonstrates his acceptance of the conventional wisdom about the beginnings of the Church in Sardis.

35 S.E. Johnson, in his article "Christianity in Sardis," in *Early Christian Origins: Studies in honor of Harold R. Willoughby*, edited by Allen Wikgren, (Chicago: Quadrangle Books, 1961): 81-89, provides a very superficial glance at Sardis based on evidence which is by and large pre-Hanfmann. He makes reference to few inscriptions and some archaeological evidence, but in the main can only tell the reader about "an important Jewish community in the city which had been absorbed by the local culture" (83).

36 See A. Seager and A.T. Kraabel, "The Synagogue and the Jewish Community," in *Sardis*, edited by G.M.A. Hanfmann, 168-190.

37 See S.E. Johnson, "Christianity."

38 Mitten, "Ancient Sardis," 65. For a more up-to-date and exhaustive study of Sardis, see Hanfmann, *Sardis*. Also see A.T. Kraabel, "Melito the Bishop and the Synagogue at Sardis: Text and Context," Studies Presented to George M.A. Hanfmann, edited by D.G. Mitten, J.G. Pedley and J.A. Scott, (Cambridge, 1971), 77-78 and notes. Not a shred of evidence has appeared to date to prove the origin of the Christian community out of the synagogue in Sardis. The opposite seems to be the case. The Jews and Judaism were such an ancient and venerable part of the Sardian culture that it is possible that Christians were attracted to the synagogue in the early days of the emergence of the church in Asia Minor. See A.T. Kraabel, "Diaspora Synagogue," in *ANRW* II.19.1: 477-510; R.L. Wilken, "Melito, The Jewish Community at Sardis, and the Sacrifice of Isaac", *TS*, 37 (1976), 68. Hanfmann, *Sardis*, 193, wrote: "The Christian community Melito represented was no longer a small, esoteric 'Jewish splinter group' but a powerful faith with ecumenical claims. Unfortunately, we have found nothing certain in the way of buildings or objects, and just possibly one grave to illustrate the life of one of the 7 churches of Asia before the Peace of the Church." See, for example, the more recent study of Melito by S.G. Wilson, "Melito," 81-102, in which there are numerous references to Kraabel's work on Sardis in Hanfmann's *Sardis*. See also Meyers and Kraabel's discussion of Sardis in "Archaeology," 184-185 and 191-192, as being "more the norm" of Judaism than Dura.

the impression that a strong and aggressive Christianity was at work in Sardis during the first two centuries of the Common Era. According to one scholar,[39] Christianity, on the rise in Asia Minor, captured the attention of Jews through contact with Christian preachers in the synagogues of the region. But the fact that the Sardis synagogue was a lively Jewish center for the first seven centuries of the common era does not support this view. It is more accurate to suggest this view as a "theological convention" made into a historical fact.

There is currently no archaeological evidence to support the conclusion that Christianity in Sardis in the second century was anything other than a fledgling movement struggling for survival. The writer of the New Testament book of Revelation seemed to be concerned about this weak and tenuous community when he wrote one of the seven letters to Sardis at the end of the first century.[40]

The only archaeological evidence from the first through the third centuries of a religious community in Sardis is the Synagogue and the pagan temples. Christian evidence[41] and some minor relics have been discovered in Sardis, but none is earlier than the fourth century C.E. G. Snyder has concluded that there was a reason for this lack of architectural evidence. They were probably meeting in houses or other public places. Constantine would change that in his building programs in the early fourth century.[42] Even without literary sources for Jews in Sardis, it is easier to reconstruct the prominence of Jews in the city because of the location of the large synagogue there.

On the basis of the evidence so far uncovered in Sardis, the picture of the second-century Jewish and Christian communities there has been revised. This revision has opened the discussion of the meaning and purpose of Melito's *Paschal Homily*.[43]

---

39 S.E. Johnson, "Christianity," 81-89.

40 See *Revelation* 3:1-7.

41 G.M.A. Hanfmann and Hans Buchwald, "Christianity: Churches and Cemeteries," in Hanfmann, *Sardis*, 191-210. For a complete discussion of the reason for little archaeological evidence of Christianity in the Roman Empire before Constantine see G.F. Snyder, *Ante Pacem*.

42 See G. Snyder, *Ante Pacem*, 67-119 and R. Krautheimer, *Early Christian and Byzantine Architecture*, The Pelican History of Art, 2d ed., (Harmondsworth: Penguin Books, 1975): 39.

43 See Meeks, "Breaking Away, in *"See Ourselves,"* edited by J. Neusner and E.S. Frerichs, 104-108. Studies of the urban setting are also necessary as a way to appreciate later writings of the early Church, especially Melito's *Homily*. For a study of a text by simply looking at the text without regard for the social context, see J.M. Espy, "Paul's 'Robust Conscience' Reexamined," *NTS* 31 (1985): 161-188.

Why is the second section (79-99) of the *Homily* so hostile toward Jews?[44] Why would a Christian Bishop (if Eusebius was correct[45]), living in a highly cultured town like Sardis, feel that it was necessary to deprecate the Jews in a place where Jews played such an important part in the cultural life for so many centuries? Which references in the *Homily* expressed actual historical and social conditions of the Jews in Sardis and which describe Jews who lived only in the mind of Melito or in the pages of Scripture which he was interpreting?

B. The Venerable Jewish Community in Sardis.

After the earthquake in Asia Minor in 17 C.E., Sardis was rebuilt with the aid of funds from emperors Tiberius and Claudius. Following the initial planning, the reconstruction took several centuries to complete. Buildings were rebuilt with much stronger foundations in the hope, apparently, that a disaster similar to the one in 17 C.E. would never again destroy the city.

The rebuilt central area was dominated by two impressive buildings: the Roman Gymnasium and, later, the large, impressive synagogue within it. The original purpose of this basilicalike structure is unclear, but the fact that it eventually became a synagogue cannot be disputed. These structures remained in place until Sardis fell to the Persian invasion in 616 C.E. The full archaeological description of the synagogue[46] provides ample evidence for a lively and prosperous Jewish community in Sardis for many centuries.

Some scholars estimate that between 5,000 and 10,000 Jews lived in Sardis during the middle of the second century C.E., approximately 10% of the total population. There is no evidence prior to the Byzantine period to determine the number of Christians in the city.[47]

The Jewish population was apparently well established and intimately involved on every level of Sardis life. The large synagogue was one of the dominant buildings as can be seen in figures 1 and 2 in the Appendix. Nothing indicates that the synagogue stood out as an unusual structure in the city. It was of a piece with the other buildings. This fact makes one wonder how involved the Jewish community was with the rest of the population. The synagogue seems to indicate that Jews of Sardis were "at home" there.[48]

---

44 See S.G. Wilson, "Passover, Easter, and Anti-Judaism: Melito of Sardis and Others," in *"See Ourselves,"* eds. J. Neusner and E.S. Frerichs, 337-355, and his more recent essay "Melito," 81-102.

45 Eus., *HE*. 4.26.1-3.

46 See the extensive bibliography in Hanfmann, *Sardis*, xvii-xxxv. Also see the summary of the Hanfmann and Mitten studies of Sardis in Goodenough, *Jewish Symbols*, 12:191-197.

47 Hanfmann, *Sardis*, 192-193, and Goodenough, *Jewish Symbols*, 12:48.

48 See Kraabel, "Impact," 178-190.

The inscriptions and the design of the synagogue suggest that it was a center for the Jewish community and not used as some kind of a "paganized" meeting place. The inscriptions found in the synagogue itself indicate that the Jews maintained a connection with their tradition even though they borrowed art and other cultural forms in which to express their rituals. Greek language itself is a cultural form which Jews in Diaspora freely employed to express their most treasured thoughts and ideas. It was often assumed[49] that "the Jewish Diaspora was syncretistic, and that substantial elements of pagan piety were mixed in with the ancestral religion." This assumption,[50] which has been challenged by Goodenough and more recently by Kraabel, is simply not the case in Sardis.

The setting of the synagogue next to a significant pagan structure indicates that the Jews were not hiding somewhere in Sardis. They had an identity which had never been completely assimilated into the surrounding pagan culture.[51]

What the evidence does not indicate is what kind of Judaism is represented by the synagogue in Sardis. Discoveries at Dura-Europos, at Bet She'-arim in Israel, and at Qumran have indicated a diverse and multifaceted Judaism both in Palestine and in the Diaspora. There is also no evidence in Sardis of the presence of the "God-fearers" in the numbers assumed by some scholars.[52] In any case, the new evidence indicates that "large numbers of God-fearers" were not hanging around the synagogue in Sardis,[53] and thus it would be inappropriate to suggest that Christianity somehow emerged out of such a group in the synagogue there.

What is more likely is that citizens of Sardis lived and worked well with Jews in the city during the middle of the second century C.E. A commonality existed on all levels, which made the synagogue an integrated part of Sardian society.[54]

C. A New Picture of the Jews in Sardis

---

49 See Kraabel, "Roman Diaspora," 450.

50 Ibid. 450 n.20-24 and Goodenough, *Jewish Symbols*, 12:185-189.

51 See Kraabel, "Impact," 178-190, for a more complete description of the Jews and Christians in Sardis.

52 See *EJ*, s.v. "Jewish Identity." Also see the discussion on and bibliography referring to the "God-fearers" in this thesis.

53 See the autobiographical comments by Kraabel, "Greeks," 150.

54 See G.M.A. Hanfmann's detailed description of the city, in which he suggests such a situation, *Sardis*, 1-16. See especially pages 5 and 14, in which the makeup of the population and the importance of the city is mentioned.

The resent discoveries in Sardis have helped scholars reconstruct a picture of the Jewish community in that city in several significant ways.

First, the Jews were longtime residents of Sardis.[55] If one accepts the arguments that 'Sepharad'[56] in Obadiah 20 (postexilic), is a reference to Sardis,[57] it is likely that the Jews survived in the Lydian capital for many centuries as an independent and identifiable ethnic group. Their community life and religious practices certainly developed and changed from the way they had lived in Jerusalem[58] in 597 B.C.E. But it is clear that a Jewish presence of some form survived nearly without a break, and possibly flourished, in Sardis until 616 C.E.

Second, all of the evidence indicates that the Jews used Greek in every area of their social, cultural, economic, and religious life in Sardis.[59] Inscriptions indicate that there was some use of Hebrew in Sardis.[60] But the extent of the use is not certain. The single inscription in Hebrew found in Sardis to date is fragmentary. Although it is not clear to whom the inscription was actually referring, it may be a dedication to the Emperor.[61] It is clear from the synagogue evidence that Greek was the language used to communicate important information, such as the names of the benefactors for the synagogue.

Kraabel states that "there is more Hebrew in the decoration of a synagogue in the American Diaspora than in the ones which have been excavated from the Mediterranean Diaspora; does that say something about the popularity of the language in each case?"[62] Certainly, to survive economically and

---

55 R.L.Wilken, "Melito," 52-55, and Kraabel, "Impact," 178-180; "Diaspora Synagogue," 487-488; "Melito," 77-85; and more recently, "Greeks," 147-157. See also Meeks, *Urban* 34-36.

56 Called "Saparda" in Persian cuneiform inscriptions. See note j, Obadiah 20, in *The Prophets, Nevi'im,* (Philadelphia: The Jewish Publication Society of America, 1978).

57 Many studies have been done in the standard commentaries on Obadiah demonstrating that "Sepharad" is Sardis (Obadiah 20). No one agrees with the exact identification of this place. See the arguments in Leslie C. Allen, *The Books of Joel, Obadiah, Jonah and Micah*, (Grand Rapids: Wm.B. Eerdmans, 1976), 168-172; John W.D. Watts, *The Books of Joel, Obadiah, Jonah, Nahum, Habakkuk and Zephaniah*, (Cambridge, England, 1975), 69, and Wilhelm Rudolph, *Joel-Amos-Obadja-Jona, in Kommentar zum Alten Testament*, (Stuttgart, 1971), 315.

58 According to Obadiah 20 the Jews who were living in Sepharad were part of the "Jerusalem exile community," (*galut yrushla'im*).

59 See the discussion of the use of Greek by the Jews in Alexandria by Cohen, *Maccabees*, 210.

60 Hanfmann, *Sardis*, 179. The Hebrew inscription honors Lucius Verus during his visit to the city about 166 C.E.

61 See Kraabel, "Diaspora Synagogue," 486.

62 A.T. Kraabel letter to R.S. MacLennan, June 10, 1985. This statement is also found in Hanfmann, *Sardis*, 189.

socially, a group must be able to do business in the *lingua franca* of the place in which it lives.

Third, Jews in Sardis maintained contact with Jewish communities around the Roman world, including Palestine. But this does not mean that they were supervised by a patriarch in Palestine.[63] The evidence from Sardis presents a portrait of a Jewish community that is international and intercultural, with some contact with Jerusalem when the temple tax was collected.[64]

The notion that Jews in Sardis were cosmopolitan accounts for the fact that some scholars have difficulty describing any one particular Jewish community in the Roman Empire during the first three centuries of the common era. There are similarities among the communities, but often they develop their own ways. When one investigates the unique expressions found in various synagogues around the world, the problem is obvious.

The sculpture pieces of animals within the synagogue in Sardis, for example, the paintings on the walls of the Dura-Europos synagogue[65] far to the East, and the zodiac on the floor of several Palestinian synagogues[66] are examples of this variety, and present more questions than answers to the discussions about the nature of Jews and Judaism in the Diaspora.

As has been pointed out by Kraabel,[67] besides the variety demonstrated in the various synagogues in the Diaspora, it is also clear that the rabbis in Palestine did not control the Jewish communities. The communities appear to have been totally independent and free to work within their own city to establish their identity there.[68]

Fourth, Jews in the Greco-Roman world, as the Greek translations of the Old Testament and the works of Josephus and Philo amply attest, were able to maintain their identity because of their flexibility and their willingness to integrate into their host culture without assimilating into it. This intellectual

---

63 See Kraabel, "Impact," 182-183.

64 Ibid., 179.

65 See M.I. Rostovtzeff, *Dura-Europos and its Art*, (Oxford, 1938) and C. Hopkins, Dura Europos 140-177.

66 See S.J. Saller, *Second Revised Catalogue of the Ancient Synagogues of the Holy Land*, (Jerusalem, 1972), 25, fig. 4, who summarizes the scholarship of the early synagogues. See also Goodenough, *Jewish Symbols* 1:241-253, for other references to the zodiac in Palestinian synagogues.

67 Kraabel, "Impact," 183.

68 See Kraabel, "Roman Diaspora," 445-464. Hirschberg, *A History of the Jews in North Africa*, vol. 1., *From Antiquity to the Sixteenth Century*, 2d revised edition, translated from the Hebrew (Leiden: Brill, 1974): 40-79 holds that there was an attempt on the part of the late second-early-third-century rabbis to send teachers out to Jewish communities in North Africa. He does not mention a similar objective for Asia Minor.

and religious agility seems to have been present in the Jewish community in Sardis.

What emerges as one examines the old data in light of the new is a Jewish culture and a form of Judaism capable of being a critical partner in its host culture. Symbols used in the synagogue, which reveal that the Jews were at home with the surrounding culture, need not suggest assimilation. Kraabel[69] suggests that early in the third century a coalition of Jews and pagans may have existed in Sardis. This "coalition" was perhaps a social necessity based on the need to oppose an aggressive (and ultimately successful) Christian mission. Kraabel further suggests that because of this coalition the synagogue did not pass into the Christians' hands during the time of Justinian, (527-565 C.E.), when there was surely a large Christian community in Sardis.

If there was a "coalition" of some kind between the Jews and the pagans in Sardis, as Kraabel has suggested, then it is understandable why Melito would have written a rather negative, even hostile, homily against the Jews. This notion will be discussed in more detail below.

Fifth, the Jews were protected by Roman Law and apparently flourished under that arrangement.[70] In Josephus's *Jewish Antiquities*,[71] in a text dated to the first century B.C.E., reference was made to long-standing laws protecting the Jews in Sardis:

> Lucius Antonius, son of Marcus, proquaestor and propraetor, to the magistrates, council and people of Sardis, greeting. Jewish citizens of ours [variant reads "yours"] have come to me and pointed out that from the earliest times they have had an association of their own in accordance with their native laws and a place of their own, in which they decide their affairs and controversies with one another; and upon their request that it be permitted them to do these things, I decided that they might be maintained, and permitted them so to do.[72]

A decree of the people of Sardis preserved in the *Antiquities* allows one to gain some insight into the interaction between Jews and pagans in Sardis:

> Decree of the people of Sardis. The following decree was passed by the council and people on the motion of the magistrates. Whereas the Jewish citizens [?] living in our city have continually received many great privileges from the people and have now pleaded that as

---

69 Kraabel, "Impact," 186.

70 Wilson, "Melito," 100, argues: "It is possible, therefore, that the need for an acceptable pedigree, a distinct identity and a respectable status contributed to the manner in which Melito attacks the Jews and asserts the Christian claim to the traditions of Israel."

71 *AJ* 14.235. As to the reliability of Josephus as a historian, see S.J.D. Cohen, *Josephus in Galilee and Rome: His Vita and Development as a Historian* (Leiden: Brill, 1979).

72 *AJ* 14.235.

their laws and freedom have been restored by the Roman Senate and people, they may, in accordance with their accepted customs, come together and have a communal life and adjudicate suits among themselves, and that a place be given them in which they may gather together with their wives and children and offer their ancestral prayers and sacrifices to God, it has therefore been decreed by the council and people that permission shall be given them to come together on stated days to do those things which are in accordance with their laws, and also that a place shall be set apart by the magistrate for them to build and inhabit, such as they may consider suitable for this purpose, and that market-officials of the city shall be charged with the duty of having suitable food for them brought in.[73]

Jews in Sardis were permitted to have their own courts and a meeting place in the center of the city. The recent archaeological discoveries in Sardis generally affirm the accuracy of Josephus's record. A letter (first century B.C.E.) from the proconsul Flaccus to the council of Sardis was confirmation of a tradition of legal rights of Jews in Sardis.[74]

With the new evidence,[75] it is no longer possible to hold the view expressed by Sherman Johnson in 1961[76] that "certainly there was an important Jewish community in the city [of Sardis] which had been absorbed by the local culture." The new data present a somewhat different view: there was an important Jewish community in Sardis in the middle of the second century; it had taken the local culture as its own, but had probably influenced it as well as being influenced by it.[77]

---

73 *AJ* 14.259-260.

74 "Gaius Norbanus Flaccus, proconsul (56 B.C.E.), to the magistrate and council of Sardis, greeting. Caesar has written to me, ordering that the Jews shall not be prevented from collecting sums of money, however great they may be, in accordance with their ancestral custom, and sending them up to Jerusalem. I have therefore written to you in order that you may know that Caesar and I wish this to be done." from Josephus, *AJ*, 16.171.

75 Kraabel summarizes the Jews' place in Sardis in concise terms: "For the understanding of Greco-Roman religions, Sardis presents us with an image of the Jews and Judaism never as clearly attested before. Still a minority, but a powerful, perhaps even a wealthy one of great antiquity, in a major city of the Diaspora, controlling a huge and lavishly decorated structure on 'Main Street' and able to retain control of it as long as the city existed. From Rome and other ancient cities we have long had the picture of Jews as just one eastern minority, often a despised minority, in a large urban population; for some sites that picture is still valid, but Sardis evidence shows that there are dramatic exceptions." Kraabel, "Diaspora Synagogue," 487-488.

76 S.E. Johnson, "Christianity," 83.

77 Compare S.E. Johnson, "Christianity," 83, with Hanfmann, *Sardis*. It is clear that the new archaeological data gathered by Hanfmann have changed the way scholars view the relationship of Jews and Christians in Sardis.

III. The Christians of Sardis in the Second Century: A Literary Approach

The evidence for Christianity in Sardis[78] from the first through the third centuries is meager and mainly literary (*The Revelation of John* and Melito's *Paschal Homily*). The text of *Revelation* obviously had a rhetorical purpose[79] and must be interpreted with this in mind. Yet, in spite of the very sketchy information about the development of the church in Sardis, S.E. Johnson[80] gives the impression that the Christian community had a long and vital history there. "When the apocalyptic prophet John wrote,[81] the church in the ancient Lydian city may have existed for some time, for it has the name of being alive but is dead. John recognizes that in Sardis there are still a few who have not soiled their garments and are worthy, but the church must awake and strengthen what little remains. Its decadence may have been a relapse into paganism or into the error of the Incognitas mentioned in the letters to Pergamum and Thyatira."[82]

The evidence, since 1962, for a venerable Jewish community in Sardis far exceeds any evidence for a strong or influential Christian community in the same period (middle and late second century of the common era). The criticism from John in Revelation, that you were "once alive and now dead,"[83] could have been a warning to the small and insignificant Christian community against conversion to an attractive form of Judaism in Sardis.

Even the commentaries on the *Revelation of John* deal with the Christian community in Sardis indirectly.[84] There is no archaeological evidence, for instance, for a church building in Sardis until c. 350 C.E., leaving the scholar with little architectural evidence about the Christians in one of the leading cities of Asia Minor.

---

78 See Kraabel, "Melito," 78.

79 See Ford, *Revelation*, 410-413, and the selected bibliography and commentary. Also the works of R.H. Charles, *The Revelation of St. John, A Critical and Exegetical Commentary*, 2 vols. *ICC*, (Edinburgh: T & T Clark, 1920), 78; G.R. Beasley-Murray, *The Book of Revelation*, New Century Bible, (London, 1974), and G.B. Caird, *A Commentary on the Revelation of St. John the Divine*, (London, 1966). For another view of Jews and Christians in Sardis see Kraabel, "Greeks," 147-157 and C.J. Hemmer, "The Sardis Letter and the Croesus Tradition," *NTS* 19 (1973): 94-97.

80 S.E. Johnson, "Christianity," 81. Compare Hanfmann, *Sardis*, 192ff.

81 See Revelation 3:1-7

82 S.E. Johnson, "Christianity," 81. The text Johnson is referring to is Revelation 2:15, 20ff.

83 Revelation 3:1.

84 See Ford, *Revelation*; Charles, *Revelation*; and C. Hemmer, "Sardis Letter," 94-97.

The literary evidence for a Christian presence in Sardis available for the late first and middle second centuries is inadequate.[85] Most commentaries avoid mentioning anything about the Church, even though *Revelation*, a first-century apocalyptic[86] writing, is meant for the Church in Sardis, as well as the other churches mentioned at the beginning of the book.

The critique in Revelation 3:1-6 was specifically directed to the Christians in Sardis. But it is too general to help establish what actually happened with Christians there.[87] The most that can be said at this time is that the seven letters at the beginning of *Revelation* were addressed to the churches founded by someone other than Paul in Asia Minor.[88] Some scholars suggest that they were letters in the form of correspondence from an "oriental despot" to his subject cities. A better way to view them would be as a form of first-century social commentary or criticism.[89]

Eusebius mentioned the Christian community during Melito's time in Sardis, but said nothing about its organization, community life, and relation to the other cultures in the city. Eusebius is understandably more concerned with the Quartodeciman debate than with the social context. For him that is the most important issue for the Church in Asia Minor. The reference in Eusebius's *Ecclesiastical History*[90] simply mentions Melito's work and calls him the "bishop of the diocese of Sardis." It is interesting that Eusebius's

---

85 Ford, *Revelation*, deals almost exclusively with the evidence for the synagogue and follows Charles, *Revelation*, commentary in describing the cultural and social background of the letter to the Church in Sardis. The evidence points to a very weak Christian presence in Sardis until the late third-early fourth centuries. For some reason the Christians could not gain a foothold in Sardis. None of the archaeological evidence to date (summer 1988) indicates a strong Christian presence.

86 96 C.E. Most commentaries simply follow the work of R.H. Charles, who sketches the social and cultural images reflected in Revelation 3:1-6, or they simply talk about the Jews in Sardis. There is no substantive description of the Christians in Sardis in R.H. Charles's commentatry. See the list of commentaries provided by Ford, *Revelation*, 59-64.

87 See W.M. Ramsay, *The Letters to the Seven Churches of Asia*, New York, 1905), 369-390. See also Meeks, *Urban*, who studies the cities to understand the messages of the writer. See Wilson, "Melito," 98, where he suggested that Revelation 2 seems to describe a problem the early Christians had with Judaism. Kraabel reviewed the two volumes of Wilson, *Anti-Judaism* 2, and Richardson, *Anti-Judaism* 1, in *CBQ* 50.2 (April, 1988): 351-353.

88 Ford, *Revelation*, 41ff.

89 Several studies are important for the interpretation of apocalyptic writings, especially D.S. Russel, *The Method and Message of Jewish Apocalyptic*, (London: SCM Press Ltd., 1964); Charles, *Revelation;* K. Koch, *The Rediscovery of Apocalyptic*, translated by M. Kohl; *Studies in Biblical Theology*, 22, (London: SCM Press Ltd., 1972); Paul D. Hanson, *The Dawn of Apocalyptic*, (Philadelphia: Fortress Press, 1975), and the more recent works of James Charlesworth and G.W.E. Nickelsburg, (see Bibliography). A comprehensive bibliography by J.H. Charlesworth, *Modern Research*, is helpful and complete to 1981.

90 Eus., *HE*. 4.26.1, 4.13.8 where Eusebius referred to *"tes en Sardesin ekklesias episcopos."*

designation *paroikia*[91] is also used to indicate a larger region, and could be interpreted as describing a diocese that included far more than simply the "center-city" Sardis. The other reference in Eusebius to Sardis is a brief comment about the burial place of Melito.[92]

Melito's *Paschal Homily*, written in the middle of the second century, is the other literary reference used as evidence for the Christian presence in Sardis. Most scholars agree that this work was the product of an extremely antagonistic anti-Jewish writer.[93] W.H.C. Frend finds this document as expressing "his attitude toward his orthodox [*sic*] Jewish neighbors,"[94] and found that the "incitement of the Jews in Smyrna against Polycarp (c.166 C.E.) was being answered in kind by Christian leaders in other towns in Asia Minor. In these years the seeds of Christian anti-Semitism were sown, and it would seem that the closer the two communities resembled each other the more deadly the enmity became."[95]

The *Homily* does seem to indicate that the writer had a concern for his *paroikia*. It is also a beautifully constructed poem or Christian midrash on the Passover and indicates that this subject was important to the Christians in or around Sardis during the middle of the second century. It is also clear that the writer of the *Homily* had some negative feelings about the Jews somewhere. Therefore the least that can be said about the *Homily* is that it was a passionate plea for an understanding of the "new"[96] thing which had taken place in Christ, but was not necessarily a polemic against the Jews in Sardis.

The *Homily* could also be used as a statement about the lack of faithfulness among all God's people, using Jews as the biblical example.[97]

According to the *Homily*, the Israelites who killed Jesus symbolized the lack of faithfulness among God's people. But certainly the warning could be

---

91 Ibid., 4.26.1.

92 Ibid., 5.24.5 "and Melito the eunuch, who lived entirely in the Holy Spirit who lies in Sardis, waiting for the visitation from heaven when he will rise from the dead?"

93 See the discussion at the beginning of this chapter about the nature of the *Homily*, especially Schreckenberg, *Adversus-Judaeos-Texte*, and Wilson, "Melito."

94 Frend, *Rise*, 240. The Jews are often referred to by Frend as a religious group; never as an ethnic community which may or may not be actively involved in some kind of religious activities. For a critical evaluation of this position see Kraabel, "Roman Diaspora," 445-464.

95 Frend, *Rise*, 241. This assumes, of course, that the Christian and Jewish communities resembled each other and that the Jewish community, like the Church, was viewed as a "religious" community. But see Kraabel's comments in "Roman Diaspora," 445-464.

96 *Homily*, 2.6-4.24.

97 See also Wilson, "Melito," 95-100 where he summarizes the reasons for the anti-Judaism of the homily.

directed to Christians as well.[98] Whatever Christian community there was in Sardis in this period must have been overshadowed by the vibrant Jewish community in the city.[99]

The Quartodeciman controversy was another issue facing the Christians during this period in Asia Minor. The controversy was about the time for the celebration of the festival of Easter. Eusebius preserves a letter from Polycrates, bishop of Ephesus, to Victor, bishop of Rome from 189 to 199 C.E., who was trying to impose the Roman practice of keeping the festival always on Sunday, the day of resurrection.[100] Eusebius reports on a dispute between the two churches, which had never really been settled to his day. S.G. Hall claims that the letter from Polycrates is "[o]ur oldest and most valuable reference to Melito."[101]

The Quartodeciman controversy pointed to a disruption within the emerging churches of Asia Minor. This makes it possible to read the *Homily* as more than a Christian defense of the meaning of the Passover before the Jewish community in Sardis. The *Homily* is an apologetic for Melito's church.[102]

With some Christians preoccupied with theological differences, it is easy to understand why they did not prove to be formidable opponents or competitors for Jews and Judaism in Sardis. In fact, the only observation the Jews might have made about Melito and his *Homily* was that he, a Church leader, tried to preserve the connections between Christianity and Israel's festival traditions.[103]

---

98 Wilson, "Melito," 93-95 insists that Melito means only the Jews and not the Christians. This is a disputable point. The writer of this book suggests that a more universal audience was the intention of the *Homily*. See also, Meeks, "Breaking Away," 114-115 where he discussed the fact that, even to the fourth century, Jews thought the Christian movement was of no real consequence. This is why there was no mention of this movement in the Mishnah, Talmuds, and early midrashim. "Too late, the Jewish leaders would be forced to recognize how dangerous the Christian movement was." (114-115).

99 Wilken, "Melito," 68.

100 Eus., *HE*. 5.23-25.

101 Hall, *ON PASCHA*, xi. Hall goes on to quote the letter of Polycrates as it is preserved by Eusebius in his *HE*. 5.24.2-6.

102 Kraabel, "Impact," 186-187. See Eus., *HE*. 5.24. See also C.W. Dugmore, "A Note on The Quartodecimans," *SP*, 79.IV.2 (1961), 411-421. S.G. Wilson thinks that "[b]y insisting on the same dating as the Jews were they not, in effect, judaizing (one of the main objections, apparently, of their opponents)? The accusation would be as natural as the response: a paradoxical determination to distance the Christian from the Jewish festival, the new from the old, the church from Israel, to show that their ostensibly closer connection with Judaism was a case of the 'Christianizing' of Judaism rather than the reverse" ("Melito," 97).

103 The Quartodeciman controversy took place between the churches in Asia Minor and the other churches, mainly the Roman Church. Melito was one of the early defenders of the custom of celebrating Easter on the 14th of Nisan along with the Jewish Passover. Polycrates,
(continued...)

Melito's supposed trip to Palestine in order to search out the "exact form of the Law and the Prophets" suggests another issue which might have been relevant to both the Christian and Jewish communities in Sardis.[104] On the one hand, the authoritative texts from Palestine would give Melito a certain edge over his opponents in Sardis. He would have an "accurate text"[105] to use in his disputes with whatever audience he addressed.[106] On the other hand, Melito might use the newly acquired texts to speak with more authority to those Jews who would listen to him, or those who still considered themselves as part of the "exiles from Jerusalem" mentioned in Obadiah 20.[107]

The Quartodeciman controversy and the acquisition of an "accurate text of the Hebrew Scriptures" suggest a reason for the rhetoric of the *Homily*: Melito's (and the Christian community's) need to defend themselves from their position of weakness. This is the same as saying they felt insecure in the face of such a well-developed and venerable sister tradition: Judaism.

In a different context, K.W. Noakes suggests that the *Homily* demonstrated a fundamental insecurity in Melito in his relation to Jews.[108] This insecurity was one of the reasons why the dialogue between Christians and Jews in Sardis, according to Noakes, "gave way to rhetorical polemic".[109]

103(...continued)
Bishop of Ephesus, was excommunicated by Victor (c. 190 C.E.) over the Quartodeciman issue. See Eus., *HE*. 5.24.2-8.

104 S.G. Wilson suggests that this trip is evidence of no contact between Melito and Jews in Sardis. See Wilson, "Melito," 98.

105 Eus., *HE*. 4.26.13.

106 Ibid., 4.26.13. The stated explanation for Melito traveling to Palestine was that he was seeking to establish for Onesimus an accurate text of Scripture so that he could know about "the Saviour, and concerning all our faith, and, moreover, since you wish to know the accurate facts about the ancient writings, how many they are in number, and what is their order . . . "

But Wilson, "Passover," 351, views the trip to Palestine this way: "Melito, it seems, had the Jews of his own day in mind. Their very existence would implicitly have challenged Christian claims to the traditions of Israel and would have encouraged extreme language and strident tone. That Melito had to travel to Judea to clarify the content of the Hebrew Bible may also suggest little formal contact with the Jews of Sardis, and perhaps a degree of animosity (Eus., *HE*. 4.26.14)." See also, Wilson, "Melito," 98.

107 Josephus reports that the Jews of Sardis maintained a connection with Palestine through the Temple tax. (Josephus, *AJ*, 14.110, 16.171).

108 K.W. Noakes, "Melito of Sardis and the Jews," *SP* 13, Part 2, (1975): 249.

109 See Hawthorne, "Paschal Homily," 148-149 where he comments on his translation this way: "The translation is presented in sense lines to give the reader some feel for the highly rhetorical nature of the *Homily*. Melito lived at the height of the Second Sophistic, a literary movement that was more concerned with *how* something was said than with *what* was said." The "Second Sophistic" began in the second century Common Era as a revivalist movement whose aim was "reviving the literary glories of the classical period sophists." Later this group was known as teachers of rhetoric. See *The Encyclopedia of Philosophy*, s.v. "Sophists"; W.
(continued...)

If one can demonstrate that a writer is "insecure with his audience" when he uses "rhetorical polemic," then this idea is supported by S.G. Hall, who suggests that the whole homily is "rhetorical and liturgical rather than exact, kerygmatic rather than dogmatic . . . "[110] While this was the way an "eastern" theologian and theological poet would speak,[111] it is clear nevertheless that Melito used this style in his own particular way to challenge his opponents in Sardis.

This "insecurity" could have been due to the fact that there was a strong and vital Judaism in Sardis. J. Neusner, in observing the early development of Christianity in the east, writes:

> It is striking that the two earliest centers of Christianity in the Euphrates valley were Edessa and Arbela, both cities containing Jewish communities but neither under Tannaite influence according to the sources available to us. On the other hand, Nisibis, which is near Edessa, and central Babylonia (Seleucia-Ctesiphon) were among the last places where Christianity was established . . . Tannaite influence gained ground among the local Jewish community, as in Nisibis and Nehardea, there Christianity made slight progress, if any, for a very long period of time.[112]

Neusner reports that the Church in Nisibis, a stronghold for the Tannaite, did not take hold until after 300.

Even though it is not suggested here that there was a Tannaite influence in Sardis, it is evident that there was a strong Jewish community which may have attracted Christians to itself, thus lessening the appeal of Christianity and slowing down the progress of Christianity in Sardis until the early third century.

One scholar has suggested that the "closer the two communities resembled each other the more deadly the enmity became."[113] But the evidence gathered from Sardis would suggest that the problem for the Christians was not

---

109(...continued)
Jaeger, *Early Christianity and Greek Paideia*, (Cambridge: The Belknap Press of the Harvard University Press, 1961).

110 S.G. Hall, "The Christology of Melito: A Misrepresentation Exposed," *SP* 13, Part 2, (1975): 168. See also Hall, *ON PASCHA*, xix-xxiii, where Hall insists that "there is no question that PP is a work of Greek rhetoric." See A. Wifstrand "The Homily of Melito on the Passion, *VC* 2 (1948): 201-223.

111 See Kraabel, "Melito," 79.

112 J. Neusner, *History*, 1: 183. Hirschberg, *History*, 40-79, suggests that there was a strong tie between Palestine and North African Jews. He sees the origin of Judaism in North Africa in the Roman slave trade and an aggressive rabbinic education program.

113 Frend, *Rise*, 241.

similarity, but the liveliness of Judaism there.[114] This would make it difficult for "outsiders" to respond to the call of the Christian gospel. Preachers would be frustrated with the lack of response.

IV. The *Homily* and the New Evidence

What is the meaning of the *Homily*[115] in the light of the new evidence from Sardis? A review of the new evidence demonstrates that the Jews had a long and respected history in Sardis (since around the 6th century B.C.E.), and that the Christians seem to have been a rather insignificant part of the city until the middle of the fourth century C.E. Also, there is no significant archaeological evidence that Christians made much of an impact in Sardis before 350 C.E. Further, there is no reason, other than historical analogy, to believe that the Christian community emerged out of the synagogue in Sardis.[116]

The Christians in Sardis during Melito's life were likely to be either non-Jews who may have known some local Jews and their form of Judaism (the importance of the Hebrew Scriptures from Palestine,[117] certain texts in those Scriptures, and the festival of Passover), or Jews who converted and were not a significant part of the community life of Sardis.

It is also likely that the Christians of Sardis did not live in "center-city" Sardis but in some outlying area, and therefore did not have much contact with the major Jewish community in the city.[118] Thus, significant contact between Jews and Christians in second-century Sardis may not have taken place.

The following description of the purpose and meaning of Melito's *Homily* is based on the new evidence recently reported.

A. Literary Form

The *Homily* is a poem or a sermon in poetic form, written by a person who led a group of Christians who did not occupy a prominent place in Sardis

---

114 See Kraabel, "Greeks," 150, where he writes about his experience in Sardis with Hanfmann.

115 For a comprehensive review of the critical issues in the *Paschal Homily*, see Hall, *ON PASCHA*, xi-xlv. Hall depends almost exclusively on Eusebius and Jerome for his understanding of the text and does not spend much time on the evidence from Sardis that was discovered before 1978, when he finished his study of *peri pascha* (see xxi).

116 There is no reference to the "God-fearers" and certainly no extant writings that suggest a similar group was involved in the synagogue. See the comments on the God-fearers above in this chapter and in the Introduction.

117 See Eus., *HE*. 4.26.13.

118 Eus., *HE* 4.26.1; 4.13.8.

during the later part of the second century. The evidence presented above indicates that the Church in Sardis might have lived under the shadow or even the threat of a venerable and well-established attractive Jewish community.

It is possible that some Christians in Sardis were moving into the synagogue as full members of the religious life of the Jewish community because of the vitality these Christians felt in the form of Judaism they experienced there. Melito may have used an effective rhetorical and kerygmatic poem to call Christians back to the Church and away from the synagogue. S.G. Wilson suggests that one of the reasons for the anti-Jewish themes in the homily was that Melito was concerned to define the uniqueness of Christianity over Judaism.[119]

Along with the threat of Christians converting to Judaism because of its great cultural and religious appeal, Judaism threatened the fundamental presuppositions of Christianity. The messianic era had not come with universal peace, and the Jews had not all converted to Christianity, so the Christian poet had to come up with reasons for its delay. As the evidence now shows, Jews were NOT converting to Christianity in great numbers, which was a constant thorn in the side of Christian missionaries beginning with Paul (see Romans 9-11). But L. Gaston[120] suggests that despite Paul's seemingly open inclusion of the Jews he is really answering the question: "Has God rejected his [sic] people?" (Rom.11.1) with a "Yes."

In fact, the data collected so far[121] suggests that Jews and their various forms of Judaism flourished during these years. Many Church historians suggest, inappropriately, that Christianity was sweeping the world, while Judaism was falling asleep.

Political positioning was another threat to Christianity from Jews and Judaism. The laws protecting the rights of Jews[122] suggest strong Jewish influence in the Empire long after the Empire became Christian under Constantine in the early fourth century.

Jon D. Levenson[123] concluded the first section of his essay with this comment:

> There is a tragicomical irony here, that a tradition which sets such a great store on love and reconciliation should have canonized literature deriving, in part, from a situation of hatred and strife.

---

119 See Wilson, "Melito," 95.

120 L. Gaston, "Retrospect," in *Anti-Judaism* 2, 173.

121 Hanfmann, *Sardis*.

122 See *The Theodosian Code and Novels and the Sirmondian Constitutions,* a translation by Clyde Pharr (Princeton: Princeton University Press, 1952).

123 J.D. Levenson, "Is there a Counterpart in the Hebrew Bible to the New Testament Antisemitism?" *JES* 22.2 (Spring 1985): 245.

However, read against their historical context, the New Testament documents exemplify a truism of human nature: We are rarely generous with our competitors, especially when the competitors have *prima facie* first claim upon the status to which we aspire. If we are to replace them, we had better show that they deserve to be replaced, and, if we dare not boast that we are better than they, then let us at least portray them as worse than we.[124]

If Melito presented his ideas out of his own feelings of insecurity and inadequacy against an established, venerable, and appealing Judaism then one may understand why he focused on "the superiority of Christianity to Judaism."[125] He tried to prove to his fellow Christians the superiority of his form of Christianity over the type of Judaism that he and they experienced in Sardis.[126]

In order to convey his message in a dramatic way, Melito used rhetoric and liturgical forms in his poem.[127] An example of the rhetorical style may be found in the section of the *Homily* that introduces the discussion about the murder of Christ (72.505-513):

> It is he that has been murdered.
> And where has he been murdered? In the middle of
>   Jerusalem.
> By whom? By Israel.
> Why? Because he healed their lame
> and cleansed their lepers
>   and brought light to their blind
>   and raised their dead,
>   that is why he died.[128]

In 14.3-15.91 Melito regards the "Pascha as an initiatory rite with apotropaie effect, and insinuates into sections 14-16 the language of Christian Baptism and unction, especially 'marked,' 'smear,' 'spirit.' Justin draws a close

---

124 But see Stanton, "Aspects," 377-392, who suggested another point of view: that possibly there were friendly relations between the Jews and Christians during this period, and even though the arguments were heated, they were not hostile. He used Justin's *Dialogue* convincingly to prove his point. This is a corrective to the notion that there was only hostility and bad feelings between Jews and Christians in the second century.

125 Wilken, "Melito," 57.

126 See Wilson, "Melito," 95, 99-100 on these issues.

127 S.G. Hall suggested that "Melito did not write the fragment (Fragment 6 which wrongly asserts that Melito wrote some theological statements [On the Incarnation of Christ] about the person of Christ). We may relieve him of the duty to pioneer the Chalcedonian doctrine in its subtle precision." See Hall, "Christology," 168. Fragment 6 is found in Hall, *ON PASCHA*, 69, and xix. See on Melito's rhetoric, Wilson, "Melito," 96.

128 Hall, *ON PASCHA*, 39.

parallel between the paschal blood and the saving faith of Christians in *Dialogue* 40.1 and 111.3."[129] Rhetoric and liturgy were a part of the way Melito conveyed, throughout his poem, his message to his audience, Christians who for some reason needed reassurance.

B. The Audience

There are two statements which can be made about the audience Melito intended to read or hear his *Homily*. First, the primary group to whom this poem was addressed was the Christian community that was in the process of defining itself.[130] They needed to clarify who they were in relation to other Christians in the Roman world (as the Quartodeciman[131] controversy implies), as well as their relationship to the Jewish communities among whom they lived.

The rabbis did something similar by codifying the Mishnah in Palestine in the beginning of the third century of the Common Era. When they discussed the fine points of the Law within the context of their relatively closed community, they referred to the *minim*,[132] those outside of their community who were not considered part of the in-group. The references to the *minim* in the Mishnah were sometimes negative, but this did not necessarily mean that all *minim* were to be considered in every circumstance in a negative way. The rabbis were working on their own identity as a group,[133] and spoke to each other about the behavior of the *minim* which was not acceptable to them.

In a similar way, the *Homily* was not directed against the Jews of Sardis, or any other Jewish group in particular, but was written to Christians who defined themselves against the Israel of the Bible (including the Israel of the New Testament). This "over-againstness" created the impression that all Jews were to be condemned by Christians, which was not necessarily the case.[134]

One of Melito's concerns was to prove that Christians possessed something that was a step beyond the Jews. This is the reason for the supersessionistic teachings found throughout the *Homily*:

---

129 Ibid. 9, n. 5.

130 See the collection of essays in E.P. Sanders, *Self-Definition* 1.

131 See Wilson, "Melito," 96-97.

132 "Minim" is translated here as "outsiders" or "those who are separated ones."

133 For the development of the rabbinic tradition, see J. Neusner's more recent works (1981-1986). For a critique of Neusner's method, see S.J.D. Cohen, "Jacob Neusner," 48-63.

134 In a way the same kind of argumentation was going on within the synagogues and the *Bet ha Midrashim* ("houses of study") in Galilee, in which the Jews were developing the Mishnah and concerned about themselves and not the *minim*. The rabbis were debating the fine points of the Law within the context of a relatively closed community. For a discussion of the intention of the rabbis during the second and third centuries, see the works of Jacob Neusner.

> [J]ust so also the law was fulfilled when the
>   gospel was elucidated,
> and the people was made void when the church
>   arose;
> and the model was abolished when the Lord was
>   revealed,
> and today, things once precious have become
>   worthless.
> since the really precious things have been
>   revealed. (43.275-279)

The Christian writer defined the Church as that which superseded Israel. But instead of interpreting these words as polemic directed at Jews in general, we must (in light of the new evidence) consider them as words which provided encouragement for the struggling church of the Sardis area. The *Homily* was written for that church.

Second, the *Homily* made a statement to a secondary and more universal audience. The Jews mentioned in the *Homily* were a type of "men" who rejected God.[135] There is an interesting shift in the argument of the *Homily*. It occurs in sections 87, 94, 103, and 104.

> Ungrateful Israel, come and take issue with me
>   about your ingratitude. (87.634-635)
> Listen, all you families of the nations,[136]
>   and see! (94.693).
> Come then, all you families of mankind who
>   compounded with sins,
>   and get forgiveness of sins. (103.766-768).
> [W]ho has power to save everyone,
> through whom the Father did his works from
>   beginning
> to eternity. (104.790-791).

---

[135] R. Bultmann makes a similar comment in his Gospel of John commentary when he writes about the Jews as those religious people who cause Jesus' death. R. Bultmann, *The Gospel of John, A Commentary*, trans. G.R. Beasley-Murray, eds. R.W.N. Hoare and J.K. Riches (Oxford: Basil Blackwells, 1971), 4. See John Ashton, "The Identity and Function of *Ioudaioi* in the Fourth Gospel" *NT*, 27.1, (1985): 40-72. Ashton seems to agree with Bultmann's view. See pages 60, 68-72 and 70-71. Also, see, S. Freyne, *Galilee from Alexander the Great to Hadrian 323 B.C.E. to 135 C.E.* (South Bend: Notre Dame University Press, 1980), 125, in which tensions between the north and the south are discussed as one problem in Palestine. But Wilson, "Melito," 99-100 suggests that we should not make too much of this. A more detailed explanation of the relation of John and Judaism in Palestine is given in R. Brown, *John, I-XII*, lix-lxvi. This "secondary audience" is more likely the "Jews" or any "religious person who should know better" who rejects the Word and not just a universal humankind.

[136] Hall, *ON PASCHA*, 53, provides a textual variant here for nations: *"ethnon"* or *"anthropon"* (both genitive plural. Either way it is clear that Melito had a universal audience in mind.

The words in these sections are harsh and do condemn Israel for the murder of "your Lord" (92.677, 93.692, 695) but there is a call in these words to "all the families of mankind," and "all you families of the nations." This is the universal appeal of the poem and becomes the "other" audience.

C. Themes and Purpose of the *Homily*

1. *The Proper Use of the Scriptures*. The first few lines of the *Homily* reported that there was a new way and an old way to understand the Scriptures.[137] Throughout, with many references to both, Melito told his reader that the new way superseded the old.[138]

There was also a proper way to interpret Exodus 12. It referred to Christ (65.449) and to an early baptismal rite (14-16).

The Scriptures, according to Melito, refer throughout to Christ (58.413-60.488). Here (69.479ff.) is one example of the typological approach to Scripture which was used by Melito to demonstrate that Christ was prefigured in the Hebrew Scriptures:

> He is the Pascha of our salvation.
> It is he who in many endured many things:
> it is he that was in Abel murdered,
>   and in Isaac bound,
>   and in Jacob exiled,
>   and in Joseph sold,
>   and in Moses exposed,
>   and in the lamb slain,
>   and in David persecuted,
>   and in the prophets dishonoured.
>   (69.479-487).

In the text of the *Homily*, Melito presented what he thought to be the proper way to interpret the Old Testament Scriptures.[139]

---

137 See conclusion in Wilson, "Melito," 100ff.

138 See 2.5-20; 9.54-62 (cf. 34-45; 36.226-234; 39.360; and 40-43 which deal with the fact that Israel was a prefiguration of the new, which was the church for Melito) where explicit references are made to the old and the new as regards Israel and the Church.

139 D.F. Winslow "The Polemical Christology of Melito of Sardis," *SP* 17.2 (1982): 766 comments on the *Homily* 96.716 and the issue of "Deicide," which he suggests is a central statement to Melito. Winslow has overstated the notion that "Melito is a hater of Jews" (771, 772). Melito does not appear to be a "misanthrope of the most bitter and spiteful kind" (774). Nor does he appear to be an unhappy man (775). Rather he is stating his case with passion and is reflecting the insecurity of the Christian community in the environs of Sardis.

2. *Christianity Replaced Judaism*. The *Homily* is also explicit about Christianity replacing Judaism, at least the Judaism that Melito knew.[140]

[A] speechless lamb was precious,
> but it is worthless now because of the spotless
Son;
the temple below was precious,
> but it is worthless now because of the Christ
above. (44.286-289)

Everything in Israel's history was merely a prefiguration of the reality which was to come (34-35; cf. 42.270-271). The model, Judaism, was made void when the real (that is, the Church) came, (40-43; 43.275-279).

A Christian community which did not seem very substantial next to the venerable and substantial Jewish community would feel affirmed if it superseded Israel in its God-given task. This theme also appears in some other *adversus Judaeos* writings.[141]

3. *Evangelistic Intent*. The *Homily* makes an appeal to "all nations" and "all families" to accept the true way which is found only in the church. The Church is the repository of the reality (40.265), and is therefore the dependable conveyor of everything necessary for salvation.

The Church also superseded Judaism (42.270) and was to be seen as the body which not only fulfilled all that was prefigured in the Scriptures; it was also to be the community through which God would continue his work in the world. The problem with Judaism was that it was limited to a "little plot" (45.294) on the earth and would never establish itself "on all the ends of the inhabited earth" (45.296). The universal appeal of Christianity for Melito demonstrated the true purpose of God.

The *Homily* seems to speak to those Christians as well as all ungrateful people (Jews and non-Jews) (87.634) who were in need of forgiveness. So in this sense the *Homily* also makes a universal appeal (94.693-705; 103.766-780; 104.790). This universal concern in the *Homily* suggests that Melito wanted his ideas to move beyond the original community he addressed.

4. *Conclusion*. The new evidence, added to what was previously available, suggests the following about Melito's *Homily* as an *adversus Judaeos* writing: It was the product of a fledgling Christian church struggling for its existence

---

140 R.L. Wilken's discussion of the *Akeda*, "Melito," 68, suggested that Jewish themes were used by Melito not to show continuity with Judaism, but to demonstrate that Christianity had replaced Judaism and was the true inheritor of the traditions of the Old Testament Scriptures. See also Wilson, "Melito," 97-98.

141 See *Barn*. 4.6-7; 6.16-19; 5.7; 7.5, among many other texts. Justin Martyr, *Dial*. 82.1; 29.2; 116; 119; 123.6; 124. Tertullian, *Ad.Jud*. 3.10; 6.1-4; 13.13; 13.19. These are only a few references in the other *adversus Judaeos* writings used in this thesis.

in or around Sardis in the latter part of the second century C.E. The Christians were overshadowed by the venerable Jewish community in the same area. Christians were insecure and defensive in relation to the Jews and the form of Judaism present there. The *Homily* was probably written in relative isolation, from within a closed community, and was not meant to directly criticize a Jewish community in Sardis.

Controversies (Quartodecimanism, the attraction of Judaism) within the emerging church at Sardis dissipated its energies; one reason, perhaps, for the church's weak showing before other Sardis groups, Jewish as well as Christian. The Christianity of Melito was not a popular force in Sardis until late in the third and early in the fourth century C.E.

The *Homily* was written or preached in a poetic form and was basically an exegesis of Exodus 12. It was not necessarily an anti-Jewish or an anti-Judaism document, but was a critique of what was perceived by the writer as Jewish parochialism.[142]

The *Homily* made it clear that even though Christianity seemed weak, it was not; it had superseded Judaism. This idea of supersessionism was intended to keep Christians from moving to the more attractive form of Judaism which existed in Sardis.[143]

The Jews in Sardis during this same period were prosperous, integrated into the society, and secure without being assimilated. Judaism threatened Christianity and its leaders' social status. But there is no evidence that Christianity disturbed the Jewish community in the same way. Jews were cosmopolitan in their outlook and international in their experience.

Melito's *Homily* can be seen as an *adversus Judaeos* writing in the sense that in it Christianity defined itself counter to Jews and Judaism. But it does not appear to have been written as an attack on Jews.[144]

---

142 This is contrary to Wilson, "Melito," 100ff.

143 See Wilson's similar point in "Melito," 97-98.

144 The following comment from *EJ* reflects their view of anti-Judaism in the Homily: "The coincident of observances (Passover and Easter) and Melito's animosity toward Judaism caused his sermon, which was written between 160 and 170, to become one of the most important documents in early Christian anti-Judaism . . . the second part of the sermon is the oldest and one of the strongest accusations of deicide made against the Jews in early Christian literature." *EJ*, s.v. "Melito of Sardis." This comment not only reflects most scholarly opinion about the *Homily* but also suggests how scholars like E. Werner in "Melito of Sardis, The First Poet of Deicide," 91-210, view the *Homily*. As has been suggested above, the original intention of the sermon was not anti-Jewish in the way the *EJ* suggests; rather, the *Homily* was made into an anti-Jewish sermon by those who used it as such.

CHAPTER FOUR

TERTULLIAN: A LEGAL DEFENSE
The *Answer to the Jews* (c. 197 CE)

I. Introduction

Tertullian's so-called *Adversus Judaeos*[1] was written in the last decade of the second century,[2] "to convert not Jews but pagans. Tertullian attempted to show that Christianity was the genuine spiritual heir of Israel in order to persuade the sympathetically inclined to join the newer religion rather than become Jewish proselytes."[3] It was not Tertullian's only anti-Jewish writing,[4] but it is the one which is specifically anti-Jewish and is the one which will be discussed in this chapter. In it Jews had lost their place as God's chosen people. There is now a new people which replaces them.[5] Tertullian "sketched the gradual revelation of God's law in the Old Testament and its replacement by the New Covenant: circumcision, observance of the Sabbath and the ancient sacrifices belong to the past... He sought to prove that Jesus was the Messiah (1.3ff)."[6]

---

1 "*Answer to the Jews*" seems to be a more appropriate translation of the first line in Latin: "*disputatio habita est Christiano et proselyto Judaeo*". It removes the polemic of "*adversus*" which some ancient manuscripts do, as in "*contra Judaeos*." J. Quasten calls it *Against the Jews* or *Adversus Judaeos*. See Quasten, *Patrology* 2: 268. The Latin text referred to throughout this chapter is the *Corpus Christianorum* edition (Turnholti, 1954).

The critical studies which have been helpful in this study are: R.H. Ayers, *Language Logic and Reason in the Church Father: A Study of Tertullian, Augustine and Aquinas* (Altertumswissenshaftliche Texte Studien, Bd. 6) (New York: Olms, 1979); C. Aziza, *Tertullien et le Judaisme*, Publication de la Faculte des Lettres et des Sciences Humanes de Nice 16 (Nice, 1977); M.M. Baney, *Tertullianius*; T.D. Barnes, *Tertullian, A Historical and Literary Study* [1971], (Oxford: Clarendon, 1985); D. Efroymson, "Tertullian's Anti-Judaism and its role in his Theology," Ph.D, Diss., (Temple University, 1976); "Tertullian's Anti-Jewish Rhetoric: Guilt by Association," *USQR* 36.1 (1980): 25-37; W.H.C. Frend, "The *Seniores laici* and the Origins of the Church in North Africa," *JTS* 12 (1961): 280-284; Schreckenberg, *Adversus-Judaeos-Texte* (1982); R.D. Sider, *Ancient Rhetoric and the Art of Tertullian* (Oxford Theological Monograph), (London, 1971); Simon, *Verus Israel*; Tränkle, *Tertulliani* (Wiesbaden: Franz Steiner Verlag, 1964); and J. Quasten, *Patrology* 2.

2 This date was determined by T.D. Barnes, *Tertullian*, 54-55.

3 See T.D. Barnes, *Tertullian*, 92. Barnes refers the reader to *Answer* 1.2.

4 See D.P. Efroymson, "The Patristic Connection," in A. Davies, *Antisemitism and the Foundations of Christianity* (New York: Paulist Press, 1979): 98-117 for a discussion of the anti-Jewish themes in all of Tertullian's writings, especially *Adversus Marcionem*. Further comments on Efroymson's thesis will be discussed below.

5 *Ad.Jud.* 3.1-13; 13.13,19; 1.1-4.

6 Barnes, *Tertullian*, 106.

The *Answer* has been described as "Christian rhetoric," which means that it is more than simply a polemic against Jews in Carthage; it becomes a theological treatise which used Jews to prove a point in favor of Christianity. R.D. Sider frames the questions and outlines the issues as follows:

> [A]ncient classical rhetoric has influenced the shape of Tertullian's work. Thus again, as in the structure of his works, we are able to point to repeated efforts to make rhetorical and theological considerations coalesce, as though he would forge a new enriched culture out of two separate traditions. Of this, we may, in the third place, find corroborative evidence in the fact that in his Biblical exposition Tertullian did not throw away the Church's exegetical tradition, but rather merged it with the insights of classical rhetoric.[7]

Tertullian's work of "Christian rhetoric" may be divided into two parts: Sections 1-8 try to prove that Israel has turned from God, rejected God's grace and the Old Testament must now be understood and interpreted spiritually.[8] Sections 9-14 continue with an attempt to establish that the Messianic references in the Old Testament were fulfilled in Jesus.[9]

According to the opening words of the document, it was occasioned by a dispute (*disputatio*) between a Christian and a Jewish proselyte (1.1).[10] In this "dispute" Christianity is shown to have vindicated the will of God in every way.

From the beginning of his disputation, Tertullian was clear that Christians have replaced Jews as the real people of Israel (13.19). In his "spiritual" interpretation of the story of Esau and Jacob (1.5-6) Tertullian reminded his readers: "The Jewish (people) must necessarily serve the "less"; and the "less" people---that is the Christians---overcome the "greater" (1.5). This theme is repeated throughout the "dispute"[11] and is used in his other writings against all heretics.

---

7 See R.D. Sider, *Ancient Rhetoric*, 126 and 129.

8 Quasten, *Patrology* 2: 268, summarizes the first section of the *Answer* in a similar way.

9 Quasten, *Patrology* 2:269. Quasten suggests that the second section of the dispute is borrowed from Book III of Tertullain's own *Adversus Marcionem*. See the studies by Tränkle, *Tertulliani* and Barnes, *Tertullian*, and Schreckenberg, *Adversus-Judaeos-Texte*, 216-225.

10 See Simon, *Verus Israel*, 271-305 on Jewish Proselytism. See especially 283 and 286 for a discussion on the *Answer to the Jews*.

11 See the discussion of Sabbath 4.2-4; 6.1; Circumcision 4.1-5; 16; The Law of Moses 6.1,; and sacrifice 5.1, where Tertullian makes clear that these are all superseded or vindicated by the Christians not the Jews. The ceremonial laws are temporary. Judaism is also parochial compared to Christianity, which is universal 7.1-8; 14.12. The Law has been obliterated by the new law 6.1-4; 2.20; 4.1. Christianity has replaced Judaism 13.19. The synagogues are worn out 13.14-16. See Simon, *Verus Israel*, 188, discussion of how "Tertullian has turned this passage upside down and seems to have forgotten that Jacob was the younger."

Several arguments are repeated throughout Tertullian's *Answer to the Jews*. The old Law was obliterated (3); circumcision and the Sabbath were temporary until the eternal would come (4-6). The New Testament would intervene and the Old would cease (6). Christ is universal and King of the world (7; cf. 14.12), and was not accepted by "all the synagogues of Israel" (8), which is one of the reasons the Jews were suffering; they deserved their sad condition (8). This theme is continued in 10.9; 11.11; 13.26-29, the second section of the dispute.

In the second half of the disputation (9-14), Tertullian continues to argue from the authority of Scripture (9), "spiritually" interpreted, for the superiority of Christianity over Judaism.[12] He appeals to the "rule of Scripture" in all of his arguments (9 and 10).[13] Israel had fallen (13) because of Jews' hardness of heart. Their predicament (13.4, 24-26) was due to their disbelief and the crucifixion of Jesus (8; 10.19; 11.11; 13.4, 24-29).

According to Tertullian, the synagogues are worn out and cannot experience the grace of God anymore (13). The Christians have replaced the Jews (13) because the Jews forsook God (13). Even though they accuse the Christians of erring (13), it is the Jews who have fallen into error (14).

This brief overview gives a broad outline of the issues which Tertullian used to persuade followers of Judaism or any other heresy out of their errors and into Christianity. It seems to be aimed mainly at a Jewish proselyte, but it is relevant to any person considering which way to go. And yet a question remains: Who are the Jews to whom Tertullian refers in the *Answer*?

Did Tertullian write this dispute for his own Christian community, or for both Jews and Christians in Carthage? Did such a dispute actually take place or is the *Answer* a "literary fiction"?[14] What information is extant that provides a basis for an answer to these questions? What can be known about the contact between Christians and Jews in Carthage? What was the purpose or intent of the disputation? Did Tertullian intend to write a treatise against the Jews in Carthage?[15]

---

12 See Simon, *Verus Israel*, 68.

13 Simon, *Verus Israel*, 139, suggests that this is due to the fact that he is arguing with biblically literate people: "If Tertullian's *Adversus Judaeos* is compared with his *Apology*, or if Justin's *Dialogue with Trypho* is compared with his *Apology*, it will be seen that the number of scriptural references is significantly less in the works addressed to pagans than in those addressed to Jews." It is suggested by this writer that the audience does not necessarily have to be Jews; it could be "biblically literate" Christians as well.

14 Schreckenberg, *Adversus-Judaeos-Texte*, 217, suggests that the *Answer* might be a literary fiction. See also Simon, *Verus Israel*, 173.

15 L. Gaston suggests that Tertullian was a "turning point" in anti-Jewish writings in the Christian Church. "In many respects Tertullian represents a turning point in the development of Christian doctrine, in which certain tentative second-century developments receive a clear formulation which will dominate all future doctrine, and that is also the case here. Anti-Judaism, then, can be defined as what Tertullian says about Jews." Gaston continues: "To judge
(continued...)

In order to answer these questions, certain literary, epigraphical, and archaeological evidence will be examined to determine what can be known about Jews and Judaism and their relationship to Christians in second-century Carthage. The last section of this chapter will summarize the meaning of the *Answer* in light of the discussion of the city as "text."

II. The City: Carthage, North Africa

A. What Can Be Known from Extant Evidence?

A summary statement in J.W. Eadie and J.H. Humphrey's recent chapter on "The Topography of the Southeast Quarter of Later Roman Carthage" in *The American Schools of Oriental Research* (about excavations of Carthage, 1976, conducted by the University of Michigan), defines the issues and the problem involved in moving beyond the old consensus in understanding Tertullian's *adversus Judaeos*, and the relation between the Jews and Christians in Carthage:

> The literary evidence alone cannot elucidate urban development or renewal much beyond the general outline traced above. The literary accounts can serve as chronological markers and occasionally as primary sources of information, but they cannot provide detailed answers to our questions. New data on the topography and urban development of later Roman Carthage can be provided only through archaeological investigations, not through further scrutiny, however systematic, of the literary evidence (or, for that matter, of some of the old excavation notices). In this connection, the importance of a close dating of building phases on the various sites under examination is paramount. The evidence of the coins and pottery should allow us to date our phases with great precision (hopefully, to within ten or twenty years). Only when this has been done can the ebb and flow of the economic fortunes of the city of Carthage during the later Roman empire be understood and seen against the larger historical picture of the world of late antiquity.[16]

15(...continued)
by the work of Tertullian, it [Christian anti-Judaism] arises out of an inner-Christian theological debate rather than out of rivalry with a living Judaism." See Gaston, "Retrospect," 163.

16 See J.H. Humphrey ed. *Excavations at Carthage 1975-1976*, conducted by the University of Michigan, (Institut National d'Archeologie et d'Art, and American School of Oriental Research) l, (Tunis 1976); 2-4, (Ann Arbor: Kelsey Museum, 1976-1978).

A short and descriptive overview of the city in the second century is found in *Carthage: A Mosaic of Ancient Tunisia*, edited by Aicha Ben Abed Ben Khader and David Soren, New York: The American Museum of Natural History in association with W.W. Norton & Company, (1987): 59-67 and 115-126. Soren describes the city with these words: "The second and early third centuries A.D. represented the golden age of Roman prosperity in ancient Tunisia. It was generally a peaceful time: and with few exceptions, competent emperors and able administrators

(continued...)

Urban sprawl in the modern city of Carthage has made it difficult to recover some ancient sites in the area.[17] Yet there have been some recent studies which are more helpful in presenting the modern reader with a "text" of the city that portrays a lively and rich cultural, political, intellectual center, competing with Rome, Athens, Alexandria, and other Roman cities in the second century.[18]

In spite of the lavish mosaics, building foundations, and maps which are available for the second and third centuries in Carthage, there is little archaeological and epigraphic evidence for the Church or Synagogue in this period. Therefore it is difficult to reconstruct the social and cultural influence of these two groups in Carthage. Most of the building materials from either churches or synagogues (if there were any) have been removed to other places and used in other structures. The only evidence left is the necropolis, which "constitutes the essence of the archaeological documentation of ancient Carthage"[19] and possibly the only evidence for a nonliterary reconstruction of Jewish and Christian life there.

Therefore any attempt to reconstruct a portrait of Jewish and Christian communities during the time Tertullian wrote his *Adversus Judaeos* is faced with difficulties. These difficulties are not impossible to overcome, but they do inhibit a more complete discussion of the relationship between these two communities. Goodenough's suggestions that the catacombs on the Gammarth Hill on the outskirts of Carthage reveal both a common bond with the ideas of the *Mishnah* in burial practices and the Jews' use of pagan art in their

---

16(...continued)
brought the blessings of civilization to a wide area." (59).

17 See C.M. Wells, "Recent Excavations at Carthage: A Review Article," *AJA*, 86 (1982): 293-296, 605-606. See Picard's comment in 1965: "Carthage for many contemporaries is the lost land, utopia, engulfed like Atlantis in an inexorable catastrophe." Picard *Carthage* (1965): 179. Since 1965 much work has been going on which has made ancient Carthage a little less like lost Atlantis.

18 See David Soren's comments in the recent A. Ben Abed ben Khader and D. Soren, *Carthage*, 123.

19 See *The Princeton Encyclopaedia of Classical Sites*, s.v. "Carthage." For more recent summaries of the evidence and a brief history of Carthage in the second and early third centuries C.E. see R.J.A. Talbert, *Atlas of Classical History*, (New York: Macmillian, 1985), 97, 100, 128, 150-154, 170-176; *Carthage*, edited by Ben Abed and Soren; and C.M. Wells "Recent Excavations."

There is a discussion about the second-century "catacombs" in Gammarth Hill on the outskirts of Carthage in Goodenough, *Jewish Symbols* 2:63-69. Goodenough suggests that some Jews were not afraid to use the "decorations" of the host society in their tombs (68) and that even though the burial practices are similar to those recorded in the *Mishnah*, "the similarity must lead us to conclude not that the Jews of Gammarth were following the prescriptions of the *Mishnah*, but that both the rabbis who wrote the *Mishnah* and the Jews of Gammarth reflected the traditional Jewish method of burial, as the catacombs in Italy did not." (65). See the same comment in Goodenough, *Jewish Symbols* 4:196 and 12:36.

tombs[20] is speculative and does not necessarily mean any real connection between the two regions.

Hirschberg suggests that the cemetery (which he dates from the beginning of the third century) provides evidence of a Jewish, but not a Christian presence in Carthage;[21] further, he thinks that there is a connection between the two regions, Palestine and North Africa.[22] His argument from the halakic and 'aggadah materials, which he assumes Tertullian knew,[23] is the evidence he uses to prove the connection. But the evidence of the cemetery alone can be used only to demonstrate the burial practices in the city.

David Soren suggests that Carthage in the second century was entering into a "golden age"[24] for the Romans in Tunisia. He also states that "[t]he meeting of African literary genius and Christianity was a happy one. African life had always been marked by strong religious feelings" (123). From the evidence in the Jewish catacombs it would be reasonable to assume that some Jews were also benefiting from and enjoying the "golden age." Yet, at the present time there is no extant literary evidence from Jewish writers living in Carthage of the second century.

If Soren is correct, and Christians and Jews were actively involved in the dynamic literary period in Carthage at this time, then it is possible to reconstruct some images of their involvement in the city.[25]

Soren suggests that from a reading of Tertullian's writings it is possible that there were a large number of Christians in Carthage by the beginning of the third century.[26] Simon reports that "Tertullian himself mentions that the Jews sometimes offered threatened Christians asylum in their synagogues, and

---

20 Goodenough, *Jewish Symbols*, 2:67; 4:196, and 12:36. Simon, *Verus Israel*, 188, suggests that the arguments which are hotly debated within Jewish and Christian circles in Carthage are the same as those talked about in Palestine. This similarity in ideas does not necessarily mean that there was an actual connection between the two regions.

21 H.Z. (J.W.) Hirschberg, *History* 1, 50, 69.

22 Ibid. 28 and 79.

23 Ibid. 76.

24 Ben Abed and Soren eds., *Carthage*, 59. See also Frend, *The Donatist Church: A Movement of Protest in Roman North Africa* (Oxford: At The Clarendon Press, 1952):112-113 for a description of a later enthusiastic movement in the North African Church.

25 See W.H.C. Frend, who offers a similar view in "A Note on Jews and Christians in Third-Century North Africa," *JTS* 21 (1970): 92-96. Also D.E. Groh, "Upper-Class Christians in Tertullian's Africa: Some Observations," *SP* 14 (=*TU* 117)(1976): 41-47, especially nn.2 & 4.

26 Ben Abed and Soren eds., *Carthage*, 124. Tertullian suggests that there were more Christians in Carthage than pagans. This is difficult to establish as a fact.

if this is true, the Jews were perhaps not so unanimously detested as he pretends."[27]

This statement helps bring balance to any reconstruction of the past and the relationship between Christians and Jews in Carthage in the last decade of the second century. That relationship was varied, depending on the memory of individuals and groups who had contact with Jews. If they were protected during a time of persecution by the Romans, then they were cordial. If they were turned away, then one would understand why some Christians were hostile to Jews.

B. The Necropolis and Other Evidence

The archaeological evidence of Jews and Christians in Carthage before 324 C.E. comes mainly from the necropolis.[28] There are no foundations for synagogues or churches prior to this time so the necropolis is important evidence.[29]

Funerary stelae indicate that there were many Jews and Christians living in close proximity to each other in Carthage in the second century. This evidence suggests that some Jews and Christians lived close to each other and were more than tolerant. In fact, the use of a common grave site indicates friendly relations and possibly a certain kind of intimate bonding. The picture of Jewish and Christian relationships is somewhat mixed in Carthage.

T.D. Barnes cautions his readers on the use of cemetery archaeological evidence to try to establish the relations between Jews and Christians in the

---

27 Simon, *Verus Israel*, 124.

28 Simon, *Verus Israel*, 124 states: "The excavations at Carthage in particular have shown that the first Christians were sometimes interred in the Jewish necropolis" (124). But Hirschberg, *History*, 50 and 69, argues that Delattre has changed his mind and thinks that the evidence can no longer be used to prove a Christian presence there.

29 See *The Princeton Encyclopaedia of Classical Sites*, s.v. "Carthage." Also see Barnes, *Tertullian*, 67, n.8 and 89, n.1. "The necropolis constitutes the essence of the archaeological documentation of ancient Carthage. There is no undeniable Christian building or inscription which survives in Africa earlier than fourth century AD." In an appendix, Barnes, *Tertullian*, 274, cautions his readers: "no evidence whatever has yet produced that Christians were buried there." For a brief summary of the evidence and maps of the sites, see Talbert, *Atlas*, 100, and for inscriptions see H.C. Leclerq, *L'Afrique Chrétienne*, par dan H. Leclerq, 1, 2d ed. (Paris, 1904), 39ff. Ben Abed and Soren eds., *Carthage*, gives an overview of the history and summaries of the evidence for the site during the Greco-Roman period. See Frend, "The Early Christian Church in Carthage," *Excavations at Carthage in 1976*, Conducted by the University of Michigan iii. (University of Michigan, Ann Arbor, 1976): 27, who suggests that it is possible that Christians shared the same location, but not necessarily the same specific graves.

last decade of the second century.[30] His comments in no way dismiss the possibility of reconstructing the close proximity of Jews and Christians in city.[31]

C. What the Evidence Does Say

The evidence which is available permits the follow assumptions:

1. The large Jewish and Christian cemetery provides evidence of a significantly well-established community with Jews and Christians living in close proximity to each other.[32]

2. The presence of *"seniores"* as a lay government which ran the church in Carthage suggests (by analogy) a basis for either the synagogues' influence on church organization or a common tradition for leadership within both institutions. This may be a clue to some major contact between Jews and Christians. This "evidence" must be carefully analyzed to discover if there is indeed any influence one on the other, or if they simply shared a common view of government.[33]

3. The literary evidence is polemical and must be read from that perspective.

---

30 See Barnes, *Tertullian*, 3-30, 56, 68, 71, 271, 280, and 281 n.8. Also see Frend, who is limited by the need to depend on later materials to talk about an earlier period in "Jews and Christians in Third Century Carthage," *Paganisme, Judaisme, Christianisme, Influences et affrontments dans le monde antique, Mélangé offert a M. Simon* (Paris: Boccard, 1978): 185-194. See J. Humphrey, "A New Museum at Carthage," *A* 38.2 (1985): 28-33, for a discussion of the work in late Roman and early Christian levels to 1986.

31 See J. Ferron, "Inscriptions juives de Carthage," *Cahiers de Byrsa* 1, Imprimerie Nationale (Paris, 1951): 175-206. This is one of the sources of Goodenough's study of the catacombs in Carthage. See Goodenough, *Jewish Symbols* 2.63-69.

32 See A. Ennabli, "North Africa Newsletter 3: Part 1. Tunisia 1956-1980." Translated by J.H. Humphrey. *AJA* 87 (1983): 199, n.28 and the bibliography on page 205, which gives the archaeological and epigraphic evidence of the necropolis. See all the comments by Goodenough, *Jewish Symbols*, 2.63-67 where he refers to other sources which provide information about the catacombs on the Gammarth Hill near Carthage.

33 See the discussion of the *seniores laici* in Frend, "Seniores," 280-284 and Barnes, *Tertullian*, 273-275 for a discussion of the *seniores* and the influence of first-century Judaism on the development of the Church in Carthage. See Frend, "Seniores," 283, where he seems to suggest something similar, and yet blurs the issue when he states: "For it seems evident that many of the peculiar features of the organization of the African Church may be explication by reference to a distinctive primitive Christian tradition, indicating, perhaps, Judeo-Christian influence." It is more in keeping with the evidence to suggest that Jews and Christians came from similar cultures and developed traditions out of that environment, rather than to state that they are somehow bound in a "Judeo-Christian" status. On the problem with the term "Judeo-Christian," see A.A. Cohen, *The Myth of the Judeo-Christian Tradition* (New York: Harper & Row, 1970), and Martin E. Marty's comments using Cohen's book: "A Judeo-Christian Looks at the Judeo-Christian Tradition," *CC* 103.29 (October 8, 1986): 858-860.

4. It appears that the relevant archaeological evidence, except the necropolis, was carried off to build other structures from pre-325 C.E. Carthage.[34]

These observations provide a broad outline of the "text" of Carthage when examining the relationship between Jews and Christians in the city.

III. Jews and Judaism in Carthage

Based on the comments above, a picture of Jews and Judaism in late second-century Carthage begins to emerge.

The presence of a public burial place for a large number of Jews indicates that Jews were long-time residents in Carthage. They had an established place for the rites of burial. The inscriptions on the graves are a kind of public notice which indicate that the burial rites were not performed in haste or in secret. Families used the burial site for many generations. However, the speculation that Christians were buried in a Jewish cemetery[35] does not necessarily add to one's understanding of the relation between Jews and Christians in Carthage. That they were buried in the same place could have been out of necessity. Another possibility is that Christians were still viewed as Jews.[36] The connection between these two groups remains ambiguous.

Second, the so-called *seniores laici* has been used to indicate a connection between Jews and Christians in Carthage. Barnes thinks that this is a questionable assumption.[37] Others suggest that the mention of them in Christian sources was an indication of Jewish influence on the Christian community in Carthage in the early years of the emergence of the Church.[38] According to

---

34 See Sider, *Ancient Rhetoric* and compare Baney, *Tertullianius*. See also G. Snyder, *Ante Pacem*.

35 Barnes, *Tertullian*, 271-273.

36 See Hirschberg, *History*, 49 and 50 for another view. He suggests that there is a possible connection in the cemetery, but because of the existence of another large cemetery where Christians are buried it is unlikely that they would be buried in a Jewish cemetery. This writer holds to the position stated in this chapter.

37 Ibid., 274-275 makes the following comment about the *seniores*: "The *seniores laici* of the African church are a remarkable phenomenon. But they come into prominence only in the fourth century. Hence the problem: are these lay elders an institution peculiar to Africa, or a survival from primitive Christianity? If the former, their origin must presumably be sought in the African background. If the latter, the institution derives from Judaism in the first century-- and becomes impossible to distinguish Jewish influence on its development in second century Africa (if any) from its ultimate Jewish origins in the first."

This reasoning assumes incorrectly that Christianity is derived from Judaism. It is not necessary for Christians to have a connection to Judaism if the *seniores laici* were from primitive Christianity.

38 See Tertullian, *Apology*, 39.4 and Frend, "Seniores," 280-284. See also, Barnes comments in *Tertullian*, 274-275.

Frend, "[t]heir functions were both administrative and disciplinary,"[39] and may indicate that the Jewish community was independent and comfortably established, organizing and running its own community life.

The problem with using *seniores* as evidence of a kind of administration present in the Jewish community in Carthage is that one tends to look at church government and then assume from the administration of the church a similar set of circumstances for the Jewish community. In other words, the *seniores* were assumed to be like the rabbis. But the evidence that Jews of late second and early third century C.E. Carthage were connected to emerging rabbinic Judaism[40] is based on a much later redacted Talmud!

In an essay on the *seniores*,[41] W.H.C. Frend made this statement about rabbinic Judaism:

> It has also been recognized that the ethical code imposed by the rigorist element in the African Church bore a striking resemblance to Jewish "halacha" of the day. Detailed comparisons can be made between Tertullian's prescription for avoiding contact with pagan society, contained in the *De Idololatria*, and those to be found in the Jewish *Abodah Zarah* of the same date.[42]

---

39 Frend, "*Seniores*," 281 and Barnes *Tertullian*, 275.

40 Simon, *Verus Israel*, 188 states: "It proves that in Africa, no less than in Palestine, this question [on Jacob and Esau] was being hotly disputed." See Simon, *Verus Israel*, 188 nn. 34 and 35. Simon seems to suggest a connection here. Hirschberg, *History*, 28 and 75-79 bases his whole argument on the origin and ongoing development of a Jewish community in Carthage on evidence he has gathered from the Talmud!
The position of this chapter is the view held by J. Neusner. See J. Neusner, *Development of A Legend, Studies on the Traditions Concerning Yohanan ben Zakkai*, (Leiden: Brill, 1970). Also consider the following: The fact that "Carthage" is mentioned in the Talmud (Men. 110a) in no way indicates that rabbinic Judaism was known about or was part of the Jewish community in Carthage. It simply means that Carthage was known about as the city on the extremity of the empire, (see *EJ* 5.214-215). The whole context of the reference to Carthage in the Talmud, Menahoth 110a (*BT*, Seder Kodashim, I, 679.) is "R. Abba b. R. Isaac said in the name of R. Hisda—others say, Rab Judah said in the name of Rab, From Tyre to Carthage the nations know Israel and their Father who is in heaven; but from Tyre westwards and from Carthage eastwards the nations know neither Israel nor their Father who is in heaven. R. Shimi b. Hiyya raised the following objection against Rab: It is not written, 'For from the rising of the sun even unto the going down of the same My name is great among the nations; and in every place offerings are burnt and presented unto My name, even pure oblations?' (Mal. 1.1)--- He replied, You, Shimi! They call Him the God of Gods." The only other references to Carthage by name in the *Babylonian Talmud* are Berakoth 29a (*BT*, Seder Zeraim, 176) and Baba Kamma 114b (*BT*, Seder Nezikin, I, 678). The indexes in *The Talmud of the Land of Israel* are incomplete and do not give complete references. Yet a reading of Baba Qamma makes no to either Kartinga (the alternative reading of Carthage) or Carthage. It is doubtful that there are any significant references to Carthage in *The Talmud of the Land of Israel*.

41 Frend, "*Seniores*," 280-284.

42 Ibid., 283. See Barnes, *Tertullian*, 275, n.5 in which he criticizes Frend: "Frend's further assertion that the seniores were 'empowered' [Frend, "*Seniores*," 282] to excommunicate unworthy members of the Christian community is not quite borne out by Tertullian's actual words."

The "traditional legalism" of the African Church might be explained with reference to this Jewish background, as well as to the secular professions of its first leaders, Tertullian and Cyprian.[43]

Third, the evidence from the Talmud for contact between Palestine and Carthage[44] is convincing but problematic. A date for the final formation of *Abodah Zarah* has not yet been settled. The "legalism" of the African Church does not necessarily have to be a legacy of a rabbinic influence. Did Jews themselves in Carthage know about the *M. Abodah Zarah* or rabbinic Judaism before it was in written form? [c.200 C.E.][45] There is no evidence other than that generously quoted by Hirschberg that there was any knowledge of the rabbinic writings.

It is not clear when *Abodah Zarah*[46] was put into its final form, or if it was used in the same way as *De Idololatria* was used. It is clear that the *Abodah Zarah* was meant for a group of Jews, and not for all people, but its intention was not so much to condemn idolatry as to help Jews live as Jews within in a non-Jewish environment.[47]

---

43 Ibid., 284 and see Frend's comments on the loyalty of the Jews in Dispersion to their traditions in *Rise*, 34. This appears to be a romantic monolithic view of the Jews in the Mediterranean World. The archaeological evidence suggests a variety of traditions which emerged in Judaism, both in and outside of Palestine. See the helios, the zodiac, and the four seasons in the mosaic of Beth Alpha synagogue in northern Israel. Goodenough has documented many Jewish houses of worship that suggest the emergence of Judaism that expressed itself in a variety of ways.
   Hirschberg, *History*, 75-79 argues for the connection between Tertullian's writings and the rabbinic *halakah* and *'aggadah*.

44 Hirschberg, *History*, 74-79.

45 It is not accurate to use the term 'rabbinic Judaism' when describing the Judaism of Carthage. As discussed extensively by J. Neusner, rabbinic Judaism was not "legalistic" but "philosophic." Or it might be more accurate to say that the "halaka" must be viewed in its larger philosophical context. See J. Neusner, *The Idea of Purity in Ancient Judaism* (Leiden: Brill, 1973), 4. Among his many other writings see *Method 10* and *Judaism*. It is more accurate to suggest that the "legalism" of the Early Church in North Africa was a result of a kind of New Testament exegesis.
   Also, see Alan J. Avery-Peck, *Mishnah's Division of Agriculture, A History and Theology of Seder Zeraim*, BJS 79, (Chico, CA, 1985), 410-411. "Ingenuity, indeed is what the Division of Agriculture, and with it the rest of Mishnah, is about" (This hardly sounds like something that would lead to a legalism in the early Church.) "For in this document, rabbinic masters envision a society in which each individual's intellect will work towards creating a perfected world, conceived by humans and yet believed to be in the holy image of God. While awaiting realization of this dream, these rabbis, powerless within their own nation, work at the elaborate puzzle that constitutes Mishnah. Their highest value is seen both in their internal intellectual life and in their legislation. This value consists of using the mind to determine what God demands and so to participate directly in the process of revelation and, ultimately, redemption."

46 Compare Frend, *"Seniores,"* 283, n.3 and Neusner, *Evidence*, 1-44, 307-328.

47 When one compares the use of scripture in each of these documents, very different agendas seem to guide the authors of each. For example, Tertullian in "On Idolatry," uses the
(continued...)

If it cannot be established, contrary to Hirschberg's view, that rabbinic Judaism was active in Carthage during Tertullian's time, then when references are made to the *seniores* they must not be seen as a type of rabbinic council in the city. It is more accurate to describe them as representing a special governing body that had oversight of the Jewish community there.

The extant evidence indicates that Judaism in Carthage[48] is something other than what Tertullian or the Christian writers describe. It is uncertain what Tertullian knew about Jews and Judaism in Carthage during the late second century.[49] But if Tertullian was dependent on the "ancient Judaism of his exemplars," then his views of Jews and Judaism would not be used as means to understand the Jewish community in Carthage, but as a way of viewing how Tertullian understood them.[50]

47(...continued)
biblical texts the way the New Testament writers use them: to prove a point as having been either foretold, or to indicate the superiority of Christianity over Judaism. This is not the way the *M. Abodah Zarah* uses scripture. The rabbis talked about the text in such a way that the original intent of the law was to be discovered. On this argument see J. Neusner, *Method and Meaning in Ancient Judaism*, Second Series, *BJS* 15, (Chico: Scholars Press,1981): 198. Tertullian also uses a variety of texts to prove his case. *Abodah Zarah* is concerned only with those texts (mainly Exodus 23 and 34, Deuteronomy 7 and 12, and Leviticus 5) which relate directly to the issue of the tractate. Tertullian has composed a law for Christians in "On Idolatry." It is apparent to this writer that *Abodah Zarah* and "On Idolatry" have very little in common.

48 See the summary Goodenough gives in his *Jewish Symbols*, 2:63-69 where he describes the freedom with which some Jews used the Greco-Roman symbols in the catacombs.

49 In his study of this period, (P. Brown, "Approaches to the Religious Crisis of the Third Century A.D.," in *Religion and Society* [1972]: 83-84), Peter Brown made the following general observation:
"The Judaism which a Christian bishop received into his community was not the Judaism of his contemporaries, the rabbis, but the ancient Judaism of his exemplars, the priests. Hence the importance of the 'neo-Judaism' of Christian adaptations of the priestly code of Leviticus in a society greatly preoccupied, in the third and fourth centuries [this statement can be made for the second century as well], with problems of organization, with hierarchy, with the divine sanctions of the imperial power, the Christian Church stood out as a group that had organized itself most effectively as a hierarchy based on the division between the sacred and the profane, and, by implication, on the superiority of the spiritual over the lay world."
Is it possible that this so-called "ancient Judaism of his exemplars," which Brown mentions in his study, is the "Judaism" one reads about in *Adversus Marcionen* and *Adversus Judaeos* or possible in all of Tertullian's works? If this is the case, then one can make the point that the Judaism and the Jews in the *Adversus Judaeos* are portraits taken from the Biblical stories, and not from the neighborhoods of Carthage.
The contrary view is Hirschberg, *History*, 40-48 and 74-79.

50 For later evidence of contact between Christians and Jews in Carthage (4th-early 5th centuries) see the *Acts of Philip*. It is referred to at this point in the discussion because it demonstrates the possibility of intimate contact between Jews and Christians---in Carthage in a later period. It seems to suggest that the synagogue still existed and viewed the Christian mission as a problem. For bibliography and texts of the *Acts of Philip*, see E. Hennecke, *New Testament Apocrypha* vol. 2 [First published, 1964], edited by W. Schneemelcher and translated by R. McL. Wilson, (Philadelphia: Westminster Press, 1976): 577.

(continued...)

IV. The Christians in Carthage

The origin of the Church in North Africa is shrouded in obscurity. Except for one documented episode, which is reported by T.D. Barnes, the evidence is sparse.[51] The episode is a martyrdom of seven men and five women of Scillium who were executed by order of the proconsul Saturnias in 180 C.E., for refusal to renounce their Christian faith.[52]

50(...continued)
In his doctoral dissertation David Efroymson summarized Tertullian's view of Jews in the following way:

1. The Jews are seen as if they were an Old Testament people or possibly a "theological abstraction" (Efroymson, *Tertullian's Anti-Judaism and its role in his Theology*, 135, 62, 56). It is clear from his writings that Tertullian "had little personal contact with our knowledge of contemporary Jews" (56, 62, 63, and 75ff., nn.40-43).

2. Tertullian needed Jews as an antitype. He uses the Jews to win arguments against his Christian opponents (64). (It is possible that Tertullian, like Melito and Justin, used the "Jews" as a way of defining his form of Christianity. See S.G. Wilson's comments on Melito in his essay "Melito," 95-96, in which Wilson suggests that one of the reasons for the *Paschal Homily* was to define Christianity in contrast to Judaism). In a sense Tertullian was not anti-Jewish, but he did use Jews to make his more pressing and important points.

3. Judaism was competing with Christians in Carthage. (56, 70 n.10). This is Simon's view and used by R. Wilken. See Efroymson, *Tertullian's Anti-Judaism and its role in his Theology*, 70 n.15, "It is primarily Marcel Simon's *Verus Israel* to which Wilken refers throughout the essay, and it is Simon, more than anyone, who has underlined both the fact and the significance of Judaism as a serious rival to Christianity. As evidence he points principally to Jewish proselytism (316-355 and 482-488), liturgical 'Judaising' within Christianity (356-393), the attraction of 'Jewish' magic (166-177 and 208-213), and the Jewish reaction to Christianity (214-238)." The debate over the existence of the "God-fearer" among recent scholars (see MacLennan and Kraabel, "Invention," 46-53; Feldman, "Omnipresence," 58-63; and Tannenbaum, "Jews," 54-57, for references to this debate over the "God-fearer" issue), suggests a continued debate over the viability of a living Judaism in the first through third centuries. Simon suggests, as Wilken has pointed out above, that Judaism was a viable and disturbing presence to Christianity in the first through third centuries C.E. (Simon, *Verus Israel*, tr., xviii). Efroymson has a rather extensive notation on the problem of competition between Jews and Christians for converts to their particular traditions (70 n.15). This could be one of the reasons for the vehemence with which Tertullian wrote "against the Jews."

4. Tertullian dealt with Judaism as if it were a worldwide monolithic religion (57). (See also the discussion by Kraabel in "Roman Diaspora," 445-464, on the monolithic view of Jews and Judaism in the Diaspora.) The Roman laws, according to Josephus (*Ant* 14.259-270), at least, seem to have dealt with Judaism as a monolithic group and as individuals. The Christian writers simply followed suit. (See Groh, "Upper Class", 41-47 for his method of interpreting Roman History.) There were no distinctions made between the various forms of Judaism.

These four statements inspired by Efroymson's thesis suggest the problems in defining the Judaism of Carthage and make one cautious in the use of Tertullian as a "source" or as "evidence" for understanding the Jews in that city.

51 W.H.C. Frend, "Early Christian," 3:21-40 and R.C.C. Law, "North Africa in the Period of Phoenician and Greek Colonization to 800," in *Cambridge History of Africa* 2, edited by J. Fage (Cambridge, 1978), 87-209. See T.D. Barnes, *Tertullian*, 60-62, summary of the *Acts of the Scillitan Martyrs*. Also appendix 16.

52 Even though this is an early (180) document (see Musurillo, *Christian Martyrs*, 86-89), (continued...)

Later in his writings, W.H.C. Frend presents a history of views on the origin of the church and its contact with Jews and Judaism[53] and concludes that there was a Jewish-Christian influence in the church there. His article on "*Seniores*" (mentioned above) is another part of the "evidence" Frend uses to support his argument. And yet, when the argument is complete, one is still left with ambiguity for the origin of the Christian Church in Carthage.[54]

At this point in his discussion, Frend, who is concerned that much research still needs to be done on the origins of the Church in North Africa, perpetuates the old consensus about Judaism and Christianity in the city; i.e., Christianity is a step higher than Judaism, by writing:[55] "perhaps Christianity came to North Africa in the Apostolic Age, brought by eastern merchants or

---

52(...continued)
and a Church was built over the site where the seven men and five women of Scillium "were executed by order of the proconsul Saturnias, for refusal to renounce Christianity," it is difficult to establish from this evidence much more than that a few Christians were martyred and later Christians (5th century) remembered them by building a church in Carthage on what was thought to be the site. No one knows where Scillium or Scilli was. Yet these *Acta* presuppose a wide dissemination of the Christian faith and quote from a Latin translation of the Bible. Hence there is a strong temptation to go further back and seek the ultimate origin of the Carthaginian church. Theories proliferate. "Perhaps Christianity came to Africa in the Apostolic Age, brought by eastern merchants or by Jews who made a pilgrimage to Jerusalem and had had the good fortune to hear from the first apostles 'speaking with tongues' at the first Pentecost. For does not the Bible say that apostles were heard by pilgrims from Libya (Acts 2.10)? Perhaps Christianity came a century or more later, in the Antonine Age, through the Jewish community of Carthage." This quote is from Barnes, *Tertullian*, 63-64. For Frend's support of the view that the Church grew out of the Jewish community in Carthage see Frend, *Martyrdom*, 361ff.

53 Frend, "Jews," 185-194.

54 Frend, "Jews," 193-194, continued his argument with these words: "Much research still needs to be done before problems relating to the origins of North African Christianity can be solved. Monceaux' view that the origins of the North African churches was not single or even double but multiple holds the field. Yet how these multiple origins produced a church so single-minded in its rigorism and acceptance of monarchial episcopacy is uncertain. More than any other community the North African Church was the 'Church of the Martyrs,' the most complete example of the 'gathered Church' in early Christianity. How did diverse origins produce this result? Solutions, however, require constructive rather than destructive criticism. It is to the lasting credit of professor Marcel Simon that he first established in detail the probable links between Judaism and Christianity in Carthage." See Simon, *Verus Israel*, 119-120 for this argument.

Another attempt to connect the origin and design of the church to the Jewish influence was made by Frend in 1976, this time using evidence of Christians (if they were indeed Christians) buried within a Jewish cemetery or Jews who were buried within a Christian cemetery. An early second-century contact between Jews and Christians in Carthage is suggested but not proved. (See Stanton, "Aspects," 381, n.25, where a connection is made between Jews and Christians by discussing the record in the *Acts of Philip* of a conversion of a Jew to Christianity.)

55 See Frend's discussion on this emphasis in *Rise*, 4.

by Jews *who had had the good fortune* [emphasis added] to hear the first apostles 'speaking with tongues' at the first Pentecost."[56]

This point of view seems to be a kind of Christian triumphalism that tends to romanticize the picture of emerging Christianity in Carthage. The more accurate statement from the evidence is that one cannot determine precisely how the Church began in that city.[57] What then can be said about the early Christians in Carthage? Several conclusions may be made based on the fragmentary evidence.[58]

(1) Christians were in every level of society. "Tertullian was writing for an audience which embraced every stratum of society. He, therefore, proffers advice to slaves, to freemen and to attendants in the service of a magistrate ... Equally a servant of God can become a magistrate or official, provided that he has not contact with sacrifices or temples."[59] He addressed the problems a Christian faced in his or her contact with the demands of the world on every social level. The cemeteries also provided evidence[60] of a multilevel involvement of Christians in Carthaginian society.

(2) The literary evidence suggests that the persecution of Christians in Carthage was done by the Romans.[61] *Ad Nationes*, according to Barnes, was an apologetic for Christianity during a time of persecution. Essentially, Tertullian argues that Christians were persecuted because "pagans are ignorant of what it is that they hate."[62] The *Apology* is aimed at informing them and therefore putting a stop to the persecutions.

According to some scholars the persecution was caused by the uncertain legality of Christianity in the second and third centuries C.E.[63] The persecution may be part of the reason for the lack of archaeological evidence of

---

56 Frend, *Martyrdom*, 361.

57 See Barnes, *Tertullian*, 71.

58 See Groh, "Upper Class," 47, for a summary.

59 Barnes, *Tertullian*, 99.

60 Frend, "Jews," 185-194.

61 See Barnes, *Tertullian*, 101. See also his "Tertullian the Antiquarian," *SP* 14 (=*TU* 117) (1976), 3-20, for more comments on Tertullian's ability with rhetoric and the use of Roman history for his own purposes.

62 Barnes, *Tertullian*, 104.

63 See Barnes, *Tertullian*, 103. "Christianity was illegal and its illegality was assumed or reaffirmed by every emperor of the second and early third centuries. Persecution, however, varied in its incidence and intensity, not according to the attitude of magistrates and the pagans whom they governed." See also *JRS* 58 (1968) 32ff. This writer concurs with the notion that there was some form of persecution of the Christians by the Romans in Carthage, but not as intense as assumed by some (Frend). There is no evidence to indicate that the Jews persecuted Christians there.

Christian buildings or markings in Carthage until 325 C.E. Roman "public works projects" may have also removed whatever evidence of Christian house-churches that might have been extant. Most scholars agree that there were no significant Christian buildings anywhere until after Constantine.[64] According to G. Snyder, Christians met in existing homes redesigned to be used as a house-church.[65]

It is also possible that Christians had to maintain a low profile in Carthage simply to survive. If they were being harassed in Carthage[66] then one can understand why they would attempt to stay out of sight.

(3) There is no discernible Christian section of the town before 400 C.E. All of the archaeological evidence gathered so far indicates a diverse population within the city, with a number of cemeteries nearly surrounding the city. It does not seem as though Carthage possessed any single exclusively Christian quarter, such as those existing in other towns, like Hippo Regius and Djemila (Cuicul).[67]

This may mean that there was no discernible or significant Christian presence in Carthage. It could be that Tertullian's Christian contemporaries were not especially significant in the affairs of the city. The so-called "persecutions" in the earlier part of the third century may be more the rhetoric of the authors than a description of an event or series of events. The presence of elaborate underground tombs suggests that the Christians desired to maintain a low profile even though some came from the upper classes in Carthage.[68]

---

64 G. Snyder, in *Ante Pacem*, suggests that Dura-Europos is the only pre-Constantinian *domus ecclesiae* we can confidently categorize as such (67). Otherwise he suggests that not until after Constantine were there any recognizable Christian structures. He considers this the third phase of emergent Christian evidence. The polemical or literary and the archaeological or nonliterary were the first and second phases (2).

65 See Snyder, *Ante Pacem*, 163ff.

66 Barnes, *Tertullian*, 110-112, 143ff., presents the literary evidence of persecution by Romans. He suggests that there were various persecutions, none of them methodical or long-lasting. But certainly there were no long periods of untroubled peace (158). See also Groh "Upper Class," 47 where he views the descriptions of the persecution of Christians in Tertullian's writings (44, 46, 47) as a way of discerning a middle- and upper-class social level in the Church. "But the *On Flight in Persecution* (212-213 A.D.) tells us in a very literary and abstract way about the churches of his own day, for it reflects a church in which individuals and whole communities can put wealth to work for their protection" (46). See *De Fuga in Persecutione* 12. Groh's approach to Tertullian's writings has helped establish one important way of uncovering a social problem facing some Christians in late second-early-third-century Carthage, which also has helped to establish the social composition of some of Tertullian's fellow Christians in Carthage.

67 Frend, "Early Christian," 28-30.

68 See Groh, "Upper-Class," 41-47 for his references to Tertullian's writings as a way of discerning the social composition of the Christians of Carthage. For comments about the available archaeological data about this period, see J.D. Pedley, *New Light on Ancient Carthage*, (Ann Arbor: The University of Michigan Press, 1980) and Ben Khader and D. Soren *Carthage*.

According to Groh, Tertullian struggled with the "meaning of social prominence and wealth for Christians."[69] This issue forced Tertullian to write a defense of those people who could pay their way out of persecution. Even though he was not writing to describe the social structure of Carthage, his arguments prepared the way for future upper-class Christians.

V. The Relationship between Christians and Jews in Carthage

There is an important difference between a discussion of the relationship of Christianity to Judaism and the relationship of Jews and Christians in Carthage during Tertullian's time. The first has to do with theological or religious concerns and questions, and the latter has to do with social and cultural issues. Often these issues are mixed, but unless one makes this distinction some important issues are missed. In this section this distinction is always an important one.

A. The "God-fearers" and Proselytes

As discussed in the Introduction of this book (Section III.B.1), scholars have long held that when a non-Jew visited a synagogue in the Diaspora to help support that Jewish institution or simply to visit it for any number of reasons, it was thought this was an indication that he or she had an intense interest in the religion of the Jews.[70]

The evidence from the Western Diaspora indicates that contact with Jews or a synagogue by the non-Jewish population is not always for religious reasons. Tertullian's *Answer* was written for that group which did have religious interest.

In the opening lines of *Answer* (1), Tertullian mentions having a dispute with a "Jewish proselyte."[71] In this case he is clear about the fact that he is talking with a convert to Judaism. This particular person has made contact with some Jews there for religious purposes.

In this case, Tertullian argues for the superiority of Christianity over Judaism in Carthage (or anywhere), and does it by using one who chose Judaism over Christianity.

---

69 Groh, "Upper-Class," 47.

70 A.T. Kraabel, "Roman Diaspora," 454, points out that that final element of the old consensus is the idea that "evidence about Jews of antiquity is best interpreted in the context of religion."

71 On the debate about "God-fearers" in the Diaspora, see MacLennan and Kraabel, "God-Fearers," 46-53. See Stern, *Authors* 2, 201. Stern states that the pagan writer Apuleius, from Carthage, was referring to the sect of God-fearers. Compare Stern's comments on Juvenal's *Saturae*; Stern, *Authors*, 2: 103. For a response to MacLennan and Kraabel, see R.Tannenbaum, "God-fearers," 54-57, and L. Feldman, "The Omnipresence of the God-Fearers," *BAR* 12.5 (1986): 58-63.

A proselyte is not necessarily a "God-fearer."[72] The proselyte is one who does have religious interests, while a God-fearer might have any number of reasons for associating with the synagogue or a community center where Jews would be present. Tertullian was trying to convince him to try the better way, i.e., Christianity.

It seems that if there were a large group of Gentiles who were interested in Judaism, as the "God-fearers" were supposed to be, then Tertullian would have introduced his *Answer* with another word for proselyte. It is clear, too, that a proselyte to Judaism has made a choice for Judaism and not Christianity.

This evidence does not help establish the relationship between Christians and Jews in Carthage as much as it indicates that Jews, like Christians, were actively encouraging converts to their tradition. Christianity and Judaism, according to Tertullian, were missionary religions.

The best way to talk about their relationship would be to say that they were in competition on one level with one another for converts.[73]

B. *Adversus Judaeos* and *Adversus Marcionem*

D. Efroymson[74] has shown that Tertullian is most anti-Jewish not in his *Adversus Judaeos* but in *Adversus Marcionem*. "Marcion's challenge and threat placed all the anti-Judaic themes in a new apologetic context, appending them to ideas of God and Christ in ways which come perilously close to permanence."[75] This statement quoted in S.G. Wilson's study of Anti-Judaism,[76] sums up the purpose of one of Tertullian's arguments in *Adversus Marcionem*, but not necessarily the purpose for all five chapters taken together.

Even though there are anti-Judaic themes in his writing against Marcion, Tertullian's main concern is in speaking against any heresy no matter where it may be found. He is trying to preserve the Christian community against all kinds of threats, including Judaism.

---

72 Stern, *Authors*, 2:201. Also see Stern, *Authors*, 2: 102-107 on the "God-fearers." See A. Overman, "God-Fearers," 17-26 for a discussion of the use of the terms "proselyte" and "*gerim*" in Hellenistic Judaism (the LXX and Philo) and a defense of the existence of Gentiles who were "God-Fearers" around the synagogues in the Diaspora.

73 Hirschberg, *History*, suggests that there were "(God-)fearing persons" "whose number was considerable" (53) and Jews were actively proselytizing (48ff.) and that Tertullian's *Answer* "gives details---no doubt historical---of a debate between a proselyte and some Christians as to whether Gentiles had part in the Divine blessings promised to Abraham's posterity (Genesis 22:18)," 75-76.

74 D.P. Efroymson, "Patristic," 100, 103-105. Efroymson states: "Against Marcion, it was simply Christianity that was defined or described in anti-Jewish ways; *God and Christ must be anti-Jewish too*" (105).

75 Ibid., 105.

76 S.G. Wilson, *Anti-Judaism*, 58.

Therefore a reading of these so-called *adversus Judaeos* writings does not necessarily indicate hostile relations between Jews and Christians in Carthage. Their purpose is, rather, to trace the outline of the issues Tertullian sees as important for a Christian interpretation of the biblical tradition. Jews and Gnostics both err.

C. "Jewish Legalism and Christian Legalism"

As it has already been pointed out above, it is a mistake to suggest that the *halakah*, in general, and the Mishnah's *Abodah Zarah*, in particular, are sources for Tertullian's *De idolatria*, and that "[t]he traditional 'legalism' of the African Church might be explained with reference to this [rabbinic] background as well as to the secular professions of its first leaders, Tertullian and Cyprian."[77] It does suggest an abiding misunderstanding of Christianity in Carthage on the part of some scholars to say that Judaism in Carthage was necessarily "rabbinic."[78]

Peter Brown, in his chapter "Approaches to the Religious Crisis of the Third Century," offers this insight for the problem of the Jewish influence as 'legalistic': "Men like Tertullian and Cyprian thought of themselves as having totally discontinued their previous life, and stressed the need to separate themselves from their previous environment."[79] This radical break with the past and search for a new expression for their behavior is likely to produce literature that seems to the outside observer as harsh and legalistic!

The source for Tertullian's so-called "legalism" was more likely Scripture and the pre-Christian gentile North African literary environment and certainly not the "legalisms" of rabbis.[80]

His enthusiastic writings were not meant to challenge Jews but were meant to stimulate his fellow Christians to take seriously their tradition. Jews who were serious about their own tradition need not be offended by his enthusiasm.

D. The Persecutions of Christians by Jews

Another way one might discover if Christians had contact with Jews in Carthage would be to determine to what extent, if at all, Jews persecuted Christians there. T.D. Barnes raises the question and refutes the arguments

---

77 See Frend, "Seniores," 284, and Barnes, *Tertullian*, 100-101.

78 See note 34 above for the few references to Carthage in the *Babylonian Talmud*. C. Aziza, *Tertullien*, 15-16 refers to references to Carthage in the Talmuds. Hirschberg, *History*, 40ff. and 74ff., uses the rabbinic *halakah* and *'aggadah* to reconstruct a Jewish community in Carthage.

79 Brown, *Religion and Society in the Age of Saint Augustine* (London, 1972): 82, 83, and 74.

80 T.D. Barnes has described Tertullian's background in pagan North Africa. See his study, *Tertullian*, 187-232.

regarding Jewish persecution of Christians. Essentially Barnes argues that some scholars still cite this famous utterance from *Scorpiace*:

"Will you plant there both synagogues of the Jews---fountains of persecution---before which the apostles endure the scourge, and heathen assemblages with their own circus, forsooth, where they readily join in the cry, Death to the third race (Christians)?"[81]

This quote is cited as proof that the Jews were prominent in fomenting the persecution of Christians in the Carthage of Tertullian's day.[82] Barnes then cites several sources who hold this view,[83] after which he counters their point of view with these comments:

> But that is to ignore, not merely the immediate context, but also a general characteristic of the writer. Tertullian is maintaining, against the Gnostics, that the Christians must be prepared to suffer for their faith here on earth, not just in heaven. The Gnostics' view entails that persecution and hatred will be encountered in heaven: hence the Gnostics must imagine that the Jews who persecuted the Apostles and the mobs howling in the amphitheater will be there, [in heaven] not here on earth. That is obviously false, and entails the falsity of the Gnostic position. Tertullian's choice of examples is careful and deliberate. The second [that is, the persecution of Christians by non-Jews] is the contemporary fact, the first [here a reference to the

---

81 *Scorpiace*, 10.10, trans. S. Thelwall. Simon, *Verus Israel*, 119, is suspicious of this (*Synagogas Judaeorum fontes persecutionum*) "epigrammatic" way of speaking. Barnes, "Tertullian's '*Scorpiace*.'" *JTS* 20 (1969): 128, suggests that *Scorpiace* was written 203 C.E. during the visit of Severus and during a time of persecution. Barnes also suggests (132) that Scorpiace, 10.10, does not implicate the Jews in the persecution (as Frend, *Martyrdom*, 334 concludes).

82 Barnes, "'*Scorpiace*,'" 132. See also Simon, *Verus Israel*, 119.

83 Frend, *Martyrdom*, 334. Barnes, *Tertullian*, 106, n.2. W.H.C. Frend, *Rivista di storia e letterature religiosa*, iv (1968) 8-9 where *Scorpiace* is used as evidence for the conduct of Jews in Carthage c. 212. Against the view is F. Millar, "The emperor, The Senate and the province," *JRS* 56 (1966): 234. See Frend, "Note on Jews," 92-96, which refutes Barnes. Frend holds on to the old view. See last lines of pages 95-96. ("The historical question is surely why in certain large cities in the empire, notably where the Jews assisted the pagans to execute Polycarp (a reference is given here by Frend to Eusebius *HE*, 4.15.26, 29, and 41) and co-operated with them against Pionius in the Decian persecution, and Carthage, and perhaps even Rome, there seems to have been an unusual degree of antipathy between the two monotheistic communities. Hitherto scholars, trusting in the catena of evidence derived from Justin, Tertullian, and Origen, may have been too sweeping in their assertion of almost universal hostility on the part of the Jews against the Christians during the second and early third centuries. There were many reasons, it has been pointed out, why the two communities should actually have co-operated in a common struggle against an oppressive and all-pervading pagan idolatry. There is little doubt, however, that in some areas this was by no means the case. Carthage was evidently one. Instead of attempting to dismiss '*synagogas Judaeorum, fontes persecutionum*' as fiction it would be more useful to try to explain why they continued for so long to be so." See also W.H.C. Frend, "The Persecutions: Some Links Between Judaism and the Early Church," *JEH* 9 (1958): 57-159, where he discusses the inevitability of Jewish-Christian conflict in the cities.

'reported' acts of persecution of Christians by Jews in Acts] is an earliest persecution of the Christians. Tertullian is employing a favorite mode of argument: he focuses attention on the origins of persecution. For he held that what was true of our object's origin was necessarily always true of the object itself: *onme genus ad originens suum censeatum necesse est* (*Praes. Haer.* 20.7).[84]

These textual analyses lead to the conclusion that Tertullian uses biblical (New Testament) images when he writes to his contemporaries about Jewish persecution. Jews were not persecuting Christians in Carthage during 197 C.E. or during the time of Tertullian's earlier works (197-202 C.E.).[85]

VI. The *Answer to the Jews*

A. A Biblical Commentary

Based on the new approach to the text and a reading of the *Answer* itself, it appears that Tertullian wrote his *adversus Judaeos* not to castigate Jews or Judaism in Carthage of the late second or early third centuries C.E., but as a kind of commentary on the superiority of Christianity over biblical Judaism. The audience was those Christians in North Africa who needed encouragement in the face of possible persecution from Roman authorities.

He moved from the biblical text in his arguments in the *Answer* to some unidentifiable context and audience. If he was thinking about the Jews at all, it was those Jews who suffered the consequences of their rejection of Christ by themselves being exiled from their land and suffering infamy.

> On your account the name of God is blasphemed among the Gentiles: for it is from them that the infamy (attached to that name) began, and (was propagated during) the interval from Tiberius and Vespasian. And because they had committed these crimes, and had failed to understand that Christ was to be found in the time of their

---

84 Barnes, "Tertullian's," 134 and 132. D.M. Scholer, "Tertullian on Jewish Persecution of Christians," *SP* 17.2 (1982): 821, agrees that the relevant texts (*Scorpiace* 10.10; *Ad Nationes* 1.14.1-2; *Apologeticum* 21.25 and 7.3; *Adversus Judaeos* 13.26) do not constitute evidence that Jews contemporary to Tertullian were either persecuting Christians or acting as instigators or persecutions against Christians." Scholer concludes: "Although these contexts represent Tertullian's strong anti-Judaism, they refer either to Jewish persecutions in the apostolic period or the enmity between Jews and Christians short of persecution or to both" (825-826). Scholer ends his argument by pointing out that in Tertullian's writings, when reference is made to a persecution it is always pre-Nero (see n.34, 828); and therefore not relevant to the relation of Jews and Christians in second- and third-century Carthage.

85 See the comment in *De Fuga in Persecutione*, 6.2. Simon, *Verus Israel*, 120 does not completely exonerate some Jews who were in a position to persecute Christians both in Palestine and in the Diaspora.

visitation, their land has been made desert and their cities utterly burnt with fire, while strangers devour their region in their sight.[86]

It is also clear that Tertullian does not speak directly to or about Jews living in his town. Some scholars have mentioned the fact that Tertullian never speaks about Jews as "you" but always as "them"; so there were never direct comments made about the Jews in his *Answer*.[87] From beginning to end in his *Answer*, Tertullian was engaged in a sophisticated biblical commentary which was not actually directed against contemporary Jews or Judaism[88] but against those "Biblepeople" who refused to accept Jesus as their Messiah.

Tränkle's suggestion that Tertullian's *Answer* was "*Scheinpolemik*" might be more in keeping with the original intention of the document or "dispute." This seems to substantiate the notion that some purpose other than a direct confrontation with Jews was intended.

Much of the argumentation in the *Answer* was a typically Christian "New Testament" polemic against the Jews and appears to have been borrowed in whole or in part from similar arguments in Barnabas, Justin, or Irenaeus.[89] As one studies these so-called *adversus Judaeos* texts, one can see many of the same arguments that appear in the biblical texts.[90] The similarities in subject matter and use of scriptural references substantiate this viewpoint.

B. Jewish or Rabbinic Influences on the *Answer*

It has been accepted by most textual critiques that, of this text at least, the first eight chapters were written sometime in the first ten years of the third century C.E.[91] It seems to be a writing that came from a time when Christians

---

86 *Answer* 13.26. See also the same ideas in 10.19; 11.11, and 13.26-29.

87 Barnes *Tertullian*, 107. See also Efroymson "Tertullian."

88 This is contrary to Rosemary Ruether's *Faith and Fratricide: The Theological Roots of Anti-Semitism* (New York: Seabury, 1974), 119, 126, 133, 139. A.L. Williams's comment on the text that "there was therefore sufficient reason for the *Adversus Judaeos* to be composed, both as a protection to Christians and as a means of winning Jews" (*Adversus Judaeos*, 43) is concerned about the contemporary situation and may be only partially true to the intention of the text.

89 Tränkle, *Tertulliani*, lxxiv.

90 See the discussion of this issue about Justin Martyr in Barnard, *Justin*, 22, 45, and 153, where there is a similar use of image in Justin's *Dialogue* (xl.4-5) and Tertullian's *Adversus Judaeos* (xiv.). Also see Schreckenberg, *Adversus-Judaeos-Texte*, 217, where he supports Tränkle. The conclusions and images which each of these writers use are so close, it is difficult to argue against the collective use of ideas about Jews and Judaism. These ideas have been referred to in each of the chapters above.

91 Tränkle would argue for the integrity of all 14 chapters, *Tertulliani*, xi-lxxxviii. But he does not dispute the date.

were under much pressure, either through direct persecution (by the Romans[92]) or some form of internal conflict.[93] The *Answer* gives one the impression of having been either hurriedly written or incomplete. If it was written during a time when Jews were putting pressure on Christians, for some reason, then why (to agree with Barnes) was it set aside?

The relationship between some of Tertullian's writings, especially his "On Idolatry," and the rabbinic writing *Abodah Zarah* has been suggested above. It was shown that the connection is highly unlikely, since they only *appear* to be dealing with the same subject but in fact are quite different. *Abodah Zarah* dealt with Jewish behavior within a pagan culture, while "On Idolatry" was dealing with Christian identity within a pagan culture.[94]

C. The *Answer* as Greek Rhetoric

As a form of Christian rhetoric, the *Answer* is something more than a polemic against the Jews in Carthage; it is a theological treatise which used the Jews (especially "New Testament" Jews, or the "Biblepeople") to prove a point in favor of Christianity; that is, Christianity was seen as superior to and as superseding Judaism.[95]

The thirteenth chapter of the *Answer* offers a supersessionistic view of Christianity over Judaism and Jews. Tertullian writes that "Israel has fallen away" (13.13), and then he quotes from various parts of the Old Testament and New: "Undoubtedly by not receiving Christ, the 'font of water of life,'[96] they have begun to have 'worn out tanks,'[97] that is, synagogues for the use of

---

[92] See the discussions of the persecution of Christians in Scillium or North Africa above. See also *De Fuga in Persecutione* 6.2: "Yes and if we are apprehended, we shall not be brought into Jewish councils, nor scourged in Jewish synagogues, but we shall certainly be cited before Roman magistrates and judgment-seats." This text indicates the source of the Christians' persecution in Carthage.

[93] See Efroymson, "*Tertullian's Anti-Judaism and its role in his Theology*," 208; Barnes, *Tertullian*, 102, and Frend, *Martyrdom*. Compare Scholer, "Tertullian," and Barnes, *Tertullian*, 107, where Barnes suggests that Tertullian in *Adversus Judaeos* actually was irrelevant to the real circumstances of Christians of Carthage and he put it aside as unfinished.

[94] Frend, "Jews," 191-192. Another argument by Frend, discussed above, was that the structure of the Church's government in Carthage indicated an influence of "legalistic" Judaism (Frend, "*Seniores*," 283-284). This so-called legalism of the Church in North Africa was seen as proof for a direct connection between the Church and rabbinic Judaism, and therefore was used as substantial evidence of the influence of Judaism on Christianity in Carthage. This unlikely connection has already been discussed above.

For an argument similar to Frend's see Hirschberg, *History*, 40-79.

[95] See Sider, *Ancient Rhetoric*, 126 and 129.

[96] Cf. John 4.10 and 11.

[97] See Jeremiah 2.13

'dispersion of Gentiles,' in which the Holy Spirit no longer lingers . . ."[98] Apparently the synagogue was viewed as no longer useful for its original purpose; it was worn out. Tertullian continues with these words: "[W]e, of course, who have succeeded to, and occupy, the room of the prophets, at the present day sustain in the world that treatment which the prophets always suffered on account of divine religion. . . . "[99]

Tertullian was arguing from a biblical text to establish theological and biblical support for the Christians in Carthage, a kind of *raison d'etre* for the Church, rather than trying to make a social or theological statement against Jews.

David Efroymson went further[100] when he demonstrated how "Jewish" became a symbol of everything that was wrong or untrue.[101] As one reads Tertullian's works, including his *Answer*, one is aware that Tertullian has taken a further step in his understanding of the designation "Jewish." He was not concerned with those Jews living in his neighborhood, but rather with writing about an adversary whom he calls "Jewish." That adversary could be any group or individual of any nationality who held an inadequate view of Jesus and his work in the world.[102]

Therefore it has been easy for most scholars who hold to the old consensus about Jews and Judaism in late antiquity, to take the step from Tertullian's symbolic use of the word "Jewish" to actual Jews living in Carthage.[103]

D. The *Answer* was written for the Nations

Simply stated, Tertullian's purpose in his *adversus Judaeos* writing known as the *Answer to the Jews*, and in his other so-called anti-Jewish writings,[104] was to make clear that Gentiles would eventually join with the Jews of the

---

98 *Answer* 13.15.

99 *Answer* 13.19; also, 4.1-5; 5.1; 6.1; 9.21; 10.6.

100 See Efroymson, "Rhetoric," 25-35.

101 Ibid. 25.

102 Ibid. 25-26.

103 Efroymson's point is that Tertullian has created "a Christian symbol-system defined or expressed in relation to, in opposition to, Judaism. There is a *God* who for centuries wanted to rid himself of Jews, and who now expects more, and better of Christians; a *Christ* whose teaching and ministry are spent in conflict with Jews, and who functions now as a symbol of Judaism's demise and Christianity's superiority . . . " Ibid., 35. Efroymson goes on to conclude with a similar statement about the Law and the Church. One problem with his argument is his failure to make a distinction between the religion (Judaism, against which Tertullian was writing) and the people (Jews, against whom Tertullian was not writing).

104 See Efroymson, "Patristic," 98-117 for a complete discussion of Tertullian's anti-Jewish view in his writings.

Bible as the new people of God. Some time later, Jews would be replaced by this new people of God through the New Covenant.

The *Answer* reports that the Old Covenant given to Israel is no longer valid or binding.[105] There are a number of passages in the *Answer* which support the argument that Tertullian's anti-Jewish writing is indeed not so much against Jews as it is for the nations; against, perhaps, Marcion or other suspect "Christians," using Jews of the New Testament as a kind of "Biblepeople" to make his point.[106]

Tertullian confirms this fact at the very beginning of his *Answer*:

> For the occasion, indeed, of claiming Divine grace even for the gentiles derived a preeminent fitness from this fact, that the man [the *proselyto Iudaeo*] who set up to vindicate God's Law as his own was of the Gentiles, and not a Jew.[107]

It may be true to say that "anti-Judaism, then, can be defined as what Tertullian says about Jews."[108] But it is also important to suggest that the *Answer* itself was not written for the purpose of degrading Jews, or creating anti-Judaism among Christians.

Contact with Jews in the second century was limited and not the cause for Tertullian's writing his *Answer to the Jews*. It is more likely that Tertullian was concerned to define Christian uniqueness and possibly bring that *proselyto Iudaeo* to the Church. For Tertullian, this definition grew out of New Testament sources.

VII. Conclusion

From the extant evidence, the following comments can be made about the relationship between Jews and Christians in late second- early third-century Carthage:

First, the literary evidence suggests that Tertullian did not need intimate contact with or knowledge of Jews and Judaism in order to write his *Answer to the Jews*. Not only was he writing to a pagan proselyte (1.1-3) to Judaism but he was addressing his comments to the biblically literate non-Jew from the

---

105 Efroymson, *"Tertullian's Anti-Judaism and its role in his Theology,"* 135.

106 See *Answer*, 17.1-9; 14.12; 6.1-4; 13.13; 13.19; 1.1-4; 13.14-16.

107 *Answer*, 1.2. Tertullian continues this line of argument by using the typological commentary of the two children in the womb of Rebecca. The first (the Jews) would be the last. The second (the Gentiles) would be the first. "[T]he prior and 'greater' people—that is the Jewish—must necessarily serve the 'less'; and the 'less' people—that is, the Christian—overcome the 'greater' (1.5).

108 Gaston, "Retrospect," 163.

pages of the biblical text. Tertullian was writing a kind of biblical commentary about the people of the Bible.[109]

Therefore it was not necessary for Tertullian to know Jews or to have knowledge about contemporary Judaism in order to challenge his readers.[110] One of the issues in the *Answer* was the thought that Judaism had lost its vitality,[111] and the synagogue was no longer lively after the Jews rejected Jesus as their Messiah, an issue within the New Testament as well as in the Hebrew

---

109 Barnes, *Tertullian*, 106, 107, suggests that Tertullian's *Adversus Judaeos* belongs to the same period as *Ad Nationes* (see Tränkle, *Tertulliani*, xxxvi; liii) and is far more obviously unfinished. It took its inception from a lengthy argument between a Christian and a Jewish proselyte, which suffered from the interruptions of ignorant bystanders. The Christian (it may plausibly be deduced) was Tertullian, himself and he decided to settle the question in writing with careful reference to the evidence of the Bible. The audience which he envisaged was not the Jewish community of Carthage, but sympathetic pagans who might be confronted by missionary efforts from both religions. Could this mean that Christians related to the Jews indirectly, as competitors, for example, who were seeking the same group of people for conversion? Or, as Barnes continues, the calculation (of the seventy weeks of Daniel's prophecy (9.24) as ending with the destruction of the Temple in the first year of the reign of Vespasian) had an academic flavor, and Tertullian realized that the *Adversus Judaeos* was irrelevant to the real situation of Christians in Carthage. [In other words Christians had little contact with Jews in Carthage and were not being persecuted by them. They also were not interested in what the contemporary Jews were doing but had already in this early period viewed them as a "Bible-people.] So he put his *Answer* aside unfinished. [See comment by Barnes, *Tertullian*, 53.] Tertullian had more important business to do. Pagan hostility entailed persecution" (107). This does not necessarily prove substantial contact. But, it is possible to suggest that Tertullian did not have an interest in speaking against Jews, or answering them. He probably wanted to answer someone else; Marcion perhaps? See the provocative suggestion in Gaston, "Retrospect," 163-164.

110 Efroymson, "*Tertullian's Anti-Judaism and its role in his Theology*," 62, 63. Efroymson makes these comments at the end of one of his chapters: "And the Jews are not those in the synagogue on the outskirts of Carthage; they are the Jews in Tertullian's imagination."

"This is not to say that there were no Jews in Carthage. They were there; their synagogue and their cemetery were visible, and Tertullian could not have been unaware of their existence. Nor is it to suggest that Tertullian was completely ignorant of post-biblical Judaism; he seems to have had some information, but nothing which would demand any significant personal contact".

"So Tertullian's anti-Judaism is an inheritance from his Christian and Roman African roots. But if he did not really know any Jews, if there were no personal confrontations and disputations with living Jews to keep this inheritance from wasting away, what kept it alive? Briefly, it can be argued that he grew to *need* anti-Judaism: he needed Jews and Judaism as a kind of anti-type to nearly everything he was and stood for. This can be demonstrated in the *uses* to which he puts his anti-Judaism. He uses it rhetorically to win arguments against his opponents, and he uses it theologically, or symbolically, to construct a Christianity, a Christian social identity which is centrally, crucially, un-Jewish, anti-Jewish, and better-than Jewish." (63-64). Earlier, Efroymson points out that Tertullian never talks directly to the Jews in his writings (63) but always indirectly, which indicates no contact. It seems that these comments suggest that Tertullian, at least, and possibly the other *adversus Judaeos* literature, is simply inventing phantom Jews to support arguments for the Christian faith.

111 Efroymson, "*Tertullian's Anti-Judaism and its role in his Theology*," 223.

Scriptures.¹¹² Tertullian could simply tell his listeners stories from the Bible to prove his point.¹¹³ He did not have to make contact with Jews in Carthage in order to draw his conclusions. In fact, it was probably better that he did not have anything to do with them, so that he could avoid facing a vital Judaism in Carthage.

Persecution of Christians, either by the Romans or as a result of some Jews encouraging the Romans to persecute them, may be another reason for avoiding social contact. This contact was more than likely negative. Barnes suggests that Tertullian's *Scorpiace* and some of his other works were written during a time when Christians were experiencing some form of persecution.¹¹⁴

Second, it is clear from the archaeological evidence that Christians and Jews were living in every level of society in the Roman cities of the late second century. Contact between Christians and Jews would be inevitable and of different kinds.¹¹⁵ But this does not mean that Christians and Jews were in a constant dialogue with each other over theological topics. It is likely that there was more contact between pagans and Jews, and Christians and pagans, than between Christians as Christians and Jews as Jews. In other words, the contact between these two groups does not mean that they related to each other through their religious traditions.¹¹⁶

There were many other reasons for being in contact with each other. Commerce, government, education and cultural activities (although this kind of activity would be limited when the "gods" were being honored in public rituals), and possibly burial rites provide a portrait of lively interaction between Jews and Christians.¹¹⁷ The ordinary contact between people in a large city was probably more likely.

Constantine was the first emperor who ordered the building of churches throughout the empire,¹¹⁸ so it would be unlikely that by the end of the second century significant church structures would be found in Carthage. What is difficult to understand, though, is why there is such a large cemetery in Carthage with a number of Jews and Christians buried there and no evidence of a synagogue.

---

112 See *Answer* 13.

113 See Barnes, *Tertullian*, 106-107 and the full footnote above on this same matter.

114 Barnes, "*Scorpiace*," 128.

115 See Groh, "Upper-Class," 41-47; Pedley, *New Light*, and Ben Abed and Soren ed., *Carthage*.

116 This is contrary to Hirschberg's view. See *History*, Chapter 1.

117 See Barnes, *Tertullian*, 271-273.

118 See G. Snyder, *Ante Pacem*, 67ff., and R. Krautheimer, *Early Christian*.

The speculation at this point is that there were synagogues and perhaps some Christian structures, which were dismantled and used to rebuild and repair other buildings, public and private, throughout Carthage.[119]

The cemetery becomes one important part of the "text" of the city. As one uses the cemetery (cautiously) as evidence for the relation between Jews and Christians, one can surmise that there might have been amicable relations between some Jews and Christians in the city.

After all, one group does not invite another to bury its dead in its own tombs unless there has been some kind of friendly contact in the past. In fact, the evidence that Christians and Jews buried their dead in the same plots suggests that there were more than hostile feelings between the two groups. This would also indicate that it was only some Jews who supported the persecution of Christians, if, indeed, any did.

Both the literary and archaeological evidence so far discovered has been interpreted to indicate that there may have been some kind of competition between Christians and Jews. Some have suggested that it was hostile and based on a feeling of competition for converts to Judaism or Christianity.[120] This argument tends to perpetuate the old consensus that Jews are to be seen in religious terms and that they would naturally be upset because of competition for converts to their tradition.

The evidence does not allow for this position. If there was any kind of competition in Carthage, though, it would have been over the reasonableness or appropriateness of Tertullian's arguments against a Jewish interpretation of Scripture. It is likely that some Jews who cared enough to listen to Tertullian might have objected to his view that Judaism is an archaic superstition.

Barnes[121] is clear that Tertullian's knowledge of Jewish customs and ideas is totally superficial and that he was ignorant of contemporary Judaism.[122] Tertullian knew neither Hebrew, nor the writings of the rabbis of the later (c. 225 C.E.) Mishnah. This notion supports Efroymson's views[123] and represents the basic position of this book.

---

119 See Barnes, "*Scorpiace.*"

120 According to Simon, *Verus Israel*, 316-355, 482-488; R.L. Wilken, "Judaism in Roman and Christian Society," *JR* 47 (1967): 313; Hirschberg, *History*, 72; and Efroymson, "*Tertullian's Anti-Judaism and its role in his Theology*," 70, n.5.

121 Barnes, *Tertullian*, 92.

122 Ibid. 107.

123 See Efroymson, "*Tertullian's Anti-Judaism and its role in his Theology*," 56, 62, 63. But see Hirschberg, *History*, 40-79.

CONCLUSION

Adversus Judaeos (against Jews) is the phrase traditionally used to describe those early Christian writings of late antiquity which tried to prove that Christianity was superior to Judaism. Few modern scholars have questioned the intention of these early writings; in fact most have themselves until quite recently perpetuated the notion of superiority.

But during the last three decades (1960 to the present), new evidence has been discovered and new methodologies for reviewing the evidence have been developing, which present the Jewish Diaspora (Jews living outside Palestine) of late antiquity in a light which has made scholars reconsider the purpose and meaning of Jewish and Christian texts of late antiquity. In the process of their studies, scholars have revised their ideas about the Jews and Judaism, resulting in a reconsideration of the relationship between early Christianity and Judaism.

The old assumptions and the old consensus about Jews, Judaism, and Christianity no longer satisfy the careful student of late antiquity. Literary analysis of the texts studied in this book is, in and of itself, inadequate for an understanding of these texts, and so the methodologies of the sociologists, anthropologists, archaeologists and other academic disciplines have supplemented the traditional study of Biblical, early Christian, and rabbinic writings. The purpose and meaning of these writings have been assessed in the light of the new evidence and methodologies. As a result of Jews' and Christians' study of each other's texts, as well as increased contact between the two groups, changes have come about in our view of Jews, Judaism, Christianity, and the relationship between the two groups that has altered our perceptions of the "other."

My concern in this book has been with the purpose and meaning of some of the earliest and most influential of the so-called *adversus Judaeos* texts: Barnabas's *Epistle of Barnabas*, Justin's *Dialogue with Trypho the Jew*, Melito's *Paschal Homily*, and Tertullian's *Answer to the Jews*.

These texts represent writings from various cities of the Mediterranean world and are from the same century. They were also very influential in the early and later Christian writings about Jews and Judaism. In fact, some (Gaston, "Retrospect," 163) would suggest that "[a]nti-Judaism, then, can be defined as what Tertullian says about Jews." This statement could also apply to the other writers as well: Justin, Barnabas, and Melito have influenced the way later Christian theologians and apologists think about Jews and Judaism.

Even today, these texts are still being used by the Church to define the questions which should be raised between Christians and Jews, even though much scholarly work has been done to present different questions and issues. For example, discussions on the floor of the General Assembly of the Presbyterian Church (USA) in Biloxi, Mississippi, as recently as June 1987, about the paper "A Theological View of Christians and Jews" seemed to echo arguments presented in the *adversus Judaeos* writings of the second century.

A problem is created when those ancient texts are used by modern Christians to propagate prejudice or create false impressions about Jews and Judaism. The New Testament, an ancient first-second century text itself, has been wrongly used as a history book in the modern sense. Modern scholars still create the history of the Church from these texts.

Reading about the Jews through the lens of the New Testament or the second-century *adversus Judaeos* writings only tells the reader the writers' views of Jews. Raising concerns about the historical value of certain reports and seeking ways to understand the context in which the New Testament was written enables the reader to discover the original intent of the authors.

In a recent article in *Biblical Archaeological Review*, A.T. Kraabel and I made the following comment: "New Testament writers were not trying to tell their readers what they already knew, namely, the facts surrounding the events of the early Church. These writers were not trying to describe the events that had occurred. They were interested, rather, in *interpreting* the meaning of those events for their readers only. They wanted to tell why the church existed, what the Cross meant, why Jesus was the Messiah, why there was a split between the Jewish Christian movement and Jews. Their concern was not simply to give an account of what happened, but rather to provide an interpretive portrait in words of the events surrounding the origin of the Church. The New Testament is not so much a history book, in a modern sense, as a collection of early Christian sermons and letters," (MacLennan and Kraabel, "Invention", 51).

The intention of my book is to suggest that, in light of the new archaeological evidence and methodologies, we can no longer read the *adversus Judaeos* writings as if they were designed to be understood universally. Rather, we must reconsider them in the light of the cities themselves as "texts," the cities in which they were written, and the specific audiences to which they were addressed.

It almost seems simplistic to suggest that we put the writings back into their original setting and then reread them there; yet without doing that, we are free to interpret them in any way we want. When we place them back in their original setting (insofar as one can do that), the city of origin becomes another text which, when examined from the perspective of archaeological and other evidence, reveals more clearly the intention of the second-century author of the writing.

We must ask straightforward questions about each city. What do we know about the city? How would the character of the city and the events in that city in the second century affect the author? What does the city tell us about the Jews and the Christians there? How large were the Jewish, Christian, or pagan populations in the city? Is there any information about the relationship between Christians and Jews in that city? What other information seems important for an understanding of how the author would feel or what he would think as a citizen of or visitor to that particular city?

In a way, New Testament scholars have concerned themselves about the context for decades. They have wondered about the "life situation" of the text, and examined the background to the questions raised in the Biblical texts. Recent scholars have provided contextual studies, placing each letter of Paul, for example, more deeply into a city or region (W. Meeks). Examining a text in the light of a context is not new to Biblical scholars.

But for some reason these works have not made, until recently, an impact on those who study the early Christian and Jewish texts of late antiquity. I began my research determined to take advantage of the new methodologies. The results are in the body of this book.

There were problems with this approach which still have not been solved. How, for example, does one allow a city to "speak"? How does one know that the questions are the right questions? Are the cities I have chosen the right ones? How, for instance, do I know that Barnabas was a native or resident of Alexandria, living there from 113 to 137 C.E., and not in Yavneh in 98 C.E., as Shukster and Richardson have suggested?

The reasons for matching the cities to the authors were given more complete attention in the text of the book, but here it is important to mention that I based my decision to choose each city on the basis of scholarly information and suggestions; the cities are the most plausible and useful for this study. Even though it is not possible to establish for sure the city in which a particular text was conceived or written, much can be learned about the authors and the writings when one has a knowledge of the cities close enough to the origin of the texts.

After I identified the cities which were the most plausible, I then examined some of the characteristics of those cities, and the evidence they provided for the presence of and relationship between Jews and Christians. The results varied. Some are rich with information about the Jews and Pagans (Sardis); others are not as complete (Neapolis).

What seems to be self-evident is that Barnabas, Justin, Melito, and Tertullian wrote their *adversus Judaeos* to particular people in a specific time and place. They were not simply writing in a vacuum, about universal truths. Further, each of them was a leader in his community. It is reasonable to assume, then, that as a leader in the church, he had a congregation, those in his charge with whom he worked to discover what it meant to be a Christian. These writings, therefore, are not abstract dissertations, but purposeful statements written with passion.

The following summary presents the conclusions I have reached based on my research into the cities and the texts:

In Chapter One, I located Barnabas in Alexandria, Egypt. Even though there is much literary evidence about this city in late antiquity, there is very little archaeological evidence about the Jews and Christians in that city until the late fourth century. Nevertheless, the city of Alexandria provided a very lively text for the study of the *Epistle*.

As I began to search for information about the Jews and Christians in Alexandria, I pieced together some of the trauma of that city in the early second century. Barnabas was faced with many disruptions during his time there. The cultural climate of early and mid-second century, as well as the social chaos of Alexandria, must have made an impression on him.

Also, Alexandria had a large Jewish population that was protected by Roman law. This fact affected Jews differently; not every citizen appreciated his privileged position. This legal status guaranteed that Jews had a secure place in the city during the second century. Barnabas benefited from this legal status.

The evidence indicates that the Jews were active in the cultural life of the city. Jews were found in every level of society. Inscriptions and papyri suggest that Jews made an impact on the city.

However, they were also fighting among themselves. As in every society and group, there are always factions which struggle for position, status, and power. Some were trying to assimilate into the culture of Alexandria; others tried to maintain their uniqueness. Some were caught up in radical and fanatical movements in the city, while others hoped to go unnoticed.

In 115-117 and 134-135 C.E., tragedy struck the Jewish communities of Palestine and North Africa, including Alexandria. The revolt of Jews in Cyrenaica, and later in Palestine under Bar-Kokhba, proved devastating to Jews in those particular locations. Large numbers of Jews disappeared from the cities in North Africa where revolts took place (see Smallwood, *Jews*, 409, 412).

During this time some Jews, both in Palestine and other cities of the Diaspora, hoped for a messianic or military leader to restore their sole jurisdiction over their own land and the rebuilding of the Temple. R. Akiba, in Palestine, thought that Bar-Kokhba was one of those persons. Jews continued to hope for the rebuilding of the Temple in Jerusalem. Alexandrian Jews were affected by this messianic excitement.

This evidence from Alexandria, and the numbers and varieties of Jews in the city, led me to conclude that the occasion of the *Epistle* (contrary to Shukster and Richardson) might be Barnabas's reaction against an emerging "fanatical Jewish messianism," fanned by either the hope of rebuilding the Temple in Jerusalem (c.113) or the coming revolt in 115.

If this was the case, then Barnabas was trying to tell his readers, and perhaps some Jewish converts, that in these "evil days" (the days of fanaticism), God's people were followers of Jesus who did not allow themselves to swerve from the truth into the "wicked ways" of those who put their "hope on the building, and not on God."

Barnabas believed that he was teaching a moderate kind of messianic Judaism which had been manifest in Jesus. Therefore, the *Epistle* was not so much an anti-Jewish writing as an antisectarian writing.

In other words, Barnabas was fighting for the life of emerging Christianity, which followed some early form of moderate messianic Jewish teaching. The *Epistle*, then, is evangelistic and apologetic---not anti-Jewish. It seeks to clarify and define Christianity as a moderate messianic form of Judaism rather than to degrade Jews.

Chapter Two deals with Justin and his unique contribution to the *adversus Judaeos* corpus. This uniqueness is principally related to the fact that Justin had intimate contact with three cities: Neapolis in Samaria, Rome, and Ephesus. It was important to look at each of the cities in turn and to gain from them what they might have contributed, as texts, to Justin's view of himself, his Christian tradition, and his perspective on Jews and Judaism.

Most studies of Justin deal with the "Jewish" content of his writings. Many discuss only his biblical commentary and Christian ideas, which leave out the fact that Justin was a cosmopolitan person. Each of these cities influenced his thinking.

Neapolis, a Roman diplomatic outpost in Palestine, provided a brief study of the Samaritan influence on Justin and his writings. Many scholars have pointed out the "Samaritanisms" in his writings, but no one has suggested that Samaritan theology might have influenced the way he looked at or understood Jews and Judaism. The questions he asked and the feelings he had about the Jews are, I propose, a result of his childhood experience with Samaritans.

Trypho, who is supposed to be a rabbi in the *Dialogue*, is not a typical rabbi. He was certainly not the one who followed Bar-Kokhba in the revolt against the Romans in 132-135, as R. Akiba did. He seems to be one of those moderates in the tradition of Johanan ben Zakkai (c.70). I suggest that Trypho is portrayed this way because of Justin's childhood memories of rabbis or other Jewish leaders he and his family had known or possibly heard about from his neighbors in Neapolis.

Ephesus, like Sardis, had a large Jewish population. This would certainly have affected Justin's view of Jews. It was a place with a long history of public lectures and debates in which teachers and philosophers would discuss their ideas. It was a center for Greek culture and philosophy. It would make sense to write a *Dialogue* in a form that would appeal to the Ephesians.

The archaeological and historical evidence, which is abundant, suggests that Justin would have had much freedom to make his case in Ephesus. I was also impressed with the fact that there was no mention of Paul in any of Justin's writings. Ephesus was a place where Paul had visited and been jailed. Why does Justin not mention Paul? Perhaps Paul's way of relating to Jews did not make sense to Justin any longer. Perhaps the writings of Paul were not as influential among some Christian groups or as important to Justin's work. Or, it is possible that Christianity was far more diverse in the late first and mid-second century than some have thought.

The city of **Rome**, where Justin taught and led a school, was another context that helped to form his ideas about Jews and Judaism. The city was also host to a number of schools within the Christian movement and groups that did not always get along. The evidence demonstrates diversity among Jews and Judaism in Rome. It is possible that these various Christian groups each had their own view of Jews and Judaism.

This diversity among the Jews and Christians in Rome certainly made an impact on Justin. How could he write a treatise or a dialogue about monolithic Christianity and Judaism when there were so many different kinds of Jews and Christians? The answer seems to be that Justin was concerned about those

Christians and Jews he encountered in his travels, and not the many others who were wrestling with their own situation.

This would mean that he had to deal selectively with both groups. He had to set out his own definitions and limit his discussions to those parts of Judaism and Christianity which, in his view, were the most legitimate.

After examining the data of the cities, I concluded that the *Dialogue* would best be described as an apologetic essay written to one of several groups: a Christian school or a house church in which Justin participated as a teacher.

The *Dialogue* is best understood not as a hostile anti-Jewish writing but, rather, as an essay dealing with a particular kind of Jew and Judaism known to Justin, possibly even created out of his own memory of Jews and Judaism in Samaria. It is with this phantom Jew, a composite of Jews from Rome, Ephesus, and Neapolis, that Justin carries on his dialogue.

Chapter Three examined **Sardis**, the city in which Melito lived; it is rich in archaeological data but poor in literary evidence. Through archaeological studies, Sardis has opened the way for a fresh look at Jews and Judaism in the second century. No longer is it possible to hold the view of Harnack, and others who hold to the old consensus, that Judaism was not vibrant during the second century. A new view of Jews and Judaism in the Diaspora has emerged as a result of the newly gathered data from Sardis and other cities of late antiquity.

We know now, and the Sardis evidence is helpful in this regard, that the Jews maintained an impressive presence, at least at some locations, in the Diaspora. They did not assimilate completely into the culture. Neither did they separate themselves totally from the culture. They were a presence that had to be dealt with, and were often in the center of the town or took some significant part in the life of the community. Jews were not ghettoized or hiding somewhere outside of the city. They were "at home" in Sardis.

The archaeological evidence for Sardis is that the Jews of Sardis were integrated into the Sardian culture. They were seen as more than a religious group. Their synagogue was used for religious purposes, but it was not limited to that use. It is more precise to say that the synagogue was a community center in which a variety of activities took place, only one of which would be the reading and study of Torah. Therefore, those non-Jews who associated themselves with the synagogue were not necessarily there for religious reasons.

Very few Jews were rabbinic, nor were they all influenced by the rabbis of the Mishnah, even though many have thought they were. In the *adversus Judaeos* writings themselves, there are "other" Jewish influences present, including Jewish sectarians. Some have suggested that early rabbinic Judaism was itself a sectarian movement within the Jewish culture. It is essential that we not think of all Jews as being influenced by or interested in the rabbinic form of Judaism.

In the context of such a diverse and important movement as Judaism seemed to be in Sardis, it is understandable why Melito would be concerned in his *Homily* to distinguish Christianity from Judaism.

Conclusion

Therefore, it seems from the evidence that it would be appropriate to conclude that Melito wrote to plead the case for Christianity against a venerable Judaism. It is likely that the small and not well-developed Christian presence in Sardis would try to find something "evil" or "satanic" about such a powerful community in the town, for the purpose of its own survival as the "true" people of God.

Melito seems to be concerned to keep Christians out of the "synagogues of the wicked" so that they would not convert to Judaism. Judaism was probably providing a rich spiritual resource for some Christians during the first and second century and this disturbed Melito and other leaders of the Church.

In the New Testament, a first-second century document, Judaism is consistently negated for its inadequacy. Scholars working in New Testament studies today demonstrate the reason for this polemic in the struggle of the early Christians (c.64-95 C.E.) with their own identity. This struggle did not cease after the first century, but continued into the next four centuries, as the Church fought its way into existence.

In order for Melito to preserve his small community, he had to convince his constituency that one must beware of the enticements of "that synagogue."

It became apparent to me as I read the *Homily* in the context of Sardis that this poetic masterpiece was really a sermon intended for a struggling community. Insofar as Melito argued for the survival of his Christian community against the Jews in Sardis, we can include the *Homily* within the category *adversus Judaeos* literature. But we must remember that it is not necessary to go from this to a generalization which suggests that the *Homily* condemns all Jews for all times. Melito was speaking to his Christian community in Sardis, attempting to present a rationale for his understanding of the Christian tradition which best represented the original intention of the God of Israel against a venerable and compelling Judaism.

Tertullian, the subject of Chapter Four, was the last writer I studied. His city was **Carthage**, North Africa. The evidence for the Christian and Jewish presence in second-century Carthage is mixed and difficult to interpret. There is no archaeological data about the interaction of Christians and Jews in Carthage.

It was not possible to determine the kind of Judaism that existed in Carthage during Tertullian's time. An obscure mention of the study of rabbinic sources in Carthage in the Talmud is hardly enough evidence to describe a particular kind of Judaism there.

A study of the large necropolis led to mixed conclusions. It seems that Christians and Jews were buried in the same area. If this can be proved, there was not a distinction between these two groups. It is difficult from this evidence, though, to establish exactly what significance this had for the two communities. I have to agree with recent analysis that all one can say is that there were large Jewish and Christian populations in the city, and they used the same area of the city to bury their dead. The literary sources and the presence of an established burial place indicate that there was a settled group of Jews and Christians in the city.

The written evidence suggests that the two communities were quite diverse. Persecution is mentioned in the literary sources, which indicates tension in the city, but it is not possible from these writings to conclude that Jews persecuted Christians, or that Christians persecuted Jews there, or that there was any significant interaction between the two groups.

The *Answer to the Jews* was written mainly as a biblical commentary to be used as a resource by Christians in their own self-definition. The *Answer* describes Jews of the Bible, not Jews living in second-century Carthage. The concerns which the New Testament writers were interested in are the important issues for contemporary Jews, as far as Tertullian was concerned. This would rule out the old view that the *Answer* was influenced by some rabbinic teachings and writings. Marcion is very important to Tertullian and, therefore, is probably the one against whom Tertullian writes. Jews and Judaism seem incidental in comparison to the real enemy, Marcion.

As a result of my study, I have drawn several conclusions about the purpose and meaning of the early *adversus Judaeos* writings in this study:

Each *adversus Judaeos* writing is unique and is a result of one writer's concern about the relationship between Christians and Jews.

Each is an attempt at Christian self-definition.

Each writer deals with his own particular view of Judaism and speaks about Jews either as he is experiencing them in his particular place and time or as he portrays them as a "Bible-people." Curiously, the writers never seem to talk directly to or about Jews, unless the Jews are invented for a dialogue. There is no dialogue taking place between these two groups.

It is unlikely that any of the authors I have studied knew anything firsthand about contemporary Judaism from a sustained relationship with the synagogue in his neighborhood.

There are many questions which remain and need further consideration. As I looked at the new evidence on the cities and thought about the more complete picture we now have about Jews and Judaism in the second-century Diaspora, I was able to draw, I believe, a more accurate conclusion about the relationship between Jews and Christians during that period. Certainly Jews did not die out or become a sterile, legalistic religion during the emergence of the Christian Church in the second-century Roman Empire.

Jews were flourishing around the Mediterranean during the second century, and their creative contributions must have upset those Jewish Christians and non-Jewish Christians who believed that the Messiah had come and the end of Israel was at hand. It must have been rather difficult to preach that message when Israel did not end after one hundred years of Christian missions.

Conclusion

The evidence from the Diaspora synagogues encourages scholars to review their conclusions about the Jews of late antiquity. The discoveries tend to support the idea that Judaism and the Jews, as well as the Christians, were more diverse, less monolithic, and more complicated that we had previously thought.

More study must be done on the nature and purpose of the ancient texts. The church saved these ancient writings. We have the texts of the "winners" and not the "losers" in the Church and Judaism. It seems certain that the "other side" will be more and more represented as we continue to dig around the sites in the Mediterranean world of late antiquity.

More work needs to be done on the cities as texts. Wayne Meeks and others have begun the task; still others need to develop further their work so that scholars can be more precise about the nature of the city as an interpretive tool in the study of ancient writings.

Christian anti-Judaism grew because third- and fourth-century readers and interpreters of Tertullian, Melito, Justin, and Barnabas read them as literally degrading Jews. After examining the *adversus Judaeos* texts, I am persuaded that these texts were not written to create the hatred of Jews and Judaism that was later to be an integral part of the Christian Church.

One question remains: Can Christians define themselves in relation to the Jews without the supersessionistic or triumphalistic overtones? It is the intention of this book to make a start in the direction of answering that question in the affirmative.

Map 1

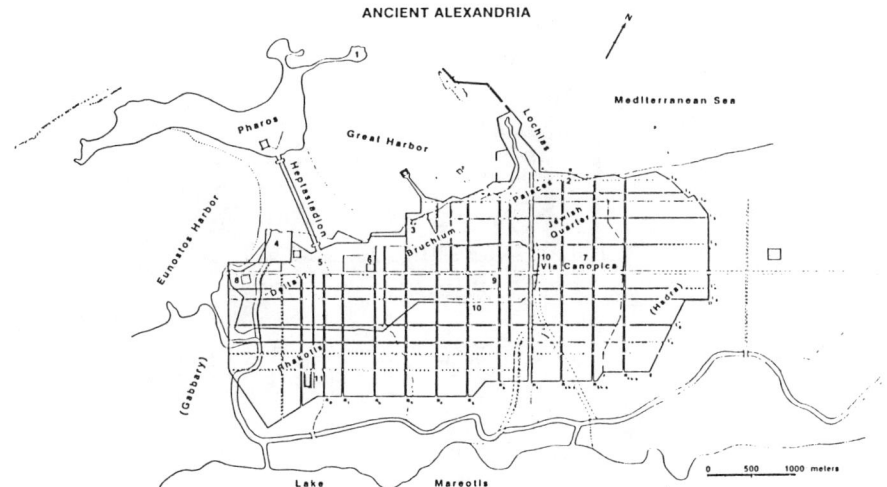

Key:
1. Pharos Lighthouse
2. *Martyrium* of St. Mark in Boukolou
3. Caesarium
4. Kibotos Harbor
5. Western Agora
6. Bendideion, St. Athanasius Church
7. Alabaster Tomb
8. St. Theonas Church
9. Gymnasium
10. Arab Wall
11. Serapeum

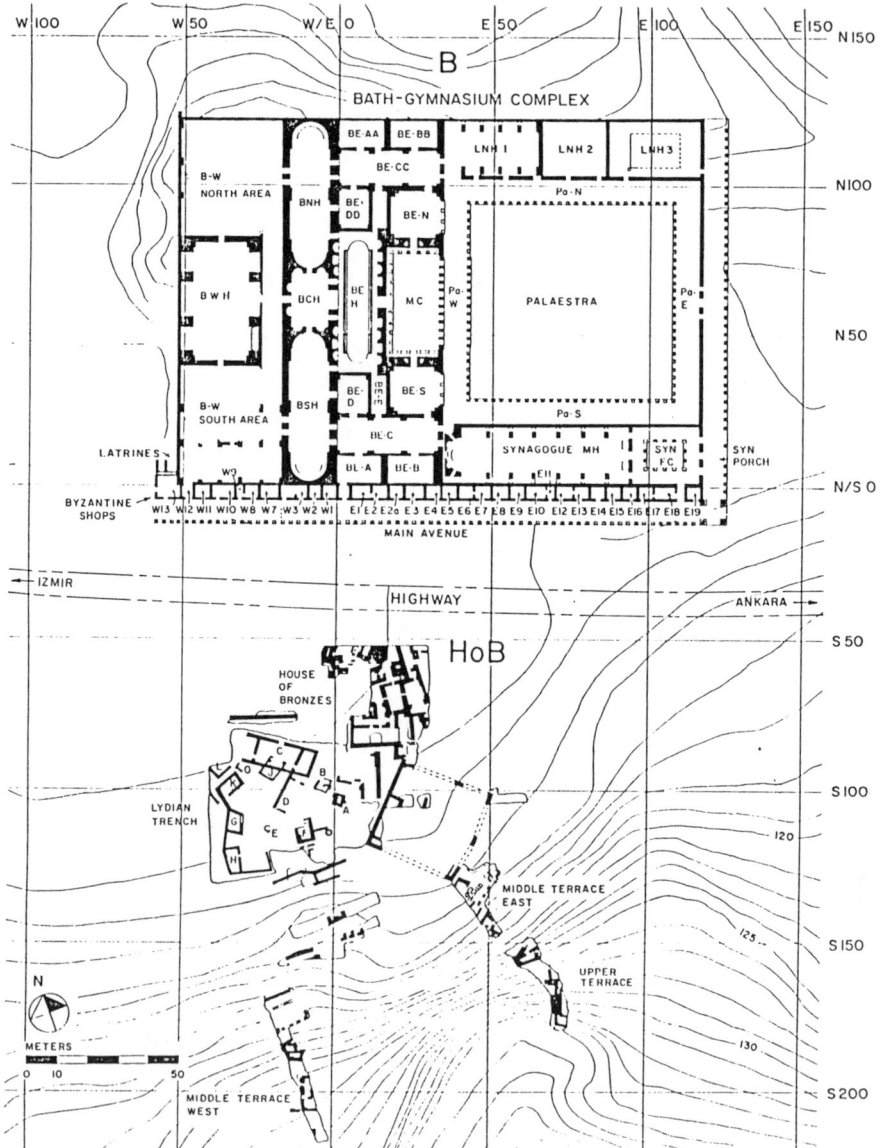

Fig. 1 Plan of the bath-gymnasium complex (B), House of Bronzes area (HoB), and terrace tunnels.

Fig. 2 Restoration of Bath-Gymnasium complex looking southwest, with Synagogue and part of south colonnade of Main Avenue (A. R. Seager, 1971).

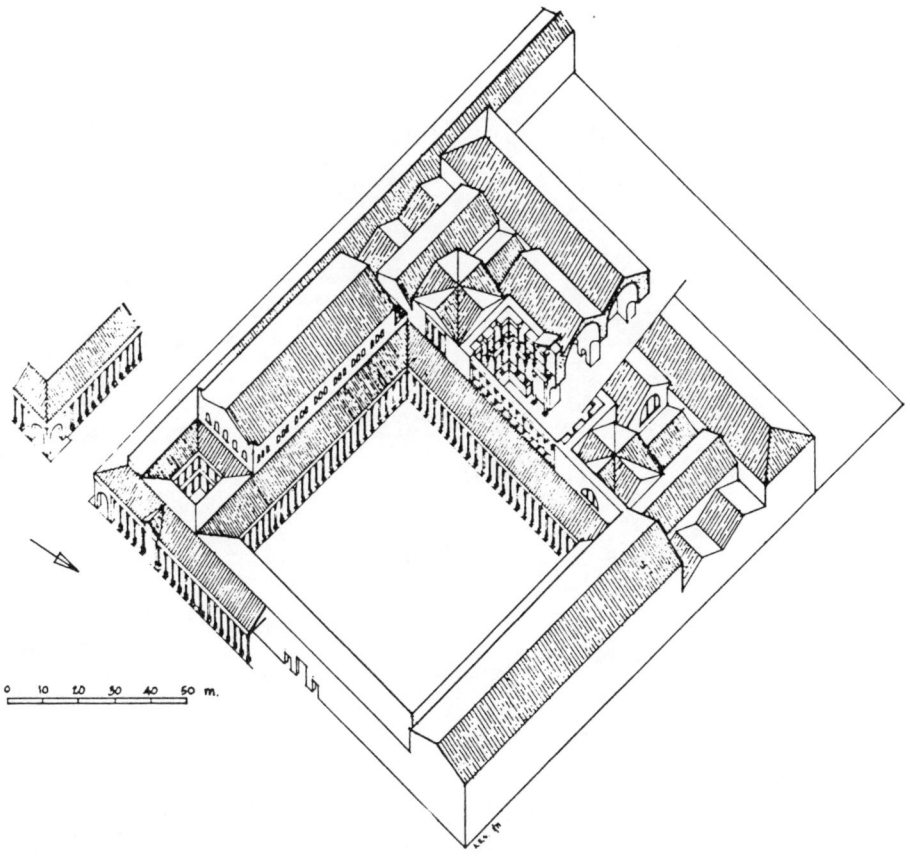

BIBLIOGRAPHY

PRIMARY SOURCES

BARNABAS

The Apostolic Fathers, 2 vols. *Barnabas*. Translation by K. Lake. LCL. Cambridge: Harvard, 1925.

Barnabas, The Apostolic Fathers. Translated by J.B. Lightfoot, London, 1926.

The Apostolic Fathers: A New Translation and Commentary, vol. 3 *Barnabas and the Didache*. Translated by R.A. Kraft, New York: Thomas Nelson & Sons, 1965.

Patres Apostolici, Epistula Barnabe, vol. 1. F.X. Funk editio II adaucta et emendata. 38-97. Tubingae, 1901.

Die Apostolischen Väter 3. Der Barnabasbrief. Edited by H. Windisch. Tübingen, 1920.

Epistola di Barnaba Introduzione, testo critico, traduzione, commento, glossario e indici a cura di Francesco Scorza Barcellona. Torino: Societa editrice Internazionale, 1975.

Epitre de Barnabe, Greek Text. Translated by K. Prigent. Edited by R.A. Kraft. Sources Chretiennes 172. Paris, 1971.

JUSTIN

Otto, E.D. *Corpus Apologetarum Christianorum*, vol. 2, *Justinus Philosophus et Martye*. Jenae, 1876.

Justin Martyr, Dialogue with Trypho. Translated by A. Roberts and J. Donaldson, 1885. Revised and edited by A.C. Coxe, *Ante-Nicene Fathers* I, Grand Rapids: Wm.B. Eerdmans, 1973.

Justin Dialogue avec Tryphon. Texte Grec. Translated by G. Archambault. Eds. H. Hemmer and P. Lejay, "Texte et Documente pour l'Etude Hist. Chr.," 2 vols. Paris, 1909.

Saint Justin Martyr. A new translation by T.B. Falls. In *The Fathers of the Church* VI. New York, 1948.

Justin Martyr, Die ältesten Apologeten, Texte mit kurzen Einleitungen. Edited by E.J. Goodspeed, Göttingen: Vandenhoecht Rupert, 1914. Reprint 1950.

MELITO

Blank, J. *Meliton von Sardes VOM PASSA: Die älteste christliche Österpredigt.* Freibourg: Lambertus, 1963.

Melito of Sardis, ON PASCHA and Fragments. Text and Translation. Translation by S.G. Hall, Oxford: Clarendon Press, 1979.

Papyrus Bodmer 13, Meliton de Sardes, Homelie sur 1 Paque, Manuscript du IIIe siecle. Translated by M. Testuz. Geneva, 1960.

The Homily on the Passion by Melito, Bishop of Sardis and some fragments of the apocryphal Ezekiel (Studies and Documents 12). Edited by C. Bonner. London and Philadelphia, 1948.

"A New English Translation of Melito's *Paschal Homily*." Translated by G.F. Hawthorne. In *Current Issues in Biblical and Patristic Interpretation.* (Studies in Honor of Merrill C. Tenney). Michigan, (1975): 147-175.

"Melito Sermon '*On the Passover.*'" *Translation, Introduction and Commentary* by R.C. White. Lexington, KY, 1976.

TERTULLIAN

Tertullian, Opera, Corpus christianorum, vol. 2. Edited by A. Kroymann. Turnhout, 1954.

Q.S.F. Tertulliani, Adversus Judaeos. Mit Einleitung und kritische Kommentar herausgegaben von Herman Tränkle. Wiesbaden: Franz Steiner Verlag, 1964.

Tertullian, Adversus Marcionem. Edited and translated by E. Evans. Oxford Early Christian Texts, 2 vols. Oxford: Clarendon Press, 1972.

Tertullian, Answer to the Jews. In *The Ante-Nicene Fathers*. Translated by The Rev. S. Thelwall [1885] Grand Rapids: Wm. B. Eerdmans Publishing Company, Reprinted 1980.

Early Latin Fathers 5, Tertullian's "*On Idolatry*." Translated and edited by S.G. Greenslade. Philadelphia: Westminster Press, 1956.

PRIMARY SOURCES: GENERAL

The Apocrypha and Pseudepigrapha of the Old Testament in English. 2 vols. Translated and edited by R.H. Charles, et al. Oxford: Clarendon Press, 1913.

The Babylonian Talmud, 18 vols. Translated and edited by I. Epstein. London: Soncino Press, 1948-1952.

Bihlmeyer, K. *Die apostolischen Väter. Neubearbeitung der Funkschen Ausgabe. SQS*, 2. Reihe 1. Tübigen, 1956.

Clement of Alexandria. *Exhortation to the Heathens, The Instructor, The Stromata*. Translated by A. Roberts and J. Donaldson, 1885. In The Ante-Nicene Fathers vol. 2. Revised and edited by A.C. Coxe. Grand Rapids: Wm.B. Eerdmans, 1979.

___. *The Exhortation to the Greeks, The Rich Man's Salvation, To the Newly Baptized, Appendix on the Greek Mysteries*. Translated and edited by. G.W. Butterworth. *Loeb Classical Library*, Cambridge: Harvard, [1919] 1982.

Corpus Inscriptionum Judaicarum 2 vols. Edited by J.B. Frey. (Rome: 1936 and 1952). Reprint of vol. 1 only with *Prolegomenon* by B. Lifshitz. New York: 1975.

Corpus Papyrorum Judaicarum 3 vols. Edited by V. Tcherikover, A. Fuks, and M. Stern. Cambridge: Harvard, 1957-1964.

Dio Cassius. *Dio's Roman History*. Translated by E. Cary. *Loeb Classical Library*. Cambridge: Harvard, 1925.

Eusebius, *Ecclesiastical History*. Translated by K. Lake and J.E.L. Oulton. *Loeb Classical Library*, 2 vols. Cambridge: Harvard, 1926 and 1932. Reprint 1965 and 1973.

The Fathers According to Rabbi Nathan. Translated by J. Goldin. New York: Schocken Paperback Edition, 1974.

Flavius Josephus, *Jewish Antiquities, Jewish Wars, The Life and Contra Apionem*. Translated by H. St.J. Thakeray, R. Marcus, A. Wikgren and L.H. Feldman, *Loeb Classical Library*, 9 vols., Cambridge: Harvard, 1925-1965.

I Maccabees, A New Translation with Introduction and Commentary Anchor Bible 41. Translated and edited by J.A. Goldstein. New York: Doubleday, 1976.

Mekilta de-Rabbi Ishmael. 3 vols. Translated and edited by J.Z. Lauterbach. Philadelphia: The Jewish Publication Society of America, 1933.

Midrash Rabbah, edited and translated by H. Freedman and M. Simon, 10 vols. London: Soncino, 1939-1951.

The Mishnah, edited by H. Danby. Oxford, 1933.

New Testament Apocrypha. Volume One: *Gospels and Related Writings*. Edited by E. Hennecke and W. Schneemelcher. [1959] English trans. edited by R. McL. Wilson. Philadelphia: The Westminster Press, 2nd ed. 1976.

New Testament Apocrypha. Volume Two: *Writings Relating to the Apostles; Apocalypses and Related Subjects*. Edited by E. Hennecke and W. Schneemelcher. [1964] English trans. edited by R. McL. Wilson. Philadelphia: The Westminster Press, 2nd. ed. 1976.

The Odes of Solomon, The Syriac Texts. Translated and edited by J.H. Charlesworth. Chico, CA: Scholars Press, 1977.

The Old Testament Pseudepigrapha, vol. 1. *Apocalyptic Literature and Testaments*. Edited by J.H. Charlesworth. New York: Doubleday, 1983.

The Old Testament Pseudepigrapha, vol. 2. *Expansions of the "Old Testament" and Legends, Wisdom and Philosophical Literature, Prayers, Psalms, and Odes, Fragments of Lost Judeo-Hellenistic Works*. Edited by J.H. Charlesworth. New York: Doubleday, 1985.

Origen, *CONTRA CELSUM*. Translated by H. Chadwick. [First published in 1953] Cambridge, England, Reprint 1965.

Origene, Contra Celse. Translated and edited by M. Borret. *Sources Chretiennes* 132, Tome I. Paris, 1967.

Philo, *Opera*. Translated and edited by F.H. Colson, H. Whitaker and J.W. Earp, *Loeb Classical Library*, 10 vols. Cambridge: Harvard, 1949-1962.

The Talmud of Babylonia. An American Translation VI. *Tractate Sukkah, BJS* 74. Translated by J. Neusner, Chico, CA: Scholars Press, 1984.

The Talmud of the Land of Israel, vol. 35. *Introduction: Taxonomy*. English translation by J. Neusner. Chicago: The University of Chicago Press, 1983.

Taylor, C. *The Teachings of the Twelve Apostles with Illustrations from the Talmud*. Cambridge, England, 1886.

The Theodosian Code and Novels and the Sirmondian Constitutions. A Translation by Clyde Pharr. Princeton: Princeton University Press, 1952.

The Tosefta. 6 vols. Division 2-4, translated and edited by J. Neusner. Division 1 edited by J. Neusner and R.S. Sarason and translated by A.J. Avery-Peck, R. Brooks, H. Essner, P. Haas, A. Havivi, M.S. Jaffee, I. Mandelbaum, L.E. Newman, M.W. Rubenstein, R.S. Sarason, D. Weiner and T. Zahavy. Division 1, Hoboken: KTAV, 1986. Divisions 2-6, New York: KTAV, 1977-1981.

SECONDARY SOURCES

Adler, E.N. and Seligsohn, M. "Une nouvelle chronique Samaritaine." *REJ* 44:188-222; 45(1902) 70-88, 160, 223-254; 46(1903) 123-146; reprint, Paris, 1903.

Adriani, A. "Saggio di una piamta archeologica di Alessandria." In *Ann. Mus. Gr.-Rom. 1*. Alexandria, 1934.

___. *Reportorio d'arte dell' Egitto greco-romano, Series C*, 2 vols., Palermo: Fondazione "Ignazio Mormino" del Banco di Sicilia, 1966.

Aland, K. "The relation between Church and State in early times." *JTS* 19 (1968): 115-127.

Albright, W.F. *From Stone Age to Christianity, Monotheism and the Historical Process*, 2nd. ed. New York: Doubleday, 1957.

___. *Yahweh and the Gods of Canaan*. Garden City, NY: Doubleday, 1968.

Alexander, M.A. Review of *Cahiers des Etudes Anciennes. 12 Carthage 4. Text and plates bound separately.* Universite du Quebec a Trois Rivieres, Quebec, by P. Senay. *AJA* 87 (1983): 415-416.

Alexander, P.S. "Rabbinic Judaism and the New Testament." *ZNW* 3/4 (1983): 237-245.

Alfoeldi, E. "Recent Excavations at Carthage: A Review Article" *Excavations at Carthage 1977, Conducted by the University of Michigan*, edited by J.H. Humphrey. (*Institut National d'archeologie et d'art. American Schools of Oriental Research*). Kelsey Museum, The University of Michigan, Ann Arbor 1981.

Allen, L.C. *The Books of Joel, Obadiah, Jonah, and Micah*. Grand Rapids: Wm. B. Eerdmans, 1976.

Alon, G. "Halacha in Barnabas Epistulae" (Hebrew). *Tarbiz* 11 (1939): 23-38.

___. *Jews, Judaism and the Classical World: Studies in Jewish History in the Times of the Second Temple, the Mishnah and the Talmud*. Jerusalem: Magnes Press, 1977.

___. *The Jews in their Land in the Talmudic Age (70-640 CE)*, vol. 1. Translated by G. Levi. Jerusalem: Magnes Press, 1980.

Alt, A. *Die Ursprünge des israelitischen Rechts. Berichte über die Verhandlungen der Sächsischen Akademie der Wissenschaften zu Leipzig*. Phil.-hist. Klasse 86/1. Leipzig S. Hirzel. Reprinted pp. 278-332 in Kleine Schriften zur Geschichte des Volkes Israel, 1. Munich: C.H. Beck, 1968.

Alverez, J. "Apostolic Writings and the Roots of Anti-Semitism." *SP* 13 (1975): 69-76.

Andresen, C. *Logos und Nomos; Die Polemische des Kelsos wider das Christentum*. Berlin, 1955.

Appelbaum, S. *Jews of North Africa*. Leiden: Brill, 1979.

Ashton, J. "The Identity and Function of the 'Judaioi' in the Fourth Gospel." *NT* 27.1 (1985): 40-75.

Attridge, H.W. Review of *Jews, Pagans and Christians in Conflict* by David Rokeah. *CQ* (1982): 46.

___. "Josephus and His Works." In M.E. Stone, *Jewish Writings of the Second Temple Period*. Philadelphia: Fortress Press, 1984.

Avery-Peck, A.J. *Mishnah's Division of Agriculture, A History and Theology of Seder Zeraim, BJS* 79. Chico, CA: Scholars Press, 1985.

Avi-Yonah, M. *The Jews of Palestine. A Political History from the Bar Kokhba War to the Arab Conquest*. Oxford, 1976.

Ayers, R.H. *Language, Logic and Reason in the Church Fathers: A Study of Tertullian, Augustine and Aquinas*. (*Altertums-wissenshaftliche Texte Studien, Bd. 6*). New York, 1979.

Aziza, C. *Tertullien et le Judaisme. Publication de la Faculte des Lettres et des Sciences Humanes de Nice 16.* Nice, 1977.

Baer, Y.F. "Israel, The Christian Church and the Roman Empire from the time of Septianus Severus to the Edict of Toleration of A.D. 313." *Scripta Hierosolymitana* VII:92 (1961): 79-145.

Bammel, E. "Christian Origins in Jewish Tradition." *NTS* 13 (1966): 317-335

___. "Origen contra Celsus 1.41 and the Jewish Tradition." *JTS* 19 (1968): 211-213.

Baney, M.M. *Tertullianius, Africa Romana: Some Reflections of Life in North Africa in the writings of Tertullian*. Washington, D.C.: The Catholic University of America Press, 1948.

Barnard, L.W. "The Date of the Epistle of Barnabas---A Document of Early Egyptian Christianity." *JEA* 44 (1958): 101-107.

___. "The Epistle of Barnabas and the Tannaitic Catechism." *ATR* 41 (1959).

___. "The Epistle of Barnabas and the Dead Sea Scrolls: Some Observations." *SJT* 13 (1960): 45-59.

___. "Saint Stephen and Early Alexandrian Christianity." *NTS* 7 (1960): 31-45.

___. "Is The Epistle of Barnabas a Paschal Homily?" *VC* 15 (1961): 8-22.

___. "The Old Testament and Judaism in the Writings of Justin Martyr." *VT* 14 (1964): 395-406.

___. "Justin Martyr's Eschatology." *VC* 19 (1965): 86-98.

___. *A History of the Early Church*. London, 1966.

___. *Studies in the Apostolic Fathers and their Background*. Oxford, 1966.

___. *Justin Martyr, His Life and Thought*. Cambridge, 1967.

___. "The New Testament and the Origins of Christianity in Egypt." *SEv.* IV/I (=*TU* 102) Berlin, (1968): 277-280.

___. "Justin Martyr in Recent Study." *SJT* 22 (1969): 152-164.

___. *Athenagoras. A Study in Second Century Christian Apologetic*. Paris: Beauchesne, 1972.

___, Review of *Barnabasbrief* by Klaus Wengst, *JEH* 23.4 (1972): 345-347.

___. *Studies in Church History and Patristics, Patriarchal Institute for Patristic Studies*. Thessaloniki, 1978.

Barnard, P.M., Review of *Contra Celsum*, edited by Koetshau, *JTS* 1 (1900): 455-461.

Barnes, T.D. "Tertullian's '*Scorpiace*'." *JTS* 20 (1969): 105-131.

___. *Tertullian, A Historical and Literary Study*. [1971] Oxford: Clarendon Press, new edition 1985.

___. "Tertullian the Antiquarian." *SP* 14 (1976): 3-20 (=*TU* 117).

___. *Early Christianity and the Roman Empire*. London: Variorum Reprints, 1984.

Baron, S.W. *A Social and Religious History of the Jews*, vols. 1-8 New York: Jewish Publication Society, 1937-1960.

Bartelink, G.J.M., Review of *Epistola di Barnaba* by Scorza Barcellona, *VC* 33 (1970): 184-186.

Barth, M. *Ephesians 1-3*. The Anchor Bible, vol. 34. New York: Doubleday, 1974.

___. *Ephesians 4-6*, The Anchor Bible, vol. 34A. New York: Doubleday, 1974.

Baskin, J.R. "Rabbinic-Patristic Exegetical Contacts in Late Antiquity: A Bibliographical Reappraisal." In *Approaches To Ancient Judaism V, BJS* 49, edited by W.S. Green, 53-80. Chico, CA: Scholars Press, 1985.

Bauer, W. *Orthodoxy and Heresy in Earliest Christianity*. Translated and edited by R.A. Kraft and G.Krodel. Philadelphia: Fortress Press, 1971.

Baumgarten, A.I. "The Pharisaic Paradosis," *HTR* 80:1 (1987): 63-77.

Baus, K. *From the Apostolic Community to Constantine*. New York, 1965.

Bean, G.E. *Aegean Turkey*. London: Ernest Benn, and New York: W.W. Norton, 1966.

Beare, F.W. *The First Epistle of Peter*. Oxford, 1970.

Beasley-Murray, G.R. *The Book of Revelation*. New Century Bible. London, Oliphant, 1974.

Beckwith, J. *Early Christian and Byzantine Art*. The Pelican History of Art. Harmondsworth:Penguin Books, 1970.

Beker, J.C. *Paul the Apostle: The Triumph of God in Life and Thought*. Philadelphia: Fortress Press, 1980.

Bell, H.I., ed. *Jews and Christians in Egypt, The Jewish Troubles in Alexandria and the Athanasian Controversy*. London, 1924.

___. "Antinopolis: A Hadrianic Foundation." *JRS* 30 (1940): 133-147.

___. "Anti-Semitism at Alexandria." *JRS* 31 (1941): 1-18.

___. "Evidence of Christianity in Egypt During the Roman Period." *HTR* 37 (1944): 185-208.

___. *Egypt from Alexander the Great to the Arab Conquest, A Study in the Diffusion and Decay of Hellenism*. Oxford, 1948.

___. *Cults and Creeds in Graeco-Roman Egypt*. Liverpool, 1953.

Bellizoni, A.J. "The Source of the Agraphon in Justin Martyr's *Dialogue with Trypho*, 47.5." *VC*, 17 (1963): 65-70.

___. "The Sayings of Jesus in the Writings of Justin Martyr." *Novem Testamentum*, Supplement 17. Leiden: E.J. Brill, (1967): 134-140.

Ben Abed ben Khader, A. and Soren, D. Editors of *Carthage: A Mosaic of Ancient Tunisia*. New York: The American Museum of Natural History in association with W.W. Norton & Company, 1987.

Ben-Sasson, H.H. *A History of the Jewish People*. Cambridge: Harvard University Press, 1976.

Berger, P. "Charisma and Religious Innovation: The Social Location of Israelite Prophecy." *ASR* 28 (1963): 940-950.

Berger, P. and Luckmann, T. *The Social Construction of Reality*. New York: Anchor Books, 1967.

Bernand, A. *Alexandrie la Grande*. Paris, 1966.

Best, T.F. "The Sociological Study of the New Testament: Promise and Peril of a New Direction." *SJT* 36 (1983): 181-194.

Bickerman, E. *From Ezra to the Maccabees, Foundations in Postbiblical Judaism*. New York: Schocken Books, 1962

___. *The Jews in the Greek Age*. Cambridge, MA: Harvard University Press, 1988.

Bietenhard, H. "Die Freiheitskriege der Juden unter den Kaisern Trajan und Hadrian und der Messianische Tempelbau." *Judaica* 4 (1948): 94-95, 101-102.

___. *Caesarea, Origenes und die Juden*, Stuttgart, 1974.

Black, M. "The Patristic Accounts of Jewish Sectarianism." *BJRL* 41 (1959): 285-303.

Bokser, B.Z. "Justin Martyr and the Jews." *JQR* 64 (1973-1974):97-122, 204-211.

Bonner, C. "A Supplementary Note on the Opening of Melito's *Homily*." *HTR* 36 (1943): 317-339.

___. "The Text of Melito's *Homily*." *VC* 3 (1949): 184-185

Borgen, P. "Philo of Alexandria." In *Jewish Writings of the Second Temple Period*, edited by M.E. Stone, 233-282. Philadelphia: Fortress Press, 1984.

___. "Philo of Alexandria. A critical and synthetical survey of research since World War II." *ANRW* 2.21.1 Berlin: Walter de Gruyter, 1984: 99-154.

Bousset, D.W. *Juedisch-Christlischer Schulbetrieb in Alexandria und Rom*. Gottingen, 1915.

Brandon, S.G.F. *The Fall of Jerusalem and the Christian Church*. London, 1951 2nd ed., 1957.

Bratton, F.G. *The Crime of Christendom: The Theological Sources of Christian Anti-semitism*. Boston, 1969.

Brin, H.B. *Catalog of Judaea Capta Coinage*. Minneapolis: Emmett Publishing Co., 1986.

___. *A New Interpretation of HVR haYEHUDIM*, Minneapolis: Emmett Publishing Co, 1987.

Brown, P. *The World of Late Antiquity: AD 150-750*. London: Harcourt Brace Jovanovich, Inc., 1971.

___. *Religion and Society in the Age of Saint Augustine*, London, 1972.

___. "Approaches to the Religious Crisis of the Third Century A.D." In *Religion and Society*. (1972): 83-84.

Brown, R.E. *The Gospel According to John I-XII*. The Anchor Bible, vol. 29, New York: Doubleday, 1966.

___. *The Gospel According to John XIII-XXI*. The Anchor Bible, vol. 29a, New York: Doubleday, 1970.

___. *The Community of the Beloved Disciple*. New York: Paulist Press, 1979.

___. "Not Jewish and Gentile Christianity but Types of Jewish/Gentile Christianity." *CBQ* 45.1 (1983): 74-79.

Brown, R.E. and Meier, J.P. *Antioch and Rome*. New York: Paulist Press, 1983.

Bruce, F.F. "The Acts of the Apostles: Historical Record or Theological Reconstruction?" In *Aufstieg und Niedergang der römischen Welt: Geschichte und Kultur Roms in Spiegel der neueren Forschung*. Edited by Hildegard Temporini and Wolfgang Haase. Berlin and New York: de Gruyter, 1984. 2570-2603.

Bull, R.J. "A Preliminary Excavation of an Hadrianic Temple at Tell er-Ras on Mount Gerizim." *AJA* 71 (1967): 387-393.

___. "The Excavation of Tell er-Ras on Mt. Gerizim", *BA* 31 (1968):58-72.

Bull, R.J. and Campbell, E.F., Jr. "The Sixth Campaign at Balatah (Shechem)". *BASOR* 190 (April, 1968): 2-41.

Bultmann, R. *The History of the Synoptic Tradition*. Translated by J. Marsh. New York and Evanston: Harper Row, 1963.

___. *The Gospel of John: A Commentary*. Translated by G.R. Beasley-Murray. Edited by R.W.N. Hoare and J.K. Riches. Oxford, 1971. Originially published as *Das Evangelium des Johannes* (Göttingen: Vandenhoeck & Ruprecht, 1964).

Burke, G.T. "Celsus and Late Second-Century Christianity." Ph.D. diss., The University of Iowa. 1981.

Burkitt, F.C. "Barnabas and the Didache." *JTS* 33 (1932): 25-27.

Caird, G.B. *A Commentary on the Revelation of St. John the Divine*. London, 1966.

Calderini, A. *Dizionario dei nomi geografici e topografici dell'Egitto greco-romano*, 1. Milan: Cisalpino-Goliardica, 1935.

Campbell, Jr., E.F., Ross, J.F., and Toombs, L.E. "The Eighth Campaign at Balatah (Shechem)." *BASOR* 204 (December, 1971): 2-17.

Campenhausen, H. van. *The Fathers of the Greek Church*. London, 1963.

___. *The Fathers of the Latin Church*. Translated by M. Hoffmann. Stanford, CA: Stanford University Press, 1972.

Cassuto, U. *Biblical and Oriental Studies*, vol. 2: *Bible and Ancient Oriental Texts*. Jerusalem: Magness, 1975.

Chadwick, H. "Origen, Celsus and the Stoa." *JTS* 48 (1947): 4-49.

___. "Origen, Celsus and the Resurrection of the Body." *HTR* (1948): 83-102.

___. "Notes on the Text of Origen, Contra Celsum." *JTS* 4 (1953): 215-219.

___. Review of *contra Celse* by J. Scherer. *JTS* (1957): 322-326.

___. "A Latin Epitome of Melito's Homily of the Pascha." *JTS* 11 (1960): 76-82.

___. "Justin Martyr's Defense of Christianity." *BJRL* 47 (1965).

___. *Early Christian Thought and the Classical Tradition: Studies in Justin, Clement and Origen*, Oxford, 1966.

Charles, R.H. *The Apocrypha and Pseudepigrapha of the Old Testament in English*, 2 vols. Oxford: Clarendon Press, 1913.

___. *A Critical and Exegetical Commentary on The Revelation of St. John*, ICC, 2 vols. Edinburgh: T & T Clark, 1920.

Charlesworth, J.H. *The Pseudepigrapha and Modern Research with a Supplement*, 7S. Chico, CA: Scholars Press, 1981.

___. "A Prolegomenon to a New Study of the Jewish Background of the Hymns and Prayers in the New Testament." *Essays in Honour of Yigdael Yadin*. Edited by G. Vermes and J. Neusner in *JJS* 33.1-2 (1982): 270, n.19.

___. *Jesus Within Judaism. New Light from Exciting Archaeological Discoveries*. The Anchor Bible Reference Library. New York: Doubleday, 1988.

___, editor. *The Old Testament Pseudepigrapha*, vol. 1 *Apocalyptic Literature and Testaments*. New York: Doubleday 1983.

___, editor. *The Old Testament Pseudepigrapha,* vol. 2 *Expansions of the "Old Testament" and Legends, Wisdom and Philosophical Literature, Prayers, Psalms, and Odes, Fragments of Lost Judeo-Hellenistic Works.* New York: Doubleday 1985.

Chiat, M.J.S. "First-Century Synagogue Architecture: Methodological Problems." In *Ancient Synagogues: The State of Research, BJS* 22, edited by J. Gutmann, 49-60. Chico, CA: Scholars Press, 1981.

___. *Handbook of Synagogue Architecture. BJS* 29. Editor J. Neusner. Chico, CA: Scholars Press, 1982.

Childs, B. *Introduction of the Old Testament as Scripture.* Philadelphia: Fortress Press, 1979.

Chouraqui, A. *Between East and West: A History of the Jews of North Africa.* Philadelphia, 1968.

Clayton, F.W. "Tacitus and Nero's Persecution of the Christians." *CQ* 41 (1947): 81-85.

Coggins, R.J. *Samaritans and Jews,* Oxford, 1975.

___. "The Samaritans and Acts." *NTS* 28 (1982): 423-434.

Cohen, A.A. *The Myth of the Judeo-Christian Tradition.* New York: Schocken, 1970

Cohen, S.J.D. *Josephus in Galilee and Rome: His Vita and Developement as a Historian.* Leiden: Brill, 1979.

___. "Yavneh Revisited: Pharisees, Rabbis and the End of Jewish Sectarianism." In *Seminar Papers 1982, SBL,* 45-61. Chico, CA: Scholars Press, 1982.

___. "Jacob Neusner, Mishnah, and Counter-Rabbinics: A Review Essay." *ConJ* 37.1 (1983): 50-51.

___. Review of *Two Powers in Heaven: Early Rabbinic Reports about Christianity and Gnosticism. Studies in Judaism in Late Antiquity* 25, Alan F. Segal. *AJS* 10.1 (1985): 114-117.

___. "The Political and Social History of the Jews in Greco-Roman Antiquity: The State of the Question." In *Early Judaism and its Modern Interpreters,* edited by R.A. Kraft and G.W.E. Nickelsburg, 31-56. Atlanta: Scholars Press, 1986.

___. "Was Timothy Jewish (Acts 16.1-3)? Patristic Exegesis, Rabbinic Law, and Matrilineal Descent." *JBL* 105 (1986): 251-268.

___. *From the Maccabees to the Mishnah. The Library of Early Christianity.* Philadelphia: Westminster Press, 1987.

Collins, J.J. *Between Athens and Jerusalem, Jewish Identity in the Hellenistic Diaspora.* New York: Crossroads, 1983.

___. "A Symbol of Otherness: Circumcision and Salvation in the First Century." *"To See Ourselves As Others See Us" Christians, Jews, "Others" in Late Antiquity*, ed. J. Neusner and E.S. Frerichs. Chico, CA: Scholars Press, 1985.

Connolly, R.H. "The Didache in Relation to the *Epistle of Barnabas*." *JTS* 33 (1932): 237-253.

Conzelmann, H. *The Theology of Luke*. Translated by Geoffrey Busswell. New York: Harper & Row, 1961. Originally published as *Die Mitte der Zeit* (Tübingen: J.C.B. Mohr, 1953).

Coote, R.B. *Amos Among the Prophets: Composition and Theology*. Philadelphia: Fortress Press, 1981.

Cosgrove, C. "Justin Martyr and the Emerging Canon." *VC* 36 (1982): 209-232.

Cranfield, C.E.B. *The Epistle to the Romans*, 2 vols. ICC. Edinburgh: T & T Clark, 1979.

Cross, F.L. Review of "Die *Passa-Homilies* des Biscofs Meliton von Sardis," by B. Lohse. *JTS* 11 (1960): 162-163.

___. "History and Fiction in the African Canon." *JTS* 12 (1961): 227-247.

Cross, F.M. *Canaanite Myth and Hebrew Epic: Essays in the History of Religion*. Cambridge, MA: Harvard University Press, 1973.

___. *The Ancient Library of Qumran and Modern Biblical Studies*, 1958. Reprint, New York: Greenwood Press, 1976.

Crouzel, H. *Bibliographie Critique d'Origene*. Haag, 1971.

___. "A Letter from Origen to Friends in Alexandria." Translation by J.D. Gauthier. In *The Heritage of the Early Church*, (1974) 13-150.

___. Review of *Origen and the Jews* by N.R.M. deLange. *Bulletin de Litterature Ecclesiastique* 79 (1978):142-144.

___. *Bibliographie Critique d'Origene*. Suppl. I. Haag, 1982.

___. "Les Etudes sur Origene des Douze Dernieres Annees." *Etudes Theologiques et Religieuses* 58 (1983): 97-107.

Crown, A.D. *A Bibliography of the Samaritans, ATLA Bibliography Series* No. 10. London, 1984.

Culley, R.C. "Structuralist Analysis: Is it Done with Mirrors?" *Interpretation* 28.2 (1974): 165-181.

Cullmann. O. *Immortality of the Soul or Resurrection of the Dead?* New York: Macmillan, 1964.

Daly, R.J. "The Hermeneutics of Origen. Existential Interpretation in the Third Century." *Essays in honor of F.L. Moriarity* (1974): 135-144.

___. "Origen studies and Pierre Nautin's Origene," *TS* 39 (1978): 508-519.

Danielou, J. *Origene*. Paris, 1948.

___. "Figure et Evenement chez Meliton de Sardes." *Neotestamentica et Patristica*. Leiden: Brill, (1962): 282-292.

___. Review of *L'omelia "In S-Pascha" dello Pseudo-Ippolito dri Roma* (Milan, 1967) by R. Cantalamessa. *RSR* 51 (1969): 79-84.

Dassmann, E. *Der Stachel im Fleisch: Paulus in der frühchristlichen Literature bis Iranäus*. Münster: Aschendorff, 1979.

Daube, D. *The New Testament and Rabbinic Judaism*. London, 1956.

Davies, A.T., editor, *Anti-Semitism and the Foundations of Christianity*. New York: Paulist Press, 1979.

Davies, W.D. *Paul and Rabbinic Judaism. Some Rabbinic Elements in Pauline Theology*. London: S.P.C.K., 1962.

___. *The Gospel and the Land*. Los Angeles: University of California Press, 1974.

de Boer, M.C. "Images of Paul in the Post-Apostolic Period." *CBQ* 42 (1980): 359-380.

deLange, N.R.M. "Jewish influence in Origen." *Origeniana*, (1976) 225-242.

___. *Origen and the Jews*. Cambridge, England, 1976.

___. "Origen and the Rabbis on the Hebrew Bible." *SP* 14 (1976): 117-121, (=*TU* 117).

Dibelius, M. *From Tradition to Gospel*. Translated by B.L. Woolf. Cambridge and London: James Clark and Co., 1971. Originally published as *Die Fromgeschichte des Evangeliums* (Tubingen: J.C. B. Mohr, 1919).

Dix, G. *Jew and Greek*. Glasgow: Dacre Press Westminster, 1953.

Donahue, P.J. "Jewish Christian Controversy in the Second Century. A Study in the Dialogue of Justin Martyr." Ph.D. diss., Yale University, New Haven, 1977.

Doran, R. "2 Maccabees 6:2 and the Samaritan Question." *HTR* 76.4 (1983): 481-485.

Douglas, M. *Purity and Danger*. London: Routledge and Kegan Paul, (1966).

___. *Natural Symbols*. New York: Vintage Books, 1973.

Dugmore, C.W. "A Note on the Quartodecimans." *SP* 79.IV.2 (1961): 411-421.

Efroymson, D. "Tertullian's Anti-Judaism and its role in his Theology." Ph.D. diss., Temple University, 1976.

___. "The Patristic Connection." In *Antisemitism and the Foundations of Christianity*. Edited by A.T. Davies. New York: Paulist Press, 1979: 98-117.

___. "Tertullian's Anti-Jewish Rhetoric: Guilt by Association." *USQR* 36.1 (1980): 25-37.

Eisman, M.M. "A Tale of Three Cities." *BA* 41.2 (June 1978): 47-60.

Eissfeldt, O. *The Old Testament, An Introduction*. Translated by P.R. Ackroyd. New York: Harper & Row, 1965.

Elliot, J.H. Review of *The First Urban Christians* by Wayne Meeks. *RSR* 11 (1985): 329-335.

___. "Social-Scientific Criticism of the New Testament and Its Social World." *Semeia* 35 (1986).

Elmslie, W.A.L. *The Mishnah on Idolatry 'Aboda Zara,' Texts and Studies*, VIII.2. Cambridge, England, 1911.

Ennabli, A. "North African Newsletter 3: Part 1. Tunisia 1956-1980." Translated by J.H. Humphrey. *AJA* 87 (1983): 197-206.

Ennabli, L. *Les Inscriptions Funeraires Chretiennes de la Basilique dite de Sainte-Monique a Carthage*, Institute Nationale d'Archeologie et d'Arts de Tunis Ecole Francais de Rome, 1. 1975.

___. *Les Inscriptions Funeraires Chretiennes de la Basilique dite de Sainte-Monique a Carthage*, Institute Nationale d'Archeologie et d'Arts de Tunis Ecole Francais de Rome, 2. 1982.

Eno, R.B. Review of *Tradition und Theologie des Barnabasbriefes* by Klaus Wengst. *CBQ* 34 (1972): 543-545.

Enslins, M.S. "Justin Martyr: An Appreciation." *JQR* 34 (1944): 179-205.

Epp, E.J. "The 'Ignorance Motif' in Acts and Anti-Judaic Tendancies in Codex Bezae." *HTR* 55, (1962): 51-62.

___. *The Theological Tendency of Codex Bezae Cantabrigiensis in Acts*, Society for New Testament Studies Monograph Series 3, Cambridge: University Press, 1966.

___. "Anti-Semitism and the popularity of the Fourth Gospel in Christianity." *CCARJ* 22 (1985): 35-57.

Epp, E.J. and MacRae, G.W, eds. *The New Testament and Its Modern Interpreters*. Atlanta: Scholars Press, 1989.

Ericksen, R.P. *Theologians Under Hitler: Gerhard Kittel, Paul Althaus, and Emanuel Hirsch*. Philadelphia: Fortress Press, 1985.

Erim, K.T. "Recent Discoveries at Aphrodisias" and "Sculpture from Aphrodisias." In *The Proceedings of the 10th International Congress of Classical Archaeology* II (Plates III), Ankara-Izmir 23-30.IX.1973. Edited by E.

Akurgal. Ankara, Turkey: Turk Tarih Kurumu, 1978: 1065-1076 and 1077-1084.

___. *Aphrodisias: City of Venus Aphrodite*. New York and Oxford: Facts on File Publications, 1986.

Esler, P.F. *Community and Gospel in Luke-Acts: The Social and Political Motivations of Lucan Theology*. SNTS Monograph Series 57. Cambridge: Cambridge University Press, 1987.

Espy, J.M. "Paul's 'Robust Conscience' Re-examined." *NTS* 31 (1985): 161-188.

Fee, G.D. "The Text of John", *Biblia* 52 (1971): 357-394,

Feldman, L.H. "The Omnipresence of the God-Fearers," *BAR* 12.5 (1986): 58-63.

Ferron, J. "Inscriptions juives de Carthage." *Cahiers de Byrsa I. Imprimerie Nationale*. Paris, (1951): 175-206.

___. "Mort-Dieu de Carthageoules Stèle Funéraires de Carthage" Collection *Cahiers de Byrsa*, Série Monographie - Tome II. Paris, 1975.

Finkelstein, L. *Akiba, Scholar, Saint and Martyr*, New York: Atheneum, 1970.

Finley, M.I. *Ancient History: Evidence and Models*. New York: Penguin Books, 1987. Originally published Great Britain: Chatto & Windus, 1985.

Finn, T.M. "The God-fearers Reconsidered." *CBQ* 47 (1985): 75-84.

Fischer, U. *Eschatologie und Jenseitserwartung im hellenistischen Diasporajudentum*. Berlin, 1978.

Fitzmyer, J.A. *The Dead Sea Scrolls---Major Publications and Tools for Study*. Missoula: Scholars Press, 1977.

___. *The Gospel According to Luke I-IX*. The Anchor Bible 28. New York: Doubleday, 1981.

___. *The Gospel According to Luke X-XXIV*. The Anchor Bible 28A. New York: Doubleday, 1985.

Ford, J.M. *Revelation*. The Anchor Bible 38. New York: Doubleday, 1975.

Forestell, J.T. *Targumic Traditions and the New Testament: An Annotated Bibliography with a New Testament Index*. Chico, CA: Scholars Press, 1979.

Forester, E.M. *Alexandria: A History and a Guide*. (1922) Revised 1982.

Foss, C. *Byzantine and Turkish Sardis*. Cambridge, MA: Harvard University Press, 1976.

___. *Ephesus After Antiquity: A late antique, Byzantine and Turkish City*. London and New York: Cambridge University Press, 1979.

Fox, R.L. *Pagans and Christians*. New York: A.A. Knopf, Inc. 1987.

Frank, K.S. *Adversus Judaeos in der Alten Kirke: Die Juden als Minderheit in der Geschichte.* Muenchen, 1981.

Fraser, P.M. *Ptolemaic Alexandria*, 3 vols. Oxford, 1972.

Frend, W.H.C. *The Donatist Church: A Movement of Protest in Roman North Africa.* Oxford: At the Clarendon Press, 1952.

___. "The Persecutions: Some Links between Judaism and the Early Church." *JEH* 9.2 (1958): 141-158.

___. "The Seniores laici and the Origins of the Church in North Africa." *JTS* 12 (1961): 280-284.

___. *The Early Church.* London, 1965.

___. *Martyrdom and Persecution in the Early Church. A Study of a Conflict from the Maccabees to Donatus.* Oxford: Basil Blackwell, 1965.

___. "The Winning of the Countryside." *JEH* 18.2 (1967): 1-14.

___. "A Note on Jews and Christians in the Third Century North Africa." *JTS* 21 (1970): 92-96.

___. "A Note on Tertullian and the Jews." *SP* 10.1 (1970): 291-296.

___. "The Old Testament in the Age of the Greek Apologists, A.D. 130-180." *SJT* 26 (1973): 139-146.

___. "The Early Christian Church in Carthage." *Excavations at Carthage in 1976. Conducted by the University of Michigan* iii. University of Michigan, Ann Arbor, (1976):21-40.

___. *Religion Popular and Unpopular in the Early Christian Centuries.* London, 1976.

___. "Jews and Christians in Third Century Carthage." *Paganisme, Judaisme, Christianisme, Influences et affrontements dans le monde antique, Mélangé offert a M. Simon*. Paris: Boccard (1978):185-194.

___. *Town and Country in the Early Christian Centuries.* London, 1980.

___. "Early Christianity and Society: A Jewish Legacy in the pre-Constantinian era." *HTR* 76.1 (1983): 53-71.

___. *The Rise of Christianity.* Philadelphia: Fortress Press, 1984.

___. "Archaeology and Patristic Studies." *SP* 18.1 (1985): 9-21.

Freyne, S. *Galilee from Alexander the Great to Hadrian, 323 B.C.E. to 135 C.E.* South Bend: Notre Dame University Press, 1980.

Gager, J. G. *Moses in Greco-Roman Paganism.* Nashville: Abingdon, 1972.

___. "The Dialogue of Paganism with Judaism: Bar Cochba to Julian." *HUCA* 44 (1973): 89-118.

___. *Kingdom and Community: The Social World of Early Christianity.* New Jersey, 1975.

___. "Shall we marry our enemies? Sociology and the New Testament." *Interpretation* 36.3 (1982): 256-265.

___. *The Origins of Anti-Semitism.* Oxford and New York: Oxford University Press, 1983.

___."Jews, Gentiles, and Synagogues in the Book of Acts." In *Christians Among Jews and Gentiles,* edited by G.W.E. Nickelsburg and G.W. MacRae. Philadelphia: Fortress Press, 1986.

Gallagher, E.V. *Divine Man or Magician?: Celsus and Origen on Jesus.* (*SBL* Diss. series 64) Chico, CA: Scholars Press, 1982.

Gaston, L. "Paul and the Torah." In *Antisemitism and the Foundations of Christianity.* Edited by Alan Davies. New York: Paulist Press, 1979: 47-71.

___. "Judaism of the Uncircumcised in Ignatius and Related Writers." In *Anti-Judaism in Early Christianity 2, Separation and Polemic.* Edited by S.G. Wilson. Waterloo, Canada: Wilfrid Laurier University, 1986.

___. "Retrospect." In *Anti-Judaism in Early Christianity 2, Separation and Polemic*, Edited by S.G. Wilson. Waterloo, Canada: Wilfrid Laurier University, 1986.

Geertz, C. *The Interpretation of Culture*, New York: Basic Books, 1973.

___. *Works and Lives: The Anthropologist as Author.* Stanford: Stanford University Press, 1988.

Gershenzon, R. and Slomovic, E. "A Second Century Jewish-Gnostic Debate: Rabbis Jose ben Halafta and the Matrona." *JSJ* 16.1 (1985): 1-41.

Goldenberg, R. Review of T*he Origins of Anti-Semitism: Attitudes Toward Judaism in Pagan and Christian Antiquity* by J.G. Gager. *RSR* 11 (1985): 335-337.

Goldfahn, A.H. "Justinus Martyr und die Agada." *Monatsschrift fuer Geschichte und Wissenshaft des Judentums.* 1973.

Goldstein, J.A. *I Maccabees, A New Translation with Introduction and Commentary* 41. New York: Doubleday, Anchor Bible, 1976.

___."Jewish Acceptance and Rejection of Hellenism." In *Jewish and Christian Self-Definition,* vol. 2, *Aspects of Judaism in the Greco-Roman Period,* edited by E.P. Sanders, 64-87. Philadelphia: Fortress Press, 1981.

Goldstein, M. *Jesus in the Jewish Tradition.* New York, 1950.

Gonzalez, J.L. "Athens and Jerusalem Revisited: Reason and Authority in Tertullian." *Church History* 43 (1974) 17-25.

Goodenough, E.R. *The Theology of Justin Martyr*. Jena, 1923.

___. *An Introduction to Philo Judaeus*. 2nd ed., rev. Oxford: Basil Blackwell, 1962.

___. "Catacomb Art" *JBL* 81 (March 1962) 113-142.

___. *Jewish Symbols in the Greco-Roman Period*. New York: Pantheon Books, 1953 (vols. 1-3), 1954 (vol. 4), 1956 (vols. 5-6), 1958 (vols. 7-8), 1964 (vols. 9-11), 1965 (vol.12), 1968 (vol 13).

___. "Symbolism, Jewish (In the Greco-Roman period)," vol. 15, 568-578. In *Encyclopaedia Judaica*. Jerusalem, 1971.

Goppelt, L. *Apostolic and Post-Apostolic Times*. Translated by R.A. Guelich. London: Adam & Charles Black, 1970.

Gorday, P.J. Review of *Der Stachel im Fleisch: Paulus in der früchristlichen Literature bis Irenäus*, by Ernst Dassmann. *The Second Century* 5:4 (1985/1986):243-244.

Grant, M. *The Jews in the Roman World*. New York: Charles Scribner's Sons, 1973.

Grant, R.M. "Aristotle and the Conversion of Justin." *JTS* 7 (1956): 246-248.

___. *Second Century Christianity, A collection of fragments*. London, 1957.

___. "Origen." In *The Encyclopedia of Philosophy* 5. Editor-in-Chief P. Edwards, 551-552. New York: Macmillan, 1967.

___. *Early Christianity and Society*, London, 1978.

___. "Theological Education at Alexandria." In *The Roots of Egyptian Christianity*, edited by B.A. Pearson and J.E. Goehring, 178-189. Philadelphia: Fortress Press, 1986.

___. "Goodenough, Erwin R." In *The Encyclopaedia of Religion*, volume 6, 76-77. Edited by Mircea Eliade. New York: Macmillan, 1987.

Green, M. *The Second Epistle General of Peter and the General Epistle of Jude*. London: Tyndale, 1968.

Green, W.S., ed. *Approaches to Ancient Judaism IV, Studies in Liturgy, Exegesis, and Talmudic Narrative*. BJS 27. Chico, CA: Scholars Press, 1983.

___. ed. *Approaches to Ancient Judaism V, Studies in Judaism and Its Greco-Roman Context*. BJS 32. Atlanta: Scholars Press, 1985.

Greenewalt, C.H. "The Sardis Campaigns of 1979 and 1980." *BASOR* 249 (1983): 1-44.

Greenwald, M.R. "The New Testament Canon and the Mishnah as Consolidation of Knowledge in the Second Century C.E." In *Seminar Papers, SBL Annual Meeting 1987*. Atlanta: Scholars Press, (1987):244-254.

Grimal, P. *Roman Cities*. Translated and edited by G.M. Woloch. Madison: The University of Wisconsin Press, 1983. Originally published as *Les villes romaines* (Paris: Presses Universitaires de France, 1954).

Groh, D.E. "Tertullian's Polemic Against Social Cooptation." *CH* 40 (1971): 7-14.

___. "Upper Class Christians in Tertullian's Africa: Some Observations." *SP* 14 (1976): 41-47. (=*TU* 117).

___. "Christian Community in the Writings of Tertullian. An Investigation into the nature and problem of North African Christianity." Ph.D.diss., Michigan State University, 1978, Microfilm.

Gunther, J.J. "The Epistle of Barnabas and the Final Rebuilding of the Temple." *JSJ* 7 (1978): 143-151.

Gutmann, J. Editor, *The Dura-Europos Synagogue: A Revaluation (1932-1972)*. (Religion and the Arts 1) Missoula, MT: Scholars Press, 1973.

___. Editor, *The Synagogue: Studies in Origins, Archaeology and Architecture*. New York: KTAV Publishing House, Inc., 1975.

___. Editor, Ancient Synagogues: The State of the Research. *BJS* 22. Chico, CA: Scholars Press, 1981.

Habbel, W. *Die Gegenwart Gottes durch das Wort in der Schrift des Origenes gegen Celsus*. Roma, 1977.

Hall, S.G. "Melito's Paschal Homily and the Acts of John." *JTS* 17 (1966): 95-98.

___. "The Melito Papyri." *JTS* 19.2 (1968): 476-508.

___. "Melito PERI PASCHA 1 and 2." *Kyriakon*, 2 vols. I:236-248. (J. Quasten Festschrift). Muenster, 1970.

___. "Melito in the Light of the Passover Haggadah." *JTS*, 22 (1971): 29-46.

___. "The Christology of Melito: A Misrepresentation Exposed." *SP* 13 (1975): 154-168.

Halperin, D.J. "Origen, Ezekiel's Merkabah, and the Ascension of Moses." *CH* (1981): 261-275.

Halton, T.P. "Stylistic Device in Melito, PERI PASKA." *Kyriakon*, 2 vols. I: 249-255. (J. Quasten Festschrift). Muenster, 1970.

Halton, T.P. and Sider, R.D. "A Decade of Patristic Scholarship 1970-1979, vol. 1." *CW* 76.2. (1982): 72-92, 104-110, 115-121.

___. "A Decade of Patristic Scholarship 1970-1979, vol. 2." *CW* 76.6. (1983): 313-314.

Handelman, S.A. *The Slayers of Moses: The Emergence of Rabbinic Interpretation in Modern Literary Theory*. Albany: State University of New York Press, 1982.

Hanfmann, G.M.A. *Sardis from Prehistoric to Roman Times: Results of the Archaeological Exploration of Sardis 1958-1975*. Cambridge: Harvard University Press, 1983.

Hanson, P.D. *The Dawn of Apocalyptic*. Philadelphia: Fortress Press, 1975.

Hanson, R.P.C. *Origen's Doctrine of Tradition*. London, 1954.

___. *Allegory and Event*. London, 1959.

___. *Studies in Christian Antiquity*. Edinburgh: T & T Clark, 1985.

Hare, D.R.A. "The Relationship Between Jewish and Gentile Persecutions of Christianity." *JES* 4.3 (1967): 446ff.

Harnack, A. von. *The Mission and Expansion of Christianity in the First Three Centuries*, (ET by J. Moffatt from 2nd German edition of 1906; London: Williams and Norgate, 1908).

___. *Judentum und Judenchristentum in Justin Dialog mit Trypho*. *TU* 39 (1913): 47-98.

___. *History of Dogma*. Translated by N. Buchanan. vol. 1. New York: Dover, 1961.

Harrington, D.J. "Sociological Concepts and the Early Church: A Decade of Research." *TS* 41, 181-190. Reprinted in D.J. Harrington. *A Light to the Nations: Essays on the Church in New Testament Research*, 148-161 (Good News Studies, 3) Jerusalem, 1982.

Harvey, A.E. "Melito and Jerusalem." *JTS* 17 (1966): 401-404.

Hawkins, P.S., editor. *Civitas: Religious Interpretation of the City. Scholars Press Studies in the Humanities*. Atlanta: Scholars Press, 1986.

Hawthorne, G.F. "Christian Baptism and the Contribution of Melito of Sardis Reconsidered." *Essays in Honor of A.I. Wiligren*. Leiden: Brill, (1972): 241-251.

Heinisch, P. *Der Einfluss Philos Auf Die Alteste Christliche Exegese*. Muenster, 1908.

Hemer, C.J. "The Sardis Letter and the Croesus Tradition." *NTS* 19 (1973): 94-97.

___. *The Letters to the Seven Churches of Asia in Their Local Setting*. Sheffield: JSOT Press, 1986.

Hengel, M. *Judaism and Hellenism, Studies in their Encounter in Palestine during the Early Hellenistic Period*. 2 vols. Translated by J. Bowden. Philadelphia: Fortress Press, 1974.

Higgins, A.J.B. "Jewish Messianic Belief in Justin Martyr's *Dialogue with Trypho.*" *NT* 9 (1967): 298-305.

Hinske, N. *Alexandrien: Kulturbegenungen dreier Jahrtausende im Schmelztiegel einer mediterranen Gross Stadt.* Mainz am Rhein: Verlag Philipp von Zabern, 1981.

Hirschberg, H.Z. (J.W.) *A History of the Jews in North Africa*, vol. 1, *From Antiquity to the Sixteenth Century*, 2nd revised edition, translated from the Hebrew. Leiden: E.J. Brill, 1974.

Hopkins, C. *The Discovery of Dura Europos.* Edited by B. Goldman. New Haven and London: Yale University Press, 1979.

Horbury, W. "Tertullian on the Jews in the Light of *De Spectaculis* 30.5-6." *JTS* 23 (1972): 455-459.

___. "The Benediction of the Minim and Early Jewish-Christian Controversy." *JTS* 33 (1982): 19-61.

Horsley, G.H.R. *New Documents Illustrating Early Christianity.* 3. *A Review of the Greek Inscriptions and Papyri Published in 1978.* North Ryde: Macquarie University, Ancient History Documentary Research Centre, 1983.

Hruby, K. "Exégèse rabbinique et exégèse patristique." *Révue des Sciences* 47 (1973): 341-372.

Hulen, A.B. "The Dialogue with the Jews as sources for the early Jewish argument against Christianity." *JBL* 51(1932): 58-71.

Humphrey, J.H. *Excavations at Carthage 1975-1976.* Conducted by the University of Michigan. (*Institut National d'Archeologie et d'Art, American Schools of Oriental Research*), 1. Tunis 1976; 2-4: Kelsey Museum, Ann Arbor, 1976-1978.

___. "A New Museum at Carthage." *A* 38 (1985): 29-33.

Humphrey, J.H. and Pedley, J.G. "Roman Carthage." *SA* 238 (1978): 111-120.

Hyldahl, N. "Tryphon und Tarphon." *ST* (1956): 77-88.

Jackson, F.J.F. and Lake, K., eds. *The Beginnings of Christianity* I, 1-5. London: Macmillan, 1920-1930.

Jacobson, R. "The Structuralists and the Bible." *Interpretation* 28.2 (1974): 146-164.

Jaeger, W. *Early Christianity and Greek Paideia.* Cambridge: The Belknap Press of Harvard University Press, 1961.

Jellicoe, S. *The Septuagint and Modern Study.* Oxford: The Clarendon Press, 1968.

Jeremias, J. "Samareia." In *TDNT*, vol. VII. S, edited by G. Friedrich. Trans. and ed. G.W. Bromiley, 88-94. Grand Rapids: Wm. B. Eerdmans, 1968.

Jervell, J. *The Unknown Paul, Essays on Luke-Acts and Early Christian History.* Minneapolis: Augsburg Publishing House, 1984.

Johnson, A.C. *Roman Egypt to the reign of Diocletian,* 2 vols. Baltimore, 1935.

Johnson, S.E. "Christianity in Sardis." In *Early Christian Origins: Studies in honor of Harold R. Willoughby.* edited by Allen Wikgren. Chicago: Quadrangle Books, 1961: 81-90.

___. "A Sabazios Inscription from Sardis." *In Religion in Antiquity: Essays in memory of E.R. Goodenough,* edited by J. Neusner. (Supplement to *Numen,* 14, (1968):542-550). Leiden: Brill, 1968.

Jones, A.H.M. *The Later Roman Empire.* Oxford, 1964.

Judge, E.A. "The Social Identity of the First Christians. A Question of Method in Religious History." *JRH* 11 (1980): 201-217.

Juster, J. *Les Juifs dans l'empire romain: Leur Condition juridique, économique, et sociale.* 2 vols., 1914. Reprint. New York: Franklin, n.d.

Kahle, P.E. "Was Melito's *Homily* on the Passion Originally Written in Syriac?" *JTS* 43 (1943): 52-56.

___. *The Cairo Geniza.* [1947] Oxford: Clarendon Press, 1959.

Kasher, A. "Les circonstances de la promulgation de l'edit de l'empereur Claude et de sa lettre aux Alexandrins (41 ap. J.C.)". *Semitica* 26 (1976): 99-108.

___. "Les Hebreux dans l'Egypt hellenistique et romaine." *Institut de recherche de la Diaspora* 23. [en Hebr. res. en angl. as "The Jews in Hellenistic and Roman Egypt."] Tel Aviv, 1978.

Kaufmann, Y. *The Religion of Israel from its beginnings to the Babylonian exile.* [8 volumes: 1937-1956] Translated and abridged from the Hebrew by M. Greenberg. Chicago: University of Chicago Press, 1960.

Kee, H.C. *Miracle in the Early Christian World: A Study in Sociohistorical Method.* New Haven and London: Yale University Press, 1983.

Kelber, W.H. *The Oral and the Written Gospel: The Hermeneutics of Speaking and Writing in the Synoptic Tradition, Mark, Paul and Q.* Philadelphia: Fortress Press, 1983.

___. "Narrative as Interpretation and Interpretation as Narrative: Hermeutical Reflections on the Gospels." *Semeia* 39 (1987): 107-134.

Kilpatrick, G.D. *The Origins of the Gospel According to Matthew.* Oxford: Clarendon Press, 1946.

Kimelman, R.R. "Rabbi Yohanan of Tiberias: Aspects of the Social and Religious History of the Third Century." Ph.D. diss., Yale University, 1977.

___. "Third Century Tiberias: The Alliance between The Rabbinate, The Patriarch, and the Urban Aristocracy." *ANRW* Suppl. to II.8, 1977.

___. "Rabbi Yohanan and Origen on the Song of Songs: A Third Century Jewish-Christian Disputation." *HTR* 73 (1980): 567-595.

___. "Birkat Ha-Minim and the lack of Evidence for an Anti-Christian Jewish Prayer in Late Antiquity." In *Jewish and Christian Self-Definition,* vol.2, *Aspects of Judaism in the Greco-Roman Period,* ed. E.P. Sanders, 226-244. Philadelphia: Fortress Press, 1981.

Klassen, W. "Anti-Judaism in Early Christianity: The State of the Question." In *Anti-Judaism in Early Christianity* 1, ed. Peter Richardson, 1-20. Waterloo, Ontario: Wilfrid Laurier University, 1986.

Klijn, A.F.J. Review of *Tradition und Theologie des Barnabasbriefes* by Klaus Wengst. *NT* 14 (1972): 332-333.

___. Review of *Origen and the Jews* by N. deLange. *JSJ* 8 (1977): 206.

___. Review of *Heiden---Juden---Christen. Auseinander-setzungen in der Literatur der hellenistisch-römischen Zeit.* Tübingen: J.C.B. Mohr, 1981, by H. Conzelmann and *Le Christianisme antique et son contexte religieux. Scripta Varia,* I and II. Tübingen: J.C.B. Mohr, 1981, by M. Simon in *NT* 24 (1982): 375-378.

___. "Jewish Christianity in Egypt." In *The Roots of Egyptian Christianity,* edited by B.A. Pearson and J.E. Goehring. Philadelphia: Fortress Press, 1986.

Klijn, A.F.J. and Reinink, G.J. *Patristic Evidence for Jewish-Christian Sects.* Supplement to NT. Leiden: Brill, 1973.

Knibbe, D. "Ephesos." *RE* Supp. 12 (1970): 293-297.

Knight, D.A. and Tucker, G.M. eds. *The Hebrew Bible and Its Modern Interpreters.* Chico, CA: Scholars Press, 1985.

Koch, K. *The Rediscovery of Apocalyptic.* Studies in Biblical Theology, 22. Napierville, Quebec: Alec R. Allenson Inc., 1970.

Koester, H. *Introduction to the New Testament. History, Culture, and Religion of the Hellenistic Age,* vol. 1. Philadelphia: Fortress Press, 1982.

___. *Introduction to the New Testament. History and Literature of Early Christianity,* vol. 2. Philadelphia: Fortress Press, 1982.

Kraabel, A.T. "Hypsistos and the Synagogue at Sardis," *Greek, Roman and Byzantine Studies,* 10 (1968): 81-93.

___. "Melito the Bishop and the Synagogue at Sardis: Text and Context." Studies Presented to George M.A. Hanfmann, edited by D.G. Mitten, J.G. Pedley and J.A. Scott, 77-85. Cambridge, MA, 1971.

___. "Ancient Synagogues." In *NCE Supplement* volume 16 (1974): 436-439.

___. "Paganism and Judaism: The Sardis Evidence." *Paganisme Judaisme, Christianisme.* (Festschrift for M. Simon) 13-33. Paris, 1978.

___. "'Syncretism' and 'Sympathizers' Among Diaspora Jews: New Archaeological Evidence." Unpublished paper presented at the University of Minnesota, June 22, 1978.

___. "The Diaspora Synagogue: Archaeological and Epigraphic Evidence since Sukenik." In *ANRW* II.19.1 (1979): 477-510.

___. "Jews in Imperial Rome: More Archaeological Evidence from the Oxford Collection," *JJS* 30 (1979): 41-58.

___. "The Disappearance of the 'God-fearers.'" *Numen* 28 (1981): 113-126.

___. "Social Systems of Six Diaspora Synagogues." In *Ancient Synagogues: The State of Research*, edited by J. Guttmann, 79-91. Chico, CA: Scholars Press, 1981.

___. "The Roman Diaspora: Six Questionable Assumptions." (Yadin Festschrift) *JJS* 33.1-2 (1982): 445-464.

___. "Impact of the Discovery of the Sardis Synagogue." In *Sardis from Prehistoric to Roman Times*, edited by G.M.A. Hanfmann, 178-190. Cambridge: Harvard University Press, 1983.

___. "New Evidence of the Samaritan Diaspora has been Found on Delos." *BA* 47 (1984): 44-46.

___. "Synagoga caeca. Systematic Distortion in Gentile Interpretations of Evidence for Judaism in the Early Christian Period." In *"To See Ourselves As Others See Us": Christians, Jews, "Others" in Late Antiquity*, edited by Jacob Neusner and Ernest S. Frerichs, 219-246. Chico, CA: Scholars Press, 1985.

___. "Greeks, Jews and Lutherans in the Middle Half of Acts." (Krister Stendahl Festschrift). In *Christians Among Jews and Gentiles*, eds. G.W.E. Nickelburg with G.W. MacRae, 147-157. Philadelphia: Fortress Press, 1986.

___, Review of *Anti-Judaism in Early Christianity*, 2 vols., eds. P. Richardson, David Granskou and S.G. Wilson. *CBQ* 50.2 (April, 1988): 351-353.

Kraeling, C.H. *The Synagogue (The Excavations at Dura-Europos. Final Report* VIII.1). New Haven: Yale University Press, 1956.

Kraft, R.A. "Barnabas' Isaiah Text and Melito's Paschal Homily." *JBL* 80 (1961): 371-373.

___. Review of P. Prigent *Les Testimonia dans le Christiennes primitif: l'Epitre de Barnabe i-xvi et ses sources*. *JTS* 13 (1962): 401-408.

___. The Apostolic Fathers, A New Translation and Commentary vol. 3, *Barnabas and the Didache*, New York, 1965.

Kraft, R.A., and Nickelsburg, G.W.E., ed. *Early Judaism and Its Modern Interpreters*. Atlanta: Scholars Press, 1986.

Krauss, S. "The Jews in the Works of the Church Fathers." *JQR* 5 (1893): 147-157.

___. "The Jews in the Works of the Church Fathers" in *JQR*, 6 (1894): 84ff and 245ff.

___. *Das Leben Jesu nach Jüdischen Quellen*. Berlin, 1902.

Krautheimer, R. *Early Christian and Byzantine Architecture. The Pelican History of Art*. 2nd. ed. Harmondsworth: Penguin Books, 1975.

Kselman, J.S. "The Social World of the Israelite Prophets: A Review Article," *RSR* 11.2 (1985): 120-128.

Kuhn, K.G. "Proselytos." In *TDNT*, vol. 6, eds. Friedrich and G.W. Bromiley, 727-744. Grand Rapids: Wm. B. Eerdmans, 1968.

Kümmel, W.G. *The New Testament. The History of the Investigation of its Problem*. Philadelphia: Westminster Press, 1973.

Last, H. "The Study of the 'Persecutions.'" *JRS* 27 (1937): 80-92.

Lattke, M. "Haggadah". *RAC* 13.3 (1985): 328-360.

___. "Halachah". *RAC* 13.3 (1985): 372-402.

Law, R.C.C. "North Africa in the Period of Phoenician and Greek Colonization to 800." In *Cambridge History of Africa* 2, ed. J. Fage, 87-209. Cambridge, 1978.

Layton, B., editor. *The Gnostic Scriptures*. New York: Doubleday & Company., 1987.

Leaney, A.R.C. *The Jewish and Christian World 200 BC to AD 200* (Cambridge commentaries on writings of the Jewish and Christian world 200 B.C. to A.D. 200, VII). Cambridge: University Press, 1984.

Leclercq, H.C. *L'Afrique Chretienne*, par Dom. H. Leclercq, 2. ed. Paris, 1904.

Leipoldt, J. "Das Evangelism nach Thanon." *SP* (=*TU* 101) 1-24. Berlin, 1967.

Lemico, E.E. "Ephesus and the New Testament Canon." *BJRL* 69.1 (1986): 210-234.

Leon, H.J. *The Jews of Ancient Rome*. Philadelphia: Jewish Publication Society, 1960.

Levenson, J.D. "Is There a Counterpart in the Hebrew Bible to New Testament Antisemitism?" *JES* 22 (1985): 242-260.

Levine, L. *Caesarea Under Roman Rule,* Leiden: Brill, 1975.

___. "Rabbi Abbahu of Caesarea." *Christianity, Judaism and other Greco-Roman Cults*. Part 4, ed. J. Neusner. Leiden: Brill, 1975.

___. ed., *The Synagogue in Late Antiquity* (A Centennial Publication of the Jewish Theological Seminary of America; Philadelphia: The American School of Oriental Research, 1987).

Lewis, N. *Life in Egypt Under Roman Rule*. Oxford: Clarendon Press, 1983.

Lieberman, S. "How much Greek in Jewish Palestine?" *Biblical and Other Studies,* ed. A. Altman. Cambridge, England, 1963.

Lightstone, J. "Christian Anti-Judaism in its Judaic Mirror: The Judaic Context of Early Christianity Revised." In *Anti-Judaism in Early Christianity* 2, *Separation and Polemic,* ed. S.G. Wilson, 103-132. Ontario: Wilfrid Laurier University, 1986.

Lohse, B. *Die Passa-Homilie des Bischofs Meliton von Sardes.* (*Textus Minores* 24). Leiden, 1958.

Lowy, S. "The Confrontation of Judaism in the Epistle of Barnabas." *JJS* 11 (1960): 1-33.

MacDonald, J. *The Theology of the Samaritans*. London: SCM Press Ltd., 1964.

Mack, B.L. "Philo Judaeus and Exegetical Traditions in Alexandria." *ANRW* 2.21.1. Berlin and New York: Walter de Gruyter, (1984): 228-271.

Mack, B.L. and Murphy, O.C. "Wisdom Literature." In *Early Judaism and Its Modern Interpreters*, edited by R.A. Kraft and G.W.E. Nickelsburg. Atlanta: Scholars Press, 1986.

MacLennan, R.S. and Kraabel, A.T. "The God-Fearers---A Literary and Theological Invention?" *BAR* 12.5 (1986): 46-53.

MacLeod, C.W. "Origen, Contra Celsum." *JTS* 32 (1981): 32.

Mainka, R.M. "Meliton von Sardes." *Claretianum* 5 (1965): 225-255.

Malherbe, A.J. *The Social Aspects of Early Christianity*. 2d ed. Philadelphia: Fortress Press, 1977.

Malina, B.J. *Christian Origins and Cultural Anthropology: Practical Models for Biblical Interpretation*. Atlanta: John Knox Press, 1986.

___. "Normative Dissonance and Christian Origins." *Semeia*, 35 (1986): 35-60.

___. "The Received View and What It Cannot Do: III John and Hospitality." *Semeia* 35 (1986): 171-194.

___. "Wealth and Poverty in the New Testament and Its World." *Interpretation* 41.4 (October 1987): 354-367.

Mantel, H. "The Causes of the Bar Kokba Revolt." *JQR* NS 58 (1967-1968): 224-241, 274-295.

Marlowe, J. *The Golden Age of Alexandria*. London, 1971.

Marshall, J.L. "Some Observations on Justin Martyr's use of testimonies." *Studia Patristica* 15-16/2, *Texte und Untersuchengen. Papers presented to the Seventh International Conference on Patristic Studies held in Oxford, 1985.* Berlin: Akademie Verlag, (1985) 197-200.

Marty, M.E. "A Judeo-Christian Looks at the Judeo-Christian Tradition." *CC* 103.2 (1986): 858-860.

Matel, H. "The Cause of the Bar-Kokba Revolt." *JQR* 58 (1967-1968): 224-296.

Matthiae, P. "Ebla in the Late Early Syrian Period: The Royal Palace and the State Archives." *BA* 39 (1979): 94-113.

McKenna, A.J. "Introduction." *Semeia* 33 (1985): 1-12.

Meeks, W.A. "The Social Context of Pauline Theology." *Interpretation* 36.3 (1982): 66-277.

___. *The First Urban Christians, The Social World of the Apostle Paul.* New Haven: Yale University Press, 1983.

___. "Breaking Away: Three New Testament Pictures of Christianity's Separation from the Jewish Communities." In *"To See Ourselves As Others See Us": Christians, Jews, "Others" in Late Antiquity*, edited by J. Neusner and E.S. Frerichs, 93-116. Chico, CA: Scholars Press, 1985.

___. Review of *Sardis from Prehistoric to Roman Times*, by George M.A. Hanfmann and W.E. Mierse. *JBL* 104.2 (1985): 367-369.

___. "A Hermeneutics of Social Embodiment." In *Christians Among Jews and Gentiles*, eds. G.W.E. Nickelsburg and G.W. MacRae, 76-186. Philadelphia: Fortress Press, 1986.

Meeks, W.A. and Wilken, R.L. *Jews and Christians in Antioch in the First Four Centuries of the Common Era*. Missoula, MT: Scholars Press 1978.

Mellink, M.J. "Archaeology in Asia Minor." *AJA* 81 (1977): 290-321.

Merlan, P. "Celsus." In *Reallexikon für Antike und Christentum* II. 954-966. Stuttgart, 1954.

Metcalf, W.E. and Bowersock, G.W. A review of *The Coinage of the Bar-Kokhba War*, by Leo Mildenberg, edited by Patricia Erhart Mottahedeh. Arrau/Frankfurt-am-Main/Salzburg: Verlag Sauerlander, 1984. In *AJA* 90 (1986): 254-256.

Meyers, E.M. "The Cultural Setting of Galilee: The Case of Regionalism and Early Judaism in the First Century." In *ANRW*, 19.2.1. (1979): 686-702.

Meyers, E.M. and Kraabel, A.T. "Archaeology, Iconography, and Nonliterary Written Remains." In *Early Judaism and Its Modern Interpreters*, edited by R.A. Kraft and G.W.E. Nickelsburg, 175-210. Atlanta: Scholars Press, 1986.

Meyers, E.M. and Strange, J.F. *Archaeology, The Rabbis, and Early Christianity: The Social and Historical Setting of Palestinian Judaism and Christianity.* Nashville: Abingdon, 1981.

Michalowski, K. *Art of Ancient Egypt.* Translated and adapted from the Polish and French by N. Guterman. New York: H.N. Abrams, 1969.

Milburn, R. *Early Christian Art and Architecture.* Berkeley and Los Angeles: University of California Press, 1988.

Millar, F. "The Emperor, The Senate and The Provinces." *JRS* 56 (1966): 156-166.

Millet, M.G. *Les Peintures de la Synagogue de Doura-Europos.* Roma, 1939.

Mitten, D.G. "The Synagogue in Sardis," *BASOR,* 170 (1963): 38-49.

___. "The Synagogue in Sardis," *BASOR,* 174 (1964): 30-44.

___. "The Synagogue in Sardis," *BASOR,* 177 (1965): 16-21.

___. "A New Look at Ancient Sardis," *BA,* 29.2 (1966): 38-67.

___. "The Synagogue in Sardis," *BASOR,* 182 (1966): 34-45.

Moffatt, J. "Two Notes on Ignatius and Justin Martyr." *HTR* 23 (1930): 153.

Moore, G.F. "Christian Writers on Judaism." *HTR* 14.3 (1921): 197-254.

___. *Judaism in the First Centuries of the Christian Era, The Age of the Tannaim,* 2 vols., 1927. Reprint, New York: Schocken Books, 1971.

Murphy-O'Connor, J. *St. Paul's Corinth: Texts and Archaeology.* Glazier, 1983.

Murray, R. "Jews, Hebrews and Christians; Some Needed Distinctions." *NT* 24 (1982): 194-208.

Musurillo, H.A. *The Acts of the Pagan Martyrs.* Oxford: Clarendon Press, 1954.

___. "The Recent Revival of Origen Studies." *TS* 24 (1963): 250-263.

___. *The Acts of the Christian Martyrs.* Oxford: Clarendon Press, 1972.

Nautin, P. "L'homelie de Meliton sur la passion." *RHE* 44.1 (1949): 429-438.

___. *Origene, sa vie et son oeuvre.* Paris, 1977.

Negev, A. Revised edition editor, *The Archaeological Encyclopedia of the Holy Land.* Nashville: Thomas Nelson, Publisher, 1986.

Neusner, J. "A Life of Rabbi Tarphon, c. 50-130 C.E." *Judaica* 17 (1961): 141-167.

___. *A History of the Jews in Babylonia,* 5 vols. Leiden: Brill, 1966-1970.

___. *Development of a Legend: Studies on the Traditions Concerning Yohanan ben Zakkai.* Leiden: Brill, 1970.

___. *A Life of Yohanan ben Zakkai ca. 1-80 C.E.* 2d ed. Leiden: Brill, 1970.

___. *The Rabbinic Traditions about the Pharisees Before 70*, 3 vols. Leiden: Brill, 1971.

___. *The Idea of Purity in Ancient Judaism*. Leiden: Brill, 1973.

___. *Method and Meaning in Ancient Judaism*. BJS 10. Missoula, MT: Scholars Press, 1979.

___. *Judaism, The Evidence of the Mishnah*. Chicago and London: The University of Chicago Press, 1981.

___. *Method and Meaning in Ancient Judaism*. Second Series. BJS 15. Chico, CA: Scholars Press, 1981.

___. *Method and Meaning in Ancient Judaism*. BJS 16. Chico, CA: Scholars Press. 1981.

___. *Formative Judaism: Religious, Historical, and Literary Studies*. BJS 37. Chico, CA: Scholars Press, 1982.

___. *Formative Judaism: Religious, Historical and Literary Studies*. BJS 41. Chico, CA: Scholars Press, 1983.

___. *Formative Judaism: Religious, Historical and Literary Studies,* BJS 46. Chico, CA: Scholars Press, 1983.

___. *Take Judaism, for Example, Studies Toward the Comparison of Religion*. Chicago: The University of Chicago Press, 1983.

___. *Ancient Judaism: Debates and Disputes*. BJS 64. Chico, CA: Scholars Press, 1984.

___. *Formative Judaism: Religious, Historical, and Literary Studies*. BJS 76. Chico, CA: Scholars Press, 1984.

___. "Judaic Studies in Universities: Toward the Second Quarter-Century." *Duke University Lecture*. Durham, NC, September 19, 1984.

___. "The Experience of the City in Late Antique Judaism." In *Approaches to Ancient Judaism* V. *BJS* 32, ed. W.S. Green, 37-52. Atlanta: Scholars Press, 1985.

___. *A History of the Mishnaic Law of Damages. Studies in Judaism in Late Antiquity*, vol. 35, Part 4, ed. J. Neusner. Leiden: Brill, 1985.

___. *Judaism in the Matrix of Christianity*. Philadelphia: Fortress Press, 1986.

___. *The Tosefta, Its Structure and Its Sources*. BJS 112. Atlanta: Scholars Press, 1986.

___. *Understanding and Seeking Faith, Essays on the Case of Judaism I, Debates on Method, Reports of Results*. BJS 116. Atlanta: Scholars Press, 1986.

___. *Understanding and Seeking Faith, Essays on the Case of Judaism II, Literature, Religion and the Social Study of Judaism*. BJS 72. Atlanta: Scholars Press, 1987.

Neusner, J. and Frerichs, E., eds. *"To See Ourselves As Others See Us": Christians, Jews, "Others" in Late Antiquity.* Chico, CA: Scholars Press, 1985.

Newman, K.J. "Celsus." In *RE*, new edition by G. Wissowa, W. Kroll, et al., Stuttgart, 1893ff.; 2d R., 1914ff.; S.3., Stuttgart: Metzler, 1939.

Nickelsburg, G.W.E. *Jewish Literature Between the Bible and the Mishnah.* Philadelphia: Fortress Press, 1981.

Nickelsburg, G.W.E. and MacRae, G.W. eds. *Christians Among Jews and Gentiles.* Philadelphia: Scholars Press, 1983.

Nilson, J. "To Whom Is Justin's Dialogue with Trypho Addressed?" *TS* 38 (1977): 538-546.

Noakes, K.W. "Melito of Sardis and the Jews." *SP* 13.2 (1975): 244-249.

Nock, A.D. Review of *Logos und Nomos* by C. Anderson. JTS 7 (1956): 314-316.

Nolland, J. "Do Romans Observe Jewish Customs?" *VC* 33 (1979): 1-11.

Norris, F.W. "Asia Minor before Ignatius: Walter Bauer Reconsidered." *SE* 7 (1982): 365-377.

Noth, M. *Geschichte Israels.* Göttingen: Vandenhoeck & Ruprecht, 2d ed., 1954. Trans. P.R. Ackroyd, *The History of Israel.* Rev. ed. New York: Harper & Row, 1960.

O'Connor, D.W. *Peter in Rome, The Literary, Liturgical and Archaeological Evidence.* New York, 1969.

Oehler, J. "Epigraphische Beiträge zur Geschichte des Judentums," *MGWJ*, 53 (1909) 293-302; 443-452; 525-538.

O'Hagan, A.P. "Barnabas: A Christian Theology of History." *Material Re-Creation in the Apostolic Fathers. SP* (=TU 100), 44-67. Berlin, 1968.

Osborn, O.E.F. "Justin's Response to Second Century Challenges." *AusBR* 14 (1966): 37-54.

___. *Justin Martyr.* Tübingen: Mohr-Siebeck, 1973.

Osborn, R.T. "The Christian Blasphemy." *JAAR* 53 (1985): 339-363.

Oster, R.E., editor. *A Bibliography of Ancient Ephesus.* American Theological Library Association; Metuchen, NJ: Scarecrow Press, 1987.

Overman, J.A. "The God-Fearers: Some Neglected Features." *JSNT* 32 (1988): 17-26.

Parkes, J. *The Conflict of Church and Synagogue. A Study in the Origins of Antisemitism.* [1934]. Cleveland and Philadelphia, 1961.

Parsons, M.C. "The Critical Use of the Rabbinic Literature in New Testament Studies." *PRS* 12 (1985): 85-102.

A Patristic Greek Lexicon. Ed. G.W.H. Lampe. Oxford, 1961.

Patte, D. *What is Structural Exegesis?* Philadelphia: Fortress Press, 1976.

___. "Response to Peter Haas: Semiotic and Jewish Ethics." *Semeia* 34 (1985): 85-92.

Pearson, B.A. "Earliest Christianity in Egypt: Some Observations." In *The Roots of Egyptian Christianity*, edited by B.A. Pearson and J.E. Goehring, 132-160. Philadelphia: Fortress Press, 1986.

Pearson, B.A. and Goehring, J.E. eds. *The Roots of Egyptian Christianity.* Philadelphia: Fortress Press, 1986.

Pedley, J.G. ed. *New Light on Ancient Carthage.* Ann Arbor: University of Michigan Press, 1980.

Pelikan, J. *The Christian Tradition: A History of the Development of Doctrine, 1, The Emergence of the Catholic Tradition (100-600).* Chicago: University of Chicago Press, 1971.

Perler, O. *Meliton de Sardes, sur la Paque et Fragments.* Paris, 1966.

___. "Typologie der Leiden des Herrn in Melitons *PERI PASCHA*." In P. Granfield and J.A. Jungmann, editors, *Kyriakon* vol.1. Münster: Aschendorff, 1970, 257-265.

Peters, F.E. *The Harvest of Hellenism: A History of the Near East from Alexander the Great to the Triumph of Christianity.* New York: Simon & Schuster, 1970.

Peterson, E. "Ps. Cyprian, *ADVERSUS JUDAEOS* und Meliton von Sardes." *VC* 6 (1952): 33-43.

Pettinato, G. "The Royal Archives of Tell Mardikh-Ebla." *BA* 39 (1976): 44-52.

Picard, G. *Carthage.* Translated by M. Kochan and L. Kochan. New York: Frederick Ungar Pub. Co., 1965.

Pichler, K. *Streit um das Christentum der Angriff des Kelsos und die Antwort des Origenes.* Bern, 1980.

Prigent, P. *Justin et l'Ancien Testament.* Paris, 1964.

Pritchard, J.B. *Ancient Near Eastern Texts*, 3d. ed. Princeton: Princeton University Press, 1969.

Pummer, R. "New Evidence for Samaritan Christianity?" *CBQ* 41 (1979): 98-117.

Purvis, J.D. *The Samaritan Pentateuch and the Origin of the Samaritan Sect.* HSM 2. Cambridge, MA: Harvard University Press, 1968.

___. "Samaritans." In *IDBS*. 776-777. Nashville, Abingdon, 1976.

———. "The Samaritans and Judaism." In *Early Judaism and Its Modern Interpreters*, edited by R.A. Kraft and G.W.E. Nickelsburg, 81-98. Atlanta: Scholars Press, 1986.

Quasten, J. *Patrology*, 3 vols., 1950. Reprint, Westminster, MD: Christian Classics, Inc., 1983.

Quispel, G. "A Jewish Source of Minicius Felix." *VC* 3 (1949): 113-122.

———. "African Christianity before Minicius Felix and Tertullian." In *Actus. Studies in Honour of H.L.W. Nelson*. ed., J. den Boeft, A.H. Kossels, 257-335. Utrecht: Inst. voor Klass. Talen, XIII, 1982.

Rache, B. "Melito of Sardis." In *The New Catholic Encyclopaedia* 9. Editorial Board of the Catholic University of America, Washington, D.C., 631-633. New York, 1967.

Räisänen, H. *Paul and the Law*. Philadelphia: Fortress Press, 1986.

Rajak, T. "Was There a Roman Charter for the Jews?" *JRS* 74 (1984): 107-123.

———. "Jews and Christians as Groups in a Pagan World." In *"To See Ourselves As Others See Us": Christians, Jews, and "Others" in Late Antiquity*. Edited by J. Neusner and E.S. Frerichs, 247-262. Chico, CA: Scholars Press, 1985.

Ramsay, W.M. *The Church in the Roman Empire*. New York, 1893.

———. *The Letters of the Seven Churches of Asia*. New York, 1905.

Rees, B.R. Review of *The Acts of Pagan Martyrs* by H.A. Musurillo. *JEA* 43 (1957): 126-127.

Remus, H. "Justin Martyr's Argument with Judaism." In *Anti-Judaism in Early Christianity, 2, Separation and Polemic*, ed. S.G. Wilson, 59-80. Ontario: Wilfrid Laurier University, 1986.

Reynolds, J. *The Inscriptions of Roman Tripolitania*. Roma, 1952.

———. "The Christians' Inscriptions of Cyrenaica." *JTS* 11 (1960): 84-294.

Reynolds, J., Beard, M. and Roueché, C. "Roman Inscriptions 1981-1985." *JRS* 76 (1986): 124-146.

Reynolds, J. and Tannenbaum, R.F. *Jews and God-fearers at Aphrodisias: Greek Inscriptions with Commentary*. Proceedings of the Cambridge Philological Society Supplement, vol. 12. Cambridge, England: University Press, 1987.

Richardson, P. and Granskou, D., eds. *Anti-Judaism in Early Christianity, 1, Paul and the Gospels*. (Studies in Christianity and Judaism 2.) Waterloo, Canada: Wilfrid Laurier University, 1986.

Richardson, P. and Shukster, M.B. "Barnabas, Nerva, and the Yavnean Rabbis." *JTS* NS 34 (1983):31-55.

Rist, J.M. "The Importance of Stoic Logic in the Contra Celsum." In *Neoplatonism and Early Christian Thought*, eds. H.J. Blumenthal and R.A. Markus, 64-78. London: Variorum, 1981.

___."Beyond Stoic and Platonist. A Sample of Origen's Treatment of Philosophy (*Contra Celsum* 4.62-70)." In *Platonism und Christentum* 228-238. (Reprint, *Platonism and its Christian Heritage*.) London, 1985.

Robert, J. and Robert, L. "Bulletin epigraphique." *Revue des etudes grecques*, 281 (1983): 123-124.

Roberts, C.H. *Manuscript Society and Belief in Early Christian Egypt*. London: Oxford Unversity Press, 1979.

Roberts, L.W. "Philosophical Method in Origen's Contra Celsum." Ph.D., SUNY at Buffalo, 1971.

Robinson, J.M. Director, *The Nag Hammadi Library in English*. New York: Harper & Row, 1977.

Robinson, J.M. and Koester, H. *Trajectories through Early Christianity*. Philadelphia: Fortress Press, 1971.

Robinson, T.A. *The Bauer Thesis Examined. The Geography of Heresy in the Early Christian Church*. Lewiston/Queenston, NY: The Edwin Mellen Press, 1988.

Rokeah, D. *Jews, Pagans and Christians in Conflict. Studia Post-Biblica*. Jerusalem-Leiden: The Magnes Press, The Hebrew University, Brill, 1982.

Rostovtzeff, M. I. *Dura Europos, The Excavations at Dura Europos, Conducted by Yale University and the French Academy of Inscriptions and Letters. Preliminary Report*. New Haven, 1928.

___. *Dura-Europos and its Art*, Oxford, 1938.

___. *The Social and Economic History of the Roman Empire*, 2 vols., 2d ed., revised by P.M. Fraser. Oxford: Clarendon Press, 1957.

Rudolph, W. *Joel-Amos-Obadja-Jona, Kommentar zum alten Testament*. 13.2. Stuttgart, 1971.

Ruether, R. *Faith and Fratricide: The Theological Roots of Anti-Semitism*. New York: Seabury, 1974.

Russel, D.S. *The Method and Message of Jewish Apocalyptic: 200 BC-AD 100*. London: SCM Press Ltd., 1964.

Saldarini, A.J. "Reconstructions of Rabbinic Judaism." In *Early Judaism and Its Modern Interpreters*, edited by R.A. Kraft and G.W.E. Nickelsburg, 437-477. Atlanta: Scholars Press, 1986.

Saller, S.J. *Second Revised Catalogue of the Ancient Synagogues of the Holy Land*. Publications of the *Studium Biblicum Franciscanum. Collectio minor* n.6., 25-26, Jerusalem, 1972.

Sanders, E.P. *Paul and Palestinian Judaism. A Comparison of Patterns of Religion*. Philadelphia: Fortress Press, 1977.

___. ed. *Jewish and Christian Self-Definition*, vol. 1, *The Shaping of Christianity in the Second and Third Centuries*. Philadelphia: Fortress Press, 1980.

___. *Jewish and Christian Self-Definition*, vol. 2, *Aspects of Judaism in the Greco-Roman Period*. Philadelphia: Fortress Press, 1981.

Sanders, E.P. and Meyer, B.F., eds. *Jewish and Christian Self-Definition*. vol. 3, *Self-Definition in the Greco-Roman World*. Philadelphia: Fortress Press, 1982.

Sanders, J.T. *The Jews in Luke-Acts*. Philadelphia: Fortress Press, 1987.

Sandmel, S. "Parallelomania." *JBL* 81 (1962): 1-13.

___. *Philo of Alexandria, An Introduction*. New York, 1979.

___. "Philo Judaeus: An Introduction to the Man, his Writings, and his Significance." *ANRW* 2.21.1. Berlin and New York: Walter de Gruyter, 1984: 3-46.

Schaff, P. *History of the Christian Church*, vol. 2, *Ante-Nicene Christianity*. 1886. Grand Rapids: Wm. B. Eerdmans, 1980.

Schneider, H.P. "Some Reflections on the Dialogue of Justin Martyr with Trypho." *SJT* 15 (1962): 164-175.

Schoedel, W.R. *Ignatius of Antioch: A Commentary on the Letters of Ignatius of Antioch*. Philadelphia: Fortress Press, 1985.

Schoeps. H.J. *Theologie und Geschichte des Judenchristentums*. Tübingen, 1949.

___. *Paul, Theology of the Apostle in the Light of Jewish Religious History*. 1959, trans. H. Knight. Philadelphia: Westminster Press, 1961.

___. *The Jewish-Christian Argument: A History of Theologies in Conflict*. New York, 1963.

___. *Jewish Christianity, Factional Dispute in the Early Church*. Philadelphia, 1969.

Scholer, D.M. "Tertullian on Jewish Persecution of Christians." *SP* 17.2 (1982): 821-828.

Schreckenberg, H. *Die christlichen Adversus-Judaeos-Texte und ihr literarisches und historisches Umfeld. (1.-11.Jh.)* Frankfurt am Main and Bern: Peter Lang, 1982.

Schürer, E. *The History of the Jewish People in the Age of Jesus Christ, (175 B.C.- A.D. 135)*. Rev. ed., G. Vermes, F. Millar and M. Black, 3 vols. Edinburgh: T & T Clark, 1973, 1979 and 1986.

Schwabe, M. "Two Inscriptions from Rome on the Tombs of a Person from Eretz Israel" (Hebrew). *Zion* 11 (1935): 46-47.

Schwartz, D.R. "The Epistle of Barnabas and the Revolt of Bar-Kokhba." *Zion* 46.4 (1981): 339-345.

Schwartz, J. "Celsus redivivus." *RHPhR* 53 (1973): 399-405.

Seager, A.R. "The Synagogue and the Jewish Community: The Building." In *Sardis from Prehistoric to Roman Times: Results of the Archaeological Exploration of Sardis 1958-1975*. Edited by G.M.A. Hanfmann, 168-178. Cambridge: Harvard University Press, 1982.

Segal, A.F. "Judaism, Christianity, and Gnosticism." In *Anti-Judaism in Early Christianity*. Vol. 2, *Separation and Polemic*. Edited by S.G. Wilson, 133-162. Waterloo, Canada: Wilfrid Laurier University, 1986.

___. *Rebecca's Children. Judaism and Christianity in the Roman World*. Cambridge: Harvard University Press, 1986.

Senay, P. *Cahiers des Etude, Anciennes*. 12 *Carthage* 4. *Text and plates bound separately*. Universite du Quebec a Trois Rivieres, Quebec, 1980, 1981.

Sevenster, J.N. *The Roots of Pagan Anti-Semitism in the Ancient World*. Leiden: Brill, 1975.

Shaw, B.D. "The Elders of Christian Africa." *CEA* 14 (1982): 207-226.

Shiffman, L.H. "At the Crossroads: Tannaitic Perspectives on the Jewish-Christian Schism." In *Jewish and Christian Self-Definition*, vol. 2, *Aspects of Judaism in the Greco-Roman Period*, eds. E.P. Sanders, A.I. Baumgarten, and Alan Mendelson, 115-156. Philadelphia: Fortress Press, 1981.

Shotwell, W.A. *The Biblical Exegesis of Justin Martyr*. London, 1965.

Shukster, M.B. and Richardson, P. "Temple and Bet Ha-midrash in the Epistle of Barnabas." In Anti-Judaism in Early Christianity 2, *Separation and Polemic*, edited by S.G. Wilson, 17-32. Waterloo, Canada: Wilfrid Laurier University, 1986.

Shutt, R.J.H. "The Letter of Aristeas." In *The Old Testament Pseudepigrapha*, 2. Edited by J.H. Charlesworth, 9. New York: Doubleday, 1985.

Sibinga, J. Smit. *The Old Testament Text of Justin Martyr*, I. *The Pentateuch*. Leiden: Brill, 1963.

___. "Melito of Sardis, The Artist and His Text." *VC* 24 (1970): 81-104.

Sider, R.D. *Ancient Rhetoric and the Art of Tertullian*. London: Oxford University Press, 1971.

Simon, M. *Verus Israel: A Study of the relations between Christian and Jew in the Roman Empire, (135-425)*. [1964] Trans. H. McKeating. Oxford, 1986.

Singer, I. "Tarphon." In *The Jewish Encyclopaedia*, 12:56. London, 1905.

Slomovic, E. and Gershenzon, R. "A Second Century Jewish-Gnostic Debate: Rabbi Jose ben Halafta and the Matrona." *JSJ* 16.1 (1985): 1-41.

Smallwood, E.M. *The Jews Under Roman Rule, From Pompey to Diocletian. Studies in Judaism in Late Antiquity* 20. 1976. Reprint. Leiden: Brill, 1981.

Smith, M. *Clement of Alexandria and the Secret Gospel of Mark.* Cambridge, MA: Harvard University Press, 1973.

Smith, M.A. "Did Justin Know the Didache?" *SP* 7.1 (1966): 287-290.

Snaith, R.H. "A Sarcophagus from Pella: New Light on the Earliest Christianity," *A* 26 (1973): 250-256.

Snyder, G. *Ante Pacem: Archaeological Evidence of Church Life before Constantine.* Macon, GA: Mercer University Press, 1985.

Sowers, S. "The Circumstances and Recollection of the Pella Flight." *ThZ* 26 (1970): 305-320.

Spawforth, A.J. and Walker, S. "The World of the Panhellenion II. Three Dorian Cities." *JRS* 76 (1986):88-105.

Spivey, R.A. "Structuralism and Biblical Studies: The Universal Guest." *Interpretation* 28.2 (1974): 133-145.

Staeger, L. *Das Leben in romischen Afrika in Spiegel der Schriften Tertullians.* Zurich, 1973.

Stambaugh, J.E. *The Ancient Roman City.* Baltimore and London: The Johns Hopkins University Press, 1988.

Stanton, G.N. "Aspects of Early Christian-Jewish Polemic and Apologetic." *NTS* 31 (1985): 377-392.

Starr, R. "The Circulation of Literary Texts in the Roman World." *CQ* 37 (i) (1987):213-223.

Stern, M., ed. and trans. *Greek and Latin Authors on Jews and Judaism*, 3 vols. Jerusalem: The Israel Academy of Sciences and Humanities, 1976-1984.

Stone, M.E., ed. *Jewish Writings of the Second Temple Period: Apocrypha, Pseudepigrapha, Qumran Sectarian Writings, Philo, Josephus.* Assen: Van Gorcum, and Philadelphia, Fortress Press, 1984.

Strack, H.L. *Jesus die Haeretiker und die Christen nach den aeltesten juedischen Angaben. Texte, Uebersetzung und Erlaeuterungen.* Leipzig, 1910.

Stylianopoulos, T. *Justin Martyr and the Mosaic Law.* Diss. Series 20, *SBL*. Missoula, MT: Scholars Press, 1975.

Suro, Roberto. "Italian Synagogue May be Oldest in Europe." *New York Times*, C3, 4 March, 1986.

Swete, H.B. *An Introduction to the Old Testament in Greek.* [1902] Revised by R.R. Ottley. New York: KTAV Publishing House, Inc., 1968.

Talbert, R.J.A., ed. *Atlas of Classical History.* New York: Macmillan Publishing Company, 1985.

Tannenbaum, R.F. "Jews and God-Fearers in the Holy City of Aphrodite." *BAR* 12.5 (1986): 54-57.

Tarn, W.W. *Hellenistic Civilization*. Third Edition, revised by the Author and G.T. Griffith. New York: New American Library, 1975.

Taylor, R.E. "Attitudes of the Fathers Toward Practices of Jewish Christians." *SP* 4.2 (1961): 504ff.

Taylor, R.O.P. "What Was Barnabas?" *CQR* 136 (1935): 59-79.

___. *The Groundwork of the Gospel*. Oxford, 1946.

Tcherikover, V. *The Jews in Egypt in the Hellenistic-Roman Age in the Light of the Papyri*, (Hebrew). Jerusalem, 1945.

___. *Hellenistic Civilization and the Jews*. Trans. S. Applebaum. 1959. Philadelphia: Atheneum, 1977.

Theissen, G. *Sociology of Early Palestinian Christianity*. Trans. John Bowden. Philadelphia: Fortress Press, 1978.

Thieme, K. "Kirche und Synagogue . . . Der *Barnabasbrief* und der *Dialog* Justin des Martyrens." *Theologisch Tijdschrift* 49 (1944): 60-383.

___. *Kirche und Synagogue*. Olten, 1945.

Thoma, C. *A Christian Theology of Judaism*. Trans. Helga Croner. New York: Paulist Press, 1980.

Tod, M.N. "Bibliography: Greco-Roman Egypt" (*Greek Inscriptions 1945-1947*). *JEA* 34 (1948): 109-113.

Tov, E. "Jewish Greek Scriptures." In *Early Judaism*, edited by R.A. Kraft and G.W.E. Nickelsburg, 221-238. Atlanta: Scholars Press, 1986.

Trakatellis, D. "Justin Martyr's Trypho." In *Christians Among Jews and Gentiles*, ed. by G.W.E. Nickelsburg and G.W. MacRae, 287-297. Philadelphia: Fortress Press, 1986.

Trigg, J.W. "A Decade of Origen Studies." *RSR* 7 (1981): 21-27.

Tsakonas, B.G. "The Usage of the Scriptures in the Homily of Melito of Sardis on the Passion." *T* 38 (1967): 609-628.

Urbach, E.E. *The Sages, Their Concepts and Beliefs*, 2 vols. Jerusalem, 1975.

___. *Halakah and History. Jews, Greeks and Christians. Studies in Judaism in Late Antiquity*, 21. edited by W.D. Davies, 112-128. Leiden: Brill, 1976.

___. "Self Isolation or Self-Affirmation in Judaism in the First Three Centuries: Theory and Practice." In *Jewish and Christian Self-Definition*, vol. 2. edited by E.P. Sanders, 269-298. Philadelphia: Fortress Press, 1981.

Van Campenhausen, H. *The Fathers of the Greek Church*. London, 1963.

Van Woerden, I.S. "The Iconography of the Sacrifice of Abraham." *VC* 15 (1961): 214-255.

Vermes, G. and Neusner, J. *Essays in Honour of Yigael Yadin*. *JJS* 33 (Spring/-Autumn 1982): viii-602.

Verweijs, P.G. *Evangelian und neues gesetz in der aeltesten Christenheit bis auf Marcion*. Utrecht, 1960.

Veyne, P., ed. *A History of Private Life* I, *From Pagan Rome to Byzantium*. Trans. A. Goldhammer. Cambridge: The Belknap Press of Harvard University Press, 1987.

Via, D.O. Jr. "A Structuralist Approach to Paul's Old Testament Hermeneutic." *Interpretation* 28.2 (1974): 201-220.

von der Osten-Sacken, P. *Christian-Jewish Dialogue: Theological Foundations*. Trans. M. Kohl. Philadelphia: Fortress Press, 1986.

Von Rad, G. *Old Testament Theology*, I: *The Theology of Israel's Historical Traditions*, [1962]. Trans. D.M.G. Stalker. Edinburg and London: Oliver & Boyd, 1962.

Walker, W. *A History of the Christian Church*. Revised by R.A. Norris, D.W. Lotz, and R.T. Handy. New York, 1985.

Walzer, R. *Galen on Jews and Christians*. London, 1949.

Watson, F. *Paul, Judaism and the Gentiles: A Sociological Approach*. SNTS Monograph Series, 56. Cambridge: Cambridge University Press, 1986.

Watts, J.W.D. *The Books of Joel, Obadiah, Jonah, Nahum, Habakkuk and Zephaniah*. Cambridge, England, 1975.

Weis, P.R. "Some Samaritanisms of Justin Martyr." *JTS* 45 (1944): 199-205.

Welborn, L.L. "On the Discord in Corinth: I Corinthians 4 and Ancient Politics." *JBL* 106.1 (March, 1987): 85-111.

Wells, C.M. "Recent Excavations at Carthage: A Review Article." *AJA* 86 (1982): 293-296, 605-606.

Wengst, K. *Tradition und Theologie des Barnabasbrief*. Berlin, 1971.

Werner, E. "Melito of Sardes, The First Poet of Deicide." *HUCA* 37 (1966): 191-210.

White, L.J. "Grid and Group in Matthew's Community: The Righteousness/-Honor Code in the Sermon on the Mount." *Semeia* 35 (1986): 61-90.

White, L.M. "The Delos Synagogue Revisited: Recent Fieldwork in the Greco-Roman Diaspora", *HTR* 80:2 (April 1987): 133-160.

White, R.C. "Melito of Sardis: Earliest Christian Orator?" *LTQ* 2.1 (1967): 82-91.

Wifstrand, A. "Die wahre Lehre des Kelsos." In *Bulletin de la Societe Royales des Lettres de Lund.* (1941-1942): 391ff.

___. "The Homily of Melito on the Passion." *VC* 2 (1948): 200-223.

Wilcox, M. "The 'God-fearers' in Acts---A Reconsideration." *JSNT* 13 (1981): 102-122.

Wilde, R. *The Treatment of the Jews in the Greek Christian Writers of the First Three Centuries.* Washington D.C.: The Catholic University of America Press, 1949.

Wilken, R.L. "Judaism in Roman and Christian Society." *JR* 47 (1967): 313.

___. *Judaism and the Early Christian Mind: A Study of Cyril of Alexandria's Exegesis and Theology.* New Haven: Yale University Press, 1971.

___. "Melito, The Jewish Community at Sardis, and the Sacrifice of Isaac." *TS* 37 (1976): 53-69.

___. Review of *Origen and the Jews* by N. deLange. *TS* 38 (1977): 578.

___. "The Jews and Christians Apologetics after Theodosius I Cunctos Populos." *HTR* 73 (1980): 451-471.

___. *The Myth of Christian Beginnings.* South Bend: Notre Dame, 1980.

___. *The Christians as the Romans Saw Them.* New Haven: Yale, 1984.

___. *John Crysostom and the Jews.* Los Angeles, CA: The University of California Press, 1984.

___. "Religious Pluralism and Early Christian Theology." *Interpretation* 40 (1986) 379-391.

Williams, A.L. *Justin Martyr, The Dialogue with Trypho.* London: S.P.C.K., 1930.

___. "The Date of the Epistle of Barnabas." *JTS* 34 (1933): 337-346.

___. *The Adversus Judaeos, A Bird's-Eye View of Christian Apologiae until the Renaissance.* Cambridge, 1935.

Williamson, C.M. "The Adversus Judaeos Tradition in Christian Theology." *Encounter* 39 (Summer, 1978): 273-296.

Wilson, S.G. "Passover, Easter, and Anti-Judaism: Melito of Sardis and Others." In *"To See Ourselves as Others See Us": Christians, Jews, "Others" in Late Antiquity*, eds. J. Neusner and E.S. Frerichs, 337-355. Chico, CA: Scholars Press, 1985.

___. ed. *Anti-Judaism in Early Christianity, 2, Separation and Polemic.* Waterloo, Canada: Wilfrid Laurier University, 1986.

___. "Marcion and the Jews." In *Anti-Judaism in Early Christianity*, 2, *Separation and Polemic*, ed. S.G. Wilson, 45-58. Waterloo, Canada: Wilfrid Laurier University, 1986.

___. "Melito and Israel." In *Anti-Judaism in Early Christianity*, 2, *Separation and Polemic*, ed. S.G. Wilson, 81-102. Waterloo, Canada: Wilfrid Laurier University, 1986.

Winden, J.C.M. van. "Notes on Origen, *Contra Celsum*." *VC* 20 (1966): 201-213.

___. "An Early Christian Philosopher. Justin Martyr's *Dialogue with Trypho*, 1-9." Leiden: Brill, 1971.

Winslow, D.F. "The Polemical Christology of Melito of Sardis," *SP* 17.2 (1982): 765-776.

Wolfson, H.A. *Philo, Foundations of Religious Philosophy in Judaism, Christianity, and Islam*, 2 vols. Cambridge: Harvard University Press, 1947.

___. *The Philosophy of the Church Fathers: Faith, Trinity, Incarnation*, 3d ed. Cambridge, MA and London: Harvard University Press, 1956.

Wright, G.E. *Shechem. The Biography of a Biblical City*. New York and Toronto: McGraw Hill Book Company, 1965.

Yadin, Y. *Masada, Herod's Fortress and the Zealots' Last Stand*. New York: Random House, 1966.

___. *Bar-Kokhba, The rediscovery of the legendary hero of the last Jewish Revolt against Imperial Rome*. 1971. Jerusalem: Steimatzky's Agency Ltd., 1978.

Yamauchi, E.M. *The Archaeology of New Testament Cities in Western Asia Minor*. Grand Rapids: Baker Book House, 1980.

Yerushalmi, Y.H. *Zakor, Jewish History and Jewish Memory*. Seattle and London: University of Washington Press, 1982.

Zaas, P. Review of *John Chrysostom and the Jews* by R.L. Wilken; *St. John Chrysostom*, ed. and trans. P.W. Harkins; and *The Origins of Anti-Semitism* by J.G. Gager. *RSR* 11.4 (October 1985): 337-340.

Zahavy, T. *The Traditions of Eleazer ben Azariah*. BJS 2, Missoula, MT: Scholars Press, 1977.

___. A review of *In Search of Talmudic Biography: The Problem of the Attributed Saying* by J. Neusner. BJS 70. Chico, CA: Scholars Press, 1984 and *The Peripatetic Saying: The Problem of the Thrice-Told Tale in Talmudic Literature* by J. Neusner. BJS, 89. Chico, CA: Scholars Press, 1985. In *JBL* 106.2 (June 1987):354-356.

Zeitlin, S. *Studies in the Early History of Judaism*. 4 vols. New York: KTAV, Publishing House, Inc., 1973-1978.

Zuntz, G. "On the Opening Sentence of Melito's Paschal Homily." *HTR* 36 (1943): 299-315.

INDEX

Aboda Zara (Abodah Zarah), 67, 126-127, 134, 139
Acta, 32-33, 38, 80
Acts of the Alexandrian Martyrs, 28
Acts of the Apostles, 41
Acts of the Pagan Martyrs, The, 32
Ad Nationes, 131
adversus Judaeos literature, 1, 7, 11, 15-19, 22, 42, 49, 51, 85, 86, 115, 117, 120, 121, 134, 137, 138, 140
    methods of study of, 2-19
    point of view in, 1-2
Adversus Marcionem, 134
Against Apion, 32
Akiba, Rabbi, 52, 53, 61
Albright, W.F., 4
Alexandria, Egypt, 2, 21, 23, 24-28, 29-31, 32-47, 121
    Great Synagogue in, 30, 37
Alon, G., 46
American Schools of Oriental Research, The, 120
Answer to the Jews, 2, 117-144
    a biblical commentary, 137-138, 141
    as "Christian rhetoric," 117-118
    not anti-Jewish but written for the nations, 140
    a "Scheinpolemik," 138
    supersessionistic views in, 139
anti-Judaism, Christian, 1, 18, 134
Antioch, 93
anti-Semitism, 28, 93, 105
Antonius, Lucius, 101
Apology, 131
Arbela, 108

Arianism, 43
Artemis, Temple to, 69
Athens, 121
Babylonia, 66, 108
Bar-Kokhba, 3, 52, 59, 60, 66
Bar-Kokhba War, 21, 52, 59-60, 79
Barnabas, 2, 21-48, 86, 138
Barnard, L.W., 67, 70-71
Barnes, T.D., 123, 125, 129, 131, 135-136, 139, 142-143, 144
Baron, Salo, 37, 65-66, 76
Bauer, W., 25, 42
Bell, H.I., 41, 42
Berakoth, T.B., 67
Bet She'arim, Israel, 98
Beth ha-midrash, 45
Bible, 3-5, 13, 112
Bokser, B.Z., 61, 86
Bollandists, 82
Brown, Peter, 134

Cairo Geniza, 42
Carthage, 2, 117-144
    catacombs in, 121, 122, 132
    "golden age" for, 122
    Jewish persecution of Christians in, alleged, 135-137
    necropolis in, 121, 122, 123-125, 143
Cassuto, U., 4
catacombs
    in Carthage, 121, 122, 132
    Roman, 81
Catechetical School, 42
Christians, 1, 2, 16, 19, 24, 29, 30, 32, 41-43, 47, 49, 53, 54, 66, 79-83, 115, 118

in Carthage, 119, 122-124, 125, 129-132, 133, 134, 135-137, 142-144
Jewish, 12, 61-63, 66-67
Jewish persecution of, 70, 75-78, 135-137, 144
relations with Romans, 78-80
in Sardis, 89, 90, 92, 93, 94, 95-96, 101, 102-113, 115-116
Chrysostom, 86
city, as background text, 7, 17-18, 24-28, 50, 54-69, 69-78, 78-84, 120-137, 143
Claudius, 97
letter to Alexandrians, 28, 36-37, 97
Clement of Alexandria, 41, 89
Commodus, 29
Constantine, 77, 96, 110, 131, 143
Conzelmann, H., 5
Corinth, 51
Corinthians, letter to the, 45
Corpus Papyrorum Judaicorum, 29-30
Cosgrove, C., 86-87
Covenant, 23-24, 47, 140
New, 117, 140
Crescens, 81, 82
Cyprian, 86, 126, 134

Damascus, 65
Daniel, 44
De Idolatria (On Idolatry), 126, 127, 134, 139
Dead Sea, 3
Dead Sea Scrolls. *See* Qumran, Kirbet, discoveries at
Delos, 57
"Demonstrations of the Gospel," 86
"Dialogue between a Christian and a Jew," 88
Dialogue with Trypho a Jew, 49-88
modern writers' opinion on, 85-88
Diaspora, 8, 34, 63, 65, 70, 97, 98, 100, 132

Mediterranean, 99
Roman, 11-12
western, 29, 72, 83, 133
Didache (Teaching of the Twelve Apostles), 23
Dio Cassius (Cassius Dio), 33, 79
"Disappearance of the 'God-fearers,' The," 11
Djemila (Cuicul), 132
Douglas, Mary, 6-7
Dura-Europos, 98

Eadie, J.W., and Humphrey, J.H., 120
Easter, 106
Ebla, 4
Ecclesiastical History, 104
Edessa, 108
Efroymson, David, 134, 140, 144
Egyptians, 27, 36, 38
"Eight Orations against the Jews," 86
Elias, 51
Enoch, 44
Ephesus, 2, 55, 69-78, 84, 106
Epistle of Barnabas, 21-48, 42, 44
two sections of, 22-23, 44
Euphrates valley, 108
Eusebius, 41, 61, 86, 89, 96, 104, 106

Flaccus, 102
Foss, Clive, 69
Fox, R.L., 78
Frend, W.H.C., 13, 46, 86, 105, 125, 130

Gager, John, 28, 34
Galilee, 64
Gaston, L., 110
Gnosticism, 42, 43, 78, 93
Gnostics, 134, 136
"God-fearers," 11, 43, 98, 133
Goodenough, E.R., 8, 64, 70, 86, 98, 121
Goodspeed, E.J., 74
Gospels, 4-5, 18
Gottwald, N.K., 5

Index

Grant, R.M., 25
Greeks, 27, 28, 32, 36, 37-38, 44
Groh, D.E., 132

Hadrian, 80
Halakah, 14, 46, 126, 134
Hall, S.G., 106, 107
Hanfmann, G.M.A., 95
Hebrew Bible. *See* Old Testament
Hellenistic Christianity, 70-71
Hippo Regius, 132
Hirschberg, H.Z. (J.W.), 122, 127
historical-critical study methods, 9, 19
Horbury, W., 68
Hulen, A.B., 86, 88

Ignatius, 74
Incognitas, 103
Irenaeus, 74, 138

Jerusalem, 36, 37, 40, 42, 55, 61, 91, 99, 107
Jesus (Christ), 2, 5, 11, 59, 60, 61, 68, 71, 73, 81, 86, 91, 105, 111, 114, 117, 118, 119, 138, 139, 140, 142
Jewish Antiquities, 101
Jewish Symbols, 70
Jews, 1, 2, 3, 8, 9, 10, 11, 18, 19, 24, 26, 28, 29-30, 31-41, 42, 43, 44-48, 49, 53, 54, 55, 59-61, 63, 69, 70-73, 79, 115
  of the Bible ("Biblepeople"), 139, 140
  in Carthage, 117-119, 122-128, 130, 133, 134, 135-144
  erring of, 119
  persecution of Christians by, 70, 75-78, 125-137, 144
  relations with Samaritans in Neapolis, 64-66
  in Rome, 82-84
  in Sardis, 90, 91, 92, 93, 94-95, 96-102, 103, 105-106, 107-113, 115-116
  Second Revolt against the Romans, 59-60, 79

Johanan ben Zakkai, Rabbi, 55, 61
John, 69, 103
Johnson, Sherman E., 102, 103
Josephus, 31-32, 59-60, 64, 100, 101-102
Judah the Prince, 66
Judaism: The Evidence of Mishnah, 14
Judaism, vitality of, 73, 107, 108, 109, 142
Judea, 64
Julian, 77
Justin Martyr, 2, 24, 49-88, 92, 138
  martyrdom in Rome, 81-82
Justinian, 101

Kaufmann, Y., 4
Kelber, W.H., 41
Koester, H., 25, 29, 42
Koina hodos, 69
Kraabel, A.T., 11-12, 98, 99, 100-101
Kraft, R.A., 25, 46

Language
  Aramaic, 63, 64
  Greek, 25, 29, 34-35, 46, 63, 71-73, 83, 92, 97, 99, 100
  Hebrew, 34-35, 63, 64, 72, 83, 99, 144
Layton, B., 78
legalism, Jewish and Christian, 134-135
Letter of Aristeas, 33-34
Letter to Theodore, 41
Levenson, Jon D., 110-111
Lowy, S., 46-47
Lusius, 33

McGiffert, A.C., 88
Maeander valley, 69
Malina, B., 7
Marcion, 74, 75, 84, 134, 140
Marcionite influence, 93
Mark, St., 41
Matthiae, P., 4
Meeks, Wayne, 5, 7, 93
Melito, 2, 24, 86, 89-116

Michigan, University of, 120
Midrash, 13, 40, 46
   Christian, 105
minim, 112
Minnesota, University of, Center for Ancient Studies, 8
Mishnah, 13, 14, 64, 66, 112, 121, 134, 144
   Tractate *Yoma*, 67
   see also Aboda Zara
Mitten, D.G., 94
Moses, 35
   Law of, 63, 66
Musurillo, H.A., 32

Nablus, West Bank, 65, 66
Nag Hammadi library, 4, 9-10
Neapolis, Palestine, 2, 54, 55, 56-57, 63, 84
   Jewish-Samaritan relations in, 64-66
Nehardea, 108
neo-Platonism, 71
Nero, 77
Nerva, 45
Neusner, J., 9, 13, 14-15, 17, 19, 108
New Testament, 2, 5, 11-12, 41, 64, 67, 68, 75, 76, 80-81, 86, 110, 112, 119, 139, 140, 141, 142
Nisibis, 108
Noakes, K.W., 107
notzrim (Nazarenes), 66-67

Obadiah, 98, 107
Old Testament, 2, 5, 29, 66, 72, 86, 100, 114, 117, 118, 119, 139
   "Word of God," 71
Origen, 41, 74-75
Orthodoxy, 43

pagans, 117, 131, 143
   in Sardis, 93, 95, 96, 97-98, 101
Palestine, 10, 31, 34, 39, 40, 42, 43, 52, 54, 55, 59, 60, 65, 66, 69, 79, 98, 99, 100, 106-107, 109, 112, 122, 127

Yavneh, 25
papyri, 26, 29-30
"Parallelomania," 67
paroikia, 104, 105
Paschal Homily, 89-116
   audience for, 112-114
   interpretations of, 89-93
   as literary form, 109, 111-112, 116
   Scriptures in, 114
   supersessionistic teachings in, 112-113, 116
Passover, 105, 106, 109
Paul, 11, 12, 45, 69, 70, 74-75, 80, 81, 104, 110
Pauline corpus, 5
Pax Romana, 70
Pearson, B.A., 25, 26
Pella, Palestine, 61
Pergamum, letter to, 103
Peri Pascha ("Concerning the Passover"), 89
Persian Royal Road, 69
Peter, 74, 80, 81
Pettinato, G., 4
Philo of Alexandria, 9, 31, 34-36, 39, 47, 70, 71, 100
Polycarp, 74, 77, 80, 82, 105
Polycrates, bishop of Ephesus, 106
"Pre-canonical synoptic transmission," 41
Pritchard, J.B., 4
proselytes, 133
Pseudo-Jonathan, 46

Quartodeciman debate (controversy), 104, 106, 107, 112, 116
Qumran, Kirbet
   discoveries at, 3, 9-10, 42, 98
   people of, 46, 47

rabbinic Judaism, 63, 64, 66, 125-126, 127, 134
Revelation of John, The, 81, 95, 96, 102-104
Richardson, P., 45

Robinson, J.M., 4
Robinson, T.A., 25, 42
Romans, 31, 36-37, 45, 59, 60, 131, 142
Rome, 2, 38, 52, 55, 78-84, 85, 106, 121
  Jews in, 82-84
Rusticus, 81

Samaria, 55, 65
Samaritans, 56-58, 59, 60, 63, 64-66
Sanders, J.T., 11, 12, 16, 18
Sandmel, S., 67
Sardis, 2, 8, 40-41, 69, 78, 89
  Christians in, 89, 90, 92, 93, 94, 95-96, 101, 102-113, 115-116
  Jews in, 90, 91, 92, 93, 94-95, 96-102, 103, 103-106, 107-113, 115-116
  pagans in, 93, 95, 96, 97-98, 101
  Roman Gymnasium in, 97
  synagogue in, 94, 95, 95, 97-98, 99, 100-101, 109-110
Saturnias, 129
Schechem, Palestine, 54, 56, 65
  Samaritan Temple in, 65
Schneider, H.P., 85
Scillium, 129
Scorpiace, 135, 143
"Second Sophistic," 92
seniores, 124, 125, 126, 127-128, 130
Septuagint, 29, 33-34, 63, 70, 71-73
Shemoneh 'Esreh Benedictions, 67-69
  Twelfth Benediction, 67
Shukster, M.B., 45
Shutt, R.J.H., 34
Sider, R.D., 118
Simon, M., 71, 122
Smith, Morton, 41
Smyrna, 105
Snyder, G., 96, 131
Soren, David, 122
Stoicism, 71
Stylianopoulos, T., 86

supersessionistic teachings
  in *Answer to the Jews*, 139
  in *Paschal Homily*, 112-113, 116
Syria, 25, 36

Tacitus, 77
Talmud, 13, 30-31, 33, 125, 127
Tannaite influence, 108
Targum(im), 46, 63
Tcherikover, V., 29, 38
Temple (in Jerusalem), 24, 36, 39, 45, 46, 47, 60, 61, 63, 65, 91
Tertullian, 2, 24, 68, 74, 87, 93, 117-144
Theissen, G., 7
"Three Books of Testimonies," 86
Thyatira, letter to, 103
Tiberius, 97, 137
"Topography of the Southeast Quarter of Later Roman Carthage, The," 120
Tosefta, 30
Trajan, 33, 42, 44
Trakatellis, D., 88
Tränkle, Herman, 138
Trypho, 2, 51-53, 54-55, 59, 60, 63-64, 66, 69, 72, 73
  eclectic Judaism represented by, 63-64, 66, 85
Tunisia, 122

Vespasian, 37, 56, 137
Victor, bishop of Rome, 106

Watson, F., 11, 12, 16
Wilken, Robert, 93
Wilson, S.G., 110, 134

Yavneh, Palestine, 25, 45, 48, 61
  rabbinical school at, 55

Zeus Hypsistos, Temple to, 57

Brown Judaic Studies

140001	Approaches to Ancient Judaism I	William S. Green
140002	The Traditions of Eleazar Ben Azariah	Tzvee Zahavy
140003	Persons and Institutions in Early Rabbinic Judaism	William S. Green
140004	Claude Goldsmid Montefiore on the Ancient Rabbis	Joshua B. Stein
140005	The Ecumenical Perspective and the Modernization of Jewish Religion	S. Daniel Breslauer
140006	The Sabbath-Law of Rabbi Meir	Robert Goldenberg
140007	Rabbi Tarfon	Joel Gereboff
140008	Rabban Gamaliel II	Shamai Kanter
140009	Approaches to Ancient Judaism II	William S. Green
140010	Method and Meaning in Ancient Judaism	Jacob Neusner
140011	Approaches to Ancient Judaism III	William S. Green
140012	Turning Point: Zionism and Reform Judaism	Howard R. Greenstein
140013	Buber on God and the Perfect Man	Pamela Vermes
140014	Scholastic Rabbinism	Anthony J. Saldarini
140015	Method and Meaning in Ancient Judaism II	Jacob Neusner
140016	Method and Meaning in Ancient Judaism III	Jacob Neusner
140017	Post Mishnaic Judaism in Transition	Baruch M. Bokser
140018	A History of the Mishnaic Law of Agriculture: Tractate Maaser Sheni	Peter J. Haas
140019	Mishnah's Theology of Tithing	Martin S. Jaffee
140020	The Priestly Gift in Mishnah: A Study of Tractate Terumot	Alan. J. Peck
140021	History of Judaism: The Next Ten Years	Baruch M. Bokser
140022	Ancient Synagogues	Joseph Gutmann
140023	Warrant for Genocide	Norman Cohn
140024	The Creation of the World According to Gersonides	Jacob J. Staub
140025	Two Treatises of Philo of Alexandria: A Commentary on De Gigantibus and Quod Deus Sit Immutabilis	David Winston/John Dillon
140026	A History of the Mishnaic Law of Agriculture: Kilayim	Irving Mandelbaum
140027	Approaches to Ancient Judaism IV	William S. Green
140028	Judaism in the American Humanities	Jacob Neusner
140029	Handbook of Synagogue Architecture	Marilyn Chiat
140030	The Book of Mirrors	Daniel C. Matt
140031	Ideas in Fiction: The Works of Hayim Hazaz	Warren Bargad
140032	Approaches to Ancient Judaism V	William S. Green
140033	Sectarian Law in the Dead Sea Scrolls: Courts, Testimony and the Penal Code	Lawrence H. Schiffman
140034	A History of the United Jewish Appeal: 1939-1982	Marc L. Raphael
140035	The Academic Study of Judaism	Jacob Neusner
140036	Woman Leaders in the Ancient Synagogue	Bernadette Brooten
140037	Formative Judaism: Religious, Historical, and Literary Studies	Jacob Neusner
140038	Ben Sira's View of Women: A Literary Analysis	Warren C. Trenchard
140039	Barukh Kurzweil and Modern Hebrew Literature	James S. Diamond

140040	*Israeli Childhood Stories of the Sixties: Yizhar, Aloni,Shahar, Kahana-Carmon*	Gideon Telpaz
140041	*Formative Judaism II: Religious, Historical, and Literary Studies*	Jacob Neusner
140042	*Judaism in the American Humanities II: Jewish Learning and the New Humanities*	Jacob Neusner
140043	*Support for the Poor in the Mishnaic Law of Agriculture: Tractate Peah*	Roger Brooks
140044	*The Sanctity of the Seventh Year: A Study of Mishnah Tractate Shebiit*	Louis E. Newman
140045	*Character and Context: Studies in the Fiction of Abramovitsh, Brenner, and Agnon*	Jeffrey Fleck
140046	*Formative Judaism III: Religious, Historical, and Literary Studies*	Jacob Neusner
140047	*Pharaoh's Counsellors: Job, Jethro, and Balaam in Rabbinic and Patristic Tradition*	Judith Baskin
140048	*The Scrolls and Christian Origins: Studies in the Jewish Background of the New Testament*	Matthew Black
140049	*Approaches to Modern Judaism I*	Marc Lee Raphael
140050	*Mysterious Encounters at Mamre and Jabbok*	William T. Miller
140051	*The Mishnah Before 70*	Jacob Neusner
140052	*Sparda by the Bitter Sea: Imperial Interaction in Western Anatolia*	Jack Martin Balcer
140053	*Hermann Cohen: The Challenge of a Religion of Reason*	William Kluback
140054	*Approaches to Judaism in Medieval Times I*	David R. Blumenthal
140055	*In the Margins of the Yerushalmi: Glosses on the English Translation*	Jacob Neusner
140056	*Approaches to Modern Judaism II*	Marc Lee Raphael
140057	*Approaches to Judaism in Medieval Times II*	David R. Blumenthal
140058	*Midrash as Literature: The Primacy of Documentary Discourse*	JacobNeusner
140059	*The Commerce of the Sacred: Mediation of the Divine Among Jews in the Graeco-Roman Diaspora*	Jack N. Lightstone
140060	*Major Trends in Formative Judaism I: Society and Symbol in Political Crisis*	Jacob Neusner
140061	*Major Trends in Formative Judaism II: Texts, Contents, and Contexts*	Jacob Neusner
140062	*A History of the Jews in Babylonia I: The Parthian Period*	Jacob Neusner
140063	*The Talmud of Babylonia: An American Translation. XXXII: Tractate Arakhin*	Jacob Neusner
140064	*Ancient Judaism: Debates and Disputes*	Jacob Neusner
140065	*Prayers Alleged to Be Jewish: An Examination of the Constitutiones Apostolorum*	David Fiensy
140066	*The Legal Methodology of Hai Gaon*	Tsvi Groner
140067	*From Mishnah to Scripture: The Problem of the Unattributed Saying*	Jacob Neusner
140068	*Halakhah in a Theological Dimension*	David Novak

140069	*From Philo to Origen: Middle Platonism in Transition*	Robert M. Berchman
140070	*In Search of Talmudic Biography: The Problem of the Attributed Saying*	Jacob Neusner
140071	*The Death of the Old and the Birth of the New: The Framework of the Book of Numbers and the Pentateuch*	Dennis T. Olson
140072	*The Talmud of Babylonia: An American Translation. XVII: Tractate Sotah*	Jacob Neusner
140073	*Understanding Seeking Faith: Essays on the Case of Judaism. Volume Two: Literature, Religion and the Social Study of Judiasm*	JacobNeusner
140074	*The Talmud of Babylonia: An American Translation. VI: Tractate Sukkah*	Jacob Neusner
140075	*Fear Not Warrior: A Study of 'al tira' Pericopes in the Hebrew Scriptures*	Edgar W. Conrad
140076	*Formative Judaism IV: Religious, Historical, and Literary Studies*	Jacob Neusner
140077	*Biblical Patterns in Modern Literature*	David H. Hirsch/ Nehama Aschkenasy
140078	*The Talmud of Babylonia: An American Translation I: Tractate Berakhot*	Jacob Neusner
140079	*Mishnah's Division of Agriculture: A History and Theology of Seder Zeraim*	Alan J. Avery-Peck
140080	*From Tradition to Imitation: The Plan and Program of Pesiqta Rabbati and Pesiqta deRab Kahana*	Jacob Neusner
140081	*The Talmud of Babylonia: An American Translation. XXIIIA: Tractate Sanhedrin, Chapters 1-3*	Jacob Neusner
140082	*Jewish Presence in T. S. Eliot and Franz Kafka*	Melvin Wilk
140083	*School, Court, Public Administration: Judaism and its Institutions in Talmudic Babylonia*	Jacob Neusner
140084	*The Talmud of Babylonia: An American Translation. XXIIIB: Tractate Sanhedrin, Chapters 4-8*	Jacob Neusner
140085	*The Bavli and Its Sources: The Question of Tradition in the Case of Tractate Sukkah*	Jacob Neusner
140086	*From Description to Conviction: Essays on the History and Theology of Judaism*	Jacob Neusner
140087	*The Talmud of Babylonia: An American Translation. XXIIIC: Tractate Sanhedrin, Chapters 9-11*	Jacob Neusner
140088	*Mishnaic Law of Blessings and Prayers: Tractate Berakhot*	Tzvee Zahavy
140089	*The Peripatetic Saying: The Problem of the Thrice-Told Tale in Talmudic Literature*	Jacob Neusner
140090	*The Talmud of Babylonia: An American Translation. XXVI: Tractate Horayot*	Martin S. Jaffee
140091	*Formative Judaism V: Religious, Historical, and Literary Studies*	Jacob Neusner
140092	*Essays on Biblical Method and Translation*	Edward Greenstein
140093	*The Integrity of Leviticus Rabbah*	Jacob Neusner
140094	*Behind the Essenes: History and Ideology of the Dead Sea Scrolls*	Philip R. Davies

140095	Approaches to Judaism in Medieval Times, Volume III	David R. Blumenthal
140096	The Memorized Torah: The Mnemonic System of the Mishnah	Jacob Neusner
140097	Knowledge and Illumination	Hossein Ziai
140098	Sifre to Deuteronomy: An Analytical Translation. Volume One: Pisqaot One through One Hundred Forty-Three. Debarim, Waethanan, Eqeb	Jacob Neusner
140099	Major Trends in Formative Judaism III: The Three Stages in the Formation of Judaism	Jacob Neusner
140101	Sifre to Deuteronomy: An Analytical Translation. Volume Two: Pisqaot One Hundred Forty-Four through Three Hundred Fifty-Seven. Shofetim, Ki Tese, Ki Tabo, Nesabim, Ha'azinu, Zot Habberakhah	Jacob Neusner
140102	Sifra: The Rabbinic Commentary on Leviticus	Jacob Neusner/ Roger Brooks
140103	The Human Will in Judaism	Howard Eilberg-Schwartz
140104	Genesis Rabbah: Volume 1. Genesis 1:1 to 8:14	Jacob Neusner
140105	Genesis Rabbah: Volume 2. Genesis 8:15 to 28:9	Jacob Neusner
140106	Genesis Rabbah: Volume 3. Genesis 28:10 to 50:26	Jacob Neusner
140107	First Principles of Systemic Analysis	Jacob Neusner
140108	Genesis and Judaism	Jacob Neusner
140109	The Talmud of Babylonia: An American Translation. XXXV: Tractates Meilah and Tamid	Peter J. Haas
140110	Studies in Islamic and Judaic Traditions	William Brinner/Stephen Ricks
140111	Comparative Midrash: The Plan and Program of Genesis Rabbah and Leviticus Rabbah	Jacob Neusner
140112	The Tosefta: Its Structure and its Sources	Jacob Neusner
140113	Reading and Believing	Jacob Neusner
140114	The Fathers According to Rabbi Nathan	Jacob Neusner
140115	Etymology in Early Jewish Interpretation: The Hebrew Names in Philo	Lester L. Grabbe
140116	Understanding Seeking Faith: Essays on the Case of Judaism. Volume One: Debates on Method, Reports of Results	Jacob Neusner
140117	The Talmud of Babylonia. An American Translation. VII: Tractate Besah	Alan J. Avery-Peck
140118	Sifre to Numbers: An American Translation and Explanation, Volume One: Sifre to Numbers 1-58	Jacob Neusner
140119	Sifre to Numbers: An American Translation and Explanation, Volume Two: Sifre to Numbers 59-115	Jacob Neusner
140120	Cohen and Troeltsch: Ethical Monotheistic Religion and Theory of Culture	Wendell S. Dietrich
140121	Goodenough on the History of Religion and on Judaism	Jacob Neusner/ Ernest Frerichs
140122	Pesiqta deRab Kahana I: Pisqaot One through Fourteen	Jacob Neusner
140123	Pesiqta deRab Kahana II: Pisqaot Fifteen through Twenty-Eight and Introduction to Pesiqta deRab Kahana	Jacob Neusner
140124	Sifre to Deuteronomy: Introduction	Jacob Neusner

140126	A Conceptual Commentary on Midrash Leviticus Rabbah: Value Concepts in Jewish Thought	Max Kadushin
140127	The Other Judaisms of Late Antiquity	Alan F. Segal
140128	Josephus as a Historical Source in Patristic Literature through Eusebius	Michael Hardwick
140129	Judaism: The Evidence of the Mishnah	Jacob Neusner
140131	Philo, John and Paul: New Perspectives on Judaism and Early Christianity	Peder Borgen
140132	Babylonian Witchcraft Literature	Tzvi Abusch
140133	The Making of the Mind of Judaism: The Formative Age	Jacob Neusner
140135	Why No Gospels in Talmudic Judaism?	Jacob Neusner
140136	Torah: From Scroll to Symbol Part III: Doctrine	Jacob Neusner
140137	The Systemic Analysis of Judaism	Jacob Neusner
140138	Sifra: An Analytical Translation Vol. 1	Jacob Neusner
140139	Sifra: An Analytical Translation Vol. 2	Jacob Neusner
140140	Sifra: An Analytical Translation Vol. 3	Jacob Neusner
140141	Midrash in Context: Exegesis in Formative Judaism	Jacob Neusner
140143	Oxen, Women or Citizens? Slaves in the System of Mishnah	Paul V. Flesher
140144	The Book of the Pomegranate	Elliot R. Wolfson
140145	Wrong Ways and Right Ways in the Study of Formative Judaism	Jacob Neusner
140146	Sifra in Perspective: The Documentary Comparison of the Midrashim of Ancient Judaism	Jacob Neusner
140148	Mekhilta According to Rabbi Ishmael: An Analytical Translation Volume I	Jacob Neusner
140149	The Doctrine of the Divine Name: An Introduction to Classical Kabbalistic Theology	Stephen G. Wald
140150	Water into Wine and the Beheading of John the Baptist	Roger Aus
140151	The Formation of the Jewish Intellect	Jacob Neusner
140152	Mekhilta According to Rabbi Ishmael: An Introduction to Judaism's First Scriptural Encyclopaedia	Jacob Neusner
140153	Understanding Seeking Faith. Volume Three	Jacob Neusner
140154	Mekhilta According to Rabbi Ishmael: An Analytical Translation Volume Two	Jacob Neusner
140155	Goyim: Gentiles and Israelites in Mishnah-Tosefta	Gary P. Porton
140156	A Religion of Pots and Pans?	Jacob Neusner
140157	Claude Montefiore and Christianity	Maurice Gerald Bowler
140158	The Philosopical Mishnah Volume III	Jacob Neusner
140159	From Ancient Israel to Modern Judaism Volume 1: Intellect in Quest of Understanding	Neusner/Frerichs/Sarna
140160	The Social Study of Judaism Volume I	Jacob Neusner
140161	Philo's Jewish Identity	Alan Mendelson
140162	The Social Study of Judaism Volume II	Jacob Neusner
140163	The Philosophical Mishnah Volume I : The Initial Probe	Jacob Neusner
140164	The Philosophical Mishnah Volume II : The Tractates Agenda: From Abodah Zarah Through Moed Qatan	Jacob Neusner

140166	*Women's Earliest Records*	Barbara S. Lesko
140167	*The Legacy of Hermann Cohen*	William Kluback
140168	*Method and Meaning in Ancient Judaism*	Jacob Neusner
140169	*The Role of the Messenger and Message in the Ancient Near East*	John T. Greene
140171	*Abraham Heschel's Idea of Revelation*	Lawerence Perlman
140172	*The Philosophical Mishnah Volume IV: The Repertoire*	Jacob Neusner
140173	*From Ancient Israel to Modern Judaism Volume 2: Intellect in Quest of Understanding*	Neusner/Frerichs/Sarna
140174	*From Ancient Israel to Modern Judaism Volume 3: Intellect in Quest of Understanding*	Neusner/Frerichs/Sarna
140175	*From Ancient Israel to Modern Judaism Volume 4: Intellect in Quest of Understanding*	Neusner/Frerichs/Sarna
140176	*Translating the Classics of Judaism: In Theory and In Practice*	Jacob Neusner
140177	*Profiles of a Rabbi: Synoptic Opportunities in Reading About Jesus*	Bruce Chilton
140178	*Studies in Islamic and Judaic Traditions II*	William Brinner/Stephen Ricks
140179	*Medium and Message in Judaism: First Series*	Jacob Neusner
140180	*Making the Classics of Judaism: The Three Stages of Literary Formation*	Jacob Neusner
140181	*The Law of Jealousy: Anthropology of Sotah*	Adriana Destro
140182	*Esther Rabbah I: An Analytical Translation*	Jacob Neusner
140183	*Ruth Rabbah: An Analytical Translation*	Jacob Neusner
140184	*Formative Judaism: Religious, Historical and Literary Studies*	Jacob Neusner
140185	*The Studia Philonica Annual*	David T. Runia
140186	*The Setting of the Sermon on the Mount*	W.D. Davies
140187	*The Midrash Compilations of the Sixth and Seventh Centuries Volume One*	Jacob Neusner
140188	*The Midrash Compilations of the Sixth and Seventh Centuries Volume Two*	Jacob Neusner
140189	*The Midrash Compilations of the Sixth and Seventh Centuries Volume Three*	Jacob Neusner
140190	*The Midrash Compilations of the Sixth and Seventh Centuries Volume Four*	Jacob Neusner
140191	*The Religious World of Contemporary Judaism: Observations and Convictions*	Jacob Neusner
140192	*Approaches to Ancient Judaism: Volume VI*	Jacob Neusner/ Ernest S. Frerichs
140193	*Lamentations Rabbah: An Analytical Translation*	Jacob Neusner
140194	*Early Christian Texts on Jews and Judaism*	Robert S. MacLennan
140196	*Torah and the Chronicler's History Work*	Judson R. Shaver
140197	*Song of Songs Rabbah: An Analytical Translation Volume One*	Jacob Neusner
140198	*Song of Songs Rabbah: An Analytical Translation Volume Two*	Jacob Neusner
140199	*From Literature to Theology in Formative Judaism*	Jacob Neusner
140202	*Maimonides on Perfection*	Menachem Kellner

DATE DUE

HIGHSMITH   # 45220